U0024365

加工出口區
與
經濟發展

余光亞　著

Process
&
Economical

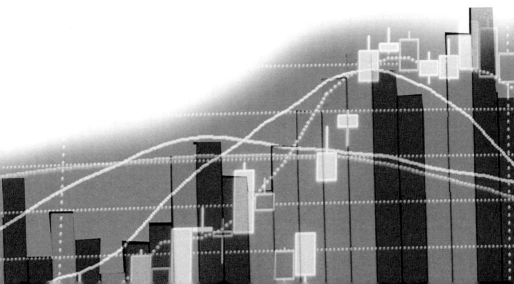

趙　序

　　中國鋼鐵公司是民國六十年代政府睿智竭力塑造的時代大
熔爐，艱辛而驕傲的建設成功國家的鋼鐵重工業，可謂「一元
之興，萬代之福」！

　　這項化時代的事業，其成功最大的因素歸功於人才的培養
及善用，中鋼公司曾有計劃的、千錘百鍊培養出公司各階層各
部門所需要的專業人才，這些人才也就是日後國家在鋼鐵行業
發展中的重要骨幹。光亞兄即是早期進入中鋼培養的基層幹部
之一，從工程師做起，負責建廠期間綜合協調的工作，建廠完
成後送往美國鋼鐵公司受訓，而轉任生產計劃的主管工作，表
現非常優異，到中鋼二期擴建時臨危受命兼任中鋼結構公司廠
長，以其機械專長及工業工程技術在極短時間內將中鋼結構公
司帶入正常生產，解決中鋼二期擴建的瓶頸，而後轉任採購處
長，以一個完全不懂商業實務的工程人員，用心學習，善盡職
守，終於達成任務，實難能可貴。至我本人奉命接任經濟部長
後，部裏也急需用有才幹的人才，因而又調光亞到加工出口區
接任處長，他也能在短時間裏促成加工出口區振衰起敝，七年
的處長工作，他已成為國內加工出口區後進專業人才，而揚名
國際。

　　我與光亞兄共事至今三十多年，他的工作能力表現得十分
出色，尤其難得的是「守法務實，廉介不苟」；在專業領域裏，

i

把自己的經驗、知識見之於文字，寫下這本「加工出口區與經濟發展」十分有參考價值的書，本書不單是台灣目前僅有的一本資料完整有系統關於加工出口區的記錄論述的書，就是當今世界也少見；它不僅提供給海峽兩岸的中國人了解參考，同時也供給世界各貧窮未開發的國家參考學習，其用心令人至為感動、欽佩，因此十分樂意為其撰寫此序言。

趙耀東 謹識

2005 年 4 月 12 日

傅　序

　　半個世紀以來，透過政府與民間的努力，台灣已經由農業社會轉型為工業社會，更進一步發展為科技化社會。社會經濟也由「未開發」，進展至「開發中」，更進而成為「已開發」國家。在這成功的發展經驗背後，「固然政府與政策有其功績，但也有許多人與機構的貢獻，才能使這小島，躋身於亞洲四小龍之列。「加工出口區」就是在政府正確的政策領導之下，做出鉅大貢獻之機構之一。

　　在當年技術、資金、人才、均匱乏的時代，「加工出口區」不僅提供就業機會，改善國家經濟，也同時引進國外先進的製造與管理技術，提昇了本土製造與管理水準。更因為外銷業務之國際聯繫，為台灣扎下國際化的基礎，而產業研究發展也奠定了台灣科技化根基。

　　本書作者余光亞先生，不僅長年服務於產業界，擔任主管與領導者，更曾奉派擔任台灣「加工出口區」處長達七年之久。在其任內運籌帷幄，改善投資環境，吸引僑外資投資，增加就業機會，並協助優秀人才之培育與獎勵。余光亞先生於 1986 年被選為「中華民國管理科學學會高雄分會」理事長，兩任期內為各大學管理學院研究生，募得獎學金達新台幣 300 萬之多。十餘年後，筆者擔任學會理事長之時，仍然依賴該獎學金孳息，鼓勵各大學管理學院研究生。

現今余光亞先生基於「改善兩岸人民之生活與福祉，進而促進世界之經濟發展」，將其多年擔任台灣「加工出口區」處長之心得與經驗，更加上對世界各國「加工出口區」之瞭解，編寫成此「加工出口區與經濟發展」著作，堪稱用心良苦。本書除可供有意借助「加工出口區」經驗，改善經濟之政府官員重要參考外，亦可供有心鑽研台灣「加工出口區」成功經驗，做學術探討與分析之重要文獻，而所附世界各國加工出口區資料，更是從事者不可或缺之重要資料。

光亞兄在本書結語中，期許「加工出口區」能帶給人類福祉，永恆的貢獻－幸福、安樂、與和平，更可見其胸懷及使命感。相信「加工出口區與經濟發展」一書，必可為兩岸及世界之經濟發展，帶來正面提昇之效果與貢獻。因此不揣簡陋，樂為此序，以就教於諸位先進。

傅勝利　謹識

2005 年 4 月 29 日於義守大學

劉　序

他山之石，可以攻玉

　　今天人們談起「加工出口區」，都不以為然了，因為無論是從理論還是到實踐都似乎已經比較熟悉了。但是在上世紀60年代中，台灣在世界上開創「加工出口區」之先河實屬不易，應該說，這是中華民族智慧之結晶，也是中國人走向工業化道路極為寶貴而重要的經驗。

　　台灣經濟在上世紀中經歷了20～30年的努力，完成了「由農到工」的過程，尤其是，積極有效地發展外向型經濟，成功地推展了產業升級，在80年代取得亞洲「四小龍」之一的稱號，應該說，台灣適時設立「加工出口區」，對發展台灣經濟猶如「助推器」一般，所作出的貢獻絕對是功不可沒。

　　祖國大陸從改革開放以來，主要是以建立經濟特區、經濟技術開發區、科技園區等不同政策目標的開放、開發模式，吸引了大量外商（包括台港澳地區）企業進駐，他們以代工（OEM）為主要經營模式設立生產工廠，進而形成完整的產業鏈生產基地，將產品供應到世界各地，但實踐表明，僅靠「經濟特區」等原有各類園區的政策都不能完全適應日益快速變化的市場需求。故此，祖國大陸從2001年開始，首先在上海、青島、深圳、天津、昆山等15個地方設立了「加工出口區」，並已取得很大成績。這是繼經濟特區、經濟技術開發區、科技園區之后的又

一重大開放舉措。「加工出口區」的出現,對引進出口型外資企業起到了關鍵性作用,同時大大提升了祖國大陸的出口能力和企業在國際市場上的綜合競爭力。據我了解,祖國大陸「加工出口區」的設立,曾吸收了一些台灣加工出口區的做法,幫助我們少走彎路。

38 年前,在台灣的「加工出口區」,今天已在美國、南美、歐洲、印度和東南亞等諸國擴散,雖然有些國家不把它稱為「加工出口區」,而大多數仍稱為「加工出口區」,無論怎樣,差異雖然存在,但主要的功能卻都是基本一致,因此還形成了一個世界性的機構(世界加工出口區協會)。為各國、各地區之間相互學習、取長補短提供了一個交流平台,這也從另一個側面反映了全世界都在關注「加工出口區」。凡事都在變化和發展之中,「加工出口區」作為一種管理模式,也在為適應不同產業特點、經營環境變化以及服務業的多項功能的提升而不斷地完善和發展。我們當然不能置身事外,而應該以不同模式參與研究和交流。

本人衷心祝賀本書出版。同時也希望本書的出版能有助於讀者進一步了解「加工出口區」模式的內涵、理念、目標,以及認真思考在世界經濟一體化過程加快的情勢下,如何做到與時俱進。

最後,我用「他山之石,可以攻玉」來共勉。

劉震濤　謹識

清華大學台灣研究所

2005 年 11 月 10 日

自 序

　　從 1966 年 12 月 3 日世界第一個高雄加工出口區成立以來，由於規劃週詳，經營成效卓著，瞬即蜚聲中外，享譽世界，影響之大，無遠弗屆，個人有幸奉前經濟部趙部長耀東先生之命，接任台灣加工出口區第五任處長，繼續經營發展，也從此與加工出口區結下不解之緣，在加工出口區七年的任期中，竭力以赴，各項工作的改進、改革、修法、擴區，加強吸引投資，擴展對外貿易，支援外交，協助友幫國家發展加工出口區，以及使台灣加工出口區恢復成為世界加工出口區協會的會員國等等，使台灣加工出口區再度展現優績，傲視國際；及至個人退除公職後，仍有機會協助友幫國家發展建設加工出口區，以及應中國國務院特區辦的邀請，協助中國發展"出口加工區"（有別於台灣的加工出口區），得有機會遍訪中國各地出口加工區，指導、協助其規劃，建設及營運理念的傳授，如此等等，其措舉、心志，乃秉承李資政國鼎先生的教誨：【你的眼光要放遠大一些，要為全世界的中國人服務】，因而愚旨及作為在以加工出口區「濟世救人，脫離貧窮，不僅殷切期盼能因而改善海峽兩岸中國人民的生活水平，增進福祉，進而企及能促使世界各落後國家或地區經濟發展，帶給人類溫飽幸福、詳和安怡的生活」，衷心企盼！

2002 年 10 月 18、19 兩日，筆者應邀訪問中國南京東南大學，並以「台灣加工出口區之創設、貢獻及轉型」為題發表演說，有幸得到該校李永泰教授（李資政國鼎先生姪子）特別的關注，建議將深入了解加工出口區的發展歷程，成效功績，個人經驗等寶貴資料，見之於文字，留待有志於加工出口區事業的後進、學者參考、研究，此建議然時回憶起 1994 年元月 9 日，李資政國鼎先生交辦撰文扶正新聞對加工出口區不實的報導時，正色道：【現在加工出口區你最了解，你不寫誰寫？】的情景，由是幾經忖量，容我自負忐忑接納李教授雅意，就個人所了解，經驗以一得之愚整理撰寫成冊，提供有識之士參考、指教；在台灣尚有多位前輩先進對加工出口區有更深入的了解，前經建會葉副主委萬安先生即是當年曾同時與李資政一起參與加工出口區計劃案規劃工作者之一，對加工出口區發展歷程更為了解，衷心懇請葉副主委對本書蕪文匡正不逮，指教是幸！

本書撰寫過程，思考理念著重在強調創設加工出口區的基本目的所在，加工出口區與國家經濟發展互動關係，尤其是初期經濟發展階段，加工出口區更顯得其重要性，而在寫作的架構思維上，在以國家整體經濟的規劃，系統運作方針，策略為主桌，而加工出口區乃國家整體經濟之一環，其權重比例，端視整體經濟需求而定，加工出口區管理處為業務執行的主管機關，以對政策的執行為要務、責任；至於加工出口區經營之所以能夠成功，其優惠條件及一元化的服務是吸引投資的最大誘因，一套加工出口區特別法的管理系統更是加工出口區經營成功的重要利器；在實務方面，以台灣加工出口區及中國出口加

工區作為範例模式，詳述其發展經過、起伏，並列舉世界各國加工出口區的發展成效彰顯與否為例，企望以實例的表達，提供世界各國在發展中或有意將要發展加工出口區的國家參考、借鏡，也許有助於彼等縮短發展加工出口區的摸索時程，而能一舉成功。

　　本書之能撰寫成冊出版，要感謝東南大學李永泰教授的倡議；前經濟部趙部長耀東先生的提拔任命個人到加工出口區服務而與加工出口區結緣；前總統府李資政國鼎先生多年的謬愛教導，經驗傳授，尤其對台灣加工出口區關懷備至，視為己出，不幸資政於 2002 年 5 月 31 日病逝，一代偉人，世界加工出口區之父，魂歸天國，留給世人無限的追思，個人更是倍極懷念，故特撰紀念文──「李資政國鼎與加工出口區之創設、發展」悼念之！（見附件六）；又中國國務院持區辦前趙副主任云棟先生十分關注鼓勵在中國出版；南京東南大學徐總編啟平先生於 2002 年 10 月 19 日筆者由李永泰教授陪同拜訪時概允協助在該校出版社出版；昆山出口加工區陸副主任宗元先生概允資助東南大學出版；世界加工出口區協會秘書長 Robert C. Haywood 概允提供該協會及部份會員國加工出口區有關資料供作參考；兒媳高毓淇女士曠日廢食辛勤地將世界加工出口區協會及有關國家英文參考資料擇重點簡要翻譯成中文，便於讀者閱讀、了解，同時還要感謝曾淑美、周含芳兩位小姐協助清稿繕打，以及張錫川、吳偉鋒、胡榮長、潘文芬等多位好友協助提供或收集資料，均此致謝！

　　本書已於 2005 年 4 月在南京東南大學出版，惟作者欲保留原文表達之精義、理念，及由世界加工出口區協會（WEPZA）

所提供之會員國專家的論著，以及亞洲生產力中心（APO）於 1999 年 11 月 23~26 日在韓國漢城由作者所主持的評鑑會議中，有關會員國的加工出口區及科學園區專家們公開發表的論文，而一併收納在本書內，難能可貴，供讀者參閱、研究、分享，故特徵得東南大學出版社於定約中同意在台灣以原稿內容出版，專此記述之。

余光亞　謹序
2005 年 9 月 30 日於台灣高雄市

目 次

緒　言

　　公元 1966 年 12 月 3 日世界首創的台灣加工出口區在台灣高雄市高雄港滀港新生地上創設成立，其創設的原由乃因國家經濟發展的需要，按世界加工出口區之父李資政國鼎先生所撰寫的【加工出口區制度之創立】文中指出：【三十年前（1956 年），我國在推動工業發展的過程中，先是由於初期發展的第一階段民生必需品進口替代工業面臨國內市場飽和，必須突破國內市場限制，拓展外銷；繼而美國經援停止，國內資金短缺，亟需大力改善投資環境，吸引僑外投資，拓展輸出，增加外滙收入，培養國際收支能力；復因人口快速增加，面對人口壓力與農村勞力過剩，需要創造試業機會；因應上述種種迫切情勢，需要採取突破性的措施並配合當時國家經濟發展條件的限制——缺乏大量資金與高級技術，決定採取先行發展勞力密集輕工業、拓展出口的策略，經過將近十年研究醞量與政策調整，克服若干制度上的困難，終於在廿年前的民國五十五年（1966 年）十二月三日創設建成了高雄加工出口區。高雄加工出口區的建立，不僅是我國第一個加工出口區，也是全世界加工出口區的首創。】此明確指出，加工出口區的創設初期原因，在於國家當時處在社會民生凋蔽的環境，經濟落後貧窮，人口壓力所造成的就業迫切需求，及在資金、技術都缺乏的條件下，而

1

以發展勞力密集的輕工業以利增加就業機會，解決了最為嚴重的問題，同時也改善了當時民生物資嚴重匱乏而需用大量外匯進口的困境，按【民國 39 年（1950）台灣主要進口商品清單】（表一），一目瞭然進口項目幾乎全為民生必需品，此一政策的推動執行，對創造就業機會及發展替代工業達到一舉兩得的效果，不僅如此，又以拓展出口政策補強國內市場過小而形成生產過剩的商品，得有機會推廣行銷國際市場，增加外滙收入，充實財政收入的不足，由是得知加工出口區首要功能在增加就業機會，拓展對外貿易，其內涵蘊藏至深，影響也大。

世界首創的台灣加工出口區自創設至今已達 39 年的歷史。亦為世界各開發中及未開發國家所效仿設置，台灣加工出口區 39 年的輝煌成就早已蜚聲中外，並且在繼續成長轉型中，而更具有意義的是，由台灣加工出口區促使世界性加工出口區模式的形成，並已然成為世界加工出口區發展中的一環，其他如中國從 1991 年前第一個昆山出口加工區成立以來，便竭力急起直追，成績斐然，有青出於藍的態勢，世界各國加工出口區的發展，也頻有成效，尤以韓國（南韓）的馬山加工出口區（Masan Free Export Zone）成效顯著，新成立營運僅及數年的越南新順加工出口區（TAN THUAN EXPORT PROCESSING ZONE）也值得稱道，中南美的巴拉圭、烏拉圭等國的加工出口區都表現得頗為出色，然而世界各設有加工出口區的國家對加工出口區的長遠發展走向，發展到何種程度？又如何與國家（區域）經濟發展產生密切的互動關係等，一連串的問題，應深入思考，宜有系統的研究

加工出口區的創設歷史演進，擴散效應及深一層的長遠發展走向，此其時，加工出口區已成為國際間經濟發展的一項工具，手段之際，在深思上述問題繼續的演進，務必要能吻合開創加工出口區的初衷目的——創造就業機會，發展國家經濟，造福人群，為人類全體的福祉而服務。

表一　民國三十九年（1950）台灣主要進口商品清單

項目	佔同年進口總金額百分比	排名次序
棉布	一四‧二九%	1
肥料	八‧八〇%	2
麵粉	五‧九二%	3
豆餅	五‧二〇%	4
大豆，豌豆	四‧一一%	5
腳踏車	三‧四二%	6
藥品	三‧三八%	7
機器及配件	二‧六五%	8
原油	一‧八七%	9
紡織機械及配件	一‧八四%	10
牛奶	一‧五〇%	11
植物油	一‧四五%	12
棉紗	一‧二七%	13
鍍鋅鋼板	一‧二五%	14
腳踏車零配件	一‧二五%	15
麻袋	一‧二二%	16
鹹魚	一‧一八%	17
電氣紡機械及配件	一‧〇四%	18
奶粉	一‧〇四%	19
鍍鋅鋼絲	〇‧九四%	20
變壓器	〇‧八九%	21
米穀	〇‧八七%	22
木材	〇‧八五%	23
未鍍鋅鋼管	〇‧八四%	24
藥材，香料	〇‧八三%	25
菜蔬	〇‧八二%	26
羊毛	〇‧八〇%	27
汽車貨車	〇‧七八%	28
汽車零件	〇‧六五%	29
發動機械及配件	〇‧六五%	30
椰子油	〇‧六〇%	31
馬口鐵	〇‧五八%	32
潤滑油	〇‧五六%	33
鐵道用客貨車	〇‧五四%	34
未鍍鋅鋼條	〇‧五四%	35
橡皮樹膠	〇‧五一%	36
其他	二五‧〇三%	

第一章　世界加工出口區首創發展的時代背景及內涵

壹、加工出口區創設發展的時代背景

　　世界首創台灣加工出口區的創設研議甚費時日、週章，絕非偶然之作，首先須要了解的是何以需要設立加工出口區？按李國鼎資政著【加工出口區制度之創立】所述【何以需要設立加工出口區論述：民國四十二年（1953 年）第一期四年經建計畫中工業部門之計畫，係由經濟安定委員會工業委員會負責籌劃推動，並以美國經緩之美金與物資銷售產生之臺幣予以支援，當時因外滙不足，依賴進口必要民生物資，以應人民需要，並可穩定物價。因此當時所支援之工業，多半以進口代替品為優先，以求節省外滙；同時發展肥料工業，增產糧食，以期減少進口；舉凡與民生必需之食衣住行有關之工業優先發展。惟國內市場究竟有限，很快的趨於飽和，記得四十五年（1956 年）紡錠已趨飽和，某投資人擬以自備外滙進口一萬紡錠，經年餘之考慮方予以核准，因此究應限制設廠或鼓勵出口之問題，以及外滙滙率多元或單元滙率，均為面臨之問題，必需解決。而進口出口手續繁多，

5

若干與原材料零組件有關之間接稅、退稅制度雖逐漸建立，但手續繁多，至於機器及零件進口時需課關稅，投資人均感不便，為求鼓勵投資，促進工業之進一步發展，必須對投資環境有所改善，乃有加工出口免稅區初期意念之產生。】由是很深刻的了解到其時代背景的迫切需要性。

一、時代背景演進概況：

中華民國政府於 1950 年完全遷至台灣後，其時台灣社會型態處於民生凋敝，百廢待舉的窮困狀態，經濟結構為農業經濟體制，人民極需就業機會，通貨膨脹影響民生，按當時環境背景而言，概述如下：

1、台灣土地面積約三萬餘平方公里，三分之二為山地，可耕面積不及四分之一，天然資源幾乎等於零。

2、1950 年代雖不到一千萬人，但人口成長率高達三·五六％，單位面積約在三百人，為世界人口密度之冠，每年需增加就業機會在十萬個之多，所幸氣候得宜，可種作二至三耕，糧食不虞匱乏。

3、1950 年代農業生產佔全國 56％，而工業僅佔 26％，故 GNP 僅為二百美元，約為美國的十分之一，屬於未開發的貧窮國家。

4、1950 年韓戰開始，美國對台灣經、軍援助，政府警覺到隨時有停止援助的可能，果真於 1965 年停止，使已脆弱的經濟頓失支持，因此政府決定從經濟發展著手改革，1953 年第一期四年經濟建設計劃應運而生。

台灣經濟發展的四個時期：

按 1950 年代所呈現的經濟貧乏，國民生活急待改善之際，政府發展國家的整體經濟是為當務之急，逐有 1953 年第一個四年經濟建設計劃之推行，而延續有以後的四個經濟發展時期。

第一時期為進口替代時期（1950~1960）

此一時期，重要的工作有：

（1）抑制通貨膨脹，建立預算制度，縮小赤字，妥善運用美援。

（2）農業改革，實施三七五減租，公地放領及耕者有其田，分三階段實施，即在使農業土地生產力提高。

（3）1953 年第一期四年經濟建設計劃中的工業發展，在發展替代進口民生必需品工業，以節省外匯支出，因此肥料工業、食品加工業、紡織工業、水泥塑膠建材工業、自行車工業、輪胎工業等，優先支持發展。

（4）改革外匯．到 1958 年物價漸趨穩定，外貿會主任委員尹仲容先生主持外匯改革，向單一匯率邁進，先於 1958 年四月將複式匯率改為兩個匯率，一為二四．七六元另一為三六．三六元兌換一美元，復於同年十一月將兩個滙率合併為單一滙率即台幣三六．三六元兌換一美元，此乃推動工業產品外銷的先決必要條件。

第二時期為出口擴展時期（1961~1970）

此一時期的主要工作在改善投資環境，大力推動進口替代產品的外銷及其工業發展，由於國內市場有限，很快趨於飽和，故而必須發展國際市場而鼓勵外銷；而外銷當以工業產品較具競爭力，附加價值亦高，故而於 1960 年由美援會成立工業發展投資小組，研究通過「投資獎勵條例」，使能簡化進出口手續，材料零組件關稅退稅手續等，以排除對資本形成，外銷不利的因素，達到鼓勵工業投資。

於此同時，農業亦開始多角化經營，如糖、米、香蕉、洋菇、蘆筍等相繼外銷，此時間人口成長率增高，失業率相對增加，唯有發展經濟，獎勵工業投資，給予投資人良好之投資環境，才能因應需求，乃有「加工出口免稅區」初期意念的產生，及至 1966 年正式創設成立高雄加工出口區。

第三時期為調整經濟結構，加速經濟發展升級時期（1971~1980）

此亦為二次進口替代時期，第一次替代是民生消費品生產，而本次為替代資本密集的中間產品，例如石油化學的中間產品供給紡織業所需，及作輕油煉解供下游工業使用，又如鋼鐵業的中間產品供下游作原料使用；另一方面農業生產力由第一時期增加土地生產力而轉變成農業人口生產力（當時美國土地生產力為我國的八分之一，然而農業人口生產力卻為我國的八倍）在此時間，遭遇到能源危機，經濟不景氣，保護主義伸張，對開發中國家十分不利，因而必須調整經濟結構，將工業生產由勞力密集轉到技術密集，再進入高科技

時代，也就進入到資本密集，此即是進入工業轉型期；此在使傳統勞力密集工業自動化，鼓勵能源少，公害少的工業投資，擬訂策略性工業，高附加價值工業。

第四時期為產業升級與科技導向時期（1981~迄今）

此一時期的目的在推動產業結構轉型，經濟自由化、國際化；將以傳統產業為主的產業結構引導轉變為以 IC 系統產業、光電產業、生化產業、耐米科技產業……等高科技產業的全面發展，同時推動六年國建計劃、亞太營運中心計劃、全球運籌中心計劃等，以達到經濟國際化、自由化的願景。

二、加工出口免稅區雛議的誘因：

因時代背景窘困的影響，政府勵精圖治，奮發圖存的堅毅意志及政府官員集一時俊彥碩儒之選，清廉剛正，殫智竭力，有守有為，乃萌「加工出口免稅區」的雛議之念，但此一構想之能最終實現成型，綜括的看應是誘因於兩點：

1、1950 年代農業經濟發展仍不能滿足社會需要，唯發展工業，創造就業機會，打開國際市場，賺取外滙，是為當務之急。

2、如何發展工業？當時香港可作為借鏡，因香港 1950 年代初由中國大陸遷往的企業家建立製造業的基礎，同時香港亦為自由港，機器及原料除極少數商品外，皆不收關稅，故前往投資者眾，發展快速，例如 1963 年香港出口總值為六億美元，且 80% 為工業加工品，而台灣僅一億美元，幾乎全為農業加工品，故以香港作為典範，從加工工業作為工業發展的起步。

此外，日本只要本國不生產的原料都一律免稅，即使收稅的貨物也有一套免稅的辦法，手續甚為簡單，此一做法亦為值得參考。

三、台灣加工出口區創設時程：

這兩項誘因加速了台灣加工出口區 1966 年的建成，其研擬創設時程簡述如下：

1、1953 年至 1958 年李國鼎先生邀請海關總稅務司張克福先生，共同研究劃出一特定區域設立加工工廠之用。

2、1956 年高雄港因濬港開闢的新生地，行政院經濟安定委員會計劃於該地設立加工工廠。（圖一）

3、1958 年美國專家加州大學 Dr. Paul Kiem 教授建議在該地設立國際貿易區。

4、1959 年，行政院長兼美援會主任陳誠先生，主持成立投資小組，開始就「自由貿易區與工業區」之得失利弊探討、研究，特別以香港為借鏡。

5、1962 年李國鼎先生隨同財政部長嚴家淦先生赴美歐開會，返國中途赴意大利 Trieste 港參觀自由貿易區作業情形，歸來後詳加研討，將自由貿區及工業區合併經營，並擬議為「加工出口區」，其同意設立加工出口區的原則架構為：

人方面：投資人出入境仍維持原有手續。

錢方面：外匯管制仍屬必要，維持原有手續，但在區內辦理。

物方面：限加工出口區產品全部外銷，其製造所需之機器及零件，與原料零組件一概免關稅及貨物稅。

6、1963 年 5 月財經部門修訂投資獎勵條例，根據上述原則架構，建議政府擇適當地區設立「加工出口區」，以發展外銷加工工業。

7、1964 年 7 月完成「加工出口區設置管理條例」草案送立法院審議，1965 年完成立法手續並呈 總統公佈實施，至此「台灣加工出口區」正式創設成立，並由曾任基隆市長的謝貫一先生擔任首任「經濟部加工出口區管理處處長」。

8、Dr. Paul Kiem 的建議國際貿易區，實為自由貿易區，此區在台灣當時國情頗不適宜，乃因三大自由問題所困擾，即（1）人員進出自由（2）物質進出口自由（3）貨幣進出自由；又自由貿易區必須有廣大腹地支持，以消化進入的物質及發揮儲存功能，故而未完全採用 Dr. Paul Kiem 建議。

9、1965 年 3 月 20 日成立高雄加工出口區，在高雄港滬港新生地上開始建區（圖二，圖三），至 1966 年 12 月 3 日完成，是為台灣第一個加工出口區開始運作，三年後相繼成立台中加工出口區及楠梓加工出口區。三十年後於 1997 年相繼成立中港園區、成功物流園區，1999 年成立臨廣園區、小港空運物流園區、屏東園區、高雄軟體科技園區及尚在進行施工的斗六絲織園區等共十個加工區。十個區的相關資料如下表：（表二）

表二　台灣加工出口區十區相關資料表

區別	轄區	土地面積（公頃）	所在位置	重點產業型態
台中分處	台中園區	26.2	台中縣潭子	相機等光電產品產製及研發
中港園區	中港分處	177	台中縣梧棲鎮、緊臨台中港	機車零組件、五金用品之產製及研發
斗六園區（絲織專區）	管理處	268	雲林縣斗六市北側之台糖農場，近六輕	計畫及彰化人纖專區纖維原料生產及其加工業、織布及染整業、成衣業及服飾配件、紡織相關之醫療生醫科技業、紡織相關之機械、設備及零件製造業
楠梓園區	管理處	97.8	高雄市楠梓區，近高雄港（15公里）、小港國際機場（23公里）、高速公路（5公里）	積體電路之封裝、測試及製程研發
高雄園區	高雄分處	72.0	高雄港區內	液晶顯示器之產製及研發等
成功物流園區	高雄分處	8.4	高雄市前鎮區成功路與中華路上。近高速公路、高雄港、小港國際機場	國際綜合型物流園區，結合「倉儲物流中心」、「加工轉運中心」、「國際會議中心」、「展覽中心」、及「商務中心」等功能
高雄航空貨運園區	高雄分處	54.5	位於高雄小港機場北側之機場用地，緊鄰高速公路及高雄港遠洋貨櫃中心	研發、設計、關鍵零組件製造及組合測試之驗證之功能為主，輔以倉儲、轉運發貨及關聯性產業服務業。
臨廣園區	高雄分處	9.0	高雄市前鎮區新生路、漁港路交	液晶顯示器之產製及研發等

			叉路口，近高速公路、高雄港貨櫃中心、小港國際機場	
高雄軟體科技園區	高雄分處	7.9	高雄市成功路與復興路口，緊臨高雄港，東側為都會商圈，南側臨近臨海工業區及高雄港貨櫃中心	軟體產業、高科技產業、自動化物流、驗證測試、倉儲發貨業
屏東園區	屏東分處	124.1	屏東縣頭前溪六塊厝農場、地處屏東市西南隅、高屏兩縣交界處	車輛組裝及零組件產製、生化產品產製及研發

資料來源：台灣加工出口區管理處

建區前之高雄加工出口區　高雄港中島原貌　The Original Appearance of Kaohsiung Harbor,Prior to the Construction of KEPZ

圖一

高雄港濬港抽沙堆積成新生地供高雄加工出口區使用

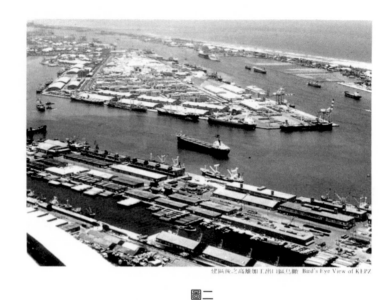

建區後之高雄加工出口區鳥瞰 Bird's Eye View of KEPZ

圖二

高雄加工出口區建設在濬港新生地上

高雄加工出口區位置圖

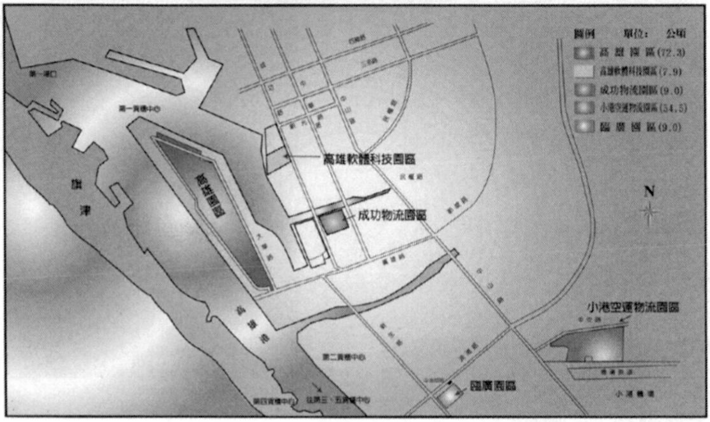

圖三

貳、台灣加工出口區創設的內涵

　　台灣加工出口區經過政府 13 年（1953~1966）漫長時間的研究討論而最後於 1962 年由李國鼎先生與當時任財政部長的嚴家淦先生擬議為「加工出口區」定案，繼而立法及建構執行，此一經過深思熟慮，規範在經濟體系中之「工商」業綜合型態的產業經營發展區，其建區的目的、理論基礎、經營理念、基本架構……等的內涵，是為極其重要的考慮思維。

　　在台灣加工出口區創設之前，世界各國只有「自由貿易區」或「工業區」等概念與設置。實際上，加工出口區既不同於自由貿易區，亦不同於一般工業區，而是兼具自由貿易區與工業區兩者之長的綜合體。若就免徵關稅和劃定隔離區域而言，它與自由貿易區完全相同，但自由貿易區却不如它有統一的規劃與完整的工業設施；若就統一的規劃與完整的工業設施而言，它又與一般工業區相似，但一般工業區既不能免徵關稅，亦不必與外界隔離。加工出口區兼具兩者的優點，為其最基本的特質。

　　加工出口區行之有年至今，除為世界各開發中及未開發國家仿效設置之外，按其特質、特性解釋也另有擴大廣範的認定，將特定的工業區，具備國家獎勵優惠條件者，如科學園區即以廣義的解釋為加工出口區的一種類型，科學園區也是界定在一定範圍內研發生產的高科技工業區，享受自由貿

15

易區的優惠條件與加工出口區類同,唯不同加工出口區者在
先由研究發展至設置工廠生產,將研發成果轉變成商品而獲
利,隨後再繼續研發,週而復始,而加工出口區則是將成熟
的市場商品先行投資生產獲利,而後研發新產品,再繼續投
資生產,亦為週而復始。這起步不同類型的「工業區」卻是
在同步的發展國家經濟,筆者曾在 1989 年 2 月 16 日答覆立
法委員質詢對加工出口區完成階段性任務後存廢問題時表
示「科學園區是加工出口區的變體,它是先研究發展而後設
廠生產,加工出口區則是先生產而後研究開發新產品,二者
在程序上雖有先後之別,但對國家發展經濟目標則是一致
的。」由是將科學園區視同加工出口區的一種類型亦甚洽
當,惟二者在產業結構上存有程度上的差異;又亦有將自由
貿易區視同加工出口區的另一類型者,因為自由貿易也包含
了一些簡易的加工,享有免稅優惠,其他如自由港區、轉運
中心以及美國稱之為外國貿易區(Foreign Trade Zone)及外
國貿易分區(Sub-foreign Trade Zone)等也都廣義的認定,
將之納入在不同型態的加工出口區的範疇之內,加工出口區
內涵,除了解其特質外,尚有其理論基礎,經營理念……等,
以下簡要說明之。

一、經營之理論基礎:

「比較利益」理論基礎,設區國(或地區)之所以願提
供設區土地及各項優惠條件,讓國外廠商來區投資設廠生產
受惠,設區國所能享受到的利益首在創造了就業機會,同時

也帶進了資金，造成國家資本財（Capital）的形成，生產技術及國際市場也是設區國的最大收益之一；而投資廠家則因免減稅優惠，低生產成本而獲最大利潤，如此得使設區國與外國投資廠商互蒙其利，各取所需。

二、經營之理念：

　　三利原則，即（1）國家的利益（2）廠商的利潤（3）員工的福利，三者缺一不可。設區國（或地區）所獲得的最大利益在發展國家經濟，解決社會民生問題，使國家經濟環境能快速成長，廠商因優惠條件低生產成本而獲利潤，參與生產的員工可得到就業機會、收入及福利，以改善家庭生活，故此三利是對國家（設區國或地區）、投資人及員工均有利可圖，合於比較利益理論要求，自然加工出口區的經營就會成功，所以加工出口區的經營理念是以三利為導向的基礎。

三、建區目標：

　　1、先期目標
　　（1）吸引工業投資
　　（2）拓展對外貿易
　　（3）創造就業機會
　　（4）引進最新技術

2、現階段目標

  （1）強化產業競爭優勢

  （2）結合國際市場需求

  （3）提升國內技術水準

  （4）引進跨國企業投資

3、將來達成之目標（將隨實際需要而修訂）

  （1）成為國際產業分工製造中心

  （2）成為國際外銷結合驗證發貨中心

  （3）成為國內共同倉儲海空運中心，為台商根留台灣基地

  （4）成為跨國企業在遠東聯絡中心及倉儲轉運供應中心

  （5）配合境外航運中心作業，成為大陸物品組合加工再出口製造轉運中心

四、建區架構：

1、在人的方面：投資人出入境仍維持原有手續。

2、在錢的方面：外滙管制仍屬必要，仍維持原有手續，但在區內辦理。

3、在物的方面：因加工出口區產品全部限外銷，其製造所需機器及零件與原料零組件一概免關稅及貨物稅。

    本架構乃政府設置加工出口區先期營運的基本政策，隨著時序的演進，今已有頗大的改變修正如下：

1、在人的方面：投資人出入境按國際貫例，辦理多次出入
　　境得到方便。
2、在錢的方面：外滙管制放寬，允許個人一年自由滙出美
　　金 500 萬元，但達到美金 50 萬滙出案須報中央銀行資
　　料列管；公司則允許達美金 1000 萬元自由滙出，如為
　　購買設備需要可報中央銀行核可，金額不限，但達到
　　50 萬元滙出者，仍須報中央銀行資料列管。
3、在物的方面：加工出口區的產品繳稅後可以內銷，不受
　　量的限制，其製造所需的機器設備、原物料、半製品等
　　均免進口稅捐、貨物稅及營業稅，若此等要輸往課稅區
　　則須補繳以上各項稅捐。

第二章　台灣加工區經營成功的因素及效益貢獻

壹、台灣加工出口區三十九年來的經營績效

　　自 1966 年 12 月 3 日加工出口區成立以來，以其特有的設置管理條例及授予吸引投資最優惠的辦法，由第一個高雄加工區成立經營，舜即三年後，於 1970 年成立楠梓加工出口區及台中加工出口區，並開始營運，自 1966 至 1986，廿年的經營，此三個加工區的產業結構為初級產品製造業，及裝配業，而區內服務業部份全由政府有關部門設置，其投資對象，初期為純僑資及外資，而後逐年增加國內中小企業投資，因而產業型態以高度勞力密集產業為主，技術密集產業為輔。1986 年以後開始區內產業升級，由勞力密集轉向資本密集，技術密集，國際化，自由化的目標發展。

　　1997 年即三十年後，又相繼成立中港園區，成功物流園區……等七區，至目前台灣總共有十個加工出口區（表二）。

　　至今三十九年來因加工出口區努力不懈的經營，已呈現出一份傲視全球的績效，無論從先期建區的目標或是現階段

目標來衡量，此其間的經營績效均已達成，茲例舉以下數項資料證明之。

　　1、歷年區內事業投資統計（表三，圖四）。

　　2、歷年進出口金額統計（表四，圖五）。

　　3、歷年勞工人數及工資統計（表五，圖六）。

　　4、歷年生產力統計

　　（1）投資生產力（表六）

　　（2）勞動生產力（表七）

　　（3）土地生產力（表八）

謹就表列數據概要說明如後：

1、歷年區內事業投資統計：（表三）

　　台灣加工出口區從 1966 年開始僅只有一個高雄加工出口區營運，1966 年投資廠商 51 家，總投資金額一千萬美元，平均每家僅 196,078 美元，至 1970 年另增加了楠梓加工出口區及台中加工出口區，共三區經營，計有 183 家廠商，總投資金額增為五千五百餘萬美元，平均每筆投資金額提高到 300,546 美元；1986 年加工出口區開始轉型，自然淘汰勞力密集，低附加價值（Low added value）的產業，至使三區投資廠家逐漸減少，而投資總金額卻相對增加，1988 年投資商家減至 246 家，投資總金額卻增加到 6.25 億美元，平均每家投資資金額提高到 2,540,650 美元，至 1998 年，台灣加工出口區數量增加，區內繼續轉型朝向高科技產業發展及增加服務轉運業，投資廠商只有 229 家，投資總金額增至 28.92 億美元，平均每家投資為 1262.8 萬美元，至 2003 年共有投

資廠商 352 家，總投資金額達 64.74 億美元，平均每家投資金額達到 1839.2 萬美元以上，投資金額呈年年上升的驅勢。

表三　台灣加工出口區歷年來區投資事業及投資金額統計表

單位：佰萬美元

投資年份	總計		高雄園區		楠梓園區		臺中園區		中港園區		其他園區	
	家數	金額	家數	金額	家數	金額	家數	金額	家數	金額	家數	金額
1966	51	10	51	10								
1967	109	26	109	26								
1968	128	25	128	25								
1969	161	36	161	36								
1970	183	55	162	41	9	7	12	7				
1971	192	63	161	46	18	10	13	7				
1972	226	77	164	50	46	18	16	9				
1973	293	140	151	55	96	57	46	28				
1974	291	156	147	64	101	63	43	29				
1975	291	176	144	72	105	71	42	33				
1976	291	208	137	78	109	85	45	45				
1977	291	229	135	89	110	89	46	51				
1978	295	255	130	96	119	105	46	54				
1979	303	281	128	104	130	120	45	57				
1980	294	301	131	120	118	124	45	57				
1981	297	346	128	132	120	142	49	72				
1982	289	365	125	145	115	146	49	74				
1983	283	382	120	150	115	145	48	87				

1984	271	417	113	160	112	165	46	92				
1985	252	397	112	166	93	133	47	98				
1986	252	459	101	140	104	211	47	108				
1987	252	552	102	155	104	273	46	124				
1988	246	625	98	166	103	329	45	130				
1989	239	706	93	176	101	384	45	146				
1990	235	796	89	190	100	441	46	165				
1991	239	878	90	225	104	495	45	158				
1992	242	923	102	521	93	210	47	192				
1993	233	914	89	198	99	545	45	171				
1994	233	969	88	189	97	601	48	179				
1995	235	1206	93	265	96	738	46	203				
1996	231	1576	90	300	96	1047	45	229				
1997	225	1930	88	356	93	1291	43	277	1	6		
1998	229	2892	97	607	89	1758	37	322	4	55	2	150
1999	238	3444	94	711	90	2038	36	405	6	76	12	214
2000	260	4384	85	794	93	2458	34	513	7	85	41	534
2001	274	5307	84	819	93	2700	33	551	9	79	55	1158
2002	305	5919	81	875	95	2868	40	641	18	91	71	1444
2003	352	6474	81	990	97	2993	51	771	32	217	91	1503

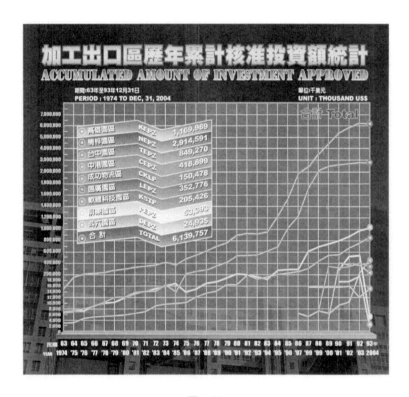

圖　四

2、歷年進出口金額統計（表四）

　　與投資相對應的業績便是進出口貿易金額的表現，1966
年開始有僑外資投資到高雄加工出口區，至 1968 年開始有
進出口貿易的發生，當年進口金額為 2960 萬美元，出口 2670
萬美元，虧損 290 萬美元，然而相對於政府當年貿易赤字，
加工出口區的貢獻為 2.55％，至 1970 年已有 183 家廠商，
進口為 9,010 萬美元，出口為 10,940 萬美元，年順差達到

1,930 萬美元；1988 年進口 17.841 億美元，出口 37.663 億美元，順差 19.822 億美元，對國家當年順差達到 18.03％的貢獻；1998 年，229 家投資，進口 51.69 億美元，出口 73.329 億美元，順差 21.639 億美元，對國家當年順差貢獻達到 36.57％，及至 2003 年，352 家，進口 47.325 億美元，出口 60.176 億美元，順差 12.850 億美元，對國家當年順差貢獻為 7.57％；此種績效及貢獻亦為當今世界加工出口區協會內會員國所驚嘆不及者。

3、歷年勞工人數及工資統計（表五）

歷年勞工人數，每年略有消長，但總括觀之，除初期五年，由約 5000 人，逐年快速成長到 40,000 人，以及隨經濟消長及廠家增減有所改變，但平均每年總員工人數均保持在六萬上下變動，其中 1987 年總員工人數達到 90,807 人，而單月總人數曾超過 10 萬人，近五、六年來，由於加工出口區轉型向高科技及轉運業發展，總人數略呈現減少，但也維持在六萬人左右。至於區內員工薪資的變動，其基本工資，根據政府勞基法執行，但各公司各有不同的福利標準，平均每年每月個人工資呈現一定比例的調漲，1968 年平均每月每人工資 NT960 元，逐年調漲，到 1984 年超過壹萬元達 NT10,711 元，1992 年超過貳萬元達 NT22,041 元，1998 年超過參萬元達 NT31.612 元，2003 年為 NT32,983 元，尤其值得注意的是，每年在加工出口區內員工工資總金數額之高甚為驚人，1968 年為 370 餘萬美元，到 1984 年提高到 2,828 餘萬美元，1992 年再提高到 6.85 億多美元，1998 年達到 7.3

億多美元，2003 年更高達 8 億多美元，38 年來總計加工出口區薪資的金額，如非加工出口區投資廠商的提供，將會變成政府一筆龐大的負擔。

表四　台灣加工出口區歷年對外貿易統計表

單位：佰萬美元

Year	Export			Import			Balance		
	Amount	Annual Growth %	%of the Country	Amount	Annual Growth %	%of the Country	Amount	Annual Growth %	%of the Country
1967	8.0		1.24%	11.6		1.44%	-3.6		2.20%
1968	26.7	233.75	3.38%	29.6	155.17	3.28%	-2.9	-19.44	2.55%
1969	62.2	132.95	5.93%	54.4	83.78	4.48%	7.8	-368.97	-4.78%
1970	109.4	75.88	7.38%	90.1	65.63	5.92%	19.3	147.44	-45.27%
1971	163.5	49.45	7.93%	110.3	22.42	5.98%	53.2	175.65	24.54%
1972	241.1	47.46	8.07%	165.4	49.95	6.58%	75.7	42.29	15.96%
1973	404.7	67.86	9.03%	299.8	81.26	7.90%	104.9	38.57	15.18%
1974	511.3	26.34	9.07%	309.9	3.37	4.45%	201.4	91.99	-15.18%
1975	459.0	-10.23	8.65%	270.6	-12.68	4.55%	188.4	-6.45	-29.30%
1976	682.5	48.69	8.36%	396.6	46.56	5.22%	285.9	51.75	50.39%
1977	761.2	11.53	8.13%	395.3	-0.33	4.64%	365.9	97.94	42.46%
1978	937.6	23.17	7.39%	564.7	42.85	5.12%	372.9	-34.10	22.46%
1979	1245.0	32.79	7.73%	680.4	20.49	4.61%	564.6	51.41	42.46%
1980	1463.5	17.55	7.39%	751.7	10.48	3.81%	711.8	26.07	918.46%
1981	1589.2	8.59	7.03%	799.4	6.35	3.77%	789.8	10.96	55.95%
1982	1626.1	2.32	7.32%	812.1	1.59	4.30%	814.0	3.06	24.55%
1983	1620.8	-0.33	6.45%	864.6	6.46	4.26%	756.2	-7.10	15.64%

1984	2036.0	25.62	6.68%	1072.3	24.02	4.88%	963.7	27.44	11.34%
1985	1872.1	-8.05	6.09%	945.8	-11.80	4.70%	926.3	-3.88	8.72%
1986	2402.7	28.34	6.03%	1231.7	30.23	5.09%	1171.0	26.42	7.47%
1987	3173.6	32.08	5.91%	1628.7	32.23	4.66%	1544.9	32.78	8.26%
1988	3766.3	18.56	6.21%	1784.1	9.54	3.59%	1982.2	27.48	18.03%
1989	3907.3	3.74	5.89%	1819.4	1.98	3.48%	2087.9	5.33	14.87%
1990	3525.1	-9.78	5.24%	1616.8	-11.14	2.95%	1908.3	-8.60	15.27%
1991	3990.6	13.21	5.24%	1919.5	18.72	3.05%	2071.1	8.53	15.58%
1992	4190.4	5.01	5.14%	2097.6	9.28	2.91%	2092.8	1.05	25.43%
1993	4325.5	3.22	5.08%	2283.3	8.85	2.96%	2042.2	-2.42	25.43%
1994	4780.2	10.51	5.14%	2800.6	22.66	3.28%	1979.6	-3.07	25.71%
1995	6272.0	31.21	5.62%	3779.8	34.96	3.65%	2492.2	25.89	30.73%
1996	6897.1	9.97	5.95%	3987.1	5.48	3.89%	2910.0	16.76	21.44%
1997	7934.1	15.04	6.50%	5105.9	28.06	4.46%	2828.2	-2.81	36.94%
1998	7332.9	-7.58	6.63%	5169.0	1.24	4.94%	2163.9	-23.49	36.57%
1999	7075.2	-3.51	5.82%	5232.9	1.24	4.73%	1842.3	14.86	16.90%
2000	8704.8	23.03	8.87%	6843.2	30.77	4.89%	1861.6	1.05	22.40%
2001	6586.7	-24.33	5.36%	4168.4	-39.09	3.89%	2418.2	29.90	15.47%
2002	6149.6	-6.64	4.71%	3827.1	-8.19	3.40%	2322.5	-3.96	12.87%
2003	6017.6	-2.15	4.17%	4732.5	23.66	3.72%	1285.0	-44.67	7.57%

圖　五

表五　歷年年平均員工人數及工資累計表

Year	Average Wage Per Month （NT$）	Average No. of Workers	Annual Wage Income + 1 Month Bonus （NT$）	Equivalent in US$	
1967	810	4600	48438000	÷40=US$	1210950
1968	962	11961	149584266	÷40=US$	3739607
1969	1075	23388	326847300	÷40=US$	8171183
1970	1183	35332	543370828	÷40=US$	13584271

1971	1358	44056	777764624	÷40=US$	19444116
1972	1424	52084	980839808	÷40=US$	24520995
1973	1713	69495	1547584155	÷38=US$	40725899
1974	2303	71387	2137255393	÷38=US$	56243563
1975	2527	60795	1997176545	÷38=US$	52557278
1976	3182	71931	2975497746	÷38=US$	78302572
1977	3641	73136	3461746288	÷38=US$	91098587
1978	4176	74182	4027192416	÷36=US$	111866456
1979	4886	77522	4924042396	÷36=US$	136778955
1980	6037	79257	6220168617	÷36=US$	172782462
1981	7562	77663	7634738878	÷38=US$	200914181
1982	8782	73078	8343022948	÷40=US$	208575574
1983	9903	73828	9504542892	÷40=US$	237613572
1984	10711	81241	11312240563	÷40=US$	282806014
1985	12030	77640	12142119600	÷40=US$	303552990
1986	12426	82437	13316708106	÷35.5=US$	375118538
1987	13162	90807	15537622542	÷28.6=US$	543273515
1988	14299	86863	16146702481	÷28.2=US$	872578102
1989	16067	77314	16148652494	÷26.2=US$	616360782
1990	18492	68196	16394045616	÷27.1=US$	604946333
1991	19935	66151	17143362405	÷25.7=US$	667056903
1992	22041	60747	17406020151	÷25.4=US$	685276384
1993	24216	53189	16744322712	÷26.7=US$	627128191
1994	26140	51792	17599957440	÷26.5=US$	664149337
1995	27820	55191	19960377060	÷26.5=US$	753221776
1996	28988	55779	21019981476	÷27.5=US$	764362963
1997	29997	57016	22234016376	÷28.7=US$	774704403

1998	31612	59598	24492155688	÷33.5=US$	731109125
1999	31693	59664	24582104976	÷32.3=US$	761055882
2000	32563	67451	28553289869	÷31.2=US$	915169547
2001	31739	65259	26926320213	÷33.8=US$	796636693
2002	35453	62165	26226729685	÷34.6=US$	757997968
2003	32983	64251	27549479529	÷34.4=US$	800856963
Total			447036022082		14455492629

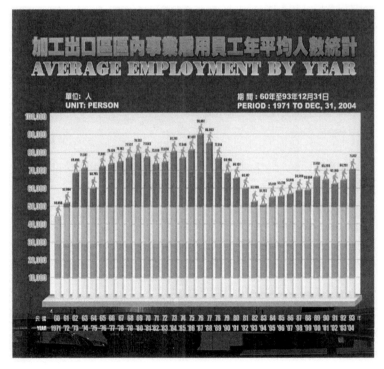

圖　六

31

4、歷年生產力統計：

（1）投資生產力（表六）：

投資生產力含意為廠商每投資一元，所獲得產值的能力，即為產出價值與投資資本額的比值，例如 1967 年，區內總投資金額為 2,600 萬美元，而年產出出口總值為 800 萬美元，故其投資生產力，或謂產值為 0.31，以後逐年成長，1970 年為 1.99；1984 年為 4.88；1987 年為 5.75，但到 2000 年轉型朝向高科技發展及其生產力大幅下降到 1.99 至 2003 年僅為 0.93，此在說明高科技產業投資資本大，而利潤率低，但就金額數字而言卻很大，所以高科技產業仍為投資大眾所喜好，加工出口區也不例外向此方向邁進。

（2）勞動生產力（表七）：

加工出口區內勞動生產力也與投資生產力的驅勢相似，建區初期勞動生產力很低，1967 年為 1,781 美元／人，以後逐年高升，1986 年轉型及勞動生產力成跳躍式的成長，1986 年提高到 29,146 美元／人，1991 年再提高到 60,325 美元／人，1995 年更高達 113,641 美元／人，到 2000 年高到 129,054 美元／人，到 2001 年開始逐年下降，2003 年降到 93,700 美元／人，此亦為高科技產業特性使然，非勞工不盡力，即便如此，此勞動生產力的數值仍傲視世界各國加工出口區的績效。

（3）土地生產力（表八）：

　　1967 年台灣加工出口區土地生產力只有 12.1 萬美元／Ha，1976 年跳躍到 379.2 萬美元／Ha，1986 年提高到 1,251.4 萬美元／Ha，年年升高，到 1996 年為最高達 3,592.2 萬美元／Ha，1997 年因新設加工出口區加入營運土地面積擴大，而短期內新區不可能有滿額的投資廠商，因而影響土地生產力開始下滑，所以 1997 年土地生產力下滑到 2,150.2 萬美元／Ha，2000 年滑至 681.4 萬美元／Ha，此項土地生產力至今世界各國也無法與之匹比。

　　這三項生產力的力道為台灣加工出口區傲視全球的珍寶，也因此珍寶才使台灣加工出口區數十年來仍能立足於台灣經濟發展的行例，而未被淘汰，同時亦為世界各國加工出口區的典範，故台灣加工出口區當應珍惜更加努力，再接再勵。

表六 台灣加工出口區投資生產力統計表

年份	年出口值 （USD$ Million）	年投資金額 （USD$ Million）	產值 USD$ /IUSD	增長值 （倍）	附註
1967	8.0	26	0.31	1	
1968	26.7	25	1.07	3.45	
1969	62.2	36	1.73	5.57	
1970	109.4	55	1.99	6.42	
1971	163.5	63	2.60	8.37	
1976	682.5	208	3.28	10.58	
1979	1,245.0	281	4.43	14.29	
1984	2,036.0	417	4.88	15.75	
1987	3,173.6	552	5.75	18.55	
1991	3,990.6	878	4.55	14.66	
1992	4,190.4	923	4.54	14.65	
1995	6,272.0	1,206	5.20	16.77	
1997	7,934.1	1,930	4.11	13.26	
2000	8,704.8	4,384	1.99	6.41	
2001	6,586.7	5,307	1.24	4.00	
2002	6,149.6	5,919	1.04	3.35	
2003	6,017.6	6,474	0.93	2.99	

※產值＝年出口值年投資總金額
（生產力）
※※增長值以 1967 年產值設定為 1，以及各年產值與 1967 年產值比即得各該年增長值

資料來源：台灣加工出口區管理處統計月報

表七　台灣加工出口區勞動生產力統計表

年份	年出口值 （US$1,000）	員工人數	產值 美元／人	增長值 （倍）	附註
1967	8,192	4,600	1,781	1	
1971	163,475	44,056	3,711	2.1	
1976	682,503	71,931	9,488	5.33	
1981	1,589,187	77,663	20,463	11.49	
1986	2,402,736	82,437	29,146	16.36	
1991	3,990,568	66,151	60,325	33.87	
1992	4,190,374	60,747	68,981	38.73	
1993	4,325,455	53,189	81,322	45.66	
1994	4,780,210	51,792	92,296	51.82	
1995	6,271,975	55,191	113,641	63.81	
1996	6,897,065	55,779	123,650	69.43	
1997	7,934,118	57,016	139,156	78.13	
1998	7,332,900	59,598	123,039	69.08	
1999	7,075,240	59,664	118,585	66.58	
2000	8,704,822	67,451	129,054	72.46	
2001	6,586,700	65,259	100,932	56.67	
2002	6,149,600	62,165	98,900	67.7	
2003	6.149,600	64,251	93,700	64	
※產值=年口值÷年平均總員工人數					

資料來源：台灣加工出口區管理處統計月報

表八　台灣加工出口區土地生產力統計表

年份	年出口值 （US$1,000）	土地面積 （Ha）	產值 （US$1,000/Ha）	增長值 （倍）	營運 區數
1967	8,192	68	121	1	1
1971	163,475	180	908	7.5	3
1976	682,503	180	3,792	31	3
1981	1,589,187	180	8,829	73	3
1986	2,402,736	192	12,514	103	3
1991	3,990,568	192	20,784	172	3
1992	4,190,374	192	21,825	180	3
1993	4,325,455	192	22,528	186	3
1994	4,780,210	192	24,897	206	3
1995	6,271,975	192	32,667	270	3
1996	6,897,065	192	35,922	297	3
1997	7,934,118	369	21,502	178	4
1998	7,270,805	415.6	17,945	148	5
1999	7,075,240	424.6	16,663	138	6
2000	8,704,822	432.5	20,127	166	7
2001	6,586,700	883.1	7,458.6	61.6	8
2002	6,149.60	883.1	6,963.7	57.6	10
2003	6,017.60	883.1	6,814	56	10

※產值=年口值÷年平均總員工人數

資料來源：台灣加工出口區管理處統計月報

貳、台灣加工出口區經營成功的因素探討

台灣加工出口區經營成功的因素很多，較為重要的有以下幾點：

1、正確的設區觀念

政府從 1953 年開始研究至 1966 年第一個高雄加工出口區的成立，共使用了十三年慎重研究的時間，而最後以合併自由貿易區及工業區的功能，截長補短成立加工出口區，俾能獲得較高的附加價值及經營積效，是為世界創舉。

2、優惠的租稅條件吸引工業投資

加工出口區除本身的設置管理法規外，全國的「獎勵投資條例」及「外國人投資條例」的優惠條件均適用於加工出口區，對吸引工業投資助益很大。

3、一元化的服務體制

加工出口區成立後，設置管理條例具有特別法的功能，區內業務授權及設置相關單位，使所有與廠商業務相關的手續，都在加工出口區圍牆內可以迅速全部辦妥，例如投資申請、公司登記、外銷簽證、勞工行政、海關報關、稅捐、產品儲運、以至郵局、銀行、醫療保健、娛樂、餐飲、消防⋯⋯等一應俱全，節省了廠商奔波各單位的辛勞及時間，此乃事權統一，簡化手續的有效制度。

4、高品質勞動力的效應

1960 至 1970 年代台灣的國民義務教育及國民好學精神，呈顯出勞動力教育水準整齊，加上工作意願強，工資低，促成勞動生產力高，形成各外國廠商爭相到台灣加工區設廠的盛況於一時。而今高品質勞動力依然存在而充沛，低成本的勞動力卻有所改變，因而外籍勞動力的引進產生替代作用。

5、土地出租、廠房出售或出租的影響

從 1966～1995 三十年產業型態由勞力密集漸進發展到技術密集，此其間區內土地只租不售，且以低價計算租金可防止土地炒作，而標準廠房出售，以成本計價，使廠商投入廠房資金有歸屬感，生根落實。1995 年後，轉型至高科技產業型態，廠房投資成本有限，不為投資成本主要考量因素之一，因而廠房也改為可租或售。

6、良好的基本設施

三區開發啟用之前完成整體的公共設施建設，如區內道路系統、電力系統、水系統、電訊系統、消防系統、安全系統、以及環境美化，使之成為最完善的花園工業區，讓廠商投資設廠無任何困擾之處。

7、管理處週密的服務作業

管理處除四大目標（投資、貿易、工商、勞工）的服務之外，另有如儲運服務、保健醫療服務、娛樂服務、餐飲服

務、消防服務、環境清潔、員工宿舍服務等等,都儘量能做到週密完善,尤其儲運服務對防止走私有極大的功效。然而服務要能做到臻於至善的境界,則必須因時制宜,適時修正作業法規或規則以達到迅速確實、便民的目標,致使區內生產、銷售、服務三者結為一鏈,因此在建區架構三方面的限制上,今已完全改觀。其中在錢方面,外匯管制上,依法定手續及法定金額內可自由匯入、匯出,不須每筆再向中央銀行申請核准;而在物的方面,機器設備、原物料的進入及成品的輸出,海關由實施已久的「圍牆式」門禁管理方式改採簡化通關作業手續,採取帳冊管理及自主管理,使「商流」、「物流」、「金流」及「資訊流」整合為一緊密的服務鏈,亦即將廠商、報關及海關一併列入關貿網路連線,使達到 e 化全球運籌管理系統的功能,如此加工區便無需再有圍牆設置,使服務作業簡化、快速、確實並節省成本。

8、加工出口區管理處自給自足的財務管理制度

台灣加工出口區設區立法之初,便法訂加工出口區管理處為自給自足的財務制度,政府僅提供初期的建區部份費用－國庫撥款,在建設高雄加工出口區時連國庫撥款也沒有,是由中美基金贈款及貸款開始建區及營運,加工出口區管理處以營運收入結餘所成立的事業基金(俗稱作業基金),作為加工出口區管理處長期經營自己自足的財源(見表九),如此將不至造成政府長期財務的負擔。加工出口區管理處為能自給自足,因此在組織架構上分成兩大部份,一部份為行政管理服務,諸如投資服務、對外貿易服務、工商行政服務、

勞工行政服務及其他尚有行政事務等方面的服務，如區內環境衛生的維護、安全及公共設施的辦理、執行等，此部份於加工出口區設置管理條例第二十條法訂得向外銷事業（即區內投資廠商）收取營業額最高千分之三為限的管理費，此便是自給自足主要的財源；另一部份為管理處本身的作業單位或謂生產單位，包括有儲運中心、保健中心、供應中心、消防隊等單位，以其對區內廠商提供的各項服務而收費，作為管理處事業基金（即作業基金）的財源，由是可知台灣加工出口區管理處自給自足作業基金的財源有二，即管理費收入及作業單位的作業服務費收入，然而管理處在基金支用上，仍然受政府預算編制的節制及審計單位的督導稽核，由於管理處在組織上分為兩部份－行政及作業，以至於財務的收支制度上也分為行政預算及作業預算，兩種不同制度併行運用執行，所以台灣加工出口區管理處在財務管理上有其複雜性及完整性（見表十），此類財務制度結構，一方面不至造成政府長時間財務的負擔，另方面因自力更生，自給自足而能永續經營，此乃之所以加工出口區經營成功，財務制度管理是為其要因之一。

9、有一部完善的法規──加工出口區法規彙編

「法」為法制之本，加工出口區三十九年來依據本法規經營發展十分順利，其間亦經多次修法以因應時宜，而世界各國加工區雖有充沛低工資的勞動力，低成本的土地，卻因法規之不夠週全或缺而窒礙難行，即為世界各國加工區所不及之所在。台灣加工出口區法規的基本精神及功能在於中央

政府授權加工出口區管理處做到「事權統一，一元化服務」
（中國稱之為一條龍的服務），高品質、高效率經營管理，
以臻於至善，所以本法規中明訂除管理處本身的業務及服務
項目外，並對區內支援的作業單位，如海關、稅捐稽徵所、
銀行、警察隊、郵局等也負有督導的責任，特別是對來區投
資案的審議核准亦授權由管理處主持審議會核准後呈報經
濟部核備，所以台灣加工出口區來區投資案的批准時間，最
長不會超過一個月，如此高效率的作業可完全得到投資人滿
意的回響；此外本法規條文至為週詳，管理處完全依法行
政，無所謂自由心證的認定，投資者依法經營，無人為的干
擾，如此順遂興旺；所以台灣加工出口區自 1966 年成立以
來，一路順暢擴大發展，邁向成功之路，乃法之使然也。

表九　經濟部加工區管理處高雄、楠梓、台中三區建區費用總表

來源別 區別	國庫撥款	中美基金贈款	中美基金貸款	銀行貸款	事業基金	合　計
高雄區		41,374,079.39	44,883,609.98	20,201,802.17	4,096,347.32	111,365,838.86
楠梓區	60,713,150.11	16,616,466.35	71,242,963.56	20,488,222.90	91,603,480.00	260,664,283.42
台中區	60,520,441.52	7,872,505.95	25,002,526.61	8,602,871.30	4,873,475.69	106,871,821.07
合　計	121,233,591.63	65,863,591.19	141,129,100.15	49,292,896.37	101,383,303.01	478,901,943.35

資料來源：台灣加工出口區管理處

表十　經濟部加工出口區管理處財務收支流程圖

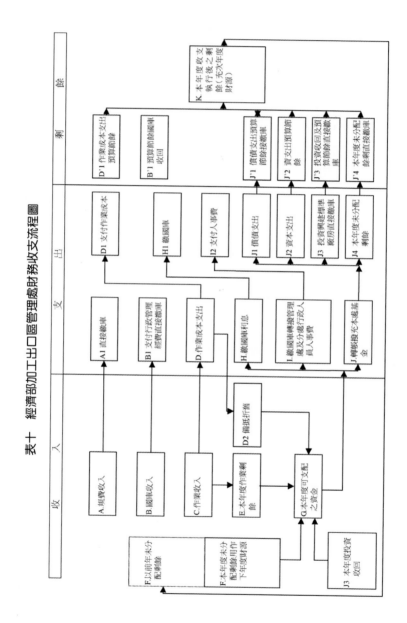

42

參、台灣加工出口區的效益貢獻

其最顯著的效益貢獻略舉以下五點說明：

1、促進國家初期資本財的形成，有利於政府外匯的使用；政府於民國 38 年（1949）遷到台灣後當時國家經濟至為貧困，拮据，外匯存底幾等於零，（表十一）直到 1961 年外匯存底才有＄9,300 萬美元，1963 年提高到＄1.77 億美元，1973 年突破了十億美元，以後一路昌旺發展，到 2004 年已高達＄2,417.38 億美元，成為世界外匯存底的第三大國；由此可知 1961 年以前國家資本財（Capital）是一無所有；至 1966 年外匯存底也才＄2.75 億美元，無法言及國力的展現，及至 1966 年台灣加工出口區成立，吸引僑外投資，並以美元為投資標的（見表三）存入國庫銀行，再加上區內國際貿易每年大量的順差（見表四）亦存入國庫銀行，如此便促成國家資本財的形成，快速成長，對政府外匯的應用上有甚大的方便及效益產生。

2、就業機會的增加促成小康社會的基礎，而至形成小資本密集，到中小企業的發展，更而促進社會經濟活力及社會安定。

3、因加工出口區的成功，1970 年促成新竹科學園區的成立，帶動國家高科技工業的發展及影響國家整體經濟轉型。

4、加工出口區外商除帶進技術，提升國內生產技術外，還帶進了國際市場及國際貿易，有利於國產品進軍國際市場，促進政府外匯存底增加，累積了國家整體財富。

5、加工出口區現已成為我國在世界的櫥窗功能，並配合政府政策協助開發中國家建設加工出口區，發展經濟。更而對欲了解我加工出口區的友邦人員開班訓練，以廣被其影響力。

表十一　中華民國歷年外匯存底統計表

新台幣億元：%

民國	流動性負債		金融機構淨超額準備	股票市場股價指數	銀行間收盤美元	支票存款	退票 *15	外匯存底	本國銀行	消費者物價
年月	期底金額	年增率	超額(+)不足(-)	(民國55年=100)	(期底)(新台幣元)	年回轉次數(次)	張數比率	(百萬美元)	逾放比率17	指數年增率
50	174	0.00	--	--	--	--	--	93	--	8.15
51	200	15.12	--	--	--	101.3	--	71	--	2.37
52	263	31.51	--	--	--	101.3	--	177	--	2.19
53	337	28.13	--	--	--	113.9	--	242	--	-0.16
54	391	16.15	--	--	--	109.6	--	245	--	-0.08
55	473	20.95	--	--	--	103.3	--	275	--	2.04
56	586	23.81	--	--	--	98.9	--	335	--	3.38
57	660	12.66	--	105	--	100.0	--	300	--	7.84
58	794	20.24	--	104	--	104.5	0.59	395	--	5.13
59	966	21.68	--	120	40.0000	104.6	0.64	482	--	3.67
60	1,247	29.11	--	127	40.0000	104.9	0.51	439	--	2.83
61	1,682	34.95	--	161	40.0000	100.2	0.55	651	--	2.97

62	2,254	33.98	--	372	38.0000	108.6	0.34	1,026	--	8.17
63	2,781	23.37	--	350	38.0000	113.4	0.44	1,055	--	48.15
64	3,542	27.39	--	317	38.0000	104.0	0.76	1,074	--	5.46
65	4,451	25.65	--	343	38.0000	104.9	0.89	1,516	--	2.52
66	5,902	32.60	--	362	38.0000	108.2	0.59	1,345	--	7.03
67	7,889	33.67	+49	554	36.0000	101.1	0.33	1,406	--	5.82
68	8,545	8.32	+43	561	36.0300	102.1	0.45	1,392	--	9.71
69	10,409	21.81	+3	547	36.0100	121.4	0.34	2,205	--	18.95
70	12,449	19.60	+123	549	37.8400	147.2	0.45	7,235	--	16.62
71	15,467	24.24	+70	477	39.9100	168.5	0.59	8,532	--	2.97
72	19,514	26.16	+20	654	40.2700	179.6	0.65	11,859	--	1.38
73	23,645	21.17	+25	873	39.4700	197.9	0.67	15,664	--	-0.02
74	28,480	20.45	+93	746	39.8500	191.9	0.74	22,556	--	-0.16
75	35,507	24.67	+27	945	35.5000	171.9	0.39	46,310	--	0.70
76	42,550	26.68	+57	2,135	28.5500	159.7	0.38	76,748	--	0.52
77	50,106	17.76	+173	5,202	28.1700	191.8	0.36	73,897	1.23	1.28
78	62,055	23.85	+159	8,616	26.1600	261.4	0.35	73,224	0.88	4.42
79	69,905	12.65	+190	6,775	27.1075	301.5	0.42	72,441	0.93	4.12
80	82,874	18.55	+116	4,929	25.7475	300.3	0.39	82,405	0.97	3.63
81	97,510	17.66	+52	4,272	25.4025	313.4	0.43	82,306	0.81	4.46
82	113,536	16.44	+39	4,215	26.6260	347.8	0.54	83,573	1.14	2.94
83	129,901	14.41	+76	6,253	26.2400	415.9	0.56	92,454	1.82	4.09
84	142,621	9.79	+50	5,544	27.2650	383.2	0.67	90,310	2.85	3.68
85	156,464	9.71	+77	6,004	27.4910	438.7	1.27	88,038	3.68	3.07
86	170,181	8.77	+2	8,411	32.6380	498.9	1.07	83,502	3.70	0.90
87	185,777	9.16	-104	7,738	32.2160	524.6	1.04	90,341	4.36	1.68
88	202,966	9.25	-3	7,427	31.3950	454.0	1.01	106,200	4.88	0.18

89	219,344	8.07	-18	7,847	32.9920	495.9	0.89	106,742	5.34	1.26
90	234,809	7.05	+79	4,907	34.9990	559.5	0.87	122,211	7.48	-0.01
91	249,750	6.36	+79	5,226	34.7530	440.9	0.61	161,656	6.12	-0.20
92	273,890	9.67	+55	5,162	33.9780	387.5	0.47	206,632	4.33	-0.28
93	301,550	10.10	+120	6,034	31.9170	294.9	0.39	241,738	2.78	1.62

15.84 年年底以前，該比率為已扣除註銷退票紀錄部分之淨退票張數比率。

17.自 82 年起，該比率除含本國一般銀行及中小企業銀行之國內營業單位逾放資料外，亦含其國際金融業務分行與海外分行資料。

第三章 台灣加工出口區經營成功的擴散效應

壹、台灣加工出口區初創經營成功震撼了全世界

台灣加工出口區於 1966 年 12 月 3 日正式成立於高雄市，稱之為高雄加工出口區，隨後因快速成長而於 1969 年分別成立楠梓加工出口區及台中加工出口區，三區之上設有管理處，各區分別設有分處，掌理各區業務的管理、執行及服務，其最主要的業務項目有吸引投資服務、對外貿易服務、勞工行政服務、工商服務、儲運服務、區內環境美化、消防、醫療保健、宿舍等服務，另有其他有關單位的配套服務如海關、銀行、稅捐、郵局、加油站等共同組合成為一元化（one stop service）的服務園區，使來區投資的廠商辦理各項業務手續簡便快捷，省時省力，而區內的水、電、電訊、道路等公共設施更是週全完善，使廠商投資設備生產順利及對外通訊聯絡便捷，廠商在此一花園工業城中安全安適的經營發展，生意興隆，家家賺錢獲益，同時也創造了就業機會，繁榮地方及增進了國家收益，Made in Taiwan 的貨品行銷到

國際市場，推廣了中華民國台灣在國際的聲譽，完全達到政府研擬設區的目的，此外，加工出口區營運的實績以數據展示出來的成就霎時震驚了世界各國，就連聯合國工業發展組織（UNIDO），世界銀行（IBRD），亞洲生產力中心（APO）等國際組織單位也投以關注的眼光和重視，尤其世界各未開發國家及開發中國家於震驚之餘，即時採取行動仿效設置加工出口區以咨發展該等國家的經濟，一時間，中華民國台灣加工出口區甚囂塵上，蜚聲國際。

貳、台灣加工出口區成功的擴散效應

根據第二章表三、四、五等統計資料上了解，從 1966 年到 1969 年僅三年的時間，來區投資設廠的廠商從 51 家增加到 161 家，投資金額也從 1000 萬美元增加到 3600 萬美元（表三），其來區投資的廠商主要是從香港、澳門、日本，由於在如此短的時間便來了那麼多投資廠商，所關連到的便是國際貿易的發生，1967 年便有 800 萬美元出口金額，1160 萬美元的進口金額，該年的營收為逆差 360 萬美元，但未及二年，1969 年，出口增加到 6220 萬美元，進口增加到 5440 萬美元，營收變為順差 780 萬美元，從此以後再也沒有逆差的情事發生（表四），從 1967 年到 1975 年，中央政府對外貿易呈現非常不穩定的現象，甚而 1969 年、1970 年、1974 年及 1975 年等四年為逆差，而這四年中，加工出口區卻為順差，表現良好，若沒有加工出口區的順差，中央政府當年

的逆差將更加擴大，加工出口區三十九年來每年貿易出口金額約為中央總出口金額的 5%至 8%，進口約為 3%至 6%，年順差約為 15%至 25%，但也有偶爾達到 50%或以上者，由此可見貢獻之巨；然而更值得令人欣慰歡愉的是創造了廣大的就業機會，從 1966 年設區成立，開始吸引廠商來區投資，1967 年便有 51 家，其所造就的就業勞工人數平均每月便達到 4600 人，平均每人每月薪資為新台幣 810 元，到 1969 年便有 161 家投資廠家，勞工人數也增加到 23,388 人，工資也隨著調升到每月新台幣 1,075 元，年薪資總額由 1,210,950 美元增加到 1969 年的 8,171,183 美元（表五），如此龐大的收入及快速成長，怎不令人興奮而震盪了世界各國，從此台灣加工出口區成功的擴散效應開始蔓衍發酵，致有：

一、世界各國開始仿效設置加工出口區：

韓國於 1970 年即時成立馬山加工出口區（Masan Free Export Zone），隨後又於 1873 年成立 Iksan Export Zone 以及 1974 年成立 Dadok Research & Science Park 等。此外，菲律賓也是繼台灣加工出口區之後於 1969 年 6 月，經中華民國政府協助之下，完成立法設置加工出口區，於 1972 年成立巴丹加工出口區（Battaan ECO Zone），而今却已有 117 個加工出口區，隨後又有 25 個國家或地區成立加工出口區。

二、世界加工出口區協會（WEPZA）如是成立：

聯合國工業發展組織（UNIDO）有鑑於台灣加工出口區發展的成功可作為借鏡，自此以後即積極鼓勵開發中國家設立加工出口區，並在該組織的推動贊助下，於 1975 年 12 月 9 日至 11 日在維也納舉行的專家會議，探討設立世界加工出口區協會，逐於 1978 年 1 月正式成立世界加工出口區協會（The World Export Processing Zones Association，WEPZA），計有 30 個國家代表出席在菲律賓馬尼拉舉行的成立大會，通過章程。該會的主要目標為鼓勵會員國採取聯合行動，相互協助，搜集與傳播統計資料，交換政府政策與激勵措施，安排計劃與作業人員的訓練，研擬並通過標準規範，以避免過度擴充與競爭。

三、亞洲生產力中心（APO）舉辦研討該會員國中，加工出口區及科學園區的評鑑：

1975 年 10 月，亞洲生產力組織（APO）也應各會員國的要求，在韓國漢城舉辦一次為期一週之加工出口區研討會，參加國家和地區計有台灣、美、日、韓、菲、泰、印尼、印度、巴基斯坦等代表。繼而 1998 年筆者應 APO 的邀請負責對 APO 會員國中，設有加工出口區及科學園區者予以研究，評鑑該等加工出口區及科學園區的經營績效及對國家的貢獻，為期一年的研究，於 1999 年 11 月 23 日至 26 日在韓國漢城召開評鑑研討會，由筆者主持，會中特別邀請到韓國

國家科學院負責人 Dr. Hyung –Sup Choi （Member, Natural Science Division, National Academy of Sciences, ROK）演講，講題是「The Role of Science & Technology Parks in the Industrialization of Developing Countries」,Dr. Hyung-Sup Choi 在韓國國家科技發展有崇高地位，相當於我國李資政國鼎先生之於中華民國一樣受國人尊敬，由是可見韓國政府對本次評鑑研討會的重視。參加研討會的國家有 Bangladesh、中華民國、Fiji、India、Indonesia、Iran、韓國、馬來西亞、Nepal、菲律賓、Sri Lanka、泰國、越南等 16 國代表，而接受評鑑加工出口區計有 13 區，科學園區 5 區，共計 18 區。

四、世界銀行對台灣加工出口區的關注及肯定：

　　世界銀行（IBRD）也於 1978 年 7 月間曾提出一份有關加工出口區之研究報告，對甚多開發中國家競相設立、廣為傳布的加工出口區就其特性、傳布情形、重要性、提供之貢獻以及一些國家的政策等深入分析探討，並對其促進國家整體工業發展及創造就業機會的角色與卓越貢獻提出肯定的結論。世界銀行對各國設置加工出口區的計劃願意提供貸款支援，其審核著眼於能促進地主國整體工業發展之裨益者為優先，該行並與世界加工出口區協會保持聯繫。

　　世界銀行對台灣加工出口區的成就，影響所及，至使甚多開發中國家競相仿效設立加工出口區，對該等國家整體工業經濟發展及創造就業機會等的卓越貢獻予以肯定，即至 1989 年 11 月 6 日至 9 日在台灣高雄市，由台灣加工出口區

負責主辦的第 10 屆世界加工出口區年會中,仍然對台灣加工出口區的成就堅信不疑,以至在研討會中,世界銀行代表 Dr.Keesing 因十分的肯定台灣加工出口區實際貢獻,而與澳洲大學經濟學教授 Dr. Healy 持相反意見,於會中彼此爭論不休,最後由筆者發言,說明加工出口區設立基本存在的要件及台灣加工出口區實績的表現,並允次日歡迎入會代表參觀楠梓加工出口區以實情作見證,才平息了此一爭論,次日 Dr.Healy 參觀後私下與筆者談,希望多保持連繫及交換資料。

五、台灣加工出口區再度應邀加入世界加工出口區協會(WEPZA)為會員國:

中華民國於 1971 年 10 月 25 日退出聯合國,隨著也退出初創成立的世界加工出口區協會的發起會員國身份,時隔 14 年,1985 年 6 月 27 日突然接到世界加工出口區協會(World Export Processing Zones Association,簡稱 WEPZA)祕書長潘納先生 TEODORO Q.PENA)來函說明該協會於當年 9 月 11 日至 15 日將在美國奧納章州開年會,討論世界各國加工出口區有關投資、貿易、市場、行政管理、優惠等問題,希望台灣加工出口區能派代表參加會議並邀請入會為會員。隨後該協會執行秘書波林先生(Richard L. Bolin)來函,強調台灣加工出口區在世界各國加工出口區中最為優秀,成就最大,且為各國學習仿效的對象,如該協會不能有中華民國的加工出口區加入,該會將失去存在的意義,彼時,筆者

正擔任台灣加工出口區管理處處長，對此項邀請至感欣慰，也多所考量，畢竟我方的參與是貢獻多於收益。經過二年多長時間的函件往反及執行秘書波林來我加工區當面溝通，終於於 1987 年 9 月 11 日於聖地亞哥的年會中通過我以中華民國加工出口區正會員入會。筆者並於 1988 年在哥倫比亞的巴蘭吉亞市（Barran-guilla）年會中爭取到 1989 年的年會在台灣高雄市召開，計有 22 會員國及 5 非會員國 121 人參加，盛況空前，十分成功。

六、中國於 1979 年開始設置出口加工區及各類經濟發展園區：

　　在世界各開發中國家仍在繼續仿效設置加工出口區作為國家經濟發展政策模式的同時，最引人注意和受到重視者，乃中華人民共和國（簡稱中國）在這方面的發展及成效。中國中央政府的整體經濟展規劃藍圖，在 1978 年 12 月 18 日至 22 日的中國共產黨第十一屆三中全會中，確立「對內經濟改革與對外經濟開放」其目標有三，第一首在「解決溫飽」，第二是在十九世紀末達到「小康水平」，第三是在二十世紀五十年內達到「中等發達國家水平」。根據此改革目標，從 1979 年 1 月深圳蛇口工業園區成立後，即時在該年 12 月決定按中共十一屆三中全會中決定全國工作重心轉移到經濟上來，至有廣義內涵的「工業園區」的成立，大致上「工業園區」有以下幾種型態區分及成立：

1、「經濟技術開發區」

它是以吸引國外的工業投資為主，產業也以工業為主、工貿結合，在區內的內商和外商投資企業均可享受其相關的優惠政策。1984 年，國務院決定開放大連、天津等 14 個沿海港口城市，這些城市都建立了「經濟技術開發區」，1992 年又批准在昆山、蕪湖、武漢等地設立，先後共設立 32 個國家級經濟技術開發區，享受沿海經濟技術開發區相同的優惠政策。近年來在內地又出現了相當一批在省、自治區的省會、首府設立的經濟技術開發區。這些經濟技術開發區，大多設在大中城市的城效結合部，實際上是城市的擴張，它既強調吸引外資，同時也鼓勵內資，但享受政策不同於沿海經濟技術開發區。

2、「高新技術產業開發區」

國際上通常稱作「科技工業園」，台灣稱之為科學園區，它以吸引高科技企業和高新產業為主，並在此基礎上推動外向型和開放型的技術與經濟的發展，它多設在科技、教育和經濟發達的地區。區內企業只有被認定為高新技術企業才能享受有關優惠政策。這種高新技術產業開發區是「工業園區」的新發展，類似美國矽谷及日本「筑波」。中國的高新技術產業開發區的出現稍晚於沿海經濟技術開發區。目前，中國國務院批准成立的國家高新區有 52 家，旨在促進科技與經濟結合，發展高新科技產業。它的任務不只是要發展經濟，壯大實力，更重要的是要發展民族高科技工業，以增進國際競爭實力。

3、「出口加工區」

自從 1966 年台灣加工出口區為世界首創以來，世界各開發中及未開發國家莫不仿效設置，中國也不例外，1979年 7 月國務院同意在廣東的深圳、珠海、汕頭及福建廈門等四市試辦「出口特區」。筆者於 1992 年 10 月應國務院特區辦的邀請參與有關出口加工區的設置及營運經驗座談會，並往昆山指導中國第一個最為成功的昆山出口加工區的創設，至今已屆滿 10 年，繼昆山出口加工區之後，全國各省，地方政府掀起一陣設置出口加工區的風潮，及至 2000 年 4月到 2002 年 6 月，中國國務院在全國相繼批准設立了 25 個國家級的出口加工區，2003 年 3 月又再度批准了 13 個國家級出口加工區，共 38 個區以後又陸續批准多區，至目前為止，總共有 56 區，其中驗收合格者有 39 區，已或開始營運，前批准的 38 區其名稱如下：

25 個出口加工區是：

已建設完成的 17 區：

吉林琿春、北京天竺、遼寧大連、山東煙台、山東威海、上海松江、浙江杭州、上海金橋、江蘇蘇州、江蘇昆山、福建廈門、廣東深圳、廣東廣州、湖北武漢、重慶、四川成都、天津。

建造中 8 區：

安徽蕪湖、浙江寧波、江蘇無錫、江蘇南通、陝西西安、河北秦皇島、內蒙古呼和浩特、河南鄭州。

新批准的 13 區：

上海青浦、漕河涇、關行、江蘇南京、鎮江、連雲港、蘇州高新區、山東濟南、青島、遼寧瀋陽、浙江嘉興、廣西北海、新疆烏魯木齊。

隨後批准的 18 個區：上海嘉定、廣東南沙、廣東惠州、雲南昆明、江蘇常州、江蘇吳中、江蘇揚州、江蘇常州、四川綿陽、遼寧瀋陽（張士）、江西九江、河北廊坊、湖南郴州、浙江慈溪、福建福州、福建福清、福建泉州出口加工區。

這些出口加工區主要分佈在沿海、沿江、沿邊、海港等開放城市的開發區內具有交通便利，信息靈敏，經濟活躍，環境典雅，人才資源豐富等優勢，前 25 區中已建設完成參與經營之 17 區 2002 年 9 月統計資料進出口總值達 38.79 億美元，其中仍以昆山出口加工區的 17.24 億元最高（表十二），最具成效。

4、「保稅工業區」

它以吸引外資企業為主，產品也全部或大部份出口，投資者享受「保稅」即關稅減、免的政策。它是專為加工、製造、裝配出口產品而開闢的新工業區。

5、「其它工業園區」

如以設區的特殊地理位置而命名的有「邊境合作區」等，又如以吸引某地域或某類型投資者命名的有「台商投資區」或「台灣工業區」、「歐洲工業園區」、「華僑投資區」等。

　　以上五類型的「工業園區」建設，是中國改革開放的一個重要產物，影響廣大深遠，對內而言，影向 13 億人民當前的生計改善，促進民富國強的實力，對外，影響全世界經濟的波動，市場走向，而以歷史進程來看，影響今後世世代代黃炎子孫生居、經濟、社會等型態，結構巨大的蛻變，出口加工區曾是此巨大影響、蛻變中的一顆因子，提供了一份莫大的貢獻；由是觀之，加工出口區的擴大效應可謂無遠弗屆，無與倫比，而倍感驕傲。

表十二　中國出口加工區招商、運作累計情況表

截至日期：2002. 9. 30

序號	加工區名稱	進區企業數量	新增投資企業	區外進入企業	投資總額（億美元）	協議入區企業數量	協議投資總額（億美元）	進口總值（億美元）	出口總值（億美元）	進出口總值（億美元）
1	江蘇昆山	37	33	4	10.98	7	0.3	10.33	6.91	71.24
2	上海松江	52	50	2	6.81	7	0.4	8.19	6.79	14.98
3	遼寧大連	58	55	3	3.59	5	0.8	0.93	0.94	1.87
4	山東煙台	62	33	29	0.66	65	2.6	0.616	0.72	1.336
5	山東威海	50	26	24	2.79	19	2.65	0.5918	0.6565	1.2483
6	蘇州工業園	8	8	0	1.3	10	5	0.9710	0.3483	1.3193
7	北京天竺	14	5	9	3.1	4	0.3	0.0215	0.0038	0.0253
8	四川成都	11	6	5	2.9648	25	1.1	0.0238	0.0129	0.0367
9	廣東深圳	16	14	2	0.407	6	1	0.078	0.019	0.097
10	廣東廣州	0	0	0	0	3	1.1730	0.0793	0.0467	0.1260
11	浙江杭州	10	10	0	1.7424	2	0.61	0.0889	0.0594	0.1483
12	吉林琿春	11	5	6	0.507	26	0.54	0.0666	0.0047	0.0713
13	湖北武漢	6	3	3	0.31	7	0.6	0.0203	0.00067	0.0210
14	福建廈門	7	5	2	0.96	0	0	0	0	0
15	天津	3	2	1	0.43	15	1.25	0.1687	0.1069	0.2756
16	重慶	5	4	1	0.1193	1	0.015	0	0	0
17	上海金橋	1	1	0	0.041	0	0	0	0	0
	總　計	351	260	91	36.71	202	18.34	22.18	16.62	38.79

第四章　加工出口區與國家(或地區) 經濟發展的互動關係

壹、未開發及開發中國家（地區）經濟、社會遭遇的共同問題

　　國家經濟之所以能夠發展，成長是在於生產產值的貢獻及包括第三類產業在內的勞務輸出所獲得報酬總產值的表現，總產值能有亮麗、可觀的表現，是國家整體經營長時間優異努力的成果，不是一蹴而起，隨手可拆取的果實，能促成經濟發展的因素，有經濟的層面及非經濟的層面，而就時序進程上看，分段執行，分初期、中期及長期發展階段，各階段有其發展的目標，擬訂不同的策略及執行手段，當然也就有不同程度的績效、成果，以展示經濟發展的實質貢獻及對人民的福祉。

　　加工出口區的建設營運是策略規劃中的一項，特別適用在初期發展階段；一般需要初期經濟發展階段的國家（或地區），都集中在未開發及開發中國家，這些國家的經濟、社會遭遇的共同問題有以下幾個現象：（１）社會普遍的貧窮，（２）急需大規模的就業機會，（３）政府資本財（capital）

嚴重匱乏，（4）缺乏技術技能，（5）急需內需替代產品
的供給，（6）政府整體經濟規劃能力明顯不足，（7）政
府及國民均缺乏經濟的法制認識及觀念，（8）普遍公共設
施不足或欠缺如自來水、電、電訊、公路……等；也就是缺
乏投資環境，這些問題，因加工出口區的設置經營，多能直
接及間接漸進的為之改善或部份解決，產生雪中送炭的功
用，解決飢腸之苦，並能延續發展。

貳、加工出口區之經營成功應有必要的經濟環境條件相配合

　　建設加工出口區，最基本的必要條件，除了要有充沛的
勞動力外，還需要有必備的基礎建設，如水、電、電訊、海
港、空港、公路……等以及財經配套措施，在開發中國家，
這些最起碼的必備條件尚可以滿足，例如菲律賓、泰國、印
尼，哥斯達尼加、巴拉馬、馬來西亞……等，都已具備發展
加工出口區的能力，事實上他們也都在朝此方向進行，然而
在未開發國家就不一定有能力備妥必要的基礎建設，更遑論
財經配套措施了，例如新內幾利亞（PNG）、柬埔塞……等；
具備勞動力，基礎建設的國家（或地區），雖可以辦加工出
口區，但不一定辦得成功，或辦得好，例如 1999 年 11 月在
韓國漢城舉辦的亞洲生產力中心對會員國的加工出口區及
科學園區評鑑（APO Survey on Export Processing Zones and
Science Parks），其結果在「Performance and Contribution of

the EPZs and Science Parks up to date」的評分中（表十三），菲律賓、馬來西亞、印度……等，都被評得很低，即表示該等國家的加工出口區經營績效並不理想；再例舉以下數例將更為明了。

例一、巴拉馬的加工出口區，由台灣的財產法人，海外投資開發股份有限公司（OiDC）出資規劃設計建設而成，同時也由 OiDC 公司派人負責經營，巴拉馬的公共基礎建設還算完善，但該加工出口區缺少一部專屬於加工出口區的法規憑作業務推動的依據，加之巴拉馬政府各項財經配套措施不能配合，以至一個新的投資案，區內管理單位無權核准，需經政府行政系統逐一批准，以至需時達數月甚而半年才能核准，投資人早已被如此工作效率嚇走了，而海關業務頗為煩瑣，缺乏服務的觀念，如此該加工區如何能經營成功？

例二、澳洲達爾文貿易發展特區（Darwin Internation Trade Development Zone），實為加工出口區，並與台灣加工出口區於 1987 年 10 月 23 日結為姊妹區，澳洲基礎建設很不錯，但該區設在北部省省會達爾文市近郊，接近達爾文港的一片空曠的砂漠地區上，一眼望去四週了無人煙，北部省總人口只有約 15 萬人，達爾文市 7 萬人，雖然達爾文貿易發展特區，對吸引投資同樣有各種法訂優惠條款，但勞動力卻要仰賴香港、澳門、馬來西亞等外地進口外勞，而澳洲外勞政策卻不如帛琉之落實，即因受限於該國的人口政策，外籍勞工只能有一年簽證一次的工作機會，對外勞而言沒有工作保障，至前往工作的外勞意願不高，踟足不前，而對投資人，每年也沒有固定的勞工工作，無法使技術成熟，產能

不穩定，因而困擾不已，而且外來勞工生活條件照顧也不週全，以至僅有的幾家投資廠商形成半停頓狀況，新的投資案則乏人問津，兩三年後該區管理局長 Mr. Ray. Mchenry 力有不逮而離職。

　　例三、馬其頓共和國，全國總面積 25,713 平方公里，總人口約 210 萬人，略有一點基礎建設，但該國為內陸國家，交通運輸管道受限制於他國，因而市場難找，資訊貧乏，幾與外界隔絕，加之社會並不安定，財政金融體制亦不健全，財經政策籌劃困難，即財經配套措施無法配合，因而欲設加工出口區解決其困境，幾不可能。

Apo Survey on Export Processing tones and scievce Parks-Nov.1999
Performance and Contribution of the EPZ and Science Parks upto date.

表十三　Final Grade and position of part 2

Name of country	Name of EPZ or Park	Group	Average grade of items														Total	Average	Position
			1	2	3	4	5	6	7	8*	9	10	11	12	13	14			
ROC	TEPZ	1	3	8	7	10	9	10	10	—	2	7	8	6	10	10	100	7.69	B+
ROK	MEPZ	1	3	6	8	10	8	10	2	—	0	2	10	6	0	6	71	5.46	C+
ROK	IEPZ	1	2	0	2	3	8	0	2	—	0	2	0	0	0	6	25	1.92	E+
ROK	DEPZ	1	2	2	5	0	10	3	0	—	0	0	0	6	8	6	42	3.23	D
India	SEEPZ	1	3	8	3	4	2	4	10	—	4	2	6	2	2	10	60	4.62	C−
Malaysia	EPZ	1	0	10	2	2	0	0	6	—	0	0	6	2	0	6	34	2.62	D−
Philippines	EPZ	2	5	0	2	10	7	0	10	—	0	0	10	2	0	6	52	4.00	C−
ROC	HSIP	2	3	2	10	10	9	4	6	—	0	3	8	6	10	10	81	6.23	B−
Bangladesh	EPZ	2	6	8	2	2	2	2	2	—	0	2	8	2	2	8	54	4.15	C−
India	MEPZ	2	3	10	2	3	2	10	10	—	2	2	6	2	4	8	64	4.92	C
India	FEPZ	2	2	10	2	2	2	10	10	—	2	2	8	6	4	10	70	5.38	C+
India	NEPZ	2	2	10	2	5	2	10	10	—	2	2	6	2	4	i0	67	5.15	C
India	BSTP	3	4	0	6	4	2	3	2	—	8	1	8	6	2	10	64	4.92	C
India	SNEPZ	3	6	8	2	6	2	6	10	—	10	3	10	6	2	10	81	6.23	B−
ROK	KHTSP	3	5	2	6	6	6	6	2	—	0	6	6	6	2	6	59	4.54	C−
Vietnam	EPZ	3	2	10	2	2	6	0	10	—	2	2	8	6	10	8	68	5.23	C

*Data not available.

資料來源：1999 年 11 月亞洲生產力中心（APO）所屬會員國之加工出口
區及科學園區在韓國漢城接受評鑑報告。

　　例四、印度是一個高科技發達的國家，尤其科技軟體設計工業特別強，而且該國的整體經濟建設近年來大有起色，外匯存底及外來投資也大有增進，但落後的基礎建設無多大改進，加上龐大的政府借貸及官僚體制，無法研擬彰顯出出色的財經政策，去年（2004）惠譽投資環境評等公司（Fitch Ratings）未對印度給予評等，原因指出「該國公共財政體質不良，乃是阻礙其信用評等升級的絆腳石」，此更說明整體經濟不振之所在；然而人口眾多，急需要就業的比率甚高，雖然從 1965 年開始在 Kandla 建設了 KAFTZ 加工出口區及隨後又建設了 SEEPZ 1974，FEPZ 1983，CEPZ 1984，NEPZ 1985，MEPZ 1984 及 VEPZ 1994 等共計七個加工出口區及科學園區，然而七個區歷年總計的產值並不儘理想（表十四），及七區創造的就業機會也有限（表十五）此顯見該國加工出口區經營管理的不善以及財經政策未臻於至善的規劃及執行。

　　例五、另一方面，基礎建設及財經政策均不儘理想，而勞動力頗為充沛的國家，因某種特殊因素促成個別加工出口區經營成功者如越南的新順加工出口區（The Tan Thuan EPZ），建區初期，除了勞動力外，國家整體的基礎建設幾乎完全沒有，而是由中華民國的光華投資公司完全負責從資金提供到軟硬體的各項規劃，建設及提供人才從事經營管理，而今非常成功，至 1993 年區內總投資開工的廠家數已達 104 家，投資總金額達美金 3.6 億多元，就業人數也達到近 37,600 多人，年進出口額 2003 年已達到進口美金 428,640,000 元，出口美金 551,560,000 元，順差美金

122,920,000 元，如此成效對越南國家的貢獻十分可觀，若政府財經政策措施能更密切配合，其貢獻就不僅止於一區個案的成就了。

　　例六、另有帛琉共合國，基礎建設也很少，亦無財經政策，而且全國（島國）總人口只有一萬八仟多人，即自有資金及勞動力幾等於零，但政府的配套政策，允許大批外籍勞工長期在該國工作，而市場因二次世界大戰後帛琉由美國託管，便視同美國之一部份，故市場也放在美國本土，凡輸往美國的產品，沒有關稅及配額限制，如此政策性配套措施彌補了勞動力不足的缺點，故此只要投資建區的單位投資部份基礎建設，即可使帛琉加工出口區順利營運有成功的機會，惟可惜該國因非經濟因素的影響，功虧一簣未能達成建區願望。

　　例七、此外，既無基礎建設，又無完備的財經政策，更無特殊原因的優勢，而要建設加工出口區經營，欲使其經營成功，實在是十分困難，

表十四　EPZ Exports and Share in Country Exports

（印度加工出口區出口點金額及所佔全國出口比率）

Year	EPZ Exports （US$ Million）	EPZ Share （%）
1980/81	56.57	0.68
1981/82	109.9	1.26
1982/83	209.2	2.30
1983/84	194.8	2.06
1984/85	303.4	2.84
1985/86	264.1	2.96
1986/87	267.8	2.75
1987/88	253.9	2.10
1988/89	357.9	2.56
1989/90	443.3	2.67
1990/91	549.9	3.03
1991/92	483.6	2.71
1992/93	476.4	2.57
1993/94	624.8	2.81
1994/95	846.8	3.23
1995/96	967.6	3.04
1996/97	1,214.2	3.67
1997/98	1,294.2	3.81

表十五　Zone-wise Employment（印度加工出口區就業人數）

as on 31 March 1998

Zone	Male	Female	Total	Tota Percentage
KAFTZ	7,268（69%）	3,232（31%）	10,500	12.92
SEEPZ	20,636（64%）	11,469（36%）	32,105	39.51
MEPZ	5,270（30%）	12,332（70%）	17,602	21.66
CEPZ	1,833（39%）	2,867（61%）	4,700	5.78
FEPZ	1,156（63%）	692（37%）	1,848	2.27
NEPZ	10,875（75%）	3,625（25%）	14,500	17.86
Total	47,038（57%）	34,217（43%）	81,255	100.00

資料來源：1999年11月漢城APO評鑑會議印度代表提供論文資料

　　例如約旦王國的經濟自由貿易區，因國家各項基礎建設闕如，財經政策，政府雖有心大力發展該區但卻不得法，又因民族性宗教的關係，以及中東地區環境的連帶影響，只能勉力的發展轉口業務，對就業機會沒有幫助，更遑論發展工業，或積極性的經濟發展體系。

　　例八、其他如柬甫塞，新內幾利亞（PNG）等條件更差，要如何發展加工出口區，端視該等國家政府睿智的決策及聰慧的執行能力了。

　　由以上這些案例，可以了解，建設加工出口區之能否成功，要有充沛的勞動力，基礎建設及政府財經政策配合措

施，此外還要有政府充份的支持，更重要的是要有一部專屬加工出口區的法規，以立法的力量促其成功，最後還要有堅強的經營團隊、管理機制，有了如此完整的配套體制，加工出口區經營成功是指日可待的了。

參、加工出口區經營成功與國家經濟發展的互動關係

加工出口區經營成功對國家（或地區）的經濟發展應該是成正面貢獻的互動關係，但加工出口區的貢獻不能代表國家（或地區）經濟發展的全部，而是在國家經濟發展過程中初期的誘導性功能的作用大於實質金額收入貢獻的影響，更坦白的說，國家長期經濟發展若不儘理想或不成功，也鮮有加工出口區經營成功者，例如菲律賓即為最明顯的實例，即使個別加工出口區經營成功，例如越南新順加工出口區，而國家（或地區）整體經濟發展因策略、法規制度，以及非經濟因素的影響等，至使加工出口區也無力承擔整體經濟發展的重任，促成國家（或地區）整體經濟發展成功，茲舉例說明加工出口區經營成功與政府經濟發展互動關係：

例一、台灣加工出口區：

於 1966 年成立至今已三十九年之久，蜚聲海內外，為國際公認成功的典範，相對的台灣整體經濟的發展，在加工

出口區成立前後，政府推動了一連串的經濟發展配套措施，加工出口區在 1966 年成立，而為了發展整體經濟，早在 1953 年開始了第一期的四年經濟建設計劃，由尹仲容先生及李國鼎先生分別擔任「工業委員會」的前後任主持人，本期的經濟建設政策及策略是「計劃式的自由經濟」和「進口替代」的產業發展，以創造就業機會，節省外匯支出，充份對民生物品的供應能自給自足；1958 年再實施外匯貿易改革，同年 1 月 16 日公布改革外匯匯率制度四月執行，先將多元匯率改為二元匯率，十一月將兩元匯率合併為一元匯率（36.36 台幣兌換 1 美元），1960 年 7 月再將匯率定在 1 元美金比新台幣 40 元；1959 年底擬訂「加速經濟發展方案」，公佈「十九點財經改革措施」，1960 年進一步的頒布「獎勵投資條例」以掃除投資的三大障礙，即一是投資關卡太多，手續太繁，二是有許多法令條文束縛了投資設廠，三是稅率太高，明顯高于香港，掃除了這三大障礙後，便達到四個預期的目標，即增加儲蓄、增加投資、增加再投資及增加外銷。終至達成國家經濟成長及穩定的雙重目標，至被世人美譽為「經濟發展奇蹟」。

　　由於以上的這些財經措施政策得宜，所以台灣在 1960 年代的經濟發展成功地自進口替代轉變為出口拓展，乃至 1966 年 12 月 3 日成立台灣加工出口區便一舉成功，在推動加工出口區的同時，仍不斷的推展各種新的財經方案，例如，1973 年至 1974 年第一次能源危機，造成台灣經濟嚴重的打擊，政府即時頒布十大建設因應，終能克服艱困，至此所應理解的是，財經政策措施得宜，只是表示經濟發展的計

劃得宜及有利的工具,執行法源的根據,而加工出口區的設
置營運才是真正達成財經政策執行項目中的一要項,填補了
就業機會的渴求,推展了國際市場,充實了外匯存底,普遍
並擴散性的發展中小企業成功,增加財政收入,所以在 1970
年代,在台灣由南至北的縱貫公路及鐵路兩邊的城鎮街道
上,有為數不少的新開設的西服店、成衣店、鞋店、電器行
等,繼而類似加工區內傳統中小型工業也在區外相繼成立,
如此可以了解到台灣中小企業之發展成功,個體戶商業市場
的繁盛及人民得以充份就業,乃歸功於台灣加工出口區誘導
性成效的發揮。從而看出,台灣經濟發展的政策制度,執行
是促成台灣加工出口區成功的基礎,而加工出口區的營運成
功,促進了社會的穩定富裕,中小企業的發展及至整體經濟
的蓬勃發展,此即是正面貢獻互動關係的結果。

例二、中國昆山出口加工區(有別於台灣的加
工出口區)

該區於 1991 年成立以來,因為地方基礎建設能夠達到
滿意的要求,政府適時訂頒適宜的財經政策,更重要的是中
央及昆山市政府全力支持,使得昆山出口加工區在一貫性法
制的信譽管理服務經營下,區內投資人無朝令夕改的困擾,
加之各種優惠條件,招商工作非常順利,區內投資廠商業績
日漸擴大,成為中國最為成功的加工出口區,以至於到 2000
年 4 月至 2002 年 6 月國務院相繼批准了全國 25 個國家級出
口加工區至 2003 年 3 月又批准了 13 個國家級出口加工區,

至此全國共有 38 個國家級出口加工區，更有意義值得稱道者，出口加工區的發展影響所及延伸到昆山出口加工區外，甚而鄰縣市的招商及長江三角洲等區域經濟也成為榮景的發展，此因昆山出口加工區誘導性影響的發展成果，在 2002 年 10 月 29、30 兩日在昆山招開的兩岸經濟發展研討會上，與會的學者專家皆一致認同，肯定此項成就及誘因，足證互動關係的密切性，此與 1989 年 11 月 6 日至 9 日在台灣高雄市舉辦第十屆世界加工出口區年會中，世界銀行代表 Dr. Keesing 所發表的論文中談到台灣加工出口區的貢獻影響到後來中國鋼鐵公司的建設，兩者有先後相呼應的效果。

例三、再看越南新順加工出口區

　　雖然基礎建設先天不足，但政府全力支持使投資建區者自帶資金及軟硬體建設進場，而建設營運成功，發揮出最基本的功能，造就了數萬勞工就業的機會，繁榮地方，但越南全國整體性的經濟發展至今仍未盡理想，仍有待財經政策的全盤得宜的規劃設計及有效執行，非新順一個加工出口區成功及能力所能及，此說明互動關係尚嫌不足。

　　由以上實例可以了解到加工出口區對國家（或地區）整體經濟發展是一顆萌芽的種子，產生誘導及原動力的功能而不是經濟發展的驅動力，換言之加工出口區是配合國家（或地區）經濟發展的一個環節，為整體經濟發展計劃的一個單元極其明顯。

　　從另一個角度來看加工出口區，它是工業及貿易結合組成的一種新型的產業經營及管理制度，到區內投資的廠商，投資低，投資報酬率高，區內投資人，沒有在區內抄土地的機會，專心從事生產，貿易事業，又因加工出口區廠商集中在區內，龐大的就業容量，可增加地方的工作機會，更有意義的是農村改革後過剩的勞動力，得有機會有效的利用，避免國家勞動力的閒置，浪費；之外，加工出口區特有的管理制度，一元化的服務（one stop service），其管理及服務的品質，極積性，使得加工出口區在生產力上有其高標準的表現，例如台灣加工出口區即為範例（附表六，七，八），這將是開發中國家，從農業經濟邁向工業化經濟發展模式的最佳途徑，繼而由工業化經濟發展轉進到多元化總體經濟發展的願景，是為可期待實現的事實，由是肯定的了解加工出口區一顆種子的功效，對國家（或地區）經濟發展互動密切的關係及其貢獻，已為當今世人有目共睹、公認、肯定，甚而成為當今開發中國家經濟發展的時尚良方。但必須切記，加工出口區不是國家整體經濟發展的萬聖丹，沒有國家整體經濟發展政策，完善的配套公共建設，專屬特設的法規依憑執行，都將枉然而興嘆！

第五章　台灣加工出口區的演變

壹、台灣加工出口區遭受疑慮的三個時段

　　世界第一個加工出口區－高雄加工出口區歷經十三年的研究、討論，到 1966 年 12 月 3 日建成，至今已歷三十九年之久，從初期的蓽路藍縷，至成長茁壯，到成熟轉型，一路走來，波濤不斷，雖艱辛有成，但時至今日，仍受國人疑慮，關注有加，區內投資人雖然滿意區內投資環境優於區外，但也怨聲時起；國人疑慮的問題，可分三個時段來看：

　　第一時段：建區的前十年，外國人壓榨本國勞力－這個觀點，在加工區成立的前十年，很多為民喉舌的民意代表，如立法委員、監察委員、縣市議員等，以及部份老學者，多質疑加工出口區以境外特區地位，提供外來投資人享受各種優惠，尤其是相較與國際的低工資，廉價勞動力，因而疑慮，憂心外國人（廠商）又在壓榨本國勞力，猶憶及滿清末年，世界列強的租界惡勢力再起，及於二次世界大戰之前，外國人在中國享有治外法權的恥辱，以及二次大戰其間日本在淪陷區的惡狀暴行，再度激起了憂心仇外之心，忿恨難忍之情，此一心情，是老一代中國人的夢魘，是可以理解和諒解的。然而 1994 年元月 4 日中國時報經濟記者張志清先生專

文報導加工出口區的「人肉機器吟悲歌」（附件一）。表達
對加工出口區勞工的悲憫與同情，認為是勞工的壓榨；筆者
針對該篇報導撰寫「加工出口區力圖轉型，何來悲歌」一文
回應（附件二），說明加工出口區內營運真實的現況及與全
國經濟發展互動的關係，以正其意。

第二時段：建區的第二個十年，區內廠商享受優惠，對
區外本國廠商不公平──在加工出口區成立後的第二個十
年，新生代的民議代表，商界名人及部份經濟學者，以各種
聲音及文字表達對加工出口區的產業（包括工業，及服務業）
享受的特殊優惠，相較與國內產業，明顯的不公平，無獨有
偶的，1994 年 8 月初，中國時報刊載中國大陸學者論壇的
文章，「地區經濟差距將危及大陸穩定」，由作者胡戰網撰
文，文中提到「特區享受優惠，不符公平競爭」，強調受惠
區與非受惠區的 GDP 相差達 17.4 倍，如此高收入區繼續享
受優惠政策，既不符合公平競爭的市場經濟原則，也會使已
經拉大的地區貧富差距變得更大，特區的「特」字應放在技
術創新，並作為今後經濟高速增長的動因和源泉；由是可以
看到兩岸的有識之士，都在為加工出口區享受優惠的公平性
提出質疑，並對國家整體經濟發展的均衡性表示關注；此
外，日本經濟研究院二次大戰後的首任院長及現任院長到台
灣加工出口區訪問，向筆者問道「貴國加工出口區給了那麼
多的優惠條件給國外投資者，對自己有什麼好處？利益？在
經濟理論上能否成立？」此亦表示國際經濟學者對加工出口
區的投資廠商享受優惠有所質疑。

　　第三時段：建區二十年以後，加工出口區是否有繼續存在的必要性－從加工出口區成立 20 年後至今，無論是民意代表，學者專家以及新聞界，均持有類似看去，認為加工出口區已營運了廿年，已完成了政府所賦予的階段性任務，對其繼續存在表示沒有必要性，甚而有新聞報導加工出口區應拆掉圍牆，還她本來面目，與一般工業區一樣的運作。

　　國人有這三個階段的疑慮及關注，是很正常的，也正因為這樣的反應，才真正顯示出加工出口區創建的意義及貢獻的價值，但這些疑慮，心意表示出國人對加工出口區了解得還不夠深入，筆者在任職加工出口區時，本持有義務及責任對社會大眾將加工出口區的實情說清楚，講明白，故對這些長年的疑慮，綜括的用以下幾點對社會各界，大眾在各種機會予以說明：

　　1、加工出口區之所以能成立並經營績效卓著經年，乃「比較利益」效益的發揮，外來投資人固然因低勞動本成及免減多種租稅而獲利，但相對的帶來國人就業的機會，得有安定的生活，同時帶進了大量的投資資金，造成國家資本財的形成，又帶進來國際市場，生產技術，機器設備，促成我國中小企業的形成及技術成長發展，所以對國家，人民及外來投資人三方面均有利可圖，而最大的收益還是國家整體經濟利益的發達，增進了國家的財富及國際形像。

　　2、加工出口區以國內境外的型式，專法（加工出口區法規彙編）管理經營，產品全部外銷，（近年來國內投資環境改善，經修法後允許科稅後內銷），所享受的優惠並不抵觸影響國內市場，當無不公平的情事存在。

75

3、加工出口區為我國工業的一環，不因階段性任務達成而不要工業，但加工出口區有一套完善的法規管理制度，理應發揚光大，再說，只有夕陽產品而無夕陽工業，加工區的工業類型及產品在不斷轉型，創新，隨著科技時代繼續發展，如此績優工業區那裡會有繼續存在的疑問呢？

為了使國人對加工出口區有更深一層，正確的認識和了解，筆者奉李資政國鼎先生指示於 1994 年 5 月 20 日、21 日再撰文「加工出口區 28 年來之貢獻及其轉型」（附件三）刊載在經濟日報上，希望國人對加工出口區深入的認識有些幫助。

貳、台灣經濟環境的變遷，影響加工出口區 獨特優惠條件的優越性

一、區外大環境的變遷：

台灣加工出口區在 1966 年建區以後的區外大環境，也在隨著時間的巨輪不停的旋轉而有所變遷，變遷的結果，影響到加工出口區原為獨特優惠條件的優越性，並逐漸衝擊到加工出口區內部的反對及回響，及衍生了應變的措施；區外大環境的變遷，概括可從三點說明：

1、1960 年代以後，政府雖建設了世界第一個加工出口區與其同時政府也在為改進台灣整體的投資環境的改善，對區外放寬了各項投資法規條款，如此相對的降低了加工出口區原先提供的優越投資條件。

2、台灣鄰近的國家，如韓國、菲律賓、泰國、馬來西亞、中國大陸等，勞動力比台灣更為充沛，工資更低，彼等也在台灣成立加工出口區之後建設了他們自己的加工出口區，因而吸引了更多，更大的投資，影響到台灣加工出口區吸引外來投資的優勢。

3、1974 至 1975 年全球經濟衰退之前，國內勞動力顯然不足，加工出口區也嚴重缺少工人，導至區內公司被迫以降低學歷，技術經驗，年齡，甚而提高工資以吸引招募工人，同時也有擴大生產量以降低成本者，但到 1974 至 1975 年間全球經濟衰退，各公司遭受嚴重的沖擊、打擊，因而不得己又探取裁員措施因應，高雄，楠梓及台中三個加工出口區一年累計減少的勞工數達到一萬二千多人，造成勞資糾紛時起，也影響到 1974 年及 1975 年全區進出口貿易大幅下降，各達 12.7%及 10.2%，年順差也降了 6.5%，此一現象，在往後第二次石油危機或經濟不景氣時都會重演，因而使加工出口區在台灣社會的評價受到負面的影響。

二、區外大環境變遷，區內廠商要求鬆綁：

區外大環境變遷，對加工出口區內部的沖擊所產生的反對及回響，表示區內投資者漸漸的體認到加工出口區專用的法規束手縛腳，捆綁住他們一些自由發揮的空間，不如區外投資者所享有的一些利益和便利，而作不平之鳴，要求鬆綁，其所經常提到要求鬆綁改進的項目有：

1、區內土地只租不售，至投資廠商未能享受到土地增值的利潤。

2、區內投資者的廠房，限制只能賣給在區內投資經營的廠商，不得任意出售，多所不便，而且閒置廠房或倉庫達六個月以上或使用不當者，管理處得依法按市價徵購。

3、區內廠商在未合法結束經營之前，不能將其進口的生產用機器設備銷售到區外市場，造成資本金不能靈活支用。

4、區內產品規定全部外銷，使投資者不能分享本地市場及市場調節功能。

5、區內投資廠商須按營業額每月繳交千分之三的管理費，此項收費抵消了一部份免稅的優惠。

6、區內儲運業務，限定由管理處所屬儲運中心辦理，缺乏服務彈性，最佳品質及發揮市場功能（指儲運費率機制的靈活性）。

7、區外因政府改善整體投資環境而對投資法規的改善，對區內的進口機器設備，原材料和半成品免稅優惠，已不再獨享，有失加工出口區特區的優異性。

三、政府及加工出口區管理處所採取的因應措施：

徵對加工出口區廠商要求鬆綁改進的聲浪，政府主管單位，經濟部及所屬加工出口區管理處，研擬可行因應措施，以配合環境變遷，時代進步的需要，其因應措施，從兩方面著手，其一為修法，其二加強對區內廠商的服務。

1、修法

修法即是將加工出口區專屬的「設置管理條例及施行細則」，按區內廠商的要求及配合台灣整體經濟發展的變遷作區內外均衡的修訂，並按需求緩急，依不同的時段進行修法，謹列舉以下幾項重點說明之：

（1）區內產品內銷的問題（即銷往台灣島內市場）

根據加工出口區設置管理條例第五條規定；「外銷事業之產品，不得內銷」，但區內廠商對此條規定，頗為不滿，彼等認為，國內市場最大的效用是發揮市場調節功能，即國際市場發生滯銷時，國內市場在短時間內作為補充國際市場停滯空檔的功效，不致造成區內廠商停產，市場中斷的現象，此即救急緩沖的功效，另一原因乃如果國內市場有利可圖，希望有公平市場競爭的機會，基於上情，經濟部及加工出口區管理處，本區內外公平合理原則而分階段性的修法，從 1987 年 5 月第一次開始修至 1993 年 5 月止，修正區內產品內銷量在年產量 50%以下者，由加工出口區管理處核定，超過 50%部份提請投資審查小組核定，至 1996 年 5 月再修正，刪除產品內銷比率的限制，只要課稅及即可內銷，至此完全開放內銷，前後共修法達六次之多，終使區內廠商完全滿意，同時也因區外投資優惠條件逐年的改變，使區內、外廠商都立足在公平合理的市場競爭基礎上合法經營。

（2）存倉 24 小時安全規定的問題

此項規定系警備總部基於從台灣境內外銷空運出口貨物，預防空中爆炸、空難事故的發生而規定，凡空運出口貨

物必須在機場倉庫存放 24 小時，而後裝機出口，警總基於國情安全需要，但對商機而言，尤其是高科技產品，爭取交貨時間十分重要，因而區內廠商怨言不斷，管理處亦反應上情到經濟部至行政院，希望取消此規定，經多年十多次與警總的溝通，於 1982 年 12 月警總同意加工出口區空運產品安全隔離時間，從駐區海關於裝運貨櫃加封時起算，不須貨到機場進倉才起算，如此可縮短一半約 12 小時的機場存倉隔離安全時間，復於 1990 年元月警總同意完全刪除 24 小時空運存倉案全隔離的規定，如此完全符合廠商的要求而不再怨聲載道了。

（3）區內廠房租，售的問題

區內廠房，分由管理處興建的標準廠房，可以出租或出售給投資在區內經營的廠商使用，另外可由投資在區內經營的廠商向管理處租地自建廠房，加工出口區設置管理條例第十二條原規定：「加工出口區內私有建築物之轉讓以供外銷事業之使用為限」，此項硬性規定，對區內廠商的流動或因業務變動，造成廠房供需彈性失調現象，使廠商多感不變而要求改進，便通處置之道，故於 1983 年 4 月修正區內租用之廠房得轉租及轉借給區內其他廠商使用；但為防止區內抄作房地產而不務生產，故於 1997 年 7 月修正設置管理條例第十二條時仍保留原條文原意，其修正後的條文為「加工出口區內私有土地或建築物之轉讓，以供在區內營業之事業使用為限」此兩次法條的修正，一方面顧及到防止區內土地、廠房抄作，同時也兼顧到廠商經營的方便。

（4）外商資本及利潤匯回的問題

外商到加工出口區來投資，對利潤及資本匯回本國，是最敏感的問題，他們都希望受到地主國最少的限制及有最便捷的手續，為了增加外商投資的信心，於 1980 年 2 月修正僑外資投資申請結匯辦法，由自投資計劃完成滿二年後逐年匯回，改為自開始營業之日起屆滿一年後逐年按 15%匯回，繼而於 1987 年 3 月再修正僑外投資資本及利潤所得可一次匯回，不受 15%的限制，並且於是年 5 月修正進出口的外匯事項免除加工出口區管理處核准，逕向銀行辦理；如此修正使得來區投資的僑外商安心樂意的投資經營。

（5）區內勞工行政管理問題

勞工行政係指勞工組織，勞動條件，勞資關係，勞工福利，勞工教育，勞工就業輔導及職業訓練協辦等事項，這些行政事項立意在協助區內廠商對所屬勞工的關注及管理規範，使來區工作的勞工得到好的照顧及工作保障，但常有適得其反的回應，效果，原立意各廠商所顧用勞工的解顧須報請管理處核准後執行，此實違背了事業主顧用勞工「顧管」合一的原則，形成部份勞工因過度保護而肆無忌憚，造成廠商人事管理上極大的困擾，影響生產，乃於 1990 年 3 月修正刪除區內廠商解顧工人應先經管理處核准的規定，解脫了廠商對員工管理上的困擾。

（6）加工出口區進出口物質管理問題

加工出口區的設置定位在「國內境外」的特性，對進出區的物質，涉及免稅優惠，又因加工出口區管理處由政府賦予一元化服務（one stop Service）的功能，因而加工出口區

設置管理條例第八條，第十五款規定管理處掌理「關於所在區物質進出口簽證事項」，於 1993 年 5 月修正進出口物質免向管理處辦理簽證，逕向海關申請驗放；此外並依海關所修訂之「加工出口區區內事業貨品及帳冊管理要點」，於2002 年 1 月 1 日起對區內廠商全面實施帳冊管理制度，以簡化海關通關作業手續，縮短通關時間，節省營運成本，提升競爭力，增進商機並精簡關員人力，此即表示廠商對自己庫存的原物料、半成品及未出貨之成品隨時要與自行填報的帳冊一致，否則若有差異，要自行負責，促使廠商真誠的做到自主管理。

以上僅列舉對區內廠商影響較大的問題，其他尚有如區間交易，工繳價值（Added Value），區外加工，樣品出區，國內採購原物料等等問題，多不勝枚舉，此修法旨在說明加工出口區管理處與區內廠商互動的真誠效應，為加工出口區的永續經營而奮力不懈。

2、加強對區內廠商的服務

加強服務，在改善行政效率，服務態度，及資訊提供等，其重點服務改善項目僅提出以下幾點說明：

（1）加強並改進了吸引投資，對外貿易，工商業務管理及勞工行政四主要工作項目的服務品質及效率，得到區內廠商滿意及肯定的認同。

（2）加強並改進倉儲及運輸的服務品質，效率及執行全天 24 小時服務，並增設小量快運服務，及爭取到海關總署同意，基於航空運輸安全考量在機場倉庫預先存放 24

小時而後裝機的規定，改按在加工出口區海關封鉛開始計算 24 小時，如此在機場存倉時間大為減少，以利廠商即早出貨。

（3）加強並改進對區內勞工朋友的照顧，服務，營造最好的工作環境，公共服務及福利，使勞工朋友能安心及穩定的在區內服務工作。

（4）協助各廠商有效及依勞基法公正的處理勞資糾紛，使公司能順利營運。

（5）配合海關協助廠商實施帳冊管理，使廠商依法正常營運，並能有效實施工廠管理，減少行政鎖事（Red tap）。

（6）有效整理美化區內環境及廢棄物處理，污水標準排放至深海放流，使廠商能順利生產營運，免受干擾之苦。

台灣加工出口區 38 年來已有顯著的演變，但也有其基本的不變，例如一元化（中國稱之為一條龍）的服務（one stop service）體制不變，區內土地只租不售的規定不變，加工出口區專屬的法規「設置管理條例及施行細則」的規範精神──「授權」加工出口區管理處準此法規執行營運不變，加工出口區經營的三利原則，即國家的利益，廠商的利潤及員工的福利不變，因其不變，台灣加工出口區真乃是以不變應萬變，或曰固本求變，臻於至善，所以成功！

參、台灣加工出口區的演變

　　台灣加工出口區的演變，並不能完全代表世界其他國家加工出口區的演變，謹能供作參考，因為加工出口區的演變是隨著國家整體經濟發展而有所改變，當今世界各國有類似台灣整體經濟發展者無幾，目前韓國及中國大陸應是整體經濟發展較為成功者，但二者對經營加工出口區的觀念及處置態度辦法不盡與台灣相同，韓國在經營加工出口區態度上不如台灣積極，認真，韓國對工業區的發展，經營重心放在科學園區上，加工出口區則任其自然發展，欠缺積極推動的力量，所以 1989 年在台灣高雄市舉行的世界加工出口區年會中，澳洲籍經濟學教授黑禮博士（Dr. Derek T. Healey）以研究韓國加工出口區的論文在會中發表，認為加工出口區對國家經濟發展的貢獻不如預期的大，尤其對技術轉移及技術升級可謂沒有績效；及至 1999 年 11 月在韓國漢城舉辦的亞洲生產力中心會員國的加工出口區及科學園區評鑑會議中，韓國參與接受評鑑的三個加工出口區的評等亦不甚理想（表十三），顯見韓國加工出口區多年來的演變不如台灣加工出口區的幅度大；中國大陸出口加工區的設置較晚，自第一個昆山出口加工區創設至今才十二年的歷史，因為建區較晚，出口加工區法規的建立，也曾參考了台灣加工出口區的設置管理條例及施行細則，所以基本管理辦法與台灣加工出口區類同，甚而近年來貨物進出口管理辦法上，台灣及中國的加工

區均改採用「帳冊管理」（按中國出口加工區貨物進口管理
辦法，採用電子底帳，取消《加工貿易手冊》，實行登記制，
通過海關聯網，實行 EDI 申報，每半年核銷一次），（表十
六及表十七），此很明顯的了解到中國的出口加工區在跟隨
台灣加工出口區成熟隱健的步履，經營運作，自不可能在短
短的幾年中有較大的演變，此為很正常的發展，但時空及區
域環境的大不同，中國出口加工區可預見的將有所演變，誠
如中國大陸學者論壇，胡戰網撰文談到「特區享受優惠，不
符公平競爭」的表達反應，以及當前中國整體經濟發展不均
衡的情況，長期的看，勢必造成區內、外不平衡的沖擊，而
衍生演變的發生，成為必然的態勢，將來衍生的演變，對中
國出口加工區應可視之為良性反應的發展，有利於中國政府
對出口加工區政策適時的修正，將更利於全國整體工業經濟
的發展，筆者對此持樂觀的看法，將拭目以待。世界其他加
工出口區，有的正隨國情發展在演變中，有的尚在努力奮鬥
中，但總而言之，演變代表了進步和希望，預祝大家成功！

表十六　中國出口加工區與一般國家級開發區優惠政策對比

	出口加工區	一般國家級開發區
功能	境內關外	中國境內
管理模式	封閉式管理	一般開發區管理
企業 所得稅	生產性企業基礎稅率15%，自利年度起「兩免三減半」。正常納稅年度按10%徵收。集成電路、軟體行業按照國家政策執行。	生產性企業基礎稅率15%，自利年度起「兩免三減半」。正常納稅年度出口額70%以上減按10%徵收。集成電路和軟體行業按照國家政策執行。
增值稅	免徵	內銷產品 17%，出口產品免徵。
進口免稅	出口加工區內加工、生產的貨物和應稅勞務，免徵增值稅、消費稅；生產所需的機器設備、模具、維修用零配件以及基礎設施所需的機器、設備和建設用基建物資、自用的辦公用品，均免徵海關關稅和進口增值稅；出口加工區和出口加工區之間的產品、原料、機器設備等進出貨物免稅。	只有國家鼓勵項目投資總額內進口自用設備可以享受免稅。進口設備零部件、基建物資、辦公用品照章徵稅。
退稅政策	在中國境內的出口加工區外企業的貨物出口到出口加工區視同出口，可享受國家有關增值稅退稅的優惠；從出口加工區外入區的國產機器、設備、原材料、零部件、元器件、包裝材料以及合理數量的建築材料等均可按出口辦理退稅。	企業使用國產原材料加工產品，其產品必須實際離境結匯後才能辦理出口退稅手續。
貨物進口	採用電子底帳，取消《加工貿易手冊》，實行登記制，通過海關聯，實行 EDI 申報，每半年核銷一次	需加工貿易合同辦理《加工貿易手冊》，並逐筆核銷

保證金和台帳	不設台帳，不收保證金	設立台帳和保證金
配額和許可證	進口不需配額和許可證	正常的配額和許可證管理
貨物通關	採用「一次申報、一次、一次查驗」的模式，可全天 24 小時快速通關	正常通關
外匯管理	不實行結售匯制度，資本金帳戶和一般項目帳戶合併，企業帳戶可全額留匯	實行規定的結售匯管理
成品內銷	區內貨物銷往境內區外按成品徵稅	內銷貨物按照成品中所含進口原料徵稅。

資料來源：中國蘇州高新出口加工區

表十七　中國出口加工區與保稅區、區外加工貿易政策、監管方式的對比:

	出口加工區內	保稅區	區　外
功能	出口加工區的功能是單一的：加工。	保稅區的功能有四個：加工、貿易、倉儲和展示。	區外加工貿易企業可擴展加工業務。
稅收政策	稅收政策同保稅區政策基本相同。	稅收政策與加工區政策基本相同。	加工貿易企業進口不作價設備予以免稅。
退稅政策	國內原材料、物料等進入加工區視同出口，稅務部門給予辦理出口退（免）稅手續。	進入保稅區的國內貨物，必須等貨物實際離境後，才能辦理出口退稅手續。	加工貿易企業使用國內原材料、物料加工產品，其產品必須實際離境後，才能辦理出口退稅手續。
國內稅收政策	國家對區內加工出口的產品和應稅勞務免征增稅、消費稅。	保稅區內國家對應稅勞務沒有免稅優惠。	
成品內銷政策	加工區內企業銷往境內區外的貨物，按制成品征稅。	保稅區內企業銷往境內區外的貨物，只有當內銷成品完全由進口料件組成時，才按成品征稅。	區外加工貿易企業內銷貨物一律按成品中所含進口原材料征稅。
管理方式	對出口加工區採取全封閉、卡口式管理，海關在及卡口設置閉路電視監控系統，並實行24小時工作制度。	海關對保稅區實行管理，並實行8小時工作制度。	海關對區外分散經營的加工貿易採取開放式的管理，並實行8小時工作制度。
審批手續	不實行銀行保證金台帳制度，合同備案只需管委會審批。審批手續簡化為一個環節、一道手續。	不實行銀行保證金台帳制度，合同備案只需管委會審批。	實行銀行保證金台帳制度。合同備案須經外經貿委－稅務－海關－銀行四個部門，十三道環節。

監管模式	取消手冊，實行電子底帳管理，企業通過 EDI 電報電子數據，經海關審核後，自動存入電子底帳。	監管模式與區外相同。	實行《登記手冊》管理。涉及合同打印，加貼防偽標簽，核發《登記手冊》等多道環節。
通關模式	貨物進出口採取「一次申報、一次審單、一次查驗」的新通關模式。	通關模式與區外相同。	貨物進出口採取地報關或轉關運輸的方式，手續繁。
監管手段	充分利用現代高科技技術，企業－主管海關－口岸海關實行計算機聯管理。	監管手段與區外基本相同（部分保稅區海關實行與企業聯）。	監管手段基本以人工監管為主。計算機在管理中的應用程度較低。海關均需進行中期下核查。
深加工結轉	加工區之間，加工區與保稅區之間，區內企業與區外企業之間可以擴展深加工結轉。	深加工結轉規定與區外基本相同。	區外加工貿易企業之間，區外加工貿易企業與保稅區企業之間可擴展深加工結轉。
合同變更	合同變更手續較簡化，直接可以辦理。	合同變更手續與區外相同。	合同變更手續較繁瑣。須按合同備案程序到各部間辦理相應的手續。
核銷管理	計算機滾動核銷。每半年核銷一次。	核銷管理手續與區外相同。	逐合同手工核銷，手續煩，效率低，每份合同核銷須 60 天。

資料來源：中國出口加工區
中國海關學會主辦　2002 年 9 月

加工出口區與經濟發展

第六章 世界加工出口區未來的 發展走向

壹、世界各加工出口區正朝向三種類型演進

從 1966 年世界第一個台灣高雄加工出口區成立以來，已邁入三十九個年頭，橫向層面的擴展，全世界各開發中及未開發國家，普遍仿效設置，成為世界經濟發展異軍突起的一股新生力量，造福了無數貧窮地區的人民，這三十九年來在加工出口區世界裡的發展，綜理歸納來看，世界各加工出口區正朝向三種類型在演進：

第一類：仍維持原來加工出口區特性模式，以創造就業機會為主的勞力密集傳統產業，繼續經營發展。

第二類：產業特性轉型朝向資本密集，技術密集，高附加價值的科技產業發展，自然淘汰無競爭能力的勞力密集傳統產業，而創造就業機會，雖然仍為其重點卻不是那麼的強調。

第三類：綜合工業生產，貿易及轉口服務業為範疇，以利潤為導向，就業機會任其自然發展的模式。

就第一類而言，多停留在落後及缺乏整體經濟發展的國家（及地區），例如越南、印尼、尼泊爾（Nepal）斯尼蘭

91

卡（Sri Lanka）巴拉馬、中國內陸省份，以及中南美洲，非洲的一些落後國家，此外尚有一些希望於此刻能設立加工出口區的國家，例如柬浦塞、新內磯利亞、馬其頓共合國，……等也都定位在勞力密集的傳統產業為目標，以利就業機會，促進該等國家的初級經濟發展。

　　第二類，如台灣、中國大陸的長江三角洲及珠江三角洲一帶，韓國等，此等著重在資本密集，技術密集，傾向往科學園區（或高新科技園區）模式發展，但仍不放棄傳統產業具有高附加價值及市場的科技產業，此即所謂加工出口區的升級轉型發展的新里程。

　　第三類如香港，台灣加工出口區企圖轉型後的型態，這一類的必備條件是海、空運輸服務能力及工業加工能力要強，金融服務週到，以及地理位置適中，這些條件的配合，絕非一般開發中國家能力所及，之外韓國業已具備此類發展的條件，但政府總體經濟發展的標的並不定位在這一類的發展上，菲律賓也具備這一類型發展的地理條件，但該國加工出口區的績效、能力實不甚理想，再則該國的社會安定、安全及國家信譽也為世人存疑而影響其發展；新加坡，偏重在金融及轉口服務，因為地小、人少，以至工業發展有限，貿易也僅稍具規模，所以加工出口區在第三類的發展尚未有顯著的成效，還有待時日觀察。

貳、世界各加工出口區未來發展的 走向及定位

　　台灣三十九年前創設加工出口區的基本目的在創造就業機會，改善人民生活，促進國家經濟繁榮，所以加工出口區定位在勞力密集的傳統產業面經營發展，換言之，加工出口區的必備條件是要有充沛的勞動力，三十九年前，台灣符合這項條件的要求，而創設了加工出口區經營成功，而今，中國大陸、印度所釋出的初級勞動力更充沛的佈滿在就業的市場上，所以，他們在加工出口區這一股「經流」中，蓬勃發展，而且有後來居上的態勢（僅限局部二、三個區），成效顯著，尤其是中國在出口加工區發展上的順利、成功更為世人所稱道，甚而延伸到高新科技園區蓬勃的發展，為中國帶進到現代科技產業之林，也於 2002 年成為世界加工出口區協會（WEPZA）的會員國之一。

　　台灣加工出口區經營成功早已成為世人所公認的事實，而中國之迎頭趕上，青出於藍，也為當今世人所讚譽，在這樣有成就的加工出口區，出自於已開發或開發中的國家（或地區），對未來加工出口區就政策而言的發展，走向又將如何？或者說國家（或地區）未來整體經濟發展中，加工出口區將如何定位？如何繼續發展才是正途？這一問題應是台灣及中國政府在經濟發展政策面所應該深刻考慮的問題，如此將可避免政府投資資源不洽當的浪費及不公平現象的發生；在這問題上若能得到正確的解答，也將有利於世界其他有加工出口區設置的國家作為參考、借鏡。

一、台灣加工出口區的部份：

1、台灣加工出口區隨台灣經濟發展而發展，達成階段性的任務：

中華民國政府自 1949 年遷到台灣後，即著手經濟發展策略規劃，至 1990 年，此其間的經濟發展策略分為七大項積極推動執行，即一、穩定與成長並重。二、農工平衡發展。三、輕重工業循序漸進發展。四、進口替代與出口擴展分段推動。五、重視公共建設。六、縮小貧富差距，平均社會財富。七、推動經濟自由化，國際化與制度化。

自 1953 年實施第一期四年經建計畫至 1989 年，經濟成長率平均每年達 8.9%，較工業化國家的 3.8%及其他開發中國家的 4.7%為高。物價方面，除兩次石油危機時期上升幅度較大外，其他各年物價均相當穩定；尤以 1960 年代最為突出，消費者物價平均每年僅上漲 3.3%，不僅較其他開發中國家漲幅為低，亦較工業國家物價穩定，為世界上能同時達成經濟快速成長及物價穩定的少數國家之一。由於經濟快速成長，每人國民所得大幅提高，1989 年平均每人國民生產毛額已達 7,512 美元，而 1952 年不及壹百美元，人民生活水準有顯著的改善，社會呈現安和樂利的景象。台灣經濟發展的成就，被聯合國經濟合作發展組織（OECD）列為十個新興工業化國家之一，並被美國基督教科學箴言報列為「明日大國」之首位。

加工出口區就是在這段時期，依七大經濟發展政策所創設的時代寵兒，肩負起時代任務的使命，而另有兩項數字的

呈現，更積極的推動促成台灣加工出口區的創設發展，第一項數字（表十八）就是在 1966 年加工出口區創設之前的失業率，1952 年是 4.4%，1955 年是 3.8%，1960 年是 4.0%，1965 年是 3.3%，第二項數字是與失業率相對的人口成長率，1952 年是 3.3%，1955 年是 3.8%，1960 年是 3.5%，1965 年是 3.0%，平均每年約成長 3.5%，此兩項高比率數據所引伸的含意是社會需要每年增加十萬個就業機會，這在當時對政府而言，是相當大的壓力和負擔，相對的當時的國民所得，1952 年之前不及 100 美元，即便到 1965 年也才達到 203 美元，民生至為疾苦，其原因在於國民生產總毛額（GDP）太低，1952 年以前小於 17 億美元，到 1965 年也才 28 億多美元，如此明顯說明，不增加就業機會，不增加生產總毛額，國民所得就不會提高，人民就不會有改善生活需求的可能，更遑論改善生活品質！

　　要增加就業機會，增加國民生產總毛額，就必須增加投資，台灣當時無論是民間或政府都無投資資金及能力，唯一途逕是吸引外國人來投資，帶進資本、技術及市場，如何吸引外人投資？政府經十多年的研究而決定以「國內境外」設立加工出口區的最佳途逕模式引進華僑，外國人的資本到台灣來投資，如此迎刃而解了迫在眉睫的就業需求問題，故台灣高雄加工出口區，也就是世界第一個加工出口區於 1966 年 12 月 3 日正式創設成立，開始營運。

　　由於加工出口區整體規劃得宜，除了關稅優惠條件之外，一元化的服務，完善的公共設施及高水準，充沛的勞動力，都是吸引僑外資來投資的誘因，與此同時政府也在加工

出口區之外，島內全面改善投資環境，所以區外也能吸引一
些不願意到加工區投資而在區外投資的僑外資，為數也不在
少數，此時，台灣整體經濟因而開始蓬勃發展，政府也鼓勵
全民拼經濟，適齡人口，無論男女，人人都投入生產，當時
政府曾喊出「客廳即是工廠」的口號，鼓勵全民參與經濟建
設，所以在加工出口區週圍的居民，尤其是眷村（軍眷村及
機關眷村）熱烈響應，如此便直接的幫助改善了民眾家庭的
生活，以當時的情景，社會一片朝氣、祥和，從政府各官員
到社會各升斗小民，無不為全國全民經濟而努力，所以從
1966 年創設加工出口區以來，五年中在區內、外共同的努
力下，（尤其區內在減少政府國際赤字貿易上的貢獻（表四）
至為明顯），逐漸的提高了國家總生產值（GDP）及國民所
得，1971 年，GDP 達到 US$65 億，國民所得提高到 400 美
元以上，1973 年 GDP 超過 100 億美元，國民所得也到 600
美元以上，到 1976 年 GDP 達 185 億美元，國民所得超過
1,000 美元，如此不斷的年年都在增長，雖有 1971、1972 年
第一次石油危機及 1979、1980 年第二次石油危機，但都因
大有為的政府及全民的努力而予以克服困境，所以到 1980
年政府創設新竹科學園區，其目的在提升台灣的產業結構，
與世界科技產業接軌，與此同時加工出口區也開始轉型，朝
向資本密集、技術密集、國際化、自由化方向發展，凡不能
配合發展的區內產業，便自然的遭到淘汰，於此必須強調
者，加工出口區不以強迫性的要求傳統產業離開加工出口
區，而代之以鼓勵轉型，提高市場競爭力及附加價值，此乃
因加工出口區成立的初衷旨意，凡能體認符合「只有夕陽產

品，而無夕陽工業」的產業，都將可以繼續在加工出口區內努力經營，創造佳績，所以加工出口區內仍然保有一部份資本密集，具有市場競爭力，技術密集的科技傳統產業，是以加工出口區每年的產值持續的增加，全國的 GDP 及國民所得保持穩定的成長，1990 年 GDP 達 183 億多美元，國民所得超過 8,000 美元，更於 1994 年，GDP 達 2439 億美元，國民所得達到 10,566 美元，至此中華民國便成為世界已開發的國家（Developed Country），至今，台灣加工出口區已歷經 39 年，隨台灣經濟發展而發展，階段性的任務，使命已圓滿達成，本身也在因時制宜的需求，而朝轉型邁進中，但就台灣當前整體經濟發展的深度及廣度而言，加工出口區將如何繼續走下去？台灣是否還需要加工出口區呢？或是現有加工出口區應轉型到更高的境界，創造更多的利基貢獻台灣人民？

表十八　台灣歷年人口成長，國民生產毛額及國民所得統計表

項目　　年份	人　口			國民生產毛額 GDP（USD 百萬元）	國民所得（USD 元）	附　註
	總人口數（1000）	成長率 %	失業率 %			
1952 以前	＜8,128			＜1,674	＜100	
1952	8,128	3.3	4.4	1,674	186	
1955	9,078	3.8	3.8	1,978	192	
1960	10,792	3.5	4.0	1,717	143	
1965	12,628	3.0	3.3	2,811	203	
1966	12,993	2.9	3.0	3,148	221	加工出口區創設
1969	14,335	5.0	1.9	4,915	320	
1971	14,995	2.2	1.7	6,589	410	第一次石油危機
1973	15,565	1.8	1.3	10,727	642	
1974	15,852	1.8	1.5	14,458	853	
1976	16,508	2.2	1.8	18,492	1,041	
1979	17,479	2.0	1.3	33,229	1,758	第二次石油危機
1980	17,805	1.9	1.2	41,360	2,155	新竹科學園區創設
1984	19,013	1.5	2.4	59,780	2,890	
1986	19,455	1.0	2.7	77,299	3,646	
1987	19,673	1.1	2.0	103,641	4,825	
1988	19,904	1.2	1.7	126,233	5,798	
1989	20,107	1.0	1.6	152,565	6,889	
1990	20,353	1.2	1.7	164,076	7,285	
1991	50,557	1.0	1.5	183,763	8,051	
1992	20,752	1.0	1.5	216,254	9,329	
1994	21,126	0.9	1.6	243,934	10,566	
1996	21,471	0.8	2.6	275,144	11,696	

資料來源：Taiwan statistical Data Book 行政院經建會

2、台灣加工區是存、廢或是轉型？

（1）加工出口區當今所面臨的經濟環境

　　台灣當今的經濟環境頹廢，從 1987 年以來，經濟成長年復一年的下降，失業率從1995年以前維持在2%以下，2000年便升至 3%，2001 年達 4.6%，2002 年更高至 5.2%（表十九），年年高升，究其原因，實非經濟因素所造成，乃因政治、社會環境不安定的因素造成了嚴重的障礙、打擊，加之世界經濟板塊的滑動，將世界經濟市場由二次世界大戰後北美主市場移動到亞洲中國大陸區域，甚而歐洲堅石的共同市場也滑向中國市場，亞洲東協國家實質上也都不得不以中國市場為依靠，亞洲最強的經濟大國日本，早在 25 年前最先搶進中國市場，韓國也以中國為它的經濟腹地，在中國北部及東北部省份投資的韓國企業不在少數，台灣雖然因政治自我設限，戒急用忍，但民間的敏銳性及商機的驅駛，民間企業早已捷足先政府而登上了對岸，尤其高科技產業的生產工廠幾乎全部移往中國大陸，或兩地同時有工廠生產，而所謂的台灣下單，大陸出貨，以及研發留在台灣，根留台灣的構想，也都幾乎破滅，因為台灣投資環境已比不上其他地區，市場經濟比較利益的誘因，自然台灣的「人與錢」就外流了，同時也帶走了技術及市場，此與 1960 年代台灣創設加工出口區時流入的情況同出一轍，真乃物換星移，世事多變！傳統產業，中小企業較難出走，但卻失去了過去強勢的競爭力，無論在土地成本，勞動成本，原料成本以及市場供應力等都無法與中國大陸匹比，至於台灣政府想重振經濟頹勢，

自我設定以亞洲為圓規中心的轉運中心，只是一種虛構的認定，從亞洲各國及美國在 1992～2002 年出口金額年平均成長率（CGR）（表二十）來看，從 1992～2002 年中國都保持在二位數的成長，美國、日本、中華民國都只有一位數的成長，尤其中華民國從 1997～2002 年都停留在低度成長中；更值得注意的是 2002 及 2003 年台灣對中國的順差大幅成長（表二十一），尤其 2003 年順差高達 US$104 億之多，此項經濟性的依靠，顯示出中國大陸經濟腹地的重要性了；此外印度當前所釋出的大量經濟勞動力，低成本的土地及高水準的科技人才，正極積登上新的經濟競爭舞台，也成為歐、美各國為抗衡中國高速經濟發展，產生擴散效應的新經濟區；另一方面，靠近中國雲南省邊界的越南也在急起直追，印度、越南都將繼中國之後形成對台灣經濟加壓的重要對手，如此看來，台灣經濟重整五十年前的雄風，再創經濟奇蹟確實是舉步維艱！即使設置再多的加工出口區及科學園區，也恐怕是望而興嘆！

（2）加工出口區未來的演變

A‧加工區是存或是廢？

台灣加工出口區已完成歷史的任務，而今台灣經濟在高科技發展的環境下，加工出口區的存廢問題為各界所關注，此一問題的答案是肯定的，可以繼續存在經營，其道理已於本章前段詳予說明。

B‧加工出口區繼續轉型發展

　　台灣加工出口區已臻於成功至上之境，而今卻處在經濟頹廢的困境時刻，當如何繼續發揮其功能，再度肩負起另一次階段性的任務，歷史性的使命呢？俗語說，「以不變應萬變」，當前現有加工出口區要能固守崗位，繼續現行的轉型發展，繼續發揮其功能輔助傳統科技產業努力經營發展，做到淘汰了夕陽產品，便無夕陽工業的市場需求，讓加工出口區自然的往科學園區演變，但不同與科學園區，不是科學園區，保持這個完善管理制度的工業區，給傳統科技產業繼續發展的空間，同時也歡迎高科技產業加入，來區投資設廠生產，使現有加工出口區完全是以高附加價值工業生產為主導的工業區，如此便創造出高附加價值的就業機會，而區內各目的事業單位當繼續留在區內擔任一元化的服務，至於純服務性的事業，轉運業，不宜設在加工出口區有限的空間裡面，而應設在加工出口區區外鄰近的地區，相乎應配合，因為只有加工出口區有大量的工業產品的產出，才有可能提供轉運業者服務的機會。

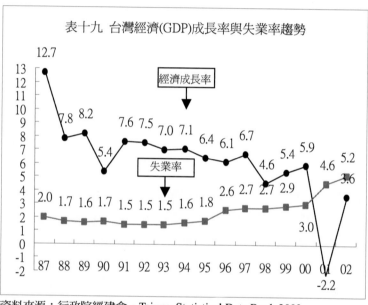

表十九 台灣經濟(GDP)成長率與失業率趨勢

資料來源：行政院經建會，Taiwan Statistical Data Book 2003

表二十　1992-2002各國年出口金額年平均成長率（CGR）

單位：%

	1992-1997	1997-2002	1992-2002
一、全球	8.2	3.0	5.5
二、前兩大國			
美國	9.0	1	4.5
日本	4.4	–0.2	2.1
三、亞洲四小龍			
中華民國	8.5	1.8	5.1
南韓	12.2	3.6	7.8
新加坡	14.5	0	7.0
香港	9.5	1.3	5.3
四、東南亞			
泰國	12.1	3.7	7.8
菲律賓	20.6	7.8	14.0
馬來西亞	14.1	3.4	8.6
印尼	9.5	1.3	5.3
五、開發中			
中國大陸	16.6	12.2	14.4
印度	12.3	7.1	9.6

註1.：1997年亞洲爆發金融危機，美國2000年進入「新經濟」尾聲。

註2.：10年期間日本陷於不振，中國大陸和印度都維持亮麗的成長，台
　　　灣的表現相對較差。

資料來源：整理自WTO：International trade statistics 2003

台灣經濟轉捩時刻——尹啟銘著

Report ID：of_o_fsr10　　　　表二十一中華民國進出口貿易值表　　　　2004/05/27

國家（地區）：CN_中國大陸（CHINA）　　　1999 年－2004 年　　　　幣別：美元

貨品號列：全部貨品　　　Total

全部貨品

年(月)別	貿易總額		出口		進口		出（入）超值	
	金額	增減比%(同期)	金額	增減比%(同期)	金額	增減比%(同期)	金額	增減比%(同期)
1999	7,062,993,161	42.829	2,536,800,171	203.937	4,526,192,990	10.115	-1,989,392,819	-39.270
2000	10,440,540,918	47.820	4,217,429,107	66.250	6,223,111,811	37.491	-2,005,682,704	0.819
2001	10,647,042,575	1.978	4,745,311,615	12.517	5,901,730,960	-5.164	-1,156,419,345	-42.343
2002	17,892,378,582	68.050	9,944,919,947	109.574	7,947,458,635	34.663	1,997,461,312	---
2003	32,377,000,074	80.954	21,416,894,791	115.355	10,960,105,283	37.907	10,453,789,508	423.504
01	1,806,799,881	87.424	1,019,665,367	109.480	787,134,514	64.930	232,530,853	2346080
02	1,560,463,244	108.583	995,802,850	177.252	564,660,394	45.173	431,142,456	---
03	2,299,278,631	59.104	1,386,398,763	82.248	912,879,868	33.380	473,518,895	520.603
04	2,172,593,325	53.255	1,264,702,104	71.995	907,891,221	33.060	356,810,883	573.301
05	2,461,239,733	75.944	1,626,444,801	114.801	834,794,932	30.094	791,649,869	585.410
06	2,592,424,322	78.855	1,714,959,554	121.656	877,464,768	29.850	867,494,786	755.027
07	2,682,205,205	74.202	1,836,625,613	114.943	845,579,592	23.400	991,046,021	485.594
08	3,053,338,385	93.521	2,126,942,283	131.781	926,396,102	40.336	1,200,546,181	366.188
09	3,175,741,362	79.547	2,161,216,172	110.366	1,014,525,190	36.841	1,146,690,982	300.985
10	3,190,986,293	82.059	2,247,362,169	120.274	943,624,124	28.829	1,303,738,045	353.013
11	3,671,267,352	100.787	2,509,399,669	132.894	1,161,867,683	54.720	1,347,531,986	312.672
12	3,710,662,341	85.372	2,527,375,446	115.125	1,183,286,895	43.099	1,344,088,551	286.301
2004	10,916,603,582	92.650	7,455,028,808	119.145	3,461,574,774	52.851	3,993,454,034	251.168
01	3,195,265,914	76.847	21,470,580,439	110.616	1,047,685,475	33.101	1,099,894,964	373.010
02	3,664,416,771	134.829	2,607,289,856	161.828	1,057,126,915	87.215	1,550,162,941	259.548
03	4,056,920,897	76.443	2,700,158,513	94.761	1,356,762,384	48.624	1,343,396,129	183.705

資料來源：中華民國關稅總局

註：---代表空白值或無法計算

在推展加工出口區轉型的意念中，政府曾有意將之轉變為科學園區的方向發展，若是果真如此，區內現有的科技型傳統產業，高附加價值的傳統產業，以及在區內推動發展的轉運中心，服務業等將如何妥善處理？如果將加工區轉變為科學園區後仍然保留這些產業在區內，則改名後的科學園區並不是真正的科學園區，也就達不到轉變的目的，徒具其名罷了！

更重要的是轉變為科學園區，試問是否還符合原創設加工出口區的宗旨，目的？世界任何一個家不可能只有高科技產業，而傳統產業的量及就業的機會對多數國家而言，都比高科技產業為大，而轉型的加工出口區是屬於傳統科技產業類，所以有其存在的價值，不宜輕言廢棄轉變。

近聞政府有意將加工出口區，科學園區及工業局所屬管理工業區的單位合組成立「產業園區管理局」，而加工出口區與科學園區相關法規維持不變，繼續運作，原工業局所管轄的工業區將可能改採法人方式經營，此一模式是將各類工業區統一單位管理，各區不同特性法規不變，此立意可嘉，只是有多大成效，有待觀察。

C．台灣還需要增設新的加工出口區嗎？

近年來，負責加工出口區經營的主管及一些發展落後的縣市，秉持土地開發而妄想必然有投資市場成功的成果，因而由原有的三個區快速發展到十個區，至今已建設完成者，數年來乏人問津，或曲指可數，而一般有識之士的看法是持否定的態度，其原因如下：

a.已開發國家要求條件的不適合性：

台灣從 1994 年便達到壹萬美元以上的國民所得，成為已開發的國家，其經濟結構已不再是以傳統產業為主體，而加工出口區的基本內涵是以傳統產業為主體，創造就業機會為目的的工業區，而且是以優惠條件吸引外資來區設廠，而今卻形成對本國類似產業不公平的競爭（因為已完全開放國內市場給加工出口區廠商），又已開發的國家，傳統工業大多數都轉移到開發中或未開發的國家（或地區）經營，以降低生產成本，繼續賺取豐厚的利潤，即使在台灣繼續設區，也不易再以低工資召募到本地的勞動力，也享受不到低土地成本及服務成本，由是便少有外資再來區投資，故而加工出口區自不宜在台灣繼續增設，而浪費公帑。

b.產業型態的不適合性：

台灣的產業，從程級來分，概括分為高科技產業及傳統產業，傳統產業又可分為傳統勞力密集產業（多屬低附加價值）及傳統科技產業（較高附加價值），原型的加工出口區是以傳統勞力密集產業為主，以創造就業機會為目的的工業區，但以台灣經濟結構的的發展現況，將不可能繼續創設新的原型加工出口區，甚而現有的加工出口區都不可能再納入在傳統勞力密集型的加工出口區內，因為現有的加工出口區，從廿年前便開始轉型，以傳統科技產業為主要的結構體發展，然而傳統科技產業，也有其特殊的條件要求存在，其一，傳統科技產業需要時間，市場及技術逐年漸進式的發展以臻於成熟，其二，這類型產業需要較多的技術性勞動力，需要較長時間專業性的訓練培養，其三，這類產業有傳統科

技重工業及傳統科技輕工業之分，加工出口區是屬於後者，由於這三個條件的要求，新創設的加工出口區很難滿足，尤其需要較長時間的經營培養，導致需要較大資本的投資，回收時間過長，非一般投資人所願意承擔的風險，所以，傳統科技工業也很難滿足新創加工出口區的要求。對於這兩項「不適合性」的理由，台灣已不再需要新增設加工出口區，除非台灣的經濟環境又回到五十年前未開發國家的水平。

　　D・台灣島加工出口區的構想：

　　台灣面積不大，35,873 平方公里，人口也不算多約 2300 萬人，但人口密度很高，平均每平方公里達 640 人以上，失業率達 5%，所以急需就業機會，1960，70 年代，建設加工出口區，以加工出口區本身功能的發揮及延伸到區外的實質效應，使台灣在短時間內失業率快速下降，但今之台灣人口數較 60 年代成長了三倍，失業人數也相對的增加，所以需要更多的就業機會，加之經濟型態的改變，加工出口區本身也正步入汰換的時刻，現有加工出口區所能彰顯出的功能貢獻較以往為少、有限，更何況過去 39 年中加工出口區內、外廠商彼此都有不盡滿意的怨言，如此，若能將台灣島整體投資環境改善，使區內、外的投資條件相同，政府服務廠商的法規一致，也一樣的能做到一元化的服務，使區內、外投資環境無所差異，則台灣島本身便是一個大型加工出口區，對外來投資者有較多的自由選擇設廠地點，不限定在加工出口區內，相對的吸引來台灣投資的機會也會增加，有如香港、新加坡自由彈性運作，如此，現有加工出口區的圍牆也可以拆除，在台灣便無個別加工出口區的存在，如此台灣整

107

體便成為一個「台灣島加工出口區」了，為台灣經濟發展創造了另一個利基的模式和機會，如果這個構想不因政治環境因素影響，可以實現，對台灣的經濟生命源將有正面的影響及貢獻，也將為全台灣人民造福。而科學園區依然繼續存在、經營，不受任何影響，因為科學園區只是另一類型的加工出口區。

E‧「台灣島加工出口區」營運平台的優勢

以整個台灣來設置「台灣島加工出口區」，以創造新的利基，其營運平台要有堅固的演進條件支撐，而建造這一平台的條件是台灣所擁有的各種優勢，台灣的優勢條件是什麼？

第一、與中國同文同種血緣關係的優勢：

台灣與中國大陸之間割捨不掉的血緣關係，具有共同的語言、文化、五仟年的歷史人文思維，摒棄現實政治利益分割外，海峽兩岸的經濟交融正不斷的在揉合成長，約有數萬家大中小各型台灣企業在中國大陸投資經營，多數並和台灣維持密切的產業關係，同時也有不少台灣優秀的人才參與了台灣的跨國企業，協助該等企業作中、外、台三方面的投資，這種狀況的產生，最主要的原因就是語言溝通，完全沒有障礙，隔閡，百分之百的相互了解，半導體教父張忠謀先生所提出的「中文優勢論」，說明在大中國市場興起的時代，中文能力已成為台灣吸引外資的人才優勢；除語言之外，還有五仟年歷史文化背景所遺傳下來兩岸中國人邏輯思想無懈的匹配及生活習慣的適應性，所以日本經濟大師大前研一說，「台灣人具備的語文優勢，全世界無與可比，而未來需

要對中國提供腦力的服務更會忙死台灣二〇〇〇萬人」,如此說明同一類思想,語文人才對大中國市場服務的重要性,具備這項優勢者,尚有新加坡的華人及海外華人,但人數較少、分散,比不上台灣五十年來與中國政治鬥爭,經濟競爭,情感紛爭不可分的親密關係。

第二、具有雄厚的產業基礎,創新能力的優勢

台灣政府從 1952 年開始推行階段性經濟成長任務,至 1972 年推動了三個階段,共五個經建計劃,其中 1966 年創設了加工出口區,創造就業機會,復於 1968 年推行九年國民義務教育,及隨後延長至十二年國民義務教育,大幅度提高了勞動力的教育水準,使外來投資者有強烈的意願,將高科技產業投入到台灣來,多項實例證實教育對產業的重要性,例如 1986 年某日資公司自韓國拆資到台灣加工出口區來投資,其主要原因是韓國國民水準較低,竟有相當比例勞工不能從 1 數到 100 者,對英文符號更是無知,所以才轉到台灣加工出口區來投資;第二例是台灣北澤公司社長於 1984 年下半年來區拜訪,說明要從中國深圳拆資來台灣投資,而選定加工出口區,主要原因有二,其一、勞工素質太差,其二、勞工由政府分派,每天派來的都是新人,無法教育訓練成熟作業,故而拆資;第三例是日本佳能公司,專門生產光學產品、照相機、影印機……等,在台中加工出口區投資生產照相機,筆者於 1983 年訪問該公司日本東京總公司時,要求該公司除在台灣生產照相機外,希望將影印機也移轉到台灣加工出口區生產,該公司董事長解釋,公司政策是將精密科技產品轉移到台灣佳能公司生產,而大件簡單的送到中

國去做，因為中國方面的技術人才不夠，果不其然，佳能總
公司將照相機由產品設計，模具製造，產品生產全系統由台
灣佳能公司選派六十三位工程師及技術勞工到東京總公司
受訓學習，而今台灣佳能公司每年都有新款式照相機上市；
其他科學園區類似情況亦比比皆是，加上工業技術研究院的
研發及技術向民間轉移、擴散，以及各大學科技人才的培
養，使得台灣的產業奠定了堅實的基礎，尤其在創新的能力
方面，更有優異的表現，這要歸功於台灣政府兩項睿智政策
的決定，即經濟結構的轉變及教育訓練人才的培養，因為這
兩項政策的實行，人才的教育及應用，使就業行業結構及就
業教育程度結構，有了巨大的變化，如圖七及表二十二，就
業行業結構，在 1952 年以農業人口佔 56.1% 為主要就業人
口，至 1971 年農業人口降至 35.1% ，工業人口增加到 29.9
% ，服務業人口達 30% ，至 1989 年農業人口更降至 12.9%
工業人口，服務業人口均上升到 40% 以上，再如圖五，就
業教育程度，1952 年國小以下人口佔 90% ，到 1989 年國小
以下人口只佔 35.9% ，中學程度者佔 48.8% ，大學以上學歷
者提高到 15.3% 之多，就因為這樣巨大的變化，台灣的科技
產業如雨後春筍般的萌芽茂盛成長，成熟，（表二十三，表
二十四）在世界科技產業中也佔有一席之地，這也是台灣當
今賴以為生的產業，工具，茲僅就 IC 產業為例，根據台灣
半導體協會（TSIA）於 2004 年 5 月 20 日公佈台灣半導體產
值，2004 年第一季為新台幣 2,396 億元，佔 WSTS 公佈全球
同期產值 483 億美元的 15% 的比重，這項比重，說明何以
台灣在 1999 年就已擠身為世界第四大 IC 生產國，而今更有

多家半導體公司例如：台積電、聯電、旺宏等高科技公司投入巨資生產 12 吋晶圓，為台灣科技產業更上一層樓而努力。此外，台灣已成為世界資訊工業重鎮，在光電產業中成為世界最大的 CD-ROM 光碟機生產國以及 CD-R 光碟片佔世界 55% 的市場，這些成就絕非偶然。台灣政府為有效掌握創新能力的優勢，而採取主動的以財產法人的模式設置各類研究發展及服務機構，以替代民間投資研究發展的不足，例如工業技術研究院，徵對高科技產品研發推廣；資訊策進委員會，以推動國家整體資訊產業及應用的發展而努力，紡託會以服務國內紡織產業面對國際市場配額分配作整體的因應，其它尚有如航空發展委員會，金屬工業研究發展中心……等，這類政府投資，非常具有創意及實質性的效果，為台灣科技產業奠定了穩固的基礎及世界競爭優勢，因而台灣榮獲科技島的美譽，2004 年 6 月 1 日滾動新聞文學城網站報導：「日人撰文震撼國人，日越來越有能力控制中國？」本報導源於日本國際經濟學家長谷慶太郎近日所發表的「中國的未來取決予日本」的文章，內容主要兩點論述，一是日本企業能向中國提供中國產業不能達到質量的產品，二是日本擁有優秀的技術實力和為確保技術優勢而研究開發的巨大投資。這兩點論述，看在台灣人的眼裡，至少有三分之二台灣有能力辦得到，事實上台灣在中國投資的企業已在輸出傳授，惟對巨額投資在研發上的資金仍是不足，差日美很多，這是台灣企業家們要省思的。

就業行業結構

1952
民國41年

農業 56.1%
2,929
千人
工業 16.9%
服務業 27.0%

1971
民國60年

農業 35.1%
4,738
千人
工業 29.9%
服務業 35.0%

1989
民國78年

農業 12.9%
工業 42.2%
8,258
千人
服務業 44.9%

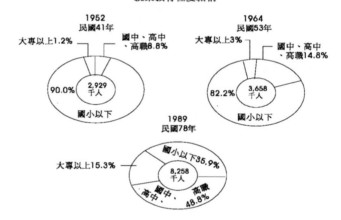

就業教育程度結構

1952
民國41年

大專以上1.2%
國中、高中、高職8.8%
90.0%
2,929
千人
國小以下

1964
民國53年

大專以上3%
國中、高中、高職14.8%
82.2%
3,658
千人
國小以下

1989
民國78年

國小以下35.9%
大專以上15.3%
8,258
千人
國中、高中、高職 48.8%

圖七

表二十二　各部門就業人力

單位：1,000 人

年	農業	工業	製造業	服務業
1985	1,297	3,088	2,501	3,044
1986	1,317	3,215	2,635	3,201
1987	1,226	3,431	2,821*	3,366
1988	1,112	3,443	2,802	3,551
1989	1,066	3,476	2,796	3,717
1990	1,064	3,382	2,653	3,837
1991	1,093	3,370	2,598	3,977

＊：就業人力達最高峰

資料來源：中華民國行政院主計處

表二十三　台灣製造業產業結構──以產值計

	1991 年	1996 年	2001 年
金屬機械	26.4%	26.7%	23.3%
資訊電子	19.3%	27.1%	36.4%
化學工業	26.0%	24.0%	24.9%
民生工業	28.3%	22.2%	15.4%

資料來源：中華民國經濟部工業局

表二十四　IC產業成為竹科的鎮園之寶（2002年）

	家數	就業人數	實收資本額 （新台幣億元）	營業額 （新台幣億元）
IC產業（A）	136	60,459	6,959	4,576
竹科合計（B）	335	98,685	9,607	7,055
（A）／（B） ×100%	41%	61%	72%	65%

資料來源：中華民國新竹科學工業園區管理局

　　台灣雄厚的產業基礎，創新的能力優勢，在加工出口區內也在同步進行，只是與科學園區有程度上的差異，畢竟加工出區不會輕易放棄創區的本意及使命，以下列舉加工出口區、科學園區、一般工業區比較表（表二十五），供讀者了解高科技產業在加工出口區內發展的驅向，程度與別區競爭力的比較。

　　台灣雄厚的產業基礎，創新能力的優勢足以彌補中國的不足，在兩岸的中國人彼此兄弟輸誠，互助互利原則下，應不會受制於日本的傲慢，是為可預見得到的事實。

　　第三、國際化發展優勢

　　國際化的條件是要自由化，包括了人、錢、物三方面的自由活動，台灣除了對中國大陸因政治因素還不能完全三通外，對世界其他國家及地區都能做到合法的自由往來，其次是制度化、法治化，台灣已屬法制，制度化的國家，尤其是國際貿易，經濟事務，完全依法行政，與世界經濟經貿法源相吻合，接軌，再則是現代化基礎建設，是外來投資人最為滿意的項目；最後是台灣的地理位置適中，衍生出橋樑，媒

介性的角色，當今世界市場焦點都轉向中國大陸，而台灣地理位置面對中國東南沿海，正是中國未來五年區域發展八大經濟區（附件四）的南部沿海地區（包括福建、廣東、海南三省）及東部沿海地區（包括上海、江蘇、浙江一市兩省），這兩區也是中國當前發展的精華區，絕大多數的台商就是在這兩區投資發展，由這兩區還可以延伸到北部沿海地區，長江中游地區及西南地區，也都是有台灣商人到達的地區，這再次顯示出大陸成為台灣經濟腹地的必然性及重要性，然而因台灣站在前哨性的地理位置，使台灣成為中國大陸與東北亞，東南亞及北美之間的樞紐及橋樑，如能摒棄對中國政治因素的考量，則可利用台灣國際化對國際事務及商務的作業經驗，信譽及作業能力水準，以及台灣語文溝通的優勢條件，可擔任及促進國際間產業投資在中國形成「物流及金流」的國際市場活動，而台灣在脈動共振條件下，也可以做到「轉運中心」互動的功能，則中台雙方相互利益輸送，相得益彰，如此，加工出口區所新賦予擔任轉運中心的任務便可落實達成。

這三項優勢條件足證「台灣島加工出口區」建構營運的可靠性，是否能成為事實，有賴台灣政府睿智的決定。

3、台灣加工出口區往後的發展走向

按台灣整體環境的變遷，加工出口區本身的發展演變，走向宜從兩方面繼續演進，走下去。

其一，仍然堅定的在製造業方面發展：

表二十五　中華民國加工區、科學園區、工業區比較表

項目 \ 區別	優劣比較	說明		
		加　工　區	科學園區	工業區（含科技園區）
地理位置	加工區＞科學園區＞工業區	加工區鄰近港口（高雄港與台中港）、機場（小港機場）及高速公路，地理位置優越，為三區最佳。	科學園區緊鄰高速公路，有利陸路運輸，惟離港口、機場較遠，而不利國內外海空運輸。	工業區分散各地，少數鄰近高速公路，交通便利性較不佳。
產業基礎及聚集性	科學園區加工區＞工業區	1. 現階段以高科技電子業為主，其中 IC 封裝測試與 LCD 模相已成為國內生產之大本營，佔全區營業額之 60%。 2. 加工區之 IC 與 LCD 產業屬中下游階段產業，而科學園區為上游廠商，故兩者之間係為垂直分工型態共存，故競合性不高。 3. 未來將繼續引進高科技高附加價值之製造業，並以其為核心，向上及向下垂直分工，以發展成為 A.高科技產業中心；B.家電關鍵	1. 竹科：以積體電路、電腦及週邊、光電、通訊為主。 2. 南科：計劃以半導體、微電子精密機械、農業生物技術為發展目標。 3. 科區產業以高科技、高附加價值產業為主。	1. 涵蓋輕工業、基礎民生工業、石化工業…等。 2. 若以高科技產業發展為評比，則難與加工區與科學園區相提並論。

		零組件、流行產品與國內外流通系統及連鎖廠商之整合管理中心；C.全球運籌管理中心三大中心為目標。		
特殊租稅優惠	科學園區加工區＞工業區 註：加工區與科學園區之相稅優惠孰優孰劣，端視事業性質而定。	1. 營所稅：從事轉運業務者，得按轉運收入 10%為所得額課徵營所稅。 2. 免徵自國外輸入之原物料、半製品、樣品、機器設備及轉運用之進口稅捐、貨物稅及營業稅。	1. 營所稅：新設事業五年免稅，增資事業可選擇四年免稅或投資抵減，且營所稅及其附加捐不超過所得額之 20%。 2. 免徵自國外輸入之原物料、半製品、樣品、機器設備及轉運用之進口稅、貨物稅及營業稅。	無特別優惠。
說明：表面上科區似乎優於加工區，惟因加工區內大型產業（投資新台幣二億元以上）若符合促產條例，亦可享五年免稅或投資抵減之優惠，故此部份僅對中小企業有差別。惟就從事轉運業務者而言，加工區則優於科學園區。				

資料來源：台灣加工出口區區刊第 42 期

區別\項目	優劣比較	說明		
		加 工 區	科學園區	工業區（含科技園區）
科技人才及研發能力	科學園區＞加工區＞工業區	1. 本區研發費用佔營業額之3%，研發能力略遜於科學園區。 2. 附近有中山、成功、義守、第一科技……等多所大學，可培養人力。	1. 本區研發費用佔營業額之5%且科技及研發人才相當充沛。 2. 附近有清大、交大、中央……等大學，另工研院則提供大量科技人力及研發資源，是本區最大的優勢。	本區是三區中最差者。
費用負擔	加工區＞科學園區＞工業區	1. 土地以租用為原則，地租每坪年租金新台幣300～400元。 2. 依行業別不同與營業額多寡收取營業額千分之0.5～2.5不等之管理費。	1. 土地以租用為原則，地租每坪年租金新台幣300～400元。 2. 依營業額千分之2.5計收。	1. 土地需價購，業者負擔頗重。 2. 土地及樓地板面積大小計收公共設施維護費，每坪每年新台幣340～1,010元。
行政效率	加工區科學園區＞工業區	1. 採單一窗口，手續簡便，由投資申請、審查、公司登記……到廠房建築許可證之核發皆由加工區管理處統籌辦理。全部核准時間約為19～21天。 2. 貨品進出採帳	1. 採單一窗口，手續簡便，由投資申請、審查、公司登記…到廠房建築許可證之核發皆由科學園區管理局統籌辦理。全部核准時間約為90天。 2. 貨品進出採帳	1. 投資申請、審查、公司、登記……到廠房建築許可證之核發，須分別向各主管機關(經濟部{僑、外資則免}、省、縣、市政府)提出申請。若為直接購地設廠者，全部

		冊式管理，需報關者亦可在 3～4 小時內完成通關，相當便捷。	冊式管理，需報關者亦可在3～4小時內完成通關，相當便捷。	核准時間約為32～47 天（以上未含建照之申請及發放）。 2. 通關時間約 1～3 天
週邊設備	加工區＝科學園區＞工業區	設有國稅局、銀行、警察局、員工宿舍、托兒所、餐廳、從業員工服務中心……等。	與加工區大致相同，而略優於加工區。	未如加工區與科學園區完善。
土地利用	加工區＞科學園區＞工業區	1. 建廠率：60%。 2. 容積率：300%～600%。	1. 建廠率：竹科60%：南科 2. 容積率：皆為200%。	1. 建廠率：20%～70%。 2. 容積率：210%～300%。
知名度	科學園區加工區＞工業區	1. 國內聲望略遜於科學園區。 2. 國外聲望與科學園區相當。	國內外聲望均佳。	國內外知名度均為三區最低者。
總評	加工區＝科學園區＞工業區	加工區在地理位置、行政效率、土地利用及費用負擔均優於科學園區，至於產業基礎及聚集性略遜於科學園區，其他事項則與科學園區相當。整體而言，加工區與科學園區具有同等之競爭力。	科學園區在租稅優惠、科技人力、研發能力、知名度等方面表現最佳，惟整體競爭力與加工區同。	工業區在各項評比均較遜於加工區與科學園區。

119

唯有固守在製造業，加工出口區才不會被時代的巨浪所席卷淹沒，然而製造業，一方面要堅持在傳統科技產業面，並督促及協助傳統產業加強研發功能，則可以使之繼續生存及升級，再創台灣在傳統產業方面的優勢，同時還繼續兼顧了就業的機會，此於數年前高雄中山大學企業管理班學員對劉維琪校長提出的疑問，為何政府只照顧高科技產業，投資大額資金建科學園區而對傳統產業於不顧，讓傳統產業投資人找不到如同科學園區的廠商一樣享有低成本投資環境的工業區，讓他們有機會生存，發展，壯大，更何況傳統產業的就業人數不比高科技的少；這一翻話，只有加工出口區還能為他們設想，也是加工出口區堅持演變中不變的原則做法。另一方面加工出口區要吸引高科技產業來區投資生產，促使加工出口區自然的往科技製造業方向發展，則加工出口區將兼顧到創造利潤，技術升級及就業機會的三項目的。

其二，承擔「物流轉運中心」功能的任務：

為配合台灣島型經濟發展的需要及面臨大環境經濟脈動的驅勢，加工出口區可以同時承擔「物流轉運中心」功能的任務，惟先決條件是加工出口區要維持堅強的生產製造的能力，如此物流轉運的功能才能為製造業服務，並為製造業協助其打開市場通路，與中國腹地市場互動，如此台灣加工出口區便增加了生存的空間及競爭力，將可永續經營。

二、中國出口加工區部份：

1、出口加工區創設發展初期

（1）出口加工區初期建設發展散漫混亂的局面

中國政府於 2000 年 4 月 27 日由國務院批准設立首批 15 個出口加工區，至 2002 年 10 月共批准 25 個出口加工區，以後又陸續批准多批，至今共 56 區，此乃國家級出口加工區，實際中國出口加工區的發展遠比國務院批准的時間要早很多，例如 1991 年昆山出口加工區就已經成立了，只不過是初期由地方政府管理推動發展，其目的在創造地方上的就業機會，促進地方經濟發展，其用心，非常明確，同時中央對地方也給予充份的自主權，所以各省、市、縣風起雲湧的建設出口加工區，彼時全國到底創設了多少出口加工區，無法得到確實的數據，各地方政府，為了吸引外來投資，盡可能的給來區投資者各種優惠，至全國優惠條件不一致，差距至為懸殊，對營利事業所得稅一項而言，有二免三減半，三免三減半，五免五減半，甚而在北方有十免十減半者，主要以達到招商為目的，導至良莠不齊，即便如此努力，其成效普遍而言，在江蘇、浙江、廣東、福建沿海一帶較為顯著，其他各地成效可謂不彰，乏善可陳，所以中央才主動介入，配合全國經濟系統發展而選定適宜定點發展出口加工區（圖八），頒行全國統一的法規制度，管理辦法，如此可避免各地方盲目的創設出口加工區；按中國出口加工區總管理單位，中國海關總署（原屬國務院特區辦主管）於 2002 年 9

121

月中國海關學會所發刊物「中國出口加工區」其概述的最新
亮點說明如下：

　　『中華人民共和國國務院于 2000 年 4 月至 2002 年 6 月在
全國相繼批准設立了 25 個出口加工區。這是中國擴大對外開
放，促進對外經濟貿易發展的一項重要舉措。出口加工區是目
前政策最優惠、通關最快捷、管理最簡便、設施最完善的海關
監管特定區域，她已成為中外客商在中國投資的最新亮點。

　　方便快捷的通關模式：海關專門開發了出口加工區管理
系統，對監管模式進行了重大改革，把通常進出口貨物需要
多個部門審批、辦理多道手續簡化為一個環節、一道手續，
在出口加工區內不實行銀行保證金台帳制度、不實行進出口
配額、許可證管理。同時，海關賦予出口加工區口岸功能，
並實現無紙化辦公。這些都為入區企業實現零庫存生產、降
低管理成本、提高市場競爭力創造了有利條件。

　　理想寬鬆的優惠政策：國家明確規定對出口加工區實行
特殊的稅收優惠政策、海關總署、外經貿部、稅務總局、外
匯管理局和質檢總局等部委也都根據國務院的規定，專門為
出口加工區制定了簡便的管理辦法。

　　得天獨厚的地理位置：已經批准成立的 25 家出口加工
區主要分布在沿海、沿江、沿邊、臨港等開放城市的開發區
內，具有交通便利、信息靈敏、經濟活躍、環境典雅、人才
資源豐富等優勢。

　　配套齊全的市政設施：大部分出口加工區都已經完成了
高質量的市政基礎設施建設，實現了「七通一平」。同時，
搭建了信息化平台，做到了光纖入區、網絡入戶。

　　現代高效的服務質量：出口加工區管委會屬於當地政府派出機構，可代替有關職能部門行使項目審批等職權，真正實現了「一門式服務、一站式辦公」的現代高效的辦事程序。

　　充滿希望的發展前景：到 2002 年 8 月底，首批成立的 17 家出口加工區均已通過驗收、正式運行。截止到 2002 年上半年、加工區已引進中外企業 313 家，投資總額 34.26 億美元，進出口累計達到 24.51 億美元。

　　中國出口加工區正張開雙臂擁抱世界，中外客商正在這裡展開翅膀飛向未來！』

　　此可以看出全國系統管理的一致性，不再是地方各自為政的散漫混亂的局面。

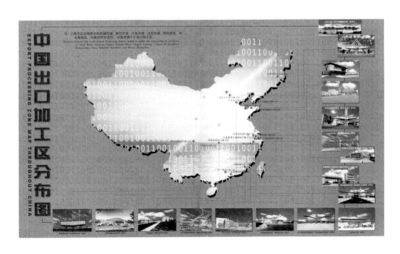

圖八　中國首先批准的二十五個出口加工區位置分布圖

（2）中央政府整體掌控發展出口加工區及各類經濟園區

出口加工區是中國整體經濟發展的一環，它所反應出來的是中國整體經濟環境的大變局及大格局，實際最迫切需要的是什麼？答案是「就業機會，社會安定繁榮，國家富強」；中國整體經濟發展改革可分成三個階段：

第一階段：從 1949 年至 1952 年，由市場經濟走向計劃經濟時期。

第二階段：從 1953 年至 1978 年，計劃經濟大規模的推展執行時期，1953 年開始第一個五年經濟計劃。

第三階段：從 1979 年至今，再由計劃經濟走向市場經濟時期，1979 年 6 月 18 日至 7 月 1 日，第五屆全國人民代表大會第二次會議，通過了中國工作重點轉移和對國民經濟實行「調整，改革，整頓，提高」八字方針重要決策，全國開始全民經濟調整工作。

這三個階段，最重要的時刻是在 1978 年 12 月中共十一屆三中全會中決議停止使用「以階級鬥爭為網」的口號，由鄧小平主政改變採取以「市場經濟取代計劃經濟」政策，這才有第三階段經濟改革的產生，然而不可諱言的，此一政策是參考了台灣（包括加工出口區的設置），新加坡、香港等華人國家及地區的經濟發展績效及貢獻為借鏡，而於 1980 年初首先在廣東深圳創設了深圳經濟特區，以及在珠海、汕頭及廈門等共創建了四個經濟特區，作為走向市場經濟起步的試點，而且是傾全國的力量促其發展成功。

　　1984 年春，鄧小平視察深圳、珠海、廈門特區後指出：
「深圳的發展和經驗證明，我們建立經濟特區的政策是正確
的。」「我們建立經濟特區，實行開放政策，有個指導思想
要明確，就是不是收，而是放。」「除現在的特區之外，可
以考慮再開放幾個港口城市，如大連、青島。」，隨後便是
出口加工區及其各類工業區，各依其特殊目的而併進有序的
在全國各地建設及發展。

2、中國大環境因素影響經濟均衡發展

　　中國全國各地經濟發展並不均衡，差距非常大，是為不
爭的事實，影響經濟不能均衡發展的因素很多，而較重要的
基本因素有以下三點：

（1）人口問題

　　人口是中國經濟發展最重要的因素，中國人口 2001 年
底，全國總人口達到拾貳億柒仟多萬人（1,276,270,000 人），
人口眾多，是中國經濟發展市場胃納的強勢，以其低勞動成
本及低土地成本，吸引了世界各國產業生產工廠的設置及貿
易兩條龐大「金流」的注入，使中國經濟以躍進式的成長，
傲視全球，反之因此而演進到不能均衡發展所造成的內損，
也十分嚴重，令人憂慮不已！

　　中國從 1980 年代鄧小平主政改革以來，二十多年確有
長足的進步，國民生產毛額，無論 GNP、GDP 1980 年代初，
每年只不過四、五仟億人民幣而已，因為改革急速的進步，
1986 年突破一兆元，1991 年達到二兆以上，1999 年突破八

兆，2001 年更高達九兆五仟多億元，（附表二十六）平均每一年都有 8%～10%的成長，成績確實驚人。但另一方面，人口成長，也令人吃驚，1980 年是 9 億 8 仟 7 佰多萬人，1985 年便突破了 10 億人，1995 年高達 12 億多萬人，至 2001 年已高達 1,276,270,000 人（附表二十七），其人口自然增長率在 1997 年以前都維持在 10%～16%的成長，到 1998 年才開始下降到 10%以下，（附表二十八），但為時似乎嫌晚了些，因為 8%～10%的國民生產毛額較人口 10‰～16%‰的成長需求要低得多，所以國民平均所得也很難改善，2001 年國民平均所得僅約為 US$900 元（按表二十一 GDP 換算；又按表二十九，農村居民家庭人均收入 2001 年為 RMB2366.4 元僅約為 US$288 元及城鎮居民家庭人均可支配收入 2001 年為 RMB6859.6 元僅約為 US$836 元），應列名在未開發國家。

國民平均所得偏低，顯現出兩大問題的存在：

其一，人民生活品質低劣，中國在二十年前的人民生活品質，確實遠不如今，至少今天全國普遍可以過得溫飽，然而全國各地家庭支出的 60%以上消費在三餐吃的部份，此乃說明中國家庭生活水平遠不及已開發國家的平均中等水平，影響家庭水平的基本指標，有每一家庭平均總收入（或國民平均所得），每一家庭的能源消耗、衛生設備的設置及每一家庭教育經費的負擔等，這些指標，在大都市如上海、北京尚可以達到平均中等水平，然而遠離城市的鄉間，村落則依舊維持從前的生活條件，改善有限，甚而據聞某些山區村莊，還維持近乎原始的生活，與外界隔絕，如此上情，表

示中國遠離大都市便沒有消費市場，自然影響到投資人怯步的心裡。

　　其二，是失業人口的增加，根據中國 2002 年中國統計年鑑資料，全國城鎮登記失業人數（年底數）及失業率如下表：（表三十）

西元年	1985	1990	1995	2000	2001
失業人數（萬人）	239	383	520	595	681
失業率（％）	1.8	2.5	2.9	3.1	3.6

　　數據所示失業人數年年增加及失業率不斷上升，此僅為城鎮登記有案者，可見其嚴重性，失業是市場經濟的副產品，是職場優生劣敗公平競爭自然產生的現象，但政府的

表二十六　中國國民生產總值和國內生產總值

單位：億元

年　　　份	國民生產總值	國內生產總值
1978	3624.1	3624.1
1979	4038.2	4038.2
1980	4517.8	4517.8
「六五」時期	32315.3	32227.0
1981	4860.3	4862.4
1982	5301.8	5294.7
1983	5957.4	5934.5
1984	7206.7	7171.0
1985	8989.1	8964.4
「七五」時期	72594.4	72550.1
1986	10201.4	10202.2
1987	11954.5	11962.5
1988	14922.3	14928.3

1989	16917.8	16909.2
1990	18598.4	18547.9
「八五」時期	187039.8	188127.8
1991	21662.5	21617.8
1992	26651.9	26638.1
1993	34560.5	34634.4
1994	46670.0	46759.4
1995	57494.9	58478.1
「九五」時期	385729.3	392163.4
1996	66850.5	67884.6
1997	73142.7	74462.6
1998	76967.2	78345.2
1999	80579.4	82067.5
2000	88189.5	89403.6
「十五」時期		
2001	94346.4	95933.3

注：本表按當年價格計算。

資料來源：2001 年中國統計年鑑

表二十七　中國人口數

（年底數）　　　　　　　　　　　單位：萬人

年　　份	總　人　口	按性別分		按城鄉分	
		男	女	城鎮人口	鄉村人口
1978	96259	49567	46692	17245	79014
1980	98705	50785	47920	19140	79565
1985	105851	54725	51126	25094	80757
1990	114333	58904	55429	30195	84138
1991	115823	59466	56357	31203	84620
1992	117171	59811	57360	32175	84996
1993	118517	60472	58045	33173	85344
1994	119850	61246	58604	34169	85681
1995	121121	61808	59313	35174	85947
1996	122389	62200	60189	37304	85085
1997	123626	63131	60495	39449	84177
1998	124761	63604	61157	41608	83153
1999	125786	64126	61660	43748	82038
2000	126743	65437	61306	45906	80837
2001	127627	65672	61955	48064	79563

資料來源：2001 年中國統計年鑑

表二十八　中國人口出生率、死亡率、自然增長率

單位：(‰)

年　份	出生率	死亡率	自然增長率	年　份	出生率	死亡率	自然增長率
1978	18.25	6.25	12.00	1990	21.06	6.67	14.39
1979	17.82	6.21	11.61	1991	19.68	6.70	12.98
1980	18.21	6.34	11.87	1992	18.24	6.64	11.60
1981	20.91	6.36	14.55	1993	18.09	6.64	11.45
1982	22.28	6.60	15.68	1994	17.70	6.49	11.21
1983	20.19	6.90	13.29	1995	17.12	6.57	10.55
1984	19.90	6.82	13.08	1996	16.98	6.56	10.42
1985	21.04	6.78	14.26	1997	16.57	6.51	10.06
1986	22.43	6.86	15.57	1998	15.64	6.50	9.14
1987	23.33	6.72	16.61	1999	14.64	6.46	8.18
1988	22.37	6.64	15.73	2000	14.03	6.45	7.58
1989	21.58	6.54	15.04	2001	13.38	6.43	6.95

注：1、以上兩表 1980 年以前數據為戶藉統計數；1985-1989 年數據根據 1990
　　 年人口普查數據有所調整；1990-2000 年數據根據 2000 年人口普查數
　　 據進行了調整；2001 年數據為人口變動情況抽樣調查推算數。

　　 2、1978-1980 年的城鎮人口是指轄區內全部人口；鄉村人口是指縣人口，
　　 但不包 1985-1999 年的城鎮人口是指設區的市所轄的區人口和不設區
　　 的市所轄街道人市所轄鎮的居民委員會人口和縣轄鎮的居民委員會人
　　 口；鄉村人口是指除城鎮 2000 年以後的城鄉人口是按國家統計局 1999
　　 年發布的《關於統計上劃分城鄉的計算的》。

資料來源：2001 年中國統計年鑑

表二十九　中國城鄉居民家庭人均收入及恩格爾系數

年　份	農村居民家庭人均純收入		城鎮居民家庭人均可支配收入		恩格爾系數（％）	
	絕對數（元）	指　數（1978 年=100）	絕對數（元）	指　數（1978 年=100）	農村居民家庭	城鎮居民家庭
1978	133.6	100.00	343.4	100.00	67.7	57.5
1980	191.3	138.99	477.6	127.02	61.8	56.9
1985	397.6	268.94	739.1	160.39	57.8	53.3
1990	686.3	311.20	1510.2	198.10	58.8	54.2
1991	708.6	317.43	1700.6	212.37	57.6	53.8
1992	784.0	336.15	2026.6	232.91	57.6	52.9
1993	921.6	346.91	2577.4	255.13	58.1	50.1
1994	1221.0	364.36	3496.2	276.83	58.9	49.9
1995	1577.7	383.67	4283.0	290.34	58.6	49.9
1996	1926.1	418.20	4838.9	301.56	56.3	48.6
1997	2090.1	437.44	5160.3	311.85	55.1	46.4
1998	2162.0	456.21	5425.1	329.94	53.4	44.5
1999	2210.3	473.54	5854.0	360.62	52.6	41.9
2000	2253.4	483.48	6280.0	383.69	49.1	39.2
2001	2366.4	503.79	6859.6	416.30	47.7	37.9

注：本表指數按可比價格計算。

資料來源：2001 年中國統計年鑑

責任是如何讓人民在各行各業中有機會發揮一己之所長，得到一份適才適所有收入能維持家計的工作，如果一年比一年失業率增高，失業人口節節上升，則表示職場容量不夠，或是人口成長數過大或職場容量擴大速度跟不上需求量的增加等，不管是何原因，總之是人口數量太過龐大所造成的結果，表示人口問題是中國經濟發展最嚴肅的問題。

（2）地理環境因素的影響

在已開發的城鎮地區、沿海、沿長江、珠江一帶的國民收入較之內陸、東北、西北地區國民收入高出近達十倍之多，呈現出嚴重的不均衡發展現象，例如根據中國 2001 年統計年鑑資料，2001 年貴州農民年收入是 1411.73 元，約為 USD\$172.2 元，西藏為 1404.01 元或 US\$171.2 元，而上海則為 12,883.5 元，約為 US\$1,571 元，北京為 11,577.8 元，或 USD\$1,412 元，平均貴州、西藏每月收入只有 RMB117 元，而上海每月達 1073 元，北京每月 965 元，如此懸殊的差異收入，長期將會形成不均則鳴的隱憂。

中國沿海、沿江快速發展，一則乃政策使然，再則地理條件、氣候、交通運輸以及滿清末年即已在這些地區開放為國際港埠等自然因素所形成，此外是這些地區龐大的市場吸引力、國際貿易互動的關係及世界資訊快速傳遞效應等的影響而促成；而政策性從沿海、沿江開始發展，是集中打點，擴展成線而廣泛成面的戰略及戰術，基本思維上是受肯定的，只是中國土地面積太大，地形多山，交通十分的不便利，需要建設發展的資金數額實在太龐大，加之人民教育水準普

遍偏低，以及需要供給溫飽的人口眾多，所以從沿海、沿江的發起攻擊線，開始全面進發時卻無法快速挺進，甚而只在原地膨脹，不斷的在原地經濟持續發展，所以從上海以下經昆山、蘇州、常州、常熟、杭州至南京一帶及沿海廣州、深圳、珠海、廈門、福州一帶，便成為大部份外商（包括台、港）的聚集投資發展地帶，而對內陸也僅武漢、成都、重慶、華北的北京、天津、濟南、青島等據點有所發展，對面積廣大的內陸，西南、西北、華北等地則裹足不前，這些佔有約四分之三中國的土地面積及近三分之二的人口，在中國建國五十年後的經濟，仍然停留在赤貧的狀況，是無法令「文明」社會的人所能想像和忍受的，目前中國全國交通網正快速發展及世界電子網路資訊的普及傳遞，民智將會很快的開啟高漲，如此這三分之二的人口，將會激發要求「均富，公平待遇」的訴求。此有待中國政府如何克服地理環境所造成經濟發展的障礙。

（3）教育對經濟發展的貢獻度有待加強

　　教育是國家百年大計，千秋萬世都不可偏廢，等閒視之的偉大事業，中華人民共合國自 1949 年 10 月 1 日建國以來，初期的 16 年中，一直都在進行國內的政治鬥爭，例如「三反」，「五反」，土地改革，社會改革，參入抗美援朝戰爭，反右派，推行大躍進，推行人民公社等一連串鬥不完的鬥爭運動，對於國家百年大計的教育渾然罔顧，接著又是 1966 年 5 月發動了文化大革命，歷時十年，國家被催殘得體無完膚，更遑論教育，無暇以顧。

如此二十六年之久教育全面中斷，影響之大，不僅是經濟發展，更擴及到國家整體性人才培養，國家長時間無人才可用，是非常嚴重到難以彌補的程度，如此嚴重無可旁貸的責任，端看歷史如何批判；教育的發展從橫向與縱向來了解，橫向是教育普及的問題，縱向則是教育深度的問題，中國與台灣的正規教育系統都類同，由小學到中學（初中、高中或高職）而大學（包括大學、獨立學院及專科）最後到研究所（碩士、博士），以下列舉 1995 年中國與台灣各級教育就學人數（由小學至大專學生）比例（表三十一）比較之：

表三一　中國與台灣各級教育就業人數比例表

區　域	中　　　國		台　　　灣	
總人口數	1,211,210,000	100%	21,304,000	100%
總學生人數	196,773,000	16.2%	4,646,134	21.8%
小學生人數	131,952,000	10.9%	1,965,515	9.23%
中學生人數	61,915,000	5.1%	2,045,148	9.6%
大專生人數	2,906,000	0.24%	635,471	2.98%
小學升中學比例	61,915,000／131,952,000	46.9%	2,045,148／1,965,515	100.4%
中學升大專比例	2,906,000／61,915,000	4.69%	635,471／2,045,148	31.1%

註：資料來源，2001 年中國統計年鑑及台灣經濟建設委員會 Taiwan Statistical Data Book 1997

按上表所顯示出一些值得探討的問題。

　　Ａ・學生的總人數，台灣達到總人口數的 21.8%，而中國只有 16.2%，相差 5.2%，相當 1/3 的中國學齡人口（由小學至大專生）未入學，表示中國教育普及率有待改進。

　　Ｂ・小學畢業生升中學，台灣達到 100%，而中國只有 46.9%，即表示中國有一半以上的小學畢業生未繼續升學而即早進入社會。

　　Ｃ・中學升大專者，台灣是 31.1%，而中國只有 4.69%，雙方比例上相差 25 個百分點。

　　小學升中學，中學升大專兩階段的學生人數大量減少，造成受教育總人口數比台灣相差 5.2%，而至影響教育深度的普及率。

　　從以上三點現象來分析，在相對比較下，中國尚有 1/3 學齡人數未就學，而即早進入社會，將形成社會的大盲點，對國家整體發展絕對不利，其次，小學升中學，不到一半的人數，即超過一半的小學畢業人口，所學僅止於啟蒙識字，初期知識教育，對人生的了解，工作的意義，家庭的責任，社會的交誼等全然無知，而所能擔任的工作，也僅限於初級勞動力的工作範圍，對往後漫長人生的認識只能在成長過程中所處的環境裡，從所見所聞，身體力行的經驗中學習，這些經驗是片斷的，有正面的，也有更多負面的，在一種沒有系統正規教育的現實環境中，全面吸取轉變為成熟經驗的認知，做人的標準，這樣的認知、標準對社會影響之大，難以估計，也很難評定自己在社會中的品位，對社會品質優化功能自然是無所幫助。

　　中國人口眾多，每年雖然有百萬以上的大學生畢業進入社會，但相對的比例，比台灣低很多，高等教育是國家人才培養最重的階段，也是國家建設基層幹部，社會優質化的中流砥柱，將來多數成為國家（各地方或事業）的領導階層，故這一階段接受教育人數的多寡較之中、小學階段教育更直接影響到國家全面進步發展現代化的成效。

　　從經濟發展的層面來看，中學及中學以上教育程度的人口數，對國家經濟發展有更直接的影響，初中學歷是龐大直接生產線上的主要勞動力，高中（含高級職業學歷）學歷是生產事業技術勞動力的主幹，而大學（含專科）以上學歷是事業單位師級，經理級以及管理經營的負責幹部或主管，國家對這類教育人才的培養欠缺或不足，自然影響整體經濟發展，也包括直接影響到加工出口區的發展，教育能不重視嗎？

　　從中國經濟開放以來的社會現象來證實教育的重要性，例如僅就商業信譽而言，約五年以前，中國境內商務必須以現金買賣，否則收不到錢，至有台灣燦坤家電公司在中國因收款困難而改變經營策略的案例，即使至今此一現象改善不大，尤其落後地區為最，大城市的大百貨公司消費者現在可以使用信用卡，是為一大進步，而國際貿易，外商多要求由中國人民銀行開狀或香港國際性的銀行如香港匯豐銀行開狀，不接受其他銀行，目前已有改進，也只限幾家大銀行，此明確的表示是商業信譽的問題；其他如衛生習慣的問題，公共道德的問題，公共秩序的問題……等，至今仍都為外人視為污點垢病，都證實教育的落後及不夠普及，因此便

影響到國家經濟快速發展的品質及全國總體經濟發展成效，此乃「教育不普及，經濟不發達」而至產生「生活貧窮，思想貧乏」的結果，何其嚴重，可怕！

　　以上三項重要的基本因素不僅影響國家經濟發展，也將影響國力及國際地位，中國政府當深思急謀改進是為當務之急！

3、中國經濟發展與出口加工區的發展走向

（1）海峽兩岸人民生活水平的落差

　　中國經濟發展不均衡現象的存在，呈現出「貧富」懸殊的差距，此懸殊的差距實際上已影響到人民心態的不平衡及社會的安定性，貧、富的認定，從兩方面來衡量，其一、是個人財富所擁有的差距，其二、是整體社會共同基本生活水平程度的差距，這兩項有互為因果的關係，後者當更形重要，因為基本生活水平是人民生活的必要條件，能夠滿足生活必要條件的國家，國民知識水平相對的比較高，人民的精神生活比較疏暢愉悅，思想情緒也較平靜、穩定，社會也會表現出朝氣蓬勃，安定祥和的景象，例如屬於華人社會國家的新加坡即是，中國社會的基本生活水平是何種程度？基本生活指數與先進國家比較達到何種標準？不可否認的，今天中國人民的生活條件，水平比 1978 年底之前要好上千百倍，社會才展現出興旺榮景的現象，此已為世界所公認的事實，尤其當今中國成為「世界工廠」，及新世紀世人希望的新市場而蜚聲國際，值得全中國人自豪，但中國社會的基本生活水平是否已達到先進國家的標準？當今的生活水平能

滿足人民普遍的要求嗎？台灣而今列入在已開發的國家，其生活水平較之美國、日本、德國等先進國家尚有一段距離，但仍為先進國家所能接受，達到基本生活水平的國家。為便於了解，謹表列海峽兩岸中國人民生活消費水平對照，呈現彼此生活水平的程度，表三十二「中國居民消費水平」（2000年中國統計年鑑）及表三十三「台灣平均每人民間消費支出」（經濟部國民所得統計摘要 2004 年 6 月）

　　表三十二，中國居民消費水平（Household consumption）是以家庭為單位計算，統計至 1999 年，平均全國每一家庭的年消費額達到人民幣 3,138 元，而城市家庭年消費額較高為 6796 元，鄉村為 1927 元，城鄉之間消費額相差達 3.5 倍之多，按中國統計年鑑資料，1999 年，中國全國家庭總戶數為 34153 萬戶，其中城市有 12545 萬戶，每戶平均為 3.1人，鄉村有 20257 萬戶，每戶平均為 4.3 人，及全國總人數為 125909 萬人，據此計算出全國平均每人年消費額為US$103.7 ，而城市平均每人年消費額為 US$267，鄉村則為US$55，此顯示鄉村個人消費只有城市個人消費的 1/5；又從表三十三，台灣平均個人年消費額 1999 年為 US$7,963，2000 年為 US$8656，2001 年為 US$8022，2002 年為US$7940，再看日本 Statistic Bureau,MPHPT 統計資料顯示平均每人每月消費額2000年為¥97881，2001年為¥95,867，2002年為¥95,965， 按當年匯率換算每人年消費額分別為US$10224，US$8748 及 US$9,648，此與台灣同期相對比，台灣平均每人年消費額約為日本的 80%，證實台灣人民生活水平與先進國家之差尚不甚遠，但與此同時，1999 年，中

138

國人民個人平均年消費額為 US$103.7，只有台灣的 1.3%，相當台灣 1951 年的水平。

（2）中國政府坦誠自暴其短而力圖上游改進

　　台灣政府有鑑於 1950 年代國民生活水平的低落，所以便於 1966 年創設加工出口區以增加就業機會，改善人民的生活，同此道理，中國政府也於十多年前開始建設出口加工區，及隨後建設各類型的經濟發展園區、特區，而所得成效至為可觀，但遺憾的不是全國全面性的設置發展，而僅限於沿海沿江的發展，局部的成就，也限於局部人民生活的改善，所以平均每人國民生產毛額也僅達到 US$977（表三十四），比同期台灣的 US$12,916 有相當大的落差，更不用提美、日等超級經濟強國了，此乃中國實在太大，人口太多所形成的經濟發展情勢，值得世人理解和鼓勵，另從中國官方宣示的數據來看，2004 年 5 月 27 日在上海舉辦的「全球扶貧大會」閉幕式上國務院副總理回良玉講話指出，「截至去年底（2003 年），中國農村仍有三千萬人沒有解決溫飽，收入水平處於最低生活保障線的城市居民有二千多萬人……」（附件五），他也在聲明同時指出：「雖然中國扶貧開發的歷史性成就得到了國內各界和國際社會的高度評價，但中國是一個人口眾多、資源不足、發展不平衡的發展中國家。特別是在廣大內陸的深山區、荒漠地區、邊疆地區以及一部分農村和城鎮，貧困現象仍然比較突出」。

表三十二　中國居民消費水平

Household Consumption

本表絕對數按當年價格計算，指數按可比價格計算。

Absolute figures in this table are calculated at current prices,while indices are calculated at comparable prices.

地區　Region 年份　Year	絕對數（元） Value（yuan）			城鄉消費 水平對比 （農村 居民＝1） Urban/Rural Consumption Ratio（Urban Households=1）
	全國 居民 All House- holds	農村 居民 Rural Households	城鎮 居民 Urban House- holds	
1978	184	138	405	2.9
1979	207	158	434	2.7
1980	236	178	496	2.8
1981	262	199	562	2.8
1982	284	221	576	2.6
1983	311	246	603	2.5
1984	354	283	662	2.3
1985	437	347	802	2.3
1986	485	376	920	2.4
1987	550	417	1089	2.6
1988	693	508	1431	2.8
1989	762	553	1568	2.8
1990	803	571	1686	3.0
1991	896	621	1925	3.1
1992	1070	718	2356	3.3
1993	1331	855	3027	3.5
1994	1746	1118	3891	3.5
1995	2236	1434	4874	3.4
1996	2641	1768	5430	3.1
1997	2834	1876	5796	3.1
1998	2972	1895	6217	3.3
1999	3138	1927	6796	3.5

2000	3397			
2001	3608			
2000 年				
北　京 Beijing	7326	3601	9054	2.5
天　津 Tianjin	6117	3414	8056	2.4
河　北 Hebei	2534	1816	5554	3.1
山　西 Shanxi	2037	1209	4312	3.6
內蒙古 Inner Mongolia	2425	1609	3930	2.4
遼　寧 Liaoning	4490	2403	6903	2.9
吉　林 Jilin	3381	1593	5639	3.5
黑龍江 Heilongjiang	3669	1665	6046	3.6
上　海 Shanghai	11546	6296	13369	2.1
江　蘇 Jiangsu	3862	2651	6589	2.5
浙　江 Zhejiang	4366	3229	8478	2.6
安　徽 Anhui	2588	1922	5323	2.8
福　建 Fujian	4428	3815	6757	1.8
江　西 Jiangxi	2396	1793	4488	2.5
山　東 Shandong	3467	2352	6572	2.8
河　南 Henan	2208	1587	4902	3.1
湖　北 Hubei	2857	1760	5719	3.2
湖　南 Hunan	2723	1981	5705	2.9
廣　東 Guangdong	5007	2855	9737	3.4
廣　西 Guangxi	2147	1478	5277	3.6
海　南 Hainan	2904	2215	4900	2.2
重　慶 Chongqing	2466	1380	6544	4.7
四　川 Sichuan	2456	1833	5236	2.9
貴　州 Guizhou	1608	1120	4517	4.0
雲　南 Yunnan	2530	2007	5444	2.7
西　藏 Tibet	1823	1144	4737	4.1
陝　西 Sheanxi	2035	1186	4891	4.1
甘　肅 Gansu	1734	993	4890	4.9
青　海 Qinghai	2255	1260	4630	3.7
寧　夏 Ningxia	2290	1393	4523	3.2
新　疆 Xinjiang	3207	2002	4402	2.2

注：城鄉消費水平對比，沒有剔除城鄉價格不可比的因素。

資料來源：2001 年中國統計年鑑

表三十三　國民所得統計摘要 2004 年 6 月台灣平均每人消費支出

年　　別 Year	平均每人 民間消費支出 Per Capita Private Consumption	
	（新臺幣元） （NT$）	（美　元） （US$）
1951	1,082	105
1973	13,413	351
1974	19,056	501
1975	21,052	554
1976	22,579	594
1977	25,617	674
1978	29,318	793
1979	34,924	970
1980	43,518	1,209
1981	51,316	1,395
1982	54,780	1,400
1983	58,369	1,457
1984	63,024	1,591
1985	65,927	1,654
1986	70,593	1,865
1987	78,843	2,474
1988	90,026	3,147
1989	105,152	3,982
1990	116,593	4,336
1991	128,842	4,804
1992	144,661	5,750
1993	160,577	6,085
1994	179,394	6,780
1995	194,426	7,340
1996	212,267	7,730
1997	228,762	7,971
1998	244,943	7,320
1999	256,978	7,963
2000	270,339	8,656
2001	271,238	8,022
2002	274,575	7,940
2003	275,086	7,992
2004	284,902	8,558

資料來源：中華民國經濟部

　　這也再度說明中國人口眾多，資源不足及發展不均衡狀況下，自然國民消費水平尚達不到國際水平，很欣慰的是中國政府很坦誠的不在意自暴其短而力圖上游努力改進，令人欽佩！但中國在繼續努力的下一步該如何走下去？要如何定向才是正確的決策？

　　2002 年 3 月 5 日中國在第九屆全國人民代表大會第五次會議上，國務院總理朱鎔基的「政府工作報告」中說明2002 年要著重做好八個方面工作：

1、擴大和培育內需，促進經濟較快增長。
2、加快農業和農村經濟發展，努力增加農民收入。
3、積極推進經濟結構調整和經濟體制改革。
4、適應加入世貿組織新形勢，全面提高對外開放水平。
5、繼續大力整頓和規範市場經濟秩序。
6、實施科教興國戰略和可持續發展戰略，加強精神文明建設。
7、進一步轉變政府職能，加強政風建設。
8、進一步做好外交工作。

　　這八個方面工作項目中，第 1，2 兩項著重在國民收入及生活水平的改善，在第 1 項中指出：

　　保持國民經濟較快增長，是擴大就業、改善人民生活和維護社會穩定的基礎，也是推進結構調整和深化改革的重要條件。

表三十四　主要國家平均每人國民生產毛額

	1996 年	1997 年	1998 年	1999 年	2000 年	2001 年	2002 年
中華民國	13260	13592	12360	13235	14188	12876	12916
美　　國	28770	30215	31433	32989	34582	35192	36085
日　　本	37646	34568	31503	35596	37859	33237	31715
德　　國	28971	25637	25997	25465	22622	22446	24082
法　　國*	26638	23992	24683	24449	22064	22169	24008
英　　國*	20588	22859	24418	25006	24573	24311	26516
韓　　國*	12242	11238	7477	9550	10887	10182	11480
新 加 坡	25362	26165	21492	21298	22971	21005	21129
香　　港*	25434	26986	25464	24543	25036	24426	23777
大國大陸	660	717	749	777	844	909	977

資料來源：中華民國經濟部網站資料
附　　　註：* 為 GDP 資料。

　　並在工作重點中指示：

　　擴大國內需求，首先必須增加城鄉居民特別是低收入群體的收入，培育和提高居民的購買力。

　　在第 2 項中也指出：

　　發展農業生產力，提高農民購買力，是擴大和培育內需十分重要的方面，關係國民經濟發展和社會穩定全局。要把加強農業和增加農民收入，作為整個經濟工作的突出任務。

　　並在工作重點中指示：

　　從根本上說，增加農民收入必須加快農業和農村經濟結構調整，大力發展農業產業化經營，積極推動傳統農業向現代農業轉變。

從這兩項指示中可以看出，朱總理的施政要旨在要保持國民經濟快速增長，則必須增加就業機會，提高國民收入，增加國民購買力，以擴大內需，如此國民生活水平便逐漸提升，而又特別強調對佔全國 2/3 總人口的農民「要採取更進一步的措施，千方百計增加農民收入……」，同時也顧及到 1/3 城市人口中貧困居民也都能得到最低的生活保障。

從政府的政策面不難了解，人民要能富裕，國家才能強盛，而富裕的基本面，在於人民的生活水平的提升，所以長遠的策略是持續經濟發展，而且要快速的發展，增長，其手段以增加就業機會，普遍增加國民購買力，擴大內需，達到「錢、貨」暢流，則市場活絡，進而促使國際貿易更形發達，以至達到民富國強的期望，而在近程的措施方面，務必確切的執行扶貧計劃是刻不容緩的工作。

（3）中國應轉向並廣泛的在內陸，北方以及西北等落後地區設置「加工區」

增加就業機會的途徑很多，建設出口加工區已為世人所公認的最佳選擇之一，中國在出口加工區的推展已達十多年之久，而多建設在沿海，沿江一帶，按目前這一帶的經濟發展已達到相當的榮景程度，而內陸、東北、西北、西南等地區，在土地面積及人口數兩方面都佔了絕多數的比率，然而根據中國統計年鑑所示，這些地區的國民所得及消費水平均偏低（表三十五，表三十六，表三十七），及根據香港東方日報 2005 年 10 月 17 日報導指明<西部四億人捱窮，貧富差距達可容忍極限>（附件七）証明屬實。

　　根據出口加工區的創設目的在協助落後國家或地區增加就業機會，改善國家或地區的經濟環境，進而改進人民的生活水平，而今中國沿海沿江經濟發展已達到一定的水平，當地人民的生活也多達到小康的程度，也有個別的特殊富

表三十五　中國各地區城鎮居民人均收支情況

（2001 年）　單位：元

地　區	全部收入	#可支配收　入	實際支出	#消費性支　出	#非消費性支　出	恩格爾系　數（%）
全國總計	6907.1	6859.6	6553.6	5309.0	1240.8	37.9
北　京	11659.0	11577.8	10676.5	8922.7	1753.5	36.2
天　津	8999.4	8958.7	8367.0	6987.2	1379.7	37.0
河　北	6027.8	5984.8	5749.7	4479.8	1267.7	35.4
山　西	5416.3	5391.1	5284.9	4123.0	1160.1	34.3
內蒙古	5561.1	5535.9	5246.7	4195.6	1044.9	33.9
遼　寧	5832.6	5797.0	5998.2	4654.4	1340.9	39.7
吉　林	5361.4	5340.5	5371.6	4337.2	1033.9	38.1
黑龍江	5461.7	5425.9	5128.4	4192.4	931.5	37.2
上　海	12981.5	12883.5	11977.4	9336.1	2641.3	43.1
江　蘇	7427.5	7375.1	6967.8	5532.7	1434.9	39.7
浙　江	10540.4	10464.7	10073.9	7952.4	2121.2	36.3
安　徽	5715.5	5668.8	5757.0	4517.7	1236.8	44.3
福　建	8384.6	8313.1	7603.6	6015.1	1583.9	44.1
江　西	5545.7	5506.0	4684.1	3894.5	777.5	40.8
山　東	7141.2	7101.1	6386.1	5252.4	1132.9	34.3

河 南	5292.1	5267.4	4894.7	4110.2	784.1	34.7
湖 北	5888.7	5856.0	5774.8	4804.8	961.5	37.5
湖 南	6832.6	6780.6	6925.5	5546.2	1377.6	35.0
廣 東	10534.7	10415.2	9607.3	8099.6	1498.8	38.2
廣 西	6722.8	6665.7	6531.7	5224.7	1302.2	37.7
海 南	5927.4	5838.8	5397.9	4367.9	976.6	46.3
重 慶	6755.5	6721.1	6668.7	5873.7	794.4	39.8
四 川	6406.6	6360.5	6114.0	5176.2	927.2	40.2
貴 州	5467.2	5451.9	5098.6	4273.9	822.1	40.9
雲 南	6849.7	6797.7	6485.5	5252.6	1228.4	40.1
西 藏	7912.4	7869.2	8431.7	5994.4	2435.3	43.8
陝 西	5513.8	5483.7	5647.7	4637.7	1008.6	34.3
甘 肅	5413.7	5382.9	5174.5	4420.3	754.0	37.1
青 海	5883.8	5853.7	5664.6	4698.6	961.8	38.1
寧 夏	5582.2	5544.2	6064.2	4595.4	1466.6	34.0
新 疆	6456.9	6395.0	5940.0	4931.4	1003.3	34.8

資料來源：2001 年中國統計年鑑

表三十六 中國各地區鄉村居民人均純收入

單位：元

地 區	1996 年	1997 年	1998 年	1999 年	2000 年	2001 年
全國 總計	1926.07	2090.13	2161.98	2210.34	2253.42	2366.40
北 京	3561.94	3661.68	3952.30	4226.59	4604.55	5025.50
天 津	2999.68	3243.68	3395.70	3411.11	3622.39	3947.72
河 北	2054.95	2286.01	2405.30	2441.50	2478.86	2603.60
山 西	1557.19	1738.26	1858.60	1772.62	1905.61	1956.05
內蒙古	1602.34	1780.19	1981.50	2002.93	2038.21	1973.37

遼　寧	2149.98	2301.48	2479.80	2501.04	2355.58	2557.93
吉　林	2125.56	2186.29	2383.60	2260.59	2022.50	2182.22
黑龍江	2181.86	2308.29	2253.10	2165.93	2148.22	2280.28
上　海	4846.13	5277.02	5406.80	5409.11	5596.37	5870.87
江　蘇	3029.32	3269.85	3376.80	3495.20	3595.09	3784.71
浙　江	3462.99	3684.22	3814.60	3948.39	4253.67	4582.34
安　徽	1607.72	1808.75	1862.90	1900.29	1934.57	2020.04
福　建	2492.49	2785.67	2946.40	3091.39	3230.49	3380.72
江　西	1869.63	2107.28	2048.00	2129.45	2135.30	2231.60
山　東	2086.31	2292.12	2452.80	2549.58	2659.20	2804.51
河　南	1579.19	1733.89	1864.10	1948.36	1985.82	2097.86
湖　北	1863.62	2102.23	2172.20	2217.08	2268.59	2352.16
湖　南	1792.25	2037.06	2064.90	2127.46	2197.16	2299.46
廣　東	3183.46	3467.69	3527.10	3628.95	3654.48	3769.79
廣　西	1703.13	1875.28	1971.80	2048.33	1864.51	1944.33
海　南	1746.08	1916.90	2018.30	2087.46	2182.26	2226.47
重　慶	1491.00	1643.21	1720.50	1736.63	1892.44	1971.18
四　川	1459.09	1680.69	1789.20	1843.47	1903.60	1986.99
貴　州	1276.67	1298.54	1334.50	1363.07	1374.16	1411.73
雲　南	1229.28	1375.50	1387.30	1437.63	1478.60	1533.74
西　藏	1353.26	1194.51	1231.50	1309.46	1330.81	1404.01
陝　西	1165.10	1273.30	1405.60	1455.86	1443.86	1490.80
甘　肅	1100.59	1185.07	1393.10	1357.28	1428.68	1508.61
青　海	1173.80	1320.63	1424.80	1466.67	1490.49	1557.32
寧　夏	1397.80	1512.50	1721.20	1754.15	1724.30	1823.05
新　疆	1290.01	1504.43	1600.10	1473.17	1618.08	1710.44

資料來源：2001 年中國統計年鑑

表三十七 中國各地區居民消費水平及增長速度

地 區	消費水平（元／人）					2000 年比上年增長（%）
	1996 年	1997 年	1998 年	1999 年	2000 年	
北 京	4208	4557	5178	5784	7326	24.5
天 津	4129	4937	5209	5551	6117	8.0
河 北	1925	2151	2207	2312	2534	9.8
山 西	1880	1985	1835	1833	2037	11.2
內蒙古	1939	2127	2141	2279	2425	5.1
遼 寧	3250	3629	3829	4128	4490	8.4
吉 林	2643	2940	3015	3148	3381	5.6
黑龍江	2994	3210	3276	3431	3669	8.5
上 海	7742	8699	9202	10328	11546	10.2
江 蘇	3121	3382	3498	3594	3862	6.6
浙 江	3412	3670	3784	3877	4366	11.7
安 徽	1945	2275	2370	2523	2588	4.3
福 建	3356	3826	3934	4066	4428	6.9
江 西	1857	1930	1973	2056	2396	16.6
山 東	2287	2722	2899	3194	3467	7.7
河 南	1686	1842	1862	1902	2708	13.5
湖 北	2398	2559	2706	2691	2857	5.8
湖 南	2199	2390	2471	2594	2723	3.2
廣 東	4235	4523	4686	4760	5007	1.6
廣 西	2008	2025	2040	2079	2147	5.6
海 南	2376	2458	2562	2729	2904	5.6
重 慶	2052	2211	2224	2336	2466	5.1
四 川	1860	2050	2121	2191	2456	11.8
貴 州	1446	1479	1511	1542	1608	1.9
雲 南	1800	1982	2059	2340	2530	9.0

西　藏	1312	1473	1551	1669	1823	7.1
陜　西	1630	1835	1852	1884	2035	6.3
甘　肅	1550	1629	1612	1650	1734	7.1
青　海	1967	1965	2047	2150	2255	6.4
寧　夏	1785	1852	1947	2014	2290	13.9
新　疆	2398	2615	2745	2936	3207	6.2

注：絕對數按當年價格計算，增長速度按可比價格計算。
資料來源：2001 年中國統計年鑑

有的現象，並正繼續的擴散中，所以這些沿海沿江的地區已
不宜再繼續建設出口加工區而應該往高科技，高附加價值，
策略性產業發展，如果在沿海沿江仍須以出口加工區的型態
及條件繼續發展，則表示這些地區的發展仍滯留在落後的水
平，所以如今已是榮景及小康經濟的地區就應該繼續更進一
步往高層次發展，如發展高新科技園區、重工業、國防工業
等，而出口加工區應轉向並廣泛的在內陸、東北、西北、西
南等較落後的地區以「加工區或加工工業區」的模式設置，
其設置所須考慮的事項：

① 設置地區：內陸、東北、西北、西南等人口眾多，經濟落
　　後的地區。

② 設置條件：

　A・給予比現在沿海、沿江更優惠的條件，尤其對本國投
　　　資人與外國投資者要一視同仁。

　B・區內產品內、外銷均可，任其自由市場選擇。

　C・區內產品不限類別，以能供應內需的替代產品及大量
　　　創造就業機會者尤為優先。

D‧ 消耗能源少，污染少的產業為優先。

E‧ 政府有責任及有效提供公共設施，如水、電、電訊，連外交通、銀行、郵局……等。

F‧ 政府以政策性的協助國內市場開發，及對中小企業融資貸款的方便。

G‧ 農、漁、畜牧加工產業及地區性特有產業，政府應廣為輔導在加工區內設廠加工生產。

H‧ 擬訂一套專屬「加工區」的法規，配合據以執行，尤為重要。

③正名：將「出口加工區」正名為「加工區」或「加工工業區」，使不受「出口」市場的限制，便於「加工區」彈性市場營運，確實有助於落後地區經濟的快速發展。

④「加工區」應列入政府策略性經濟發展的要項之一，宜由中央政府督導，地方政府執行，使能達到有效的成果。

　　為促使中國政府對內陸、西北、西南、北方等經濟落後地區立法建設「加工區」，再提出以下兩點觀點供作參考：

〈1〉藏富於民，國庫滿盈：

　　國家對各類經濟開發區的投資建設，其目的在促使經濟發達，社會繁榮，人民富裕，但對落後地區則政府有責任政策性的輔助以適當的措施促其迎頭趕上，如何輔助及採取措施呢？在於「經濟市場」的培養，漸進到「人民財富」的培養，最後達到「藏富於民，國庫滿盈」，社會才是真正的豐盛祥和，如此乃國家人民之福！

〈2〉加工出口區內投資廠商的「基本消費」也是一筆可觀的貢獻，投資人以賺錢為目的，在貧饑地區沒有政府

優惠條件是不可能有人願意投資的，但政府也要了
解，投資廠商除了賺取利潤之外，也有對等的貢獻，
最起碼在投資經營期間，有各項「消費額」的提供，
如表三十八，台灣加工出口區三區投資廠商歷年支付
國內各項費用累計表，自 1966 年至 1985 年，累計在
台灣消費的各項費用達到 US$5,452,283,255，如此龐
大的費用如非區內廠商提供，則必須由政府國庫支
應，以配合經濟發展，這不是一筆小金額的負擔，所
以，可以了解區內投資廠商最基本的消費也是一筆可
觀的貢獻。

表三十八　經濟部加工出口區三區廠商歷年（1966～1985）

支付國內各項費用累計表

項　　目	金　　額
國內課稅區採購	82,244,944,755
員工薪資	72,567,853,185
員工年終獎金	8,145,943,931
勞保費用	3,859,109,248
稅捐	8,270,080,608
報關費用	1,303,476,945
海關業務費	1,037,743,757
土地租金	616,472,080
銀行利息及手續費	6,189,378,054
公共設施建設費及進出口簽證費	2,257,113,588
電力費用	6,261,333,035
用水費用	421,247,440
郵匯費用	244,479,236

出口推廣費	419,057,429
電報電話費	1,288,613,035
其他銷管費用	10,084,441,983
儲運費用	2,431,962,937
運輸行運費	252,416,882
空運費用	3,005,559,216
海運費用	6,472,401,662
保險費用	412,037,857
醫療保健費	305,663,346
合　計	台　　幣 折合美元（1：40）	N.T. 218,091,330,209 US$ 5,452,283,255

資料來源：台灣加工出口區管理處　　　　單位：元

（4）綜觀中國出口加工區的發展走向

　　A・不宜再在沿海沿江繼續增設或擴大出口加工區。

　　B・中央政府應以政策性在內陸、西北、北方、西南等經濟落後地區建設「加工區」，要以更優惠的條件吸引中、外投資，培養內需市場，發展該等地區的經濟，走向均富的社會。

　　C・中央必須以立法推動「加工區」的政策，由中央督導，地方確實執行，則「加工區」的發展必然會走向成功之路，中國整體經濟發展將更興旺發達！

三、世界其他國家（或地區）加工出口區部份：

　　世界設有加工出口區發展的國家，除韓國之外，其他國家（或地區）的整體經濟發展絕多數仍處在開發中國家，此等國家要如何有效的經由加工出口區的發展而擴展到國家

153

整體經濟快速的發展？台灣及中國在不同環境條件下創設加工出口區發展成功的經驗，案例可供作參考，借鏡，但必須再三強調者，不同國家（或地區）有各自不同的經濟環境及國情，雖然加工出口區已被公認為開發中國家經濟發展的一帖良方，但仍要根據各國的經濟環境，國情擬訂發展政策，惟對加工出口區的經營理念，目的則是一致不變的，謹提供以下三點參考：

1、建議請詳細了解台灣及中國加工出口區發展的過程及與國家經濟策略擬訂執行相配合的經驗案例，而其中若有類似中國狀況，在局部城鎮設置加工出口區頗具績效，並已促成局部地區經濟改善，人民生活達到小康程度者，希望這些國家能將國家有限的財力資源再用到比較落後的城鎮，建設新的「加工區」如此可連鎖性的擴散發展國家整體經濟至均富小康的社會。

2、凡有意設置或增設加工出口區的國家，限於本國財力之不足，無法達成所願者，建議可採取 BO 或 BOT 等方式，提供最優惠條件吸引外國資金來投資設區，以達到創造本國就業機會為首務，繼之可充實國家資本財的能力，而後漸次發展本國的中小企業，如此漸進的可以達到國家經濟環境的改善。

3、凡有意設置加工出口區的國家（或地區），必須建立「三利原則」的邏輯思維（國家利益，廠商利潤及勞工福利），而更重要者，欲促使設置加工出口區經營成功，則必須擬訂一套完善可行的【加工出口區特別法】，並經國家立法成立，據以執行，則所設置的加工出口區必有成功的可能。

參、中國出口加工區宏觀發展的探討

　　本書第四章強調加工出口區的發展與國家經濟發展的互動關係，並舉例說明獨自加工出口區的成就，不能代表國家整體經濟發展的成就，例如越南即是，另一方面國家經濟政策不完備，落實，即便設置再多的加工出口區也是枉然，例如菲律賓、印度等國；中國從 1980 年鄧小平主政改革，推動市場經濟至今已約 25 年，此期間國家整體經濟發展的成效為世人所讚譽稱道，出口加工區的互動成長也有點綴性的成就，然而國民所得仍只有不到壹仟美元，列為世界未開發或低度開發中國家，究其原因乃是中國大環境因素影響全國經濟未達均衡發展，即「人口，地理環境及教育」三大問題所形成的障礙，這些問題已在前節討論，不再贅述。

　　出口加工區是中國經濟發展的一環，在加工出口區與經濟互動的關係上，國家的經濟政策是影響互動關係的成功之鑰，而中國的經濟政策是什麼？何種經濟理論基礎？由 1978 年 12 月中共十一屆三中全會的決議是以「市場經濟取代計劃經濟」，這項經濟政策從 1980 年開始執行至今將近 25 年，其成效有目共睹，為世人所讚譽，也是中國擺脫貧窮的起步，因為中國必竟還未達到均富的條件，出口加工區的貢獻也僅止於對局部地區的影響，所以這項政策應該是繼續的推行發展下去，但是從市場經濟，宏觀性的考量，出口加工區應該不是漫無目標的任其海濶天空的發展，因為國家的財力

155

是有限的，改善人民生活，均富要求是有時間性的，所以市場經濟發展應該考慮到時程區間目標達成為目的，因而台灣在經濟發展政策的擬訂，是經由楊繼曾先生於民國 47 年 3 月至 54 年元月（1958.3－1965.1）任經濟部長期間擬訂出「計劃自由經濟」政策，簡單的解釋是政府根據時段的需求擬訂經濟發展目標計劃，並由政府、國人根據此計劃目標，自由的發揮執行達成，尤其鼓勵民間參與投資配合發展，所以才有台灣經濟發展成功的四個時期，此部份已在第一章簡要敘述，茲再根據行政院經濟建設委員會資料簡述台灣經濟現代化的歷程如下：。

一、引述台灣經濟發展的政策及策略參考：

台灣經濟政策，策略發展現代化的歷程可分成五個階段逐步達成：第一階段是自民國 34 年至 41 年（1945 至 1952）為復舊時期，即二次大戰後台灣光復，但社會貧窮，經濟不穩定，所以政府首在恢復舊的社會次序，實施貨幣改革，提高人民對貨幣的信心，推動農工業及交通建設等的復舊工作，以穩定物價及促進社會安定。

第二階段自民國 42 年至 49 年（1953 至 1960）為四十年代替代進口時期，自民國 42 年（1953 年）開始實施第一期四年經濟建設計劃，在「以農業培養工業，以工業發展農業」，實施耕者有其田，三七五減租及公地放領等政策，至農工業快速成長，全國經濟成長平均每年達到 7.6%，社會因而穩定並開始繁榮。

　　第三階段是自民國 50 年至 61 年（1961 至 1972），為出口擴張時期，完成第三、四、五期的四年經濟建設計劃，此時期以創造就業機會，解決失業問題，提高國民所得，因而成立加工出口區，開擴國際市場等，年經濟平均成長達10.2%，達成了穩定與成長的雙重目標，是為中華民國經濟發展的黃金時期。

　　第四階段是自民國 62 年至 72 年（1973 至 1983）為經濟結構轉變時間，本階段因兩次石油危機影響經濟緩慢成長，政府政策以「穩定中求成長」，穩定物價為重心，並推動十大建設，繼之推動十二項建設，如此本階段經濟成長平均每年達到 8.1%。

　　第五階段自民國 73 年至 78 年（1984 至 1989），為加速推動經濟自由化及國際化時期，此時間有經濟失衡現象產生，乃因國家累積了鉅額出超帶來國際貿易摩擦及物價膨脹壓力，另一方面國人大量超額儲蓄引發不利經濟發展導至工業升級緩慢，流動資金過剩，威脅金融安定等問題，因而成立「經濟革新委員會」檢討，策劃經濟革新原則與方向，總計在財政、金融、產業、貿易與經濟行政等五方面提出五十六項興革建議方案，其後並據以積極推動經濟自由化與國際化，迄民國 78 年（1989）年底，經濟自由化已採取的重要措施包括：財稅方面大幅降低進口關稅、取消進口關稅價格附加；金融方面廢除「利率管理條例」、放寬外匯管制、貿易收支結匯完全自由化、開放黃金進口及國內自由買賣；產業方面取消石化業產銷協議及中鋼進口加簽規定、加油站開放民營、適度開放及增設石化碼頭槽區；貿易方面逐步解除

157

進出口管制及簡化簽證手續、檢討並大幅減少應實施進出口檢驗的產品項目、取消有關貿易商與生產事業間稅負之差別待遇；經濟行政方面取消僑外投資有關外銷比率與自製率的限制、放寬僑外投資事業轉投資符合僑外投資範圍之國內事業等。在世界經濟恢復高度繁榮及國內經濟體系更趨自由化與國際化的帶動下，民國73年至78年間（1984至1989），我國年平均經濟成長率高達 9.4%，消費者物價則呈平穩，年增率平均僅1.1%。

台灣在 1989 年以後為新階段的開始，至今國人看不出明確的新經濟政策或策略，拼經濟卻無從著手，徒具口號而已，遺憾！

台灣在「計劃自由經濟」政策推動經濟現代化歷程五個階段的執行方案中，有其經濟發展策略的擬訂，規劃，其策略規劃如下：

1、穩定與成長並重

2、農工平衡發展

3、輕重工業循序漸進發展

4、進口替代與出口擴展分段推動

5、重視公共建設

6、縮小貧富差距，平均社會財富

7、推動經濟自由化，國際化與制度化

這七項策略在不同時段，以其不同的需求而演進執行，所以從台灣經濟發展的過程看「計劃自由經濟政策」是正確及有其必要性的。

據此政策，擬訂策略，循序漸進執行以至於成功，此證明台灣經濟奇蹟的美譽其來有自，絕非偶然。

二、中國經濟發展政策與策略的演進：

觀乎中國從 1980 年開始實施「市場經濟」、「對內改革，對外開放」的政策，25 年來經濟策略是什麼？

中國總體經濟發展，概略而言，可分成兩個階段：

第一階段是從 1949 至 1978 年，此階段初期的發展不同與台灣初期的復舊經濟活力的發展，而是改變革除由中華民國留下原有的經濟體制，取而代之的是推行農村農業集體化，從「家庭聯產承包責任制」開始推行，到城市工商業社會化，推動「放權讓利」，並集中主力進行重工業，國防工業為中心的工業建設，以機械，鋼鐵為主要項目，甚而到 1953 年開始實行經濟中央集權制，更積極推動工業化經濟發展；本階段是項經濟發展策略，一方面是基於共產主義思想及受到國際共產舊經濟體制輸入的堅實信念的影響，另一方面就國防而言，國家在求生存的時刻，發展重工業，國防工業是事實上的需要，這一點實非純經濟發展理論學者專家們所能體認或完全認同，但這樣的經濟發展模式，出現了兩種結果，其一對國防而言，有了堅強自衛能力的國防，不再畏懼強權外力的侵入，是對國家民族存續歷史負責的表現，為後代子孫造福，其二對國家人民當前的生活環境，留下了近卅年貧窮痛苦的生活記錄，也將受到歷史責任公平的批

判，真乃魚與熊掌不可兼得，主政者當有勇氣面對歷史，熟重熟輕作決斷。

　　這樣的經濟發展也有可觀的成就，1952 至 1978 年共 26 年的時間，國民生產總值增長 5.3 倍，工業總產值增長 12 倍，農業總產值增長 3 倍，居民消費水平增長 2.3 倍，各方多有成長，（詳見表三十九），但增長數若按每年平均值計，都比較偏低，即表示這種模式的經濟發展，還缺少了一點總體深度規劃的積極性及缺乏認識參與世界經濟活動受其正面影響的效益評估。

表三十九　1952 至 1999 年中國的經濟發展

項　目	1952 年（1）（當年價,億元）	1978 年（2）（當年價,億元）	1999 年（3）（當年價,億元）	（4）=（2）/（1）	（5）=（3）/（2）
國民生產總值	680.9	3,624.1	80,729.8	5.3	22.5
工業總產值	349	4237.0	35,356.5	12.1	8.3
農業總產值	461	1,397.0	24,519.0	3.0	17.6
國家財政收入	183.7	1,132.3	11,377.0	6.2	10.1
職工工資總額	68.3	568.9	9,876.0	8.3	17.4
居民消費水平（元）	76	175	3,180.0	2.3	18.2
全民所有制單位固定資產投資	43.6	668.7	21,719.0	15.4	32.5
全社會商品零售總量	175.0	1,588.6	31,135.0	9.1	17.9
進出口貿易總額（億美元）	19.4	206.4	3,607.0	10.6	17.5
能源生產總量標準煤（萬噸）	4,871	62,770	110,000.0	12.9	1.7
貨物週轉量（億噸公里）	762	9,829	40,273.0	12.9	4.1
郵電業務量	1.64	11.65	3,311	7.1	284.2

說明：①1952 年，以國內生產總值代替國民生產總值。由於 1950 年代之初，中共的對外關係極其微弱，所以當時兩者的差別幾乎為零。

資料來源：《中國統計摘要 2000》（北京）：國務院發展研究中心 UNDP 項目組，《經濟發展改革與政策》第一卷（上），頁 20。

　　第二階段，自 1979 至今，將近 25 年，其經濟策略重點在市場化，制度法制化，地方化而追續到國際化，市場化在恢復市場機制，讓市場機能決定經濟的發展，因而中央政府決然採取減少政府行政權力的干預，要能確實做到這一點，必須要法制化，首要在去經濟體制的公有制，因而國營企業便成為首先改革的對象，與其同時也發展與國際經濟接軌，改善投資環境及法規，因而大量吸引了國際產業的投資，及資金流入，形成國家龐大的資本財及獲得世界工廠的美譽，至有大經濟市場活動的空間與利基的產生，由是累積成為世界第二大的外滙儲備國，達七千億美元之多；而在實質的執行上，首先在發展地方，使地方首先快速發展繁榮，所以先選擇較易開發的重點地區先行發展，乃決定從華南地區的長江三角洲及珠江三角洲城鎮開始發展，而後漸進的往華中、華北，內陸地區延伸發展，乃至 90 年代初擬訂了「沿海、沿江、沿邊」的明確發展策略，到「九五」計劃時再強調指向中、西部的發展，至有大西北開發計劃；惟地方開發成功，全國才會有大的成就，因而對地方採取「讓權」的策略，但是如果沒有法制化的制約，「讓權」將導至地方「濫權」，所以法制化在建立各類制約的管理制度，最明顯的是財稅，海關關稅，工業管理等制度的革新，甚而制訂有關稅務，外滙，進出口貿易，金融，財務管理，法人登記，經營管理，用人制度等新法規，使國家在經濟體制能完全法制化，取信於民及對國際經濟可獲得誠信的支持及通滙，在這樣的策略推動執行後，確有巨大的效益產生，從 1978 至 1999 年，20 年間的成就上看，（表三十九）國民生產總值由 3,624.1 億

元成長到 80,729.8 億元，成長 22.5 倍，十分可觀，國家財政收入增加了 10.1 倍，尤其值得欣慰的是全國居民消費水平也隨之增長了，由年消費額 175 億元增加到 3180 億元，達 18.2 倍之多，這才是真正政府造福國民的責任表現。

三、中國經濟發展宏觀的思維與出口加工區需要變革發展：

1、三次產業不均衡的發展

中國在第二階段的經濟發展，雖有亮麗的成績單，但仍值得檢討；前已述及中國經濟不均衡發展的原因，茲再就三次產業分析，其國內歷年生產值（表四十），1980 年國內生產總值為人民幣 4517.8 億元，到 2001 年成長到 95933.3 億元成長達 21.2 倍，其間 22 年，平均每年成長約一倍，非常可觀，但就三次產業分別來看，1980 年各產業的產值比是 30：48.5：21.4，隨後各年，第一產業，農業產值率逐年降低，至 2001 年降至 15.2%，下降達 6.2%；第二產業，工業及建築業，1980 年以後各年時有小量的起伏平均維持在 50%上下，成長幅度高達 20%；第三產業，服務業由 21.4% 逐年上升，至 2001 年升到 33.6%，上升幅度也達 12.2%。再按就業人數觀之（表四十一）1980 年總就業人數為 42361 萬人，至 2001 年達到 73025 萬人，增加量達 30664 萬人，增加率為 72.4%，此乃全國總人口大幅成長之故，而第一產業從 29122 萬人上升到 36513 萬人，增加數為 7391 萬人，25.4%，但人員構成比率却從 68.7%降至 50%

降幅為 18.7%；第二產業就業人數的變化從 7707 萬人增加到 16284 萬人，而構成比由 18.2%提升到 22.3%，升幅僅約 4%；第三產業就業人數由 5532 萬人，升到 20228 萬人，構成比率由 13.1%進升到 27.7%，升幅為 14.1%。

表四十　中國國內歷年生產值

單位：億元，%

項目＼年份	1980	1985	1990	1995	2000	2001
國內生產總值	4517.8 100%	8964.4 100%	18547.9 100%	58478.1 100%	89403.6 100%	95933.3 100%
第一產業	1359.4 30%	2541.6 28.4%	5017.0 27%	11993.0 20.5%	14212.0 15.9%	14609.9 15.2%
第二產業	2192.0 48.5%	3866.6 43.1%	7717.4 41.6%	28537.9 48.8%	45487.8 50.9%	49069.1 51.1%
第三產業	966.4 21.4%	2556.2 28.5%	5813.5 31.3%	17947.2 30.7%	29703.8 33.2%	32254.3 33.6%

註：資料來源 2002 年中國統計年鑑

表四十一　按三次產業分的就業人員

（年底數）

年份	就業人員總計（萬人）	第一產業	第二產業	第三產業	構成（以合計為100） 第一產業	第二產業	第三產業
1978	40152	28318	6945	4890	70.5	17.3	12.2
1980	42361	29122	7707	5532	68.7	18.2	13.1
1985	49873	31130	10384	8359	62.4	20.8	16.8
1990	64749	38914	13856	11979	60.1	21.4	18.5
1991	65491	39098	14015	12378	59.7	21.4	18.9
1992	66152	38699	14355	13098	58.5	21.7	19.8
1993	66808	37680	14965	14163	56.4	22.4	21.2
1994	67455	36628	15312	15515	54.3	22.7	23.0
1995	68065	35530	15655	16880	52.2	23.0	24.8
1996	68950	34820	16203	17927	50.5	23.5	26.0
1997	69820	34840	16547	18432	49.9	23.7	26.4
1998	70637	35177	16600	18860	49.8	23.5	26.7
1999	71394	35768	16421	19205	50.1	23.0	26.9
2000	72085	36043	16219	19823	50.0	22.5	27.5
2001	73025	36513	16284	20228	50.0	22.3	27.7

註：資料來源：2002 年中國統計年鑑

　　由以上三次產業的產值與就業人數配合來看，第一產業，農業佔了 70 至 50%高比率的就業人數，而所得產值為最低，由 30%降至 15.2%，而第二產業人口比率只佔 18.2%至 22.3%，不及第一產業的一半，然而產值 2001 年為第一產業的 3.36 倍，產值相差 34,459 億元；第三產業人口數變化頗大，至 2001 年才提升為 27.7%，而產值構成比保持在 30%～33%，還算適中。

　　由於三次產業比此間就業人數與產值不成比例的結果，而導至各產業間勞動力平均年收入有頗大的差別水平（表四十二），職工年平均工資（包含國有單位，城鄉集體單位，股份合作，聯營，有限責任公司，港澳台商投資企業，外商投資企業等）1985 年為 1148 元，逐年調升，至 2001 年達 10870 元，調升 9.5 倍，而農村居民平均每人年收入 1985 年為 547.31 元逐年調升，至 2001 年調升到 3306.92 元，調升 6 倍，但 2001 年農村居民平均每人年收入僅為職工年平均收入的 30%，即便是城鎮居民也高出農村居民約一倍之多，如下列職工，城鎮居民及農村居民收入比較（表四十三）

表四十二　中國產業居民平均每人每年收入

年份 產業	1985	1990	1995	2000	2001
職工年平均 工資	1,148	2,140	5,500	9,371	10,870
農村居民年 平均收入	547.31	990.38	2,337.87	3,146.21	3,306.92
城鎮居民年 平均收入	748.92	1,522.79	4,288.09	6,316.81	6,907.1

註：資料來源 2002 年中國統計年鑑

表四十三　職工、城鎮居民、農村居民收入比較表

	2000		2001	
	年收入（元）	構成比	年收入（元）	構成比
職工	9371	1	10870	1
城鎮居民	6316.8	0.67	6907.1	0.64
農村居民	3146.21	0.34	3306.92	0.30

　　除平均年收入有頗大的差異之外，各產業間的年人均產值，對國家的貢獻度也有相當大的落差（表四十四），第一產業，1980 年人均產值為 467 元，2001 年成長 8.5 倍，達到 4001 元，但第二產業成長更多 10.6 倍，2001 年為 30133 元，是第一產業的 7.5 倍，即便是第三產業也是第一產業的 4 倍，可見農業人員生產力的微弱，對國家整體經濟貢獻的比重顯得是「事倍功半」的效果。

2、中央政府宏觀思維的改革政策

　　中國中央政府也深為了解三次產業不均衡發展的嚴重差異，所以在 2001 年朱鎔基總理的「政府工作報告」中說明 2002 年要著重做好八個方面工作的議題，其中第二議題便是「加快農業和農村經濟發展，努力增加農民收入」，「把加強農業和增加農民的收入，作為整個經濟工作的突出任務」；第一議題「擴大和培育內需，促進經濟較快增長」，及第三議題「積極推進經濟結構調整和經濟體制改革」（請參考本章第貳節第二段第 3 小段：中國經濟發展與出口加工區的發展走向）。

表四十四　三次產業每年人均產值表

單位：元／人一年

產業＼年份	1980	1985	1990	1995	2000	2001
第一產業	467	816	1289	3375	3943	4001
第二產業	2844	3724	5570	18229	28046	30133
第三產業	1747	3058	4853	10632	14985	15945

註：年人均產值是根據表 A,B 各產業每年生產值除以就業人數

這三項策略性的議題即擬訂出中國今後經濟發展的明確方向,是邏輯性的宏觀思維,有見地,有膽識的政治思考及政策。

3、出口加工區需要變革

出口加工區當前的發展與經濟開發區,高新科技園區等在內容上有些重疊,類同的做法與結果,及繼續不斷的在開發成熟的地區,城鎮發展,形成錦上添花,失去原設計「加工出口區」功能的意義-增加就業機會,發展落後地區經濟;而從中國整體經濟發展的實績及廣大人口在經濟面的需求兩方面檢討,其經濟發展的走向,應該是「全國普遍性的創造就業機會,改善人民的基本生活」不宜完全採用韓國跳躍式的經濟發展,以使扶貧計劃早日達成,使全國能達到均富的社會;創造了就業機會,擴大內需也能自然的接踵而至;如何創造就業機會?出口加工區往變革的方向發展是為必要的途徑,也是洽逢其時。

出口加工區變革發展意見供作參考:

①現有已成熟的出口加工區維持發展,不再增設,但允許區內產品不受限制的內銷,以配合擴大內需的要求。

②在全國各落後省縣、市、地區(內陸、華中、華北、西北等)普遍設置「加工區或加工工業區」,而非「出口加工區」,以為擴大就業機會,而區內產品以內銷為主,不限外銷,配合擴大內需策略的推動。

③政府對各「加工區」給予比「出口加工區」更優惠或同等的優惠條件,鼓勵中,外廠商不限科技產業到「加工區」

168

來投資，同時政府要做好各項公共建設項目，便利投資者設廠生產。

　　④各省、縣、市、地區等依其當地環境，資源設置具有特色的「加工區」（例如農產品加工，水產殖加工，……等），即不限定產業類別，尤其要鼓勵幫助年青人，中小企業創業，踏實的做好國家「民族產業」生根的目的。

　　全國在落後地區普遍設置「加工區」其目的在創造就業機會，改進落後地區的經濟環境，提高國民所得，擴大內需，有利「物流與金流」的活動力發展，則均富的目的，指日可待！

（1）出口加工區的變革須與三次產業發展的改革相配合

　　「加工區」經營策略的推動，執行，必須與三次產業的發展改革相配合，尤其是第一產業，農業的改革，刻不容緩，政府將以何種方法，策略改革，是政府與專家的工作，責任，但以常識的看法，期盼，是希望農業產值與工業產值的差距拉近，企望能由現在的1：3改善到1：1.5或更接近，另方面農業人口必須要大量的減少，此在以提高土地生產力及農業勞動生產力為手段達成目標，則農業人口由現在佔三次產業50%的比率降至40%或35%，如按2001年農業人口數來計，要減少約1億至1.5億農業生產人口，此減少的農業生產人口，將轉業到第二次及第三次產業，這也就是要普設「加工區」以「容納農業過剩勞動力」的目的，如此，農業生產力提高，農民收入才能提高，生活便得到改善，擴大內需自然形成，如將鼓勵消費政策配合推動，將會更有利，扶貧的

計劃也能迅速達成，落後地區的經濟也會相應的改進，國家整體經濟總成長也會相對的大量增加。

（2）比較利益看出口加工區變革的需要性

再從比較利益的觀點看出口加工區變革的需要性，中國經濟改革以 1980 年為分界點，1980 年以前可以稱得上是赤貧的國家，是最迫切需要出口加工區的國家，以當時的時空背景，經濟發展非首要目標，1979 年決定改革政策後，從1980 年在廣東深圳開始設置「深圳經濟特區」以後，經濟發展日漸成長，國內生產總值從 1980 年的 4517.8 億元至2001 年增加到 95933.3 億元，增加了 21 倍之多（見表四十），外商直接到中國投資的金額也年年增加（表四十五），自1992 年開始，每年投資金額都達到 100 億美元以上，2004年為 561.4 億美元；同時進出口貿易自 1980 年以後年年增長（表四十六），1980 年進、出口金額各為 195.5 億美元及182.7 億美元，逆差 12.8 億美元，1989 年以前每年為逆差，而 1990 年起，以後除 1993 年外，均為順差，而且每年順差金額相當大，以至國家外滙儲備至本 2005 年上半年已超過7000 億美元（表四十七），這樣為世人稱道的成就，也包含了出口加工區的貢獻在內，再按「出口加工區招商，運作累計情況表」（表四十八）從 2000 年 9 月至 2005 年 2 月全國三十三個出口加工區的投資總金額為 101.6 億美元，進出口貿易總值為 662.1 億美元，順差 88 億美元，此貢獻值，與全國同期（2000 年至 2005 年）比較（見表四十九），出口加工區 2000 年至 2005 年總投資額為同期全國外來總投資

額的 4%，總貿易值為全國總貿易值的 2%，貿易順差即貢獻
度為全國總順差的 6.3%，以上各項比值對全國而言是很小
的，所起作用，貢獻不大；而在全國 33 個營運的出口加工
區中，投資總額以松江，昆山及蘇州工業園區等三區較具規
模，共約 37 億美元，佔各區投資總額的 36.4%，而進出口
貿易總值，則以松江及昆山較具規模達到 510 億美元，佔各
區進出口總值的 77%，由此可見中國十多年來出口加工區的
發展業績僅只有二或三個區較具績效，成功，而這三區均設
置在沿長江，已開發的地區如上海、蘇州等地區，按松江出
口加工區及昆山出口加工區各有勞動人數約為 45000 人及
42860 人，土地面積各約為 6 km 2 及 2.86 km 2，此其間的生
產力計算如下表五十：

　　與其同期，台灣加工出口區平均每年的生產力如下表五
十一

表四十五　中華人民共和國商務部規劃財務司

Ministry of Commerce of the People's Republic of China Department of Planning and Finance

1979 年以來外商直接投資

金額單位：億美元

年份	實際金額	同比％
1979-1982	17.7	-
1983	9.2	-
1984	14.2	54.9
1985	19.6	37.8
1986	22.4	14.7
1987	23.1	3.1
1988	31.9	38.0
1989	33.9	6.2
1990	34.9	2.8
1991	43.7	25.2
1992	110.1	152.1
1993	275.2	150.0
1994	337.7	22.7
1995	375.2	11.1
1996	417.3	11.2
1997	452.6	8.5
1998	454.6	0.5
1999	403.2	-11.3
2000	407.2	1.0
2001	468.8	15.1
2002	527.4	12.5

數據來源：中華人民共和國海關統計 561.40（實際）2.05%

表四十六 中華人民共和國商務部規劃財務司
Ministry of Commerce of the People's Republic of China Department of
Planning and Finance
1978 年以來進出口額

金額單位：億美元

年份	進出口額	出口額	進口額	順差
1978	206.4	97.5	108.9	-11.4
1979	293.3	136.6	156.8	-20.2
1980	378.2	182.7	195.5	-12.8
1981	440.2	220.1	220.2	-0.1
1982	416.1	223.2	192.9	30.3
1983	436.2	222.3	213.9	8.4
1984	535.5	261.4	274.1	-12.7
1985	696.0	273.5	422.5	149.0
1986	738.5	309.4	429.0	-92.6
1987	826.5	384.4	432.2	-37.8
1988	1027.8	475.2	552.7	-77.5
1989	1116.8	525.4	591.4	-66.0
1990	1154.4	620.9	533.5	87.4
1991	1357.0	719.1	637.9	81.2
1992	1655.3	849.4	805.9	43.5
1993	1957.0	917.4	1039.6	-122.2
1994	2366.2	1210.1	1156.2	53.9
1995	2808.6	1487.8	1320.8	167.0
1996	2898.8	1510.5	1388.3	122.2
1997	3251.6	1827.9	1423.7	404.4
1998	3239.5	1837.1	1402.4	434.7
1999	3606.3	1949.3	1657.0	292.3
2000	4743.0	2492.0	2250.9	241.1
2001	5096.5	2661.0	2435.5	225.5
2002	6207.7	3255.7	2952.0	303.7

註：1981 年以前的數據來自於外經貿業務統計。
數據來源：中華人民共和國海關統計

表四十七　中華人民共和國商務部規劃財務司

Ministry of Commerce of the People's Republic of China Department of Planning and Finance

1979 年以來國家外滙

金額單位：億美元

年份	年末金額	當年增減額
1979	8.4	6.7
1980	-13.0	-21.4
1981	27.1	40.0
1982	69.9	42.8
1983	89.0	19.2
1984	82.2	-6.8
1985	26.4	-55.8
1986	20.7	-5.7
1987	29.2	8.5
1988	33.7	4.5
1989	55.5	21.8
1990	110.9	55.4
1991	217.1	106.2
1992	194.4	-22.7
1993	212.0	17.6
1994	516.2	304.2
1995	736.0	219.8
1996	1050.3	314.3
1997	1398.9	348.6
1998	1449.6	50.7
1999	1546.8	97.2
2000	1655.7	109.0
2001	2121.6	465.9
2002	2864.1	742.5
2003	4032	1167.9
2004	4033	0.1

數據來源：中華人民共和國海關統計

表四十八　出口加工區招商、運作累計情況表

統計時段：2000.9-2005.2.28

序號	加工區名稱	外資項目批准數	投資總額（億美元）	內資項目批准數	註冊資本（億元）	進口總值（萬美元）	出口總值（萬美元）	進出口總值（萬美元）
1	上海松江	63	13.02	0	0	1221505.7	1711693.5	2933199.2
2	江蘇昆山	74	13.1996	0	0	948194.1	1218111.4	2166305.5
3	江蘇蘇州工業園區	56	10.815957	0	0	176778.1	197111.2	373889.3
4	浙江杭州	29	3.9639	1	0.1	172642.7	182546.6	355189.3
5	上海漕河涇	4	2.978	0	0	144065.2	196996.6	341061.8
6		86	7.8025	8	3.04	32076.5	61959.2	94035.7
7	廣東深圳	36	5.303	9	10.92	35729.3	43951.7	79681.0
8	山東威海	50	2.9601	5	3.08	29949.1	33997.9	63947.0
9	江蘇南京	4	0.993	2	0.502	24560.7	17519	42079.9
10	山東烟台	79	1.95201	28	2.64	17422.3	17282.2	34704.5
11	上海金橋	19	1.5277	1	1.06	10093.3	10952.4	21045.7
12	天津	6	1.9114	9	1.02	7199.6	12466.3	19665.9
13	浙江波	23	4.481	1	0.17	5935.6	13256	19191.8
14	湖北武	4	0.458	3	0.18	8386.4	5710.6	14097.0
15	福建廈門	18	1.082	6	0.6215	6834.5	7255.0	14089.5
16	蘇州高新區	20	3.7754	0	0	7254.4	6256.9	13511.3
17	江蘇南通	13	1.181	1	0.03	4365.9	3495.6	7861.5
18	北京天竺	14	2.50411	0	0	3591.1	2050.3	5641.4
19	江蘇	16	4.9798	2	7.78	4180.7	1124.5	5305.2

	无錫						
20	四川成都	16	8.788	4	0.107	2221	1057.4	3278.4
21	陝西西安	5	0.1834	6	0.92	32.3	2940.5	2972.8
22	上海青浦	15	2.0364	1	0.1	2422.3	183.8	2606.1
23	重慶	7	0.1619	3	0.18	932.2	1549.7	2481.9
24	廣東廣州	1	0.963	0	0	1992.1	41	2033.1
25	吉林春	11	0.3822	4	0.69	617.1	437.6	1054.7
26	江蘇鎮江	10	1.181	0	0	555.5	86	641.7
27	安徽湖	10	0.104	7	0.145	266.5	316.7	583.2
28	江蘇連云港	3	0.325	2	0.125	315.7	175	490.6
29	山東青島	9	1.618	10	0.6627	192.3	24.7	217.0
30	河北秦皇島	11	0.3741	1	0.01	135.3	6	141.4
31	上海行	5	0.3105	1	0.1	2.1	27	28.9
32	廣西北海	1	0.0183	2	0.4318	0	0	0.0
33	河南鄭州	9	0.2583	10	0.5061	0	0	0.0
	總計	727	101.592577	127	35.1211	2870449.6	3750582.7	6621032.3

表四十九 2000 至 2005 年全國與出口加工區進、出口值比較表

單位：億美元

	投　　　資	貿　　　易	
全　國	2500	進出口總值	33802.3
		進口值	16203.9
		出口值	17598.3
		順差值	1394.4
出口加工區	101.6	進出口總值	662.1
		進口值	287
		出口值	375
		順差值	88
比　值 （全國：加工區）	1：0.0406	總值	1：0.0196
		順差	1：0.0631

表五十 2000 至 2005 年松江及昆山出口加工區生產力統計表

單位：萬美元

	勞動生產力	土地生產力	投資生產力
松江出口加工區	$7.6 萬元／人一年	$57,056 萬元／km^{2}一年	$2.63 萬元／萬元一年
昆山出口加工區	$5.7 萬元／人一年	$85,183 萬元／km^{2}一年	0~0.36 萬元／萬元一年
其它區	0~2.2 萬元／人一年	0~13,594 萬元／km^{2}一年	0~0.36 萬元／萬元一年

註：生產力＝出口總值÷（勞動人數或土地面積或投資金額）

表五十一　2000 至 2005 年台灣加工出口區生產力統計表

單位：萬美元

	勞動生產力	土地生產力	投資生產力
2000 年以前	$12 萬元／人一年	$200,000 萬元／$km^2$一年	$4.5 萬元／萬元一年
2000 年以後	$9.5 萬元／人一年	$68,000 萬元／$km^2$一年	$1 萬元／萬元一年

　　由以上兩表比較觀之，松江出口加工區及昆山出口加工區的三項生產力在 2000 年以前，遠低於台灣加工出口區，而 2000 年以後則有項目略高於台灣加工出口區者，後來居上，可賀可喜！

　　但是，除松江，昆山等出口加工區外，其他三十個區的生產力業績極低，乏善可陳。

　　由以上兩表可以了解到，台灣的加工出口區自 1997 年增加第四個加工出口區開始，業績便呈現下滑的現象，台灣自 1994 年國民所得達到 10566 美元，成為已開國家後，就不宜再以加工出口區作為經濟發展的推動力量，也就是不宜再設置新的加工出口區，但是台灣加工出口區主政者盲目的建設新的加工出口區增至十個區，並妄想以加工出口區作為亞太營運中心及轉運中心為主軸的發展，以至忽視了以工業為主的生產事業的發展，至有 2000 年以後區內業績不彰的表現。

　　同理中國已參與營運的三十三個出口加工區，只有二或三個區有較優異的表現，不適合比較利益的要求，表示中國也已不再適合設置出口加工區

（3）從創造就業機會，擴大內需要求看出口加工區變革的需要性

繼而從創造就業機會，擴大內需來看，以松江及昆山出工加工區所提供的勞動力，就業機會，一個區約達 45000 人，三十三個區若全部營運成功則可創造的就業機會最多 200 萬人，又若第一產業，農業經濟改革成功，農村過剩的勞動力一億人，如全部轉業到第二類產業，工業就業，則需要興建類似松江或昆山出口加工區規模的新出口加工區 2200 多區，即便有二分之一的人口轉業到第三產業，服務業，另二分之一的轉業人數也需要興建約 1100 區，試問全世界現有的企業數量能夠填滿 1100 個新的出口加工區麼？更何況是要設置在同一個國家之內的可能性更是微乎其微；又出口加工區原有的特性，目的在創造就業機會，繁榮地方經濟，此與擴大內需的經濟政策是相吻合的，但中國出口加工區，凡經營成功的區均位在已開發或開發中的地區，如上海、昆山、蘇州等地並以高科技為吸引投資的對象，對落後地區的創造就業機會及提高地方經濟能力，沒有幫助。

（4）綜合分析不再適合設置出口加工區的原因

所以總括的分析，中國雖然還有廣大面積及低成本勞動力的落後地區，應是符合發展出口加工區的條件之一，但却因以下原因不再適合設置出口加工區：

①在已開發或開發中的城鎮中，已發展成熟的出口加工區目前已演進到科學園區的模式，自不再適合設置新的出口加工區，以避免錦上添花，國家資源分配不公的現象。

　　②中國廣大面積需要設置數量龐大的出口加工區，才能滿足就業的需求，然而世界有意海外投資的企業有一定的限量，不太可能滿足中國的需求。

　　③設置一個完善的出口加工區，投資費用不低，又現有出口加工區普遍績效不彰，以及廣大土地非經濟性的使用，政府的投資成本應該精細考量。

　　④從比較利益，三利原則分析：不利於再設置出口加工區。

　A・國家的利益：貢獻極其有限

　　a.能創造多少就業機會呢？按現有營運的三十三區全部滿額，也才 200 多萬人就業，解決不了薪火之急。

　　b.對國家資本財的形成，按中國當前外滙儲備達 7000 億美元之普，出口加工區的貢獻甚微。

　　c.工業先進技術的引進，絕大多數已由高新科技園區，經濟開發區等所引進，出口加工區所引進的層次略低，規模也較小，對中國整體技術引進而言，意義不大。

　　d.帶進國際市場方面，出口加工區的對外貿易額只佔全國的 2%，貢獻有限，龐大的國際市場也已由經濟開發區，高新科技園區等引進。

　B・廠商的利潤：中國境內市場獲利不易。

　　a.廠商在生產成本方面，中國各落後地區是可以提供低價位的勞動力及土地成本，但環境成本如運輸，原料，公共設施，非管銷內的事務費都比東南亞的

國家如越南，緬甸等國為高，尤其是加值稅及進口關稅令人聞之色變，影響投資廠商的獲利。

　　b.市場獲利方面，中國現為世界製造工廠，但國內龐大的消費市場却因國民所得普遍偏低，購買力不足，只呈現出虛有的市場空間，影響獲利。

　C‧員工的福利：

員工可維持基本工資，少有較多的福利，只要有外資到區內投資設廠，員工的基本工資是必然有的，但要求高幅度的調漲，改善員工收入，提高國民所得，可能性非常小，其他福利，視個別企業而定，可遇而不可求。

四、以出口加工區為發展經濟的國家，在觀念上的認知：

　　當今世界各未開發或低度開發的國家需要加工出口區，而達到一定程度的開發中或已開發的國家，便不再適宜了，中國當前外滙儲備高達 7000 億美元，自不適宜再設置出口加工區；若中國至今仍需要以出口加工區的模式作為經濟發展的手段，即表示中國仍處在貧窮落後的環境，如此過去二十多年辛勤努力的經濟發展是不成功的，而事實中國的經濟發展是二次世界大戰以落後國家中發展較為成功的國家之一，為世人所公認，所以中國不再適宜發展出口加工區了。

　　中國既不適宜再發展出口加工區，而其變革發展的方向，如前節「出口加工區變革發展」的意見，在全國各落後

地區普遍設置「加工區或加工工業區」，如此可使全國經濟普遍繁榮昌旺，奠定「民族產業」的基礎，達到全國均富的目的。

五、中國經濟發展宏觀思維落實的重點：

最後要強調中國經濟發展宏觀思維若能實現才具有實質的意義，果能執行，則落實的重點，概括而言有以下數點提供參考：

1、要迅速確實改善中國大環境因素影響經濟不均衡發展的三項基本問題，即人口，地理環境及教育發展。

2、加速三次產業的均衡發展。

3、加強推動內需政策，鼓勵消費市場，使「金流與物流」活動加速。

4、積極推動出口加工區的變革並與三次產業的均衡發展及擴大內需政策相配合，以奠定堅實的民族產業基礎。

5、防止泡沫經濟的演進。

6、建置完善且與國際接軌的金融，財稅制度，早日使人民幣成為可信度的國際貨幣，有利國家金融長期發展，全民受益。

7、健全法制化，使經濟發展循法制正軌運行演進。

第七章　結語

　　自 1966 年 12 月 3 日世界首創的台灣高雄加工出口區成立至今已達 39 年的歷史，一路艱辛的經營發展，成就彪炳，享譽國際，然而從其發展的歷程來看，與台灣近半世紀經濟發展的三個里程碑－從僑外資企業的引進（1950~1970），繼之加工出口區的年代（1966~1985），到科學園區的發展（1980 至今）是相吻合的，但僅就加工出口區而言，約可分成三個階段在演進，第一階段為創設初期加工出口區的第一個十年（1966~1975），亦為國家整體經濟發展最慘淡的時期，此時加工出口區尚在嬰兒般羸弱體質培育的時刻，卻已然擔負起國家所賦予的歷史重任，由於政府規劃得宜，所以這一階段發展工作頗為順利、快速，才會於三年內有第二及第三個加工出口區的增設，而享譽中外；第二階段即第一階段後的 15 年（1976~1990），加工出口區隨著國家經濟的成長，社會環境的變遷，進而逐漸大幅成長及改進經營運作，尤其加強對區內廠商的服務、溝通及必要的制度法規的修訂，更重要的是擴大了就業機會的容量。第三階段即營運 25 年以後至今（1991~）的這一段時間，加工出口區已完成了國家交賦的時代使命，並促成了科學園區的創設，國家科技工業、重工業的發展，以及十大建設、十二大建設、亞太營運中心等國家超大型計劃的推動，而加工出口區本身卻面

臨必須轉型發展的時刻；從加工出口區的價值觀而言，由初創、艱辛的奮鬥到茁壯茂然有成，傲視國際之時，至今卻為社會各界檢討存廢轉型之際，只不過三十九年的歲月，這三十九年裡國家也因有加工出口區的一份貢獻而成就為世界已開發的國家，及為世人讚譽為經濟奇蹟的國家，故而了解到台灣加工出口區貢獻的價值實無法用百億或千億金額來衡量其成就的偉大或重要性；再說，台灣加工出口區一本完整的發展演變史，也證實是國家正常發展歷程的必然結果，因為如果三十九年後的中華民國仍然停留在需要設置加工出口區來創造就業機會及改善國家整體經濟的發展，即表示國家沒有進步，仍然停留在貧困不振落後的經濟情況，果如此，則國家三十九年的經營成效乏善可陳，人民何來希望！

然而當今台灣經濟賡續的發展又將如何定向？因台灣境內及國際大環境的巨大變遷，故而必須要從宏觀的層面來思考國家經濟策略的擬訂，「資金市場」應該是列為台灣今後經濟主軸的思維議題，而不再只局限在「加工出口區」（包括科學園區），「工業生產」領域的「創造就業機會」，「高附加價值」等範圍內的利益追求而已。

再就中國出口加工區的發展觀之，國家整體經濟發展受制於整體大環境的影響，尤其是受到「人口，地理環境因素及教育」三大問題的鉗制，使出口加工區的發展也受到關連性的影響，致其成效並未達到臻於至善的目標，人口問題是一切障礙的根源，人口問題涉及到至為嚴肅及嚴重「教與養」的問題，這也是政府責無旁貸的沈重責任和使命，因為「教與養」衍生到一個國家的「國民生活水平」及「民族優質化」

的議題，而表現在人口實質上的問題則是「就業與失業，國民所得的水平及社會進步的表徵」的存在事實，出口加工區確為這些問題提供了一份貢獻，但中國全體出口加工區的功能仍然有待努力、發展，在上海、江蘇、浙江及廣東，福建這兩大區域已發展成熟的出口加工區則應轉型往科技，高產值，高附加價值的產業發展，而更深一層的看，中國經濟發展也應該考慮到「資金市場」發展的效益，在上述兩區域已不宜只停留在「生產市場」，「世界生產工廠」的範疇，而「生產市場」的功能，效益應向內陸經濟落後地區擴展，包括「加工區」的配合發展，此即說明中國整體經濟不均衡發展現況的前景規劃，兼顧到「開發中驅向已開發的長江三角洲及珠江三角洲」區域與「尚待開發的內陸、西北、西南等」落後地區，兩個截然不同程度的經濟區塊同時並進發展，則一方面使國家濟發展走在世界經濟熱潮宏流的行列中，不致落伍、落差，另一方面則可即早改善三次產業不均衡發展的實質需求及達成扶貧的目標，使全國經濟早日達到均衡發展，脫離過去均貧思維所造成全民的艱苦生涯，而轉變成為均富優渥的國家。

　　從台灣加工出口區這一段歷史的演進，可提供世界各開發中及未開發國家最寶貴的參考資料，但卻要深切體認的是世界各國各有其不同的環境因素，不能仍以同一模式規範發展，而要因時地制宜，但一項最基本的信念，乃是已有加工出口區設置的國家，也要有宏觀的理念、思維，要能更上層樓往高附加價值，高技術經濟領域發展，尤其重要的是要如何以有限的資金，可行性的模式，協助待開發的落後地區建

設「加工區」，而非「加工出口區」，這完全是為了創造就業機會，擴大內需加惠貧困的人民，使之能改善生活，同時也推動外銷，使國內外市場兼顧發展，以能達到發展國家或地區的初級經濟為目的，此乃是加工出口區初衷、意念規範的神聖使命，永不改變；台灣及中國兩類絕然不同的地理條件、社會環境及國情，皆建設加工出口區經營成功，可作為參考、借鏡，則加工出口區將帶給人類福祉，永恆的貢獻－幸福、安樂與和平，是為可期！

第八章　世界加工出口區相關
參考資料（中、英文）

壹、世界加工出口區協會（WEPZA）簡介
及參考資料

一、世界加工出口區協會簡介

　　世界第一個台灣加工出口區於 1966 年 12 月 3 日創設成立於高雄，在短時間內便成效卓越，震驚世界各國，聯合國工業發展組織（UNIDO）至為肯定台灣加工出口區的成效貢獻，可用以協助世界開發中或未開發國家仿效建設，以增加就業機會，協助該等國家經濟發展，逐大力推動，並促進世界加工出口區協會（WEPZA）的成立，於 1974 年由 UNIDO 支助在哥倫比亞首都 Barranquilla 召開首次「工業自由區經理專家工作會議」，繼於 1975 年 12 月專家工作小組會議在越南召開，起草協會規章，復於 1977 年 2 月在埃及 Alexandria 召開協會成立有關文件最後定案會議，最後於 1978 年 2 月 4 日在菲律賓馬力拉召開世界加工出口區協會成立第一次會議，參與成立大會者計有 29 個國家的加工出口區或自由工業區的負責人，大會由 UNIDO 贊助。

二、世界加工出口區協會成立的目的

1、建立會員間正常的連繫，促進彼此相互的了解及協助。

2、培養會員間和諧的關係及鼓勵相互支助。

3、促進國際相關機構間為共同的目的、興趣而合作。

4、促進會員間資訊的交流。

5、在投資者及市場方面有效提升工業投資計劃及資訊交換。

6、加工出口區管理技術訓練課程的規劃及加工出口區彼此間幕僚及高階人員間互訪。

7、鼓勵技術交流。

8、採取有效可行的行動以達到協會未來的目標。

世界加工出口區協會理事會議由入會會員投票產生，再由各理事票選出理事長及秘書長，第一任理事長是埃及投資及自由區的局長 Gamal El Sahrawi 博士，秘書長是由菲律賓加工出口區管理局長，Teodoro Q.Pena 先生擔任；1981 年在菲律賓的賓城會議中重選協會理事長由斯里蘭卡的 Upali Wijewardene 先生擔任，而 Pena 先生仍被認命為秘書長；至今協會理事長由 Pena 先生擔任，秘書長由前任的 Richard L.Bolin 先生交由現任的 Robert C.Haywood 接任。

世界加工出口區協會會址，設在美國奧納章納州的 Flagstaff Institute 內，F.I 屬於北奧納章納州立大學商學院，此亦為世界加工出口區協會的永久會址。

有關世界加工出口區的詳細資料請參考後頁有關文件。

World Export Processing Zones Association （**WEPZA**）

Table of Contents

THE PRIVATIZATION OF WEPZA

Export Processing Zones investors and managers will benefit from the 22 papers presented here for ideas and experience of many of the most successful early EPZs on how they grew in spite of difficulties they faced. Of particular note are Noe Koenig's suggestions for EPZ success as Motorola, Inc. saw them, John Kent's risk management plan for startup of a new EPZ and Richard Campbell's Nogales Shelter Plan, an innovative promotion idea.

These are memoirs of the International Conference and 3rd General Assembly of the World Export Processing Zones Association held at Flagstaff, Arizona, USA September 11-15, 1985 attended by 78 persons from 20 countries. The conference provided renewed contact and exchange of information among WEPZA members and was called to convert WEPZA to a non-government organization (NGO). From its founding by United Nations Industrial Development Organization (UNIDO) at Manila in 1978 WEPZA had been constrained by its inter-governmental nature from acting quickly on relatively simple matters such as accepting new members. Also, its budget decision to operate its Secretariat from the Secretary General's EPZ placed an increasing burden on that EPZ office as WEPZA grew.

The WEPZA Statutes were amended to make WEPZA an organization of export processing zones, public or private, and to place responsibility for membership in the hands of zone leadership. The WEPZA Secretariat was provided a permanent location at Flagstaff to be operated as a project of The Flagstaff Institute. This document was originally published in the Journal of The Flagstaff Institute, Volume X No. 1, March 1986 (Library of Congress Card Number 77-649702) and is reproduced here by permission.

Edited by Richard L. Bolin

A PUBLICATION OF THE FLAGSTAFF INSTITUTE

@1997, the flagstaff institute

all rights reserved

ISBN 0-945951-18-3

THE WEPZA CONFERENCE AT FLAGSTAFF

Richard L. Bolin Director

The Flagstaff Institute

Flagstaff, Arizona, USA

This issue of the Journal of The Flagstaff Institute is devoted entirely to the papers presented at the International Conference of Managers and Users of Export Processing Zones held at Flagstaff September 11-15, 1985. The conference was sponsored by the World Export Processing Zones Association (WEPZA), The Flagstaff Institute, and the Management Development Center of the College of Business Administration of Northern Arizona University.

WEPZA is a child of UNIDO, The United Nations Industrial Development Organization ,which became independent of UNIDO at its founding in Manila in February, 1978. Its history is described in the remarks of Teodoro Pena, President of WEPZA, in the first paper of this issue. The Flagstaff Conference of Managers and Users of EPZs was the first held in the United States, and the first to which non-members were invited. A total of 78 persons from 20 countries exchanged views during a 3-day session.

In order to improve its organization, WEPZA's 3rd General Assembly modified its charter at Flagstaff and adopted new regulations. These change WEPZA from an organization of governments to an organization of EPZ's and Export Industrial Parks, public and private. The General Assembly further established a permanent Secretariat for the period 1986-90 at Flagstaff under the management of The Flagstaff Institute. It is the Secretariat's responsibility to increase membership of EPZs and Users, publish a quarterly newsletter, carry out two research projects per year, and supply statistical information through the Journal of The Flagstaff Institute. Teodoro Pena of the Philippines was elected President of WEPZA and Guillermo Ochoa, Head of the Bermudez Industrial Parks of Juarez, Mexico, was named Secretary General.

The Flagstaff Institute is pleased to accept the responsibility for the WEPZA Secretariat as a major project of the Institute and has assigned Robert C. Haywood and Richard L. Bolin as co-Directors of the Secretariat. The work will enhance the information available to the Institute and broaden its contact with the many countries operating EPZs, or interested to establish them. Our Journal will, from time to time, include information about WEPZA among its research projects and statistical analyses, but the Institute will continue as before to be an independent center dedicated to improved world trade and business and to pursuing its unique research on the internationalization of manufacturing.

THE WORLD EXPORT PROCESSING ZONES ASSOCIATION

Teodoro Q. Pena

President of WEPZA

Manila. Philippines

It is my pleasure to welcome you all to the first conference of the World Export Processing Zones Association in the United States and the first to which non-members have been invited.

This International Conference of Managers and Users of Export Processing Zones and similar facilities marks the realization of a foremost objective of WEPZA's creation, the establishment of a forum where there will be free exchange of views, information and experiences and an opportunity for dialogue and that may guide the EPZ managers and developers in the planning and operation of their EPZs.

The wealth of experience and success in the field of export processing zones and free zones is not the monopoly of WEPZA members. The majority who are not members of this organization are equally successful and have plenty of experience and information which the are ready to share with the other EPZ practitioners all over the world. The experts and corporate representatives present here in response to our invitation have come at their own expense in the name of fellowship, and in the earnest desire to improve and learn existing practices in the development, organization, management and operation of an industrial free zone or export processing zone.

We are thankful to the Flagstaff Institute and to Northern Arizona University for agreeing to co-sponsor and manage this conference. Flagstaff's Richard

Bolin has been with us since the inception of WEPZA and in all its meetings, sharing his wisdom and thoughts to improve the services of EPZs. Mr. Bolin decided to play a greater role. He made this conference possible and unselfishly and generously poured his time and effort in bringing us together in the interest of understanding and world trade.

We are likewise thankful to the United Nations Industrial Development Organization and the governments of our member countries for the support they have given WEPZA since its inception. UNIDO has laid the groundwork for the organization of WEPZA since the idea was first discussed in meetings in Barranquilla in 1974 and developed in Vienna and Alexandria, until WEPZA was formally organized in Manila in 1978.

In this conference, we shall be discussing formally and informally, our respective zones. We shall examine the relevance of our systems and procedures, incentives, our advantages and disadvantages to our investors. We shall hear from users of EPZs and industrial estates on how we can further improve our services. We shall learn the latest trends in the development and operations of EPZs from experts. I'm afraid that we may not have enough time to accommodate all the knowledge and experiences from all participants as a result of this three-day conference.

Teodoro Q. pena received law degrees from the University of the Philippines and Yale University. He has served as a member of the Philippine Parliament, as Minister of Natural Resources, and as Chairman and Administrator of the Export Processing Zone Authority of the Philippines. He has been secretary General of WEPZA since its founding in 1978 and was elected President by the General Assembly at Flagstaff.

However, I hope that our prime objective which is to learn how to improve the operations of our EPZs will be beneficial and that the projects which we have started or we plan to start will achieve the results for which they were established.

Historical Background of WEPZA

The idea of setting up some form of free zone association was first broached in the Regional Expert Working Group of Managers of industrial free zones in Barranquilla, Colombia in 1974.The meeting was held under the auspices of the United Nations Industrial Development Organization. An expert working group was thereafter constituted at Vienna in December 1975 to draft the Association's constitution and by-laws. In another meeting in Alexandria, Egypt in Feburary 1977, the working papers for the association's establishment were finalized.

On February 4, 1978, the World Export Processing Zones Association came into being. Its creation was endorsed by the authorities of export processing zones and industrial free zones of 29 countries who attended the first conference held in Manila, Philippines under the auspices of UNIDO.

The Wpr;d Export Processing Zones Association (WEPZA) was

established, for the following purposes:

(a) establishing and maintaining regular contact between members in order to improve their mutual understanding and their appreciation of each other's problems and requirements;

(b) fostering harmonious relationships and encouraging common action and mutual assistance among the members;

(c) co-operating with international agencies having similar aims and interests;

(d) producing and circulating between members relevant information;

(e) exchanging methods of evaluating industrial investment proposals and information on investors and marketing;

(f) arranging training courses in EPZ management techniques and also appropriate exchange visits of EPZ staff or potential staff;

(g) encouraging the transfer of technology;

(h) taking all necessary and appropriate action to further the objectives of the Association.

The principal organs are the General Assembly, which shall be composed of all the founding members and a WEPZA Council, composed of a President and ten members duly elected by the General Assembly. These two bodies determine the general policies and program of work of the Association. The Policies and program of work of the association shall be implemented by a WEPZA Secretariat to be headed by a Secretary General.

For its first President, Dr. Gamal El Sahrawi of the Investments and Free Zones Authority of Egypt was elected. The

EPZ authorities of the following countries were elected as Council Members:

EPZ AUTHORITIES	REPRESENTED BY
Zona Franca Industrial y Commercial de Barranquilla, Colombia	Mr. Julio Gerlain Comelin
Santa Cruz Electronics Export Processing Zone, India	Mr. S. Rajgopal
Shannon Free Airport Development Company, Ltd. Ireland	Mr. Niall A. O'Brien
Liberia Industrial Free Zone Authority, Liveria	Mr. Joseph G. Richards
Mauritius Export Processing Zone System, Mauritius	Mr. Edward L. Lim Fat
Direccion General de Fomento Industrial Fronteriza y Maquiladora, Mexico	Mr. Guillermo Teutli Otero
Zona Libre de Colon, Panama	Mr. Harry Z. Castro
Export Processing Zone Authority, Philippines	Mr. Roberto P. Villa
Greater Colombo Economic Commission, Sri-Lanka	Mr. Sivali H. Ratwatte
Syrian-Jordanian Industrial Free Zone Company, Syria	Mr. Taha M. Bali

Mr. Teodoro Q. Pena of the Philippine Export Processing Zone Authority was appointed as Secretary-General.

Because of fund limitations, the Secretary-General and his staff were appointed on a part time basis until such time as a full-time Secretary General and permanent secretariat is established. Temporarily, the location of the Secretariat followed the domicile of the Secretary-General.

Guided by the objectives of the WEPZA creations, the Secretariat went about its tasks. A data bank on free zone operations as established. The WEPZA News was published. Inquiries from various international and local institutions were attended. WEPZA was promoted in various international meetings of EPZ authorities. An official logo was adopted. Spanish and French were included as working languages in addition to English. [Ed. Note:mandating translation into second, third, and potentially more languages placed a difficult and costly burden on a small EPZ office. This requirement for multiple languages was dropped at Flagstaff when English was adopted as the sole language.]

The WEPZA Council met in Panama City in October 1979. By then, official membership of WEPZA was reduced to 16, based on their fulfillment of financial obligations as called for in the WEPZA Statutes. A new program of work was established to further strengthen the organization. A WEPZA Code of Ethics was proposed.

The WEPZA General Assembly again met in Baguio City, Philippines in March 1981 to elect a new President and members of the Council. Elected as President was Mr. Upali Wijewardene of the Sri-Lanka Greater Colombo Economic Commission. The WEPZA Code of Ethics was adopted, New members were elected to the Council namely:

NEW MEMBERS   REPRESENTED BY

NEW MEMBERS	REPRESENTED BY
Export Processing Zone Authority, Pakistan	Mr. G. Yazdani Khan
Free Zones Corporation H.K. of Jordan	Mr. Mohammad Abdalat
P.T. (Persero) Bonded Warehouse Qty., Ltd. Indonesia	Mr. Hardjo Oetmo
Masan Export Processing Zone Administration, Korea	Mr. Byeng Ku Kwak

Re-elected to the Council were the following:

RE-ELECTED MEMBERS   REPRESENTED BY

RE-ELECTED MEMBERS	REPRESENTED BY
General Establishment for Free Zones, Syria	Mr. Fouad Al-Sayed
Sectorial de la Industria Electronica Fronteriza y Maquiladora, Mexico	Mr. Guillermo Teutli Otero
Liberia	Mr. Paul H. Perry
Egypt	Mr. Gamal El Sahrawi
India	Mr. Bishambar N. Makhija
Zona Franca de Colon, Panama	Mr. Jose Montenegro

To better promote the association in Africa and the Americas, Messrs. Paul Perry of Liberia and Guillermo Teutli Otero of Mexico were designated Vice Presidents for these regions respectively.

The General Assembly adopted the program of work proposed at the WEPZA Council meeting in Panama and other measures to boost the organization's international standing. Recognizing the accomplishment of the WEPZA Secretariat in the past three (3) years of operations, Mr. Teodoro Q. Pena was re-appointed as Secretary-General.

REVIEW OF THE MAIN POINTS OF THE WEPZA CONFERENCE

Robert C. Haywood, Rapporteur

The flagstaff Institute

Boulder, Colorado, USA

It is an honor to be the rapporteur at this conference. It is also an enviable task since the content of this conference, both formally and informally, has been so rich. I wand to thank all of the speakers who have made my task a little easier. Before I begin, let me say that what criticisms, if any, I am about to make do not apply to any of the countries or participants that are present here. Present company is always excepted from any comments. And I will also take the prerogative of the rapporteur to start at the end.

For a conference of this size and type, the users of Export Processing Zones have provided a refreshing, candid and valuable critique, and I thank them for their participation. But, what have they told us?

What they have told us is that they need economic stability throughout their operations, and no just political stability; that they need cheap labor, but with all respect to David Miller, they need more than just cheap labor; and that many other items are also primary. Three fourths or so of the worlds' population provides cheap labor. Yet, Eden Toys is only in Korea and Haiti, and neither of those is the cheapest labor available. What is it these companies are saying that they need?

They need the products of cheap labor in part, delivered to their markets in saleable condition in a timely manner. They are interested no in the cost of wages but in the cost of that hour of labor embodied in their product delivered to their customers, and that is more than low wages.

I have taken the liberty of borrowing Noe Koenig's list of suggestions for improving EPZs. Note that it does not include proving cheap labor nor increasing the fiscal incentives for moving. In fact, three of the items call for a reduction in the barriers of entry.

Reducing Entry Barriers

Now the barriers of entry can be number of thins. Richard Campbell has shown us how he reduces the barriers of getting a company into Nogales, Mexico – The one-stop shopping – and it was a very effective presentation of what he offered his customers. But his way may only be possible in an environment wher the government has enacted enabling legislation that applies with relative uniformity to most investors. In Mexico, this has been done very well for the maquila industry. There is, as this list shows, particularly for this export industry, simplified government approval and control procedures. There is a clarity in the legislation, or else in the way it is developed and practiced over a period of years.

Robert C. Haywood is a physicist with an MBA from Harvard Business School who has managed factories in Hong

Kong and the peoples republic of China. A candidate for the DBA and PhD degrees at the University of Colorado, he is Director of the WEPZA Secretariat at The Flagstaff Institute.

Some governments have created a single agency, with the power to negotiate on behalf of other agencies and to reach final agreements. The has been a typical road.　Singapore has done that fairly well.　But when you take authority away from an agency that already had it, you create additional political and legal problems that I'm sure Michael van Notten would recognize .

Other countries have created and agency that coordinates negotiation. We had a discussion just earlier today on how effective that type of procedure is when applied to a country that is known to be hard to deal with. Other countries require independent negotiations with different ministries to be essentially coordinated by the foreign investor himself. I know of a country (not at this meeting) in which you need the unanimous consent of 26 ministers of government. This country had an excellent location, appropriate skill, and raw materials for the product we were interested in. There was to be provided by our venture an import substitute product for that country and an export product. But, because of the impossibility of negotiating an agreement with 26 separate ministers, one of the ministers expressed astonishment that I had even bothered to come.

This reduction of the early entry barriers is one of the major oncepts we have heard here, in terms of how to attract investment. What are the other items on the list?

Some governments have created a single agency, with the power to negotiate on behalf of other agencies and to reach final agreements. That has been a typical road. Singapore has done that fairly well. But when you take authority away from an agency that already has it, you create additional political and legal problems that I'm sure

Michael van Notten would recognize.

Other countries have created an agency that coordinates negotiation. We had a discussion just earlier today on how effective that type of procedure is when applied to a country that is known to be hard to deal with. Other countries require independent negotiations with different ministries to be essentially coordinated by the foreign investor himself. I know of a country (not at this meeting) in which you need the unanimous consent of 26 ministers of government. This country had an excellent location, appropriate skills ,and raw materials for the product we were interested in. There was to be provided by our venture an import substitute product for that country and an export product. But, because of the impossibility of negotiating an agreement with 26 separate ministers, one of the ministers expressed astonishment that I had even bothered to come.

This reduction of the early entry barriers is one of the major oncepts we have heard here, in terms of how to attract investment. What are the other items on the list?

Maintaining Stability of Operation

Well, we have four other items that refer to maintaining the stability of operations once you have arrived in the country. The country must remain internationally competitive, must avoid unreasonable requests, must maintain an unrestricted flow of currency and avoid inflationary policies.　This too is a task of managing policies but it is also the management of the risks that are associated with beginning a new investment.

Just as the first three involve reducing the risk of entry, there four involve reducing the risk or uncertainties of continued operations. And the last two involve making available the country's resources to promote this type of investment. There are some countries that have not yet decided whether their industrial promotion agency or their foreign investment board has the task of promoting investment or regulating investment and the two can be in direct conflict.

Tax Incentives

What Mr. Koenig's list tells me is that, while tax incentives may have a place, the place is not at the forefront of attracting new companies. We heard from Bourns, Inc., that in one country they were delayed by the lack of information available to them. They really never got to the point of asking about tax incentives. They hadn't yet figured oout if they could get a building built. And that question was far more important to them at the time. Tax incentives have a place, but where is it?

Some governments have provided tax incentives to make up for deficiencies in what they felt they were offering – or merely because other countries do so. And perhaps in place of some of the tax incentives they should think about getting rid of some of their deficiencies in infrastructure, transportation, or communications needed to attract industry.

Role of Export Processing Zones in Development

We have talked about the economic development role of the Export Processing Zone, and have seen it defined with different emphasis by different people. At one level we have been told that it is to provide jobs and foreign exchange – period. But many countries would also like it to provide technology and use local resources and raw materials; the list can go one and on. Just what is the EPZ role in this?

It seems to me that EPZ managers are in the forefront of a major industry: the management of information and how their EPZ (country/location) fits into the international network of manufacturing for world markets. You are managing an important information interface.

Many EPZs can construct roads and buildings, but that's not the important factor in an export processing zone. What makes a successful EPZ is the information that the zone management provides to the companies on how to operate in that environment and to its own government on how to improve that environment. It's the information on what the laws are, on how to deal with labor, on employees, on skills, on resources – on how to do business. That is in many cases where money in the successful zone is spent. We have heard about EPZs putting too much money into infrastructure, into buildings, into roads because that's the easy part of the EPZ, the one that banks understand. The hard part – the expensive part – is getting the information to the right people, getting the decisions made, and supporting those decisions.

We have heard from EPZs that have proven the success of this concept. It is growing in favor as a means of developing a country's economy. Again, when we talked about transfer of technology, we did not talk about the transfer of production equipment. Instead, we talked about the transfer of soft products, knowledge, management skills, management technology. And that is what is being seen as having value. We looked at a city like Juarez, where some of the industrial park managers are now setting up their won companies to do subcontracting in order to provide the management skills they have learned to running the parks. We heard Richard Campbell tell us that his Mexican industrial park has 2 sourcing operation in Asia to help support the clients operating in his park. And the information age that we are moving into requires that the value of a product be more in this "soft" knowledge that it is in hardware. And this is what you learn from managing an EPZ because the EPZ is a key information interface in this new information age.

The Role of　WEPZA in Economic Development

As more countries develop an interest in EPZs, and we have heard of over 40 sent to various UNIDO training programs in recent years, the need for WEPZA as an organization increases. I think this conference will appropriately end with a consensus to make WEPZA into an organization to assist you. WEPZA may also play an important role in educating the developed countries as to the importance of export processing in the developing world in advancing their own development and security.

WEPZA's President, Mr. Pena, has outlined the goals of the organization, among which are to maintain regular contact, interchange information and ideas, establish high standards of conduct, and work together in training managers of EPZs and of user organizations to the benefit of host countries and user companies. This conference has advanced these goals. I would like to be able to report later that this conference marked the growth of WEPZA from its infancy to its vigorous adolescence. The growing opportunities for EPZs in the increasingly complex and difficult environment that all of us face pose a greater need for WEPZA than perhaps even when it was founded.

The process of developing Export Processing Zones has gone on for a long time. I think Michael van Notten mentioned some of them going back to the 30's in Europe, and since 1942 in Puerto Rico. Many of the zones hav started however in the last 5 years; and many of the people that are here today were not operating zones when WEPZA was organized. Peter Drucker has been quoted as saying that 7-9 million manufacturing jobs will probably have to be moved from the United States offshore before the end of the Century. By inference, some 20 million jobs would move from all of the developed nations of the world to the developing countries in roughly the same period as the information revolution impacts Japan and Europe. And this organization has an opportunity with this conference and with what follows to be in the forefront of seeing those promises develop.

WEPZA CODE OF CONDUCT

A full member of WEPZA in good standing agrees that the following code of conduct will govern its dealings with the public:

1. To be truthful in advertising and promoting its EPZs.
2. To be fair and impartial toward its clients in the administration of its EPZs and of the laws, regulations, incentives and policies within its power to apply.
3. To report to the Secretary General of WEPZA its experience with any client failing to meet ethical standards of behavior as an EPZ client.
4. To conduct itself at all times as a highly ethical professional industrial development organization so as to reflect favorably on itself and on other WEPZA members.

THE WEPZA CODE OF CONDUCT

The WEPZA Code of Conduct was approved by the 2nd General Assembly of WEPZA at Baguio City, Philippines on March 26, 1981. The ad hoc committee which drafted the resolution for the General Assembly on March 25, 1981 was:

Chairman: G. Yasdani Khan, Chairman EPZA Pakistan

Members: G. Teutli Otero, Maquila Officer, Governmemt

of Mexico

Upali Wijewardene, Chairman, GCEC, Sri Lanka

Lorenzo Castillo, Attorney, EPZA Philippines

ex officio:

Niall O'Brien, Director, Shannon Devel, Co., Ireland

Mark Lester, Consultant, East-West Center, Hawaii, USA

Secretary: Richard Bolin, The Flagstaff Institute, Arizona, USA

While the code applies only to WEPZA Members, it is a true multinational agreement since at that time WEPZA was a body of governments founded by UNIDO in 1978. WEPZA was changed to a private non-profit non-government organization (NGO) in 1985. As such it is accredited to UNIDO as NGO advisor on EPZs and was invited as an NGO by the new World Trade Organization (WTO) to its Singapore Trade Ministers meeting in December 1996.

PUBLICATIONS OF THE FLAGSTAFF INSTTTUTE

JOURNAL OF THE FLAGSTAFF INSTITUTE
WEPZA INTERNATIONAL. DIRECTORY OF EXPORT
PROCESSING ZONFS AND FREE TRADE ZONES

MEMOIRS OF WEPZA CONFERENCES

EXPORT PROCESSING ZONES MOVE TO HIGH
TECHNOLOGY

(How Can Government Amint)-TIANJIN, PEOPLES
REPUBLIC OF CHINA

FREE ZONES AND EXPORT PROCESSING ZONES IN
CENTRAL EUROPE/CIS

TO SPEED TRADE WITH WESTERN EUROPE –
VIENNA, AUSTRIA

THE IMPACT OF 57 NEW EXPORT PROCESSING
ZONES IN MERCOSUR – RIO DE JANEIRO, HRAZII.

MAINLINE FREE ZONES:MEDITERRANEAN, GUIR,
INDIAN SUBOONTINENT – DUBAI, U.S.E.

THE WORLD IMPACT OF NAFTA – JUAREZ,
MEXICO

PUBLIC VS. PRIVATE FREE ZONES – COLOMBO,
SRILANKA

FREE ZONES IN THE NEW EUROPE CADIZ, SPAIN

THE NEW ZONES:EAST/WEST EUROPE AND NORTH/SOUTH AMERICA – CURACAO, N.A.

RECHING THE GLOBAL, MARRET THROUGH FREE ZONES – ST, PAUL, MINNESOTA, USA

TECHNOLOGY TANSFFR AND MANAGEMENT IN EXPORT PROCCESSING ZONES – BARCELONA, SPAIN

LINKING THE EXPORT PROCESSING ZONE TO LOCAL INDUSTRY – KAOHSIUNG, TAIWAN, ROC.

THE GLOBAL NETWORK OF EXPORT PROCESSING ZONES – BARRANQUILLA, COLOMRA

PRODUCTION SHARING: A CONFERENCE WITH PETER DRUCKER – SAM DOFGP. CA;OFPRMOA. USA

To order books of for more information please contact:

THE FLAGSTAFF INSTITUTE

P.O.BOX 986

FLAGSTAFF

ARIZONA 86002-0986

U.S.A.

TEL(520)779-0052

FAX(522)774-8589

E-mail:instflag@aol.com

WEPZA Web Site: http://www.wepza.org/world/

ISBN 0-945951-18-3

貳、世界相關國家加工出口區介紹

一、孟加拉加工出口區（Bangladesh EPZS）：

（一）孟加拉加工出口區現況

　　目前孟加拉有二個加工出口區，分別設在 Chittagong 及 Dhaka, Chittagong 加工出口區於 1983.03.06 建成，Dhaka 加工出口區於 1993.07.20 建成，其佔地面積分別為 255 公頃及 144 公頃，Chittagong 區已有 87 單位進入生產中，另有 59 個單位尚待完成中；而 Dhaka 區已有 39 個單位參與生產，另 54 個單位列入下一階段即 1998 年 2 月發展。總投資金額至 1998 年 2 月二區分別為美金＄244.61 百萬元及＄107.70 百萬元，各區的幹部及勞工人數分別為 50863 人及 26667 人，此兩區建設完成後，外國在該國的投資增加到 1994 年及 1998 年從美金＄8,300 萬元提升到＄8 億 7 佰萬元。

　　來區投資者分別來自 16 個國家，其主要投資的國家有南韓（27 家）、日本（17 家）、美國（11 家）及香港（17 家）；累計兩區進出口金額達到美金＄420.89 百萬元及＄309.34 萬元，順差為＄111.55 百萬元；由當地採購佔總進口的 4.6% 約＄14.086 百萬元，而區內產品銷產售到國內市場佔總出口的 6.6% ，附加價值達到 25.5% ，主要投資行業類別有三、1.成衣、針織及成衣配件 2.電子及電器產品 3.皮革

及皮製品。兩區出口營利額在 1990／91 年佔全國的 2.69% 提升到 1998／99 年為 13.40% 。

（二）設備及優惠條件

1、設備：

（1）區內提供土地及廠房出租。

（2）區內備妥電訊、天然氣及水供應。

（3）區內進出口物質 24 小時內放行。

（4）工作許可由管理局核定。

（5）加工出口區內為安全管制區。

（6）區內設有各項娛樂設施。

（7）區內對外籍人員供應極少稅收的食物及飲料。

（8）具有實力的投資者只要向管理區辦理投資手續及所有關於生產目的事務。

（9）外國人投資最少金額，US＄75,000 便可拿到永久住留權（不退還），而投資 US＄500,000 便可成為公民或過戶 US＄1,000,000 到任何知名的孟加拉財務機構。

2、優惠條件：

（1）免稅：

①十年免營利所得稅。

②借入資本免利息所得稅。

③經雙方談妥同意減輕雙重稅。

④基於某種條件在免稅期間三年股息稅全免。

⑤基於某種條件外籍技術人員薪資三年免稅。

（２）進出口免稅

　　①機器、設備及原料進口免稅。

　　②在某種條件下，供廠商自用的汽車三輛免進口
　　　稅。

　　③在區內供建廠房用的材料免進口稅。

　　④區內生產的產品銷售輸出免出口稅。

　　⑤優良廠商（ＧＳＰ）設備允許輸出到美國、歐洲
　　　及日本市場。

　　⑥最惠國待遇（ＭＦＮ）國家輸出者可經孟加拉到
　　　美國。

（３）加工出口區內海關法規，詳細內容如下：

　　①進出加工出口區的貨物免關稅及營業稅。

　　②免關稅及加值稅。

　　③進口的機器、設備及原料免關稅及營業稅。

　　④1984 年加工出口區海關法。

　　⑤加工出口區的貨物可以輸出到國內市場（DTA）。

　　⑥加工出口區廠商產品項目表。

　　⑦加工出口區進口貨品物海關清除程序。

　　⑧國內市場的營建材料依法可供應到加工出口區
　　　內。

　　⑨加工出口區內廠商自用進口的汽車免關稅及營
　　　業稅。

　　⑩加工出口區內各廠商進口自用的汽車免加值稅。

⑪加工出口區內各廠商進口自用的小轎車免加值稅。

⑫加工出口區內各廠商可以外幣在特定為100%出口的保稅倉庫支付。

⑬加工出口區內土地轉移免50%的印花稅及

⑭加工出口區內土地轉移免印花稅。

（4）加工出口區營利所得稅法

①加工出口區廠商免所得稅。

②出口金額免所得稅。

③外國技術專家薪資所得免稅。

④加工出口區內廠商免50%出口營業稅。

⑤加工出口區內外國國民在惠稅期內免個人稅。

⑥加工出口區內工廠或機器可加速折舊。

⑦進口到加工出口區及由出口加工區輸出規定。

（三）孟加拉設加工出口區管理局的目的

1、鼓勵及提昇區內外國廠商來投資以培育及促成國家經濟發長。

2、經由加工出口區增加出口而賺取外匯。

3、鼓勵、培育建立及發展區內工商業以增強孟加拉經濟力。

4、創造就業機會，提高勞工素質及管理技術以達到先進技術。

BANGLADESH

Muhammad Rowshon Kamal
Ashanulla University of Science and Technology

CONCEPT OF EXPORT PROCESSING ZONE （EPZ）

Whatever be the present status of EPZs the world over, the concept is not a new one. They are extended version of 「Free Trade Zones,」 combining both trade and manufacturing. The essence of an EPZ is the establishment of modern manufacturing units in the customs-bonded industrial estate by providing suitable package of incentives for foreign and local investors. Though in concept EPZs are meant both for the local and foreign investors, in reality all-out attempt is made to attract multinationals and industrial combines, which are the leading manufacturers of the world. Zones are thus essentially special enclaves created for the benefit of foreign investors for export manufacture, though incentives are equally applicable to the domestic investors also. But 「in the whole approach there is the presumption that the search for low-cost labor is the main motivation of foreign investment and further that multinational firms can be induced through incentives to locate their labor intensive stages of production in the EPZs of developing countries」（Monsur, A.Hamid, GM BEPZ, 1999）. The main thrust of EPZs is to attract foreign investors who have established marketing network all over the world. An attempt has been made in this paper to examine how far these conceptual frames have been effective in the contest of EPZs in Bangladesh. It is, however, clear that the developing countries mainly focus on employment generation in view of high incidence of unemployment in these countries.

BACKGROUND

The oldest EPZ （whatever may have been the shape） was established in Gibraltar in 1705 and the one in Macao（Free Zone）in 1829. Since their inception, EPZs have not been free from criticism. For example, a Canadian business journal described EPZs as an age-old concept with little weight in the current world's economic system. Many critics consider EPZs as the new from of economic colonization. But the fact remains that within the shortest possible time EPZs have been able to develop in many countries a large number of industries and generate huge employment and export earnings for them. According to a World Bank Report there are about 30 million people working in 900 EPZs all over the world. In this context, special reference may be made of Mauritius （with 60% of employed population in the EPZs）, UAE and Costa Rica where EPZs have helped in transforming the economies and lessening the sufferings of the poor through employment generation.

In terms of regional distribution, North America has 320 EPZs, Central America 42, the Caribbeans 43, Europe 81, Africa 47 and Asia and Pacific 275. But country-wise, USA has 213 EPZs which is the highest, followed by China and Mexico with 123 and 108 EPZs respectively. In terms of employment generation, China ranks first with 18 million employed with foreign investors and many more with the local investors, while Mexico ranks second in this regard. The most dynamic EPZ, however, is Taiwan's Science Park where labor intensive assembly industries have shifted towards advanced technology.

RATIONALE FOR BANGADESH EPZs

Since independence in December 1971, Bangladesh inherited an economy characterized by high pressure of population （perhaps one of the highest in the world）, very low literacy rate, low saving, poor health and sanitation conditions （thus causing low life expectancy）, poor industrial base and growth, poor infrastructural system, high unemployment rate （may be about 40% of the working population）, too much dependence on agriculture and above all precarious law and order situation. In addition, the country is faced with unprecedented trade-gap, acute shortage of hard currency, shortage of entrepreneurial personnel and lack of technical know-how. This state of the economy of Bangladesh forced the economic planners to search for an alternative strategy, which could ensure industrial devel9opment and resolve these chronic problems within the shortest possible time.

A distinctive demographic feature of the developed countries, on the other hand, is the chronic shortage of working population and increasing percentage of aging population, which is likely to accentuate in the future. Thus, most of these countries with a view to save themselves form ever increasing labor costs, require an alternative location to continue their industrial activities. Even Malaysia is faced with the problem of labor shortage and is therefore taking recourse to importing labor from countries like Bangladesh, Indonesia and Philippines etc. The performance of EPZs in Malaysia is, of course, noteworthy. Setting up of industrial units in the EPZ areas in Bangladesh, which has large unemployed population though untrained, offers tremendous attraction to the developed countries to mitigate the problem of labor shortage and reducing costs. With this background in mind, the government of Bangladesh took the bold step to promote and develop EPZs in the country and provide appropriate incentives to foreign investors.

LEGAL FRAMEWORK

In order to promote the development of export processing zones, Bangladesh Export Processing Zones Authority Act, 1980 was enacted（Act No. XXXVI of 1980 dated 26 November 1980, as modified up to 13 December 1994）. The objectives of the Zones Authority are：

• To foster and generate economic development of Bangladesh by encouraging and promoting foreign investment in the Zones;

- To diversify the sources of foreign exchange earnings by increasing exports through zones;
- To encourage and foster the establishment and development of industries and commercial enterprises in zones in order to widen and strengthen the economic base of Bangladesh; and
- To generate opportunities for productive employment and to upgrade labor and management skills through acquisition of advanced technology.
- To achieve these objective, a Board of Governors has been set up which consists of：-
- Chairman （the Prime Minister of her nominee in the rank of Minister）；
- Minister-in-charge of Industries or divisions dealing with industries, finance, commerce, planning, foreign affairs, energy, posts and shipping;
- Governor Bangladesh Bank; and
- Secretaries dealing with industries, finance, commerce, planning, foreign affairs, energy, ports and shipping and internal resources.

Besides this high level Board of Governors which has defined functions, there is an executive board a consultative committee. All these measures are in line with the government's sincere efforts to induce investors to set up industries in the EPZs. The next task is that of identifying the types of industries that should be promoted in EPZs. This is important for the purpose of meting the aspiration of the people for creating additional employment opportunities, as the country has one of the highest unemployment rate in the world. Besides, it is necessary to upgrade the age old technology used in the country. The extent to which EPZs have achieved these objectives can be evaluated only after examining the nature and types of industries actually operating in the zones.

INDICATIVE LIST

The list of industries promoted in the zones in Bangladesh is given in Annex – 1. A closer look at this list would suggest that it is not much different from other developing countries which have currently or in the past, encouraged the development of EPZs. But the exception, in case of Bangladesh, perhaps is that there is a bias in favor of labor intensive industries. This is for the obvious reason of high unemployment rates and low level of technical experience of the labor force.

FACILITIES AND INCENTIVES

Various facilities and incentives offered by the zones in Bangladesh are detailed in Annex – 2. Here again we find that the position in regard to incentives, in almost all the developing countries is more or less similar. A booklet brought out by the zone authority contains details of facilities offered in Bangladesh zones. It provides comprehensive information in respect of labor costs, laws relating to working hours and leave etc., land prices and rental charges, rates of electricity, water, telephone and other means of communications and natural gas. It also provides other relevant information which the investors would like to have to calculative fixed and recurring costs, before deciding to set up an industrial unit in the zones. But the investors are also equally interested in knowing the law and order situation in the host country. Here perhaps, most of the countries are either silent or paint a rosy picture, which could somewhat mislead the investors. At times, it becomes a focal point of dissatisfaction amongst investors and in some cases results in tension between the investors and the host country. For the time being we would refrain from making any further comment on this subject.

PARTICIPATING COUNTRIES, INVESTMENT AND NATURE OF INDUSTRIES IN THE ZONES

Details regarding types of industries set up in the zones are given in Annex – 3. Countries practically from all over the globe have participation in the zone, through there are no investors from the Latin American countries. Actual achievement in respect of investment and employment against projections for the Dhaka zone has been 16.74% and 38.59% respectively and for Chittagong zone it is 56.71% and 60.90% respectively （employment figures pertain to local employers only）. The combined achievement in respect of investment and employment for the two zones works out to 32.78% and 50.89% respectively （till 2 June 1999）. Country-wise details for major investors regarding number of units proposed or set up in the zones are given below：

Table – 1 : Chittagong Export Processing Zone

Country	Units	Country	Units
Bangladesh	37	USA	13
China	4	Taiwan	4
Hong Kong	11	Japan	21
UK	7	ROK	34

Table – 2 : Dhaka Export Processing Zone

Country	Units	Country	Units
Bangladesh	23	USA	5
Hong Kong	7	Japan	4
Malaysia	3	Singapore	3
ROK	27		

ROK is leading in terms of proposed investment of US$382.430 million followed by Bangladesh –US$119.693million, Hong Kong –US$84.90 million and Japan –US$60.25 million （actual investment）. Number of enterprises proposed or actually set up in the zones country-wise are : ROK-61, Bandladesh-60, Japan-25, USA-18, Hong Kong-18 and UK-12.

PRESENT CONDITION OF EPZs IN BANGLADESH

At present, Bangladesh has two EPZs located in Chittagong and Dhaka. Their dates of establishment are 6 March 1983 and 20 June 1993 and they have an area of 255 and 144 hectare respectively. In Chittagong EPZ 87 units are in operation, besides 59 are under implementation. In the Dhaka zone, 39 units are in operation and 54 were at various stages of development in

February, 1998. The total investment so far （up to February 1998） in the two zones was US$244.61 million and US$107.70 million respectively. The strength of staff and workers for Chittagong and Dhaka EPZs was 50,863 and 26,667 respectively. With the setting up zones, foreign investment in the country has gone up between 1994 and 1998 from US$83 million to US$807 millions.

Zones have investors from about 16 countries, but the majority of them are from South Korea（27）, Japan（17）, USA （11） and Hong Kong（7）. The cumulative imports and exports form the zones are US 420.89 million and US$309.34 million, which gives a favorable balance of US$111.55 million. However, local purchase of inputs was US$14.086 millions only which accounts for 4.6% total imports. Sales of zone products in the domestic market was low at 6.6% of exports. The aggregate value added ratio for the zones is 25.5%. Three sectors which account for most of investment are：（1） garments, textiles and garment accessories; （2）electronics and electrical; and （3） leather and leather goods. The share of zones in export earnings for the earnings for the country has gone up from 2.69% in 1990/91 to 13.40% in 1998/99 （Table - 3）.

From the data it is clear that Bangladesh has benefited tremendously from the operation of zones in so far as export earnings are concerned. This factor alone should be enough to support the promotion and development of the EPZs in Bangladesh in view of its limited capacity to earn foreign exchange which is badly needed to accelerate the pace of development in the country.

Table – 3 : Share of Zones in Export Earnings

Year	Hare in Export Earnings （%）
1990/91	2.69
1991/92	3.86
1992/93	5.32
1993/94	5.80
1994/95	6.56
1995/96	8.86
1996/97	10.56
1997/98	12.32
1998/99	13.40

Some Observations

It may be clarified at the very outset that observations in this section may not be applicable to the zones in many other countries, while these have intimate connection with Bangladesh. It is, therefore, appropriate to consider these observations to avoid future problems for the country in general and the EPZs in particular.

Lack of Zoning : The plan for locating industrial enterprises in the zones is based on plot-wise demarcation and the area fixed for the industries. But there is no zoning for specific industries. At this stage, planners do not visualize any problem and thus industrial enterprises are allowed to be set up as per investor preferences. This has already led to environmental pollution problems in the Dhaka zone. The textile units, specially the printing and dyeing plants, are carelessly discharging waste dyes from their plants, adversely affecting nearby areas by this unrestricted practice. But the future implications will be far more serious when the chemical industries will be developed near the food industries. Therefore, it is time for the EPZ authorities in Bangladesh to enforce zoning of industrial enterprise based on product lines. The typical classical type of plot based development will surely create environmental problems and lead to tensions among the enterprises and the local inhabitants. This can adversely affect agriculture, fisheries, drinking water, air and what not ?

Need for Updating Technology for the Domestic Enterprises : Though dissemination of information on new technologies and their introduction are included in the EPZ objectives, but in reality it is found that the maximum units in both the two zones are ready made garments and textiles related. Bangladesh has already achieved maturity in these sectors. Foreign investors are presently exploiting the quota allotted by countries like USA, EEC, though their presence would be well justified after 2005 when the quota system would come to an end. But the real problem is that Bangladesh is unable to attract technology oriented industries, which may be due to lack of suitable and appropriate industrial facilities in the country.

Use of Local Inputs : This is another area where the country has not been able to maximize benefits from the EPZs. As imports are tax free, mostly imported inputs are used. Domestic industries therefore do not derive much benefit from the development of export oriented industries in the zones. In the case of developed countries, the position is completely different. Their industries in zones use locally produced inputs and hence they are benefited both ways i.e. by use of local inputs also increased share in added value. For Bangladesh the most significant advantage of zones has been in terms of employment generation. However, in a country of millions of unemployed persons, zones have not been able to create so much employment as to arrest the pace of ever-increasing educated unemployment. Again, in this respect Mr. Kihak Sung, Chairman of Youngone Group has categorically denied the fact that his industrial group has established units in the EPZs in Bangladesh because of availability of cheap labor（The Bangladesh Observer, 1 July 1999）. Thus the foreign investors are not coming here to capitalize cheap labor only. The question then remains for what?

Share in Export Trade : The share of EPZs in the export trade of Bangladesh is quite significant. As stated earlier, it has gone up from 2.69% in 1991 to 13.4% in 1998/99. This has so much encouraged the government that it is planning to establish two more zones-one at Ishurdi and the other in Comilla. Now the question is if the share of EPZs in the export trade increases to the extent of, say 60%, will it help the country or the government? Sure enough there will be employment for another 60,000-70,000 workers but what about the revenues of the government? All imports and exports in the zones are tax free. Besides, foreign employees are exempt from paying income tax （who are very highly paid） and profits are allowed to be repatriated without payment of taxes. There will be no contribution in the collection of taxes on all these accounts. Reserves of foreign exchange may swell, but there will be hardly any local currency available with the government as it would not get enough taxes. This aspect of zone development needs to be examined carefully. Of course, the problem may be a special one for Bangladesh due to limited items which are taxed and where taxed on imports contribute about 25% to total tax collection of the government. Price manipulation by the enterprises in the import of materials and other import is also a common feature leading to tax evasion.

Trade Unions : One of the objectives of the development of EPZs is that there shall be no labor union activities in the zones. This is mainly because of the absence of union culture in the country. Two major political parties in the country are constantly engaged in a war like situation which is again very much reflected in the unions also. Strikes are every day affair in Bangladesh. Foreign investors are encouraged to come to Bangladesh because there is no place for labor unions in the zones. But very recently, USA has openly advocated a policy which will compel the enterprises in the zones to permit labor unions. This may be a devastating step for Bangladesh. Bangladesh do not have any development oriented labor unions and if these are allowed to formed, the very base of the zones will be destroyed. Already, foreign investors have threatened to withdraw from the EPZs if unions are allowed to operate. This is a dilemma, for which solution is not in sight right now （because USA is the single largest buyer of EPZ products）. One would have imagined that USA companies operating in the zones will not support the view of American government.

Facilities for Workers : Though is the last section we talked about the denial of permission for labor unions in the zones, a critical situation has arisen because of poor residential facilities around the zones. First, these zones are far from the residential areas which have inefficient and insufficient transport system and secondly, the workers have to live far away from their families. The solution of these problems is entirely dependent on the officials of the zones and the entrepreneurs. But how far we can rely on them to resolve the problems of the workers? Are they working as slaves? Sooner we solve this problem, the better it would be for the country is general and the zones in particular. USA has simply pin-pointed the problem and the responsibility to resolve the same depends on the willingness of the government authorities and the management of enterprises. This must be to the mutual benefit of all the three parties viz. government, enterprises and the workers. Let us hope that an amicable solution emerges soon which should not only pave the way for the survival of existing zones but also be an inducement to prospective investors. This could usher in a new chapter for industrialization to solve the severe economic problems of Bangladesh.

CONCLUSION

From the above discussion, it can be concluded that promotion and development of EPZs can be an effective means for eliminating much of the chronic problems in Bangladesh. Zones can also be effective instruments for updating the age old technology and bringing in new and modern technology in the industrial sector in the country. But the zones are not the magic lanterns to solve all the problems. Hence, besides revolving the issues raised above, attention needs to be paid to the under-mentioned critical problem areas persisting in Bangladesh：

- Chronic shortage of electricity resulting in frequent breakdown of the supply system;
- Transit time through Cittagong and Mongla pots is very long. Even though ports may be in operation, a country-wide strike would jeopardize delivery schedules; and
- Technology transfer in the zones has been negligible, which is contrary to the fundamental objectives of EPZs.

To improve the situation：-

- Rule of law and not rule of thumb should be enforced;
- There has be less of bureaucratic red-tapism and corruption;
- Law and order situation should improve;
- There is need for building industrial peace by social and political consensus; and
- Support services viz., power, water, gas, transport and communication should be improved.

EPZs are only a means and not an end. In order to maximize benefits through the development of EPZs, we have to develop requisite environment to foster and develop local industries. The local industries should be extensively utilized for subcontracting and creating linkages – both forward and backward. In the absence for these linkages, the value added from the EPZ in many cases would be nil. There should be close contact of local industries with the high technology oriented EPZ industries for providing support in respect of technology, management, marketing and human resource development. The existing policy entirely favors the promotion and development of industries within the zones, with little importance given for the development of local industry. There are hardly any positive incentives for the development of industries outside the zones. Thus, though the export trade and earning form EPZ industries are increasing continuously, the imports are also increasing enormously. This is mainly because the local market is increasingly becoming dependent on the imported items. This situation has to be corrected.

If the problems identified in this paper are properly considered, we can visualize a bright future for the EPZs in Bangladesh, which could resolve her chronic problems and thereby accelerate the tempo of economic development.

Annex － 1 :

Indicative List of Industries

- Electrical equipment
- Electric components
- Electronic products
- Software
- Optical goods
- Woven and knitted fabric
- Engineering products
- Leather products
- Foot-wear
- Toys
- Medical and Biological instruments
- Pharmaceutical products
- Plastic molded products
- Industries based on new uses of jute
- Cutting/polishing of precious and semi-precious stones
- Household fittings and equipment
- Specialized ferments
- Head-wear
- Jewelry
- Horological instruments
- Scientific measuring instruments
- Aircraft instruments
- Laboratory ware
- Printing and publishing
- Printing & copying equipments and accessories

- Do-it yourself tools and equipments
- Musical instruments
- Products based on laser technology

NB : This is not exhaustive, only indicative.

Annex – 2 :

Facilities and Incentives

Facilities

1. Land and factory buildings are available on rental basis.

2. Electricity tele-communications, gas and water are provided by the zones.

3. Imports and exports permits are issued by EPZ within 24 hours

4. Work permits are issue by BEPZA.

5. EPZ is a secured and protected area.

6. Recreational facilities are available.

7. Food stuff and beverages are available on payment of nominal fax for foreigners working in EPZs.

8. Potential investors are required to deal only with BEPZA for investment and all other operational purposes.

9. Permanent residentship to a foreign citizen investing a minimum of US$75,000 or equivalent amount （non-repatriable）; similarly citizenship to any foreign citizen investing US$500,000 or transferring US$1,000,000 to any recognized Bangladesh financing institution （non-repatriable）.

Incentives

Fiscal：

Tax Exemptions：

1.0Tax holiday for 10 years.

2.Exemption of income tax on interest on borrowed capital.

3.Relief from double taxation subject to bilateral agreement.

4.Complete exemption from dividend tax for tax holiday period for 3 years subject to certain conditions.

5.Exemption of income tax on salaries of foreign technicians for 3 years subject to certain conditions.

Duty Free Import and Export：

1.Duty Free import of machineries, equipment and raw materials.

2.Duty Free import of three motor vehicles for use of the enterprises in EPZs under certain conditions.

3.Duty Free import of materials for construction of factory building in the zones.

4.Duty Free export of goods produced in the zones.

5.GSP facilities available for export to USA, European and Japanese markets.

6.Most Favored Nation （MFN） status for exports from Bangladesh to USA.

Non Fiscal：

Investment：

1.All foreign investments are secured by law.

2.No ceiling on the extent of foreign investment.

3.Full repatriation of profit and capital permissible.

4.Repatriation of investment including capital gains, if any, permissible.

5.Remittances are allowed in the following cases：

- All post tax profit and dividend on foreign capital
- Savings from earnings, retirement benefits, personal assets of individual on retirement/termination of services.
- Approved royalties and technical fees.

6.No permission is required for expansion of the project or product diversification.

Project Financing and Banking：

1.Off-shore banking facilities are available.

2.Local and international banking facilities are also wide-open.

Import：

1.Freedom from national import policy restrictions.

2.Import of raw materials are also allowed on Documentary Acceptance （DA） basis.

3.Advantage of opening back to back L/C for certain types of industries for import of raw material s.

4.Import of goods from the Domestic Tariff Area （DTA） is permissible.

5.Enterprises can sell 10% of production in the DTA on payment of duties and taxes under certain conditions.

Project Implementation：

1.Re-location of existing industries from abroad allowed.

2.Re-location of industries from one to another zone within the country permissible.

Operation：

1.Sub-contracting within EPZ is allowed.

2.Inter-zone and intra-zone exports permitted.

3.All customs formalities are done at the gate site of the respective factory building within the zone.

4.Permission for import/export is given on the same day.

5.Repairing and maintenance of machineries and capital equipment from domestic tariff area allowed.

Employment：

1.Liberal employment of foreign technicians/experts is allowed.

2.Foreigners employed in the zones enjoy equal rights similar to those of Bangladesh nationals.

3.Law forbids formation of any labor union in the zones. Strike within the zones prohibited.

Support Services：

　　Customs office, post office, medical center, fire station and police station are within the zone.

Annex – 3 :

List of Item Produced by the Enterprises in the Export Processing Zones
（Excepting Garments Industries）

* Toys	*Aluminum ingot
* Cycle	*Audio video tapes
* Zipper	*Electronic goods
* Gloves	*Electronic ballast
* Plywood	*Metal pipe fittings
* Software	*Steel marine chain
* Vinyl belt	*Printed jute bags and ropes
* Plastic bags	*Fishing reel and golf shaft
* Fan motor	*Hanger and its accessories
* Carton box	*Parts of optical instruments
* Crystal blank	*sports shoes and leather shoes
* Parts of cycle	*Woven dyed and printed fabric
* Sweater yarn	* Padding and quilting materials
* Circuit board	*Knitted dyed and printed fabric
* Quartz crystal	*hand bag, school bag & luggage
* Sewing thread	*Marine/industrial mechanical parts
* Plastic granules	*Metal parts for vehicle and other parts
* Electrical goods	*Terry towel, shop towel and surgical towel
* Floppy diskette accessories	*Label, polybag and other garment
* Parts of dye-cast chair.	*Chair, table, basket, folding and compact
* Artificial	

Customs Regulations for EPZs

Details of custom exemptions and regulations are given below：

- Exemption of customs duties and sales tax on goods imported into and exported from EPZs;
- Exemption of s=customs duties and value added tax;
- Exemption of customs duties and sales tax on the import of machineries, equipment and raw materials;
- The customs （EPZs） rules, 1984;
- Export of goods from EPZs to DTA;
- List of items produced by the enterprises in EPZs;
- Customs clearance procedure for imported goods for EPZs;
- Rules relating to supply of construction materials from DTA to EPZs;
- Exemption of customs duties and sales tax on imported motor vehicles for use by the executives of EPZ enterprises;
- Exemption of value added tax on imported motor vehicles for industrial unit in EPZs;
- Exemption of value added tax on imported car and micro-bus for industrial units in EPZs;
- Customs duty and value added tax on imported motor vehicles for industries in EPZs;
- Export of goods of the EPZ industries against payment in foreign currency from special bonded warehouse established for 100% export;
- Exemption of 50% stamp duty on transfer of land in EPZs; and exemption of stamp duty on transfer of land in EPZs.

Income Tax Regulations for EPZs
- Exemption of income tax for EPZs industries;
- Exemption of income tax on the export value;
- Exemption of income tax on salaries of foreign technicians;
- Exemption of 50% tax on export sales for EPZ industries;
- Exemption from dividend tax for tax holiday period for foreign nationals in EPZs;
- Accelerated depreciation for machinery or plant in EPZs; and import into and export from EPZs

二、印度加工出口區（India EPZS）

　　我必須事先聲明我既不是個經理人也不在加工出口區工作，我只是名獨立的學術研究學者，而我目前所做的關於加工出口區的研究報告獲得印度政府的資助。

　　所以我要說的是我的這篇研究並不是代表官方的正式聲明，而只是一份我的學術言論。首先，讓我先告訴您關於印度發展加工區的現況，接下來，我會針對印度這些年將所學的經驗套用於設立加工出口區作簡短的評論。

　　對於印度，我想您會記得它是全世界第三個國家設立加工出口區的。早在 1965 年之前，印度在其西海岸位於旁遮普省設立了 Kandla 加工出口區。到了 1974 年，又在孟買設立了另一個加工出口區，Santa Cruz 電子加工出口區（簡稱 SEEPZ），專門從事電子產品的生產與裝配出口。

　　今日，這兩個加工出口區已出口價值約 3 億的貨品並且雇用了約 50,000 名員工。據統計，在 Kandla 加工出口區約有 80 家開工廠商，而在孟買的 SEEPZ 加工出口區也有約 44 家。在 1981 年，印度政府決定再增設至少四個加工出口區，這四個加工出口區將設立在大城市而不是在落後的偏遠地方（Cochin, Madras 及 Noida 三區在 Delhi 附近，而 Falta 區設在 Calcutta 附近），因為他們考量到大城市已有完善的工業公共建設以及工業活動。

　　雖然這四個尚未正式營運，但已經有一家公司進駐並準備在年底開始生產。其餘的加工出口區將會在 1986 年的三

月正式開始運作。然而印度政府及四個加工出口區的當地政府並不太支持這四個加工區的成立，印度的商業部長宣稱這四個加工區對印度出口業務進行實驗性質的運作，關於這一點，此時政府正遭受國內很大的關注。

這些加工出口區的貨物輸出終點站是到西方市場，除了 Kandla 加工出口區出口之產品有將近 80%的貨物在過去的 6, 7 年間都出口到東德。大致上來說，有 60%的貨物是出口至西方市場，其中包含了 30%是出口到歐洲及美洲市場。

到加工出口區來投資的投資者多是因為穫得財務優惠條件的外國投資人而非本國公司，最好的例子就是通用電器公司。通用電器公司在加州已經有一間很大的工廠，他們在孟買的 SEEPZ 加工出口區也擁有一間電子零件裝配廠。像這樣的公司在 Kandla 加工出口區和孟買的 SEEPZ 大約有 30 多家。隨著德州儀器也選擇於印度設廠，他們將工廠設在印度的南方而不是在加工出口區內。我很榮幸有這個機會能跟德儀的經理見面，他認為這四個加工區未來會成為外國公司選擇設廠的地方，我的研究報告就是要讓大家知道這些加工出口區內還存在哪些大問題需要去克服及改進，對於正發展中的加工區多少會有些助益。

印度政府之所以會成立這些加工出口區其原因是這些投資公司需要有更好的環境和政策來配合，尤其是那些從事大量進口免稅原物料的公司。有些國外當地的公司轉移到這些加工出口區內。這讓我想到在好幾年前政府也實行一個政策，就是鼓勵外國投資人來國內的任何地方設廠，並規定他們要將生產的產品外銷出去。但是印度政府要的不只是這

些；所以這些外國投資者覺得受限於印度的加工出口區政策。因此目前的鼓勵外國投資人的財務優惠條件是為將來成立加工出口區所準備的。

　　為了讓加工區有更好的環境，現在印度政府已著手成立加工出口區管理局。管理局將負責六個加工出口區全部的進出口業務也包括印度銀行，進出口銀行及國外出口部門的業務，並且出口管理局也是這六個加工出口區的最後決策者。國會預計在冬季會期完成立法，出口管理局預計在 1986 年初正式運作。

　　接下來，是我對這些加工出口區概括的意見（或評論）。首先，我們發現將卸貨及倉儲作業與生產結合在一起是沒有產能的。倉庫通常不被鼓勵於加工區內設置。

　　第二點，區內廠商的產品是不允許在國內市場銷售的。

　　第三點，印度政府發覺到成立這些加工出口區並不能改善落後地區的經濟。以 Kandla 加工出口區為例，當初設立Kandla 加工出口區是想要繁榮當地的經濟，後來他們馬上警覺到當地沒有公共設施，缺乏技術，更缺乏通訊及運輸設備，造成 Kandla 加工出口區無法再吸引更多的投資者上門。印度政府的新政策是將新的加工出口區設置接近大城市，因為那裡已具備工業所需要的公共設施。

　　第四點，我們確信加工區內的廠商不會將最新科技引進到我們的國家。因為有些經理人發現即使公司引進了最新科技他們也不願意將這技術傳給區內的其他公司——怕樹立競爭對手。

　　第五點，有時他們相信這些區內的公司會將員工送至擁有先進科技的地區受訓，即使已完成訓練，他們還是相信這些科技還不是最先進的。

　　根據以上所述，我認為加工出口區有兩個目的；一為提昇印度整體出口水平，二是增加全國就業人口。我們必需瞭解加工出口區的出口成長就是全印度出口成長，出口成長也相對刺激勞力提昇及技術成長，最後，我必須指出印度加工出口區並沒有扮演一個將高科技普及的角色，這方面的進度仍然很緩慢。不管如何，SEEPZ 加工出口區在電子產品出口方面已有超過 60% 的供獻。寄望新的加工出口區在往後的十年能超越現況而達到三十億美金的出口產值。

THE EXPORT PROCESSING ZONES OF INDIA

Ashok Kumar Kundra
Ministry of Environment and Forests

I am neither a manager nor a user of an Export Processing Zone, but rather an independent researcher who is supported in my research on export processing zones by the Government of India. So what I am going to say is really not an official statement but the observations of an independent observer. But first, let me give you an update on the Indian export processing zone situation and then very briefly I will try to make some general comments on what India has learned about setting up these zones.

India you will recall was the third country to establish a zone which was in the State of Punjab, the Kandla Export Processing Zone, on the western coast of India, before 1965. It was followed by another zone in Bombay in 1974, the SEEPZ, the Santa Cruz Electronic Export Processing Zone, exclusively for the manufacturing and assembly of electronics goods.

Today the two zones export about 300 million dollars worth of goods and employ about 50,000 people. They have about 80 units working in Kandla and about 44 in SEEPZ in Bombay. In 1981 the Government of India decided to establish four more zones in the country. It was decided that these new zones would not be used to promote regional development of backward areas of the country, so they were established in cities （Cochin, Madras, Noida near Delhi, and Falta near Calcutta） which already have industrial infrastructure and some industrial activity going on.

These four zones are not yet operational, but the first unit in one of the new zones will start producing by the end of this year. The other zones will become operational by some time in March of 1986. The Government of India and the State governments are nor strong supporters of these zones. The Minister of Commerce has said that these zones will be a kind of an experiment for Indian export activity, which at the moment under the present government is now receiving the greatest publicity in the country.

The destination of export in these zones has been to western countries except that Kandla has provided 88% of its exports to Ease Germany for the last 6 or 7 years. However, overall, 60% of exports go to western markets including 30% to the European and American markets.

The investors in these zones are by large non residents who invested because of the fiscal incentives that have been allowed. The best example is Standard Electronics which has a very large facility in California and which established component assembly in SEEPZ. There are about 30 other companies in Kandla and SEEPZ in the foreign products division distributing a variety of other products. With the arrival of Texas Instruments, not in one of the zones but in an area in South India, the managers that I have spoken to recently in Bombay are very keen that these new zones will become the exclusive locations for foreign companies. My survey is to define the biggest problems within these zones so that the right kind of environment will be created in the new zones as they grow.

The reason the Indian government establish these zones is that companies needed a better environment and policy package to work in, especially to handle large volume imports of duty-free raw materials. Some companies have shifted from the domestic market to these zones. This occurred a couple of years ago when the government also had a policy of starting projects anywhere in the country and import units could establish themselves anywhere in the country provided they agree to export their output. The Government wanted out of that; so the exporters are being confined to the Indian EPZs. The incentives package is not in preparation for use in future export processing zones.

And to follow up on this the government is now preparing the administrative setup, the Export Processing Zone Authority, which will manage imports and exports at all six zones of the departments including the Bank of India, the Export Import Bank, and Foreign Export Department. The body will have final decision making authority in the managing of the zones. Legislation is expected to be introduced in the winter session of Parliament, and the Authority is expected to be in effect by the beginning of 1986.

Now to my general comments on the export processing zones. First, we have found out that combining break-bulk and warehousing activities with manufacturing is not productive. Warehousing is generally not encouraged within these processing zones.

Secondly, the manufacturers in the EPZs are generally not allowed in the domestic market.

Third, India has found that these zones are not a way to carry out regional development in backward areas. Kandla was set up to develop a backward area; it was soon discovered that the lack of infrastructure facilities, the lack of skills, the lack of communications and transport facilities and other problems prevented Kandla from attracting new export companies in large numbers. India's new policy is to put such EPZs near larger cities with industrial infrastructure already developed so they will work.

Fourth, we now believe the zones will not serve to bring the latest technology to the country. The Indian zone managers have found that even when a firm brings in new technology it is very reluctant to pass it on to other firms within the area – a logical position for a competitor.

Fifth, sometimes it is believed that the zones would train the workforce in higher technological areas. Even when this is done, there is a belief that the technology is not very high.

I say these things because I now believe that these zones should have two objectives：1）to raise the whole level of Indian exports and 2）to increase employment within the country. We must come to understand that exports from these zones are effectively everybody's export. Exports of everybody's output encourages the development of labor and expands the development parameter. Lastly, may I just say that the India Export Processing Zones have not yet played a tremendous role in high technology exposure for the country; their progress in this area is still very slow. However the SEEPZ contributes today more than 60% of the electronics export of our country. It is our hope that the new zones will follow in its path with something like 3000 million dollars worth of export in the next 10 years.

三、大韓民國加工出口區
（Republic of Korea EPZS）

（一）政策

　　韓國加工出口區的興建可視為全韓國發展策略計劃的一部份。在 1960 年代底，韓國政府決定要進行一項策略來吸引投資，於 1970 年。頒布了自由出口區設立法案。

　　加工出口區的設立是為了幫助經濟發展以吸引外國投資，技術移轉，推銷出口以及增加就業率。另外，韓國政府藉著興建加工出口區致力於促進地域性平衡的工業發展。馬山加工出口區於 1970 年成立，隨即 Iksan 加工出口區也在 1973 年成立。

（二）優惠條件

　　加工出口區為設廠的公司均提供「全套性」的服務。所有關於外國投資進駐事宜及進出口工廠設備核准事宜皆由管理局全權處理。為了方便投資人，一切有關工廠建造的問題均由自由出口區管理局來負責。

　　工廠用廠房及發展小塊用地均以較市價低 1/5 計算租金給投資人。租期可長達 10 年之久另外可在延長 10 年。只要獲得營運許可證，就馬上可以入廠開始營運。

標準廠房租金（請參照表一，Table-1）：

稅金的優惠條件：

商業稅及所得稅——

> 1、享有 100%的削減以及從營業的那天起可享有 7 年
> 的免稅。
>
> 2、在接下來的 3 年享有 50%削減以及免稅。

房地產稅，獲得稅，土地稅及註冊稅——

> 1、享有 100%的削減以及 5 年的免稅。
>
> 2、在接下來的 3 年享有 5%削減以及免稅。

企業稅及外國投資所得稅退稅——

> 1、從營業的那天起算可享有 7 年 100%的減免稅。
>
> 2、在接下來的 3 年享有 50%削減以及免稅。

關稅，特別貨物稅及首次取得的資本貨物增值稅——

> 1、享有 100%的減免。

　　在自由出口區內所有進口的原物料以及消耗品是免繳交關稅的。所以，在區內當區內進口的原物料被加工再輸出銷售時。不需要繁複的關稅退稅手續，目前當區內進口的原物料被加工再銷售至當地市場時卻要徵收關稅。從 1999 年 1 月至今，就開始針對進口的原物料徵稅了。

（三）馬山加工出口區及 Iksan 加工出口區簡介

1、馬山加工出口區

　　馬山加工出口區是一個沿海地區工業區位於韓國的東南方，距離南方的漢城 412 公里而距離西方的斧山港市約 40 公里。總面積有 793,010 平方公尺且劃分為兩個區域。區

253

內有 31 家外國投資公司，17 家公司是屬於企業合資經營的；
本國公司 31 家。這些公司生產的產品有 98% 外銷出口。馬
山加工出口區就佔了有 79 家公司，員工數達到 12,987 人。

這些跨國企業之中包括有：SONY（松下企業），SANYO
（三洋），NOKIA（諾基亞），CASIO（卡西歐），以及
CITIZEN（星辰錶）。設在馬山加工出口區的用意是要吸引
外國資本家來此投資的而它也被世界加工出口區協會
（WEPZA）公認為標準的工業區。

自建廠房面積（請參照表三，Table-3）：

標準廠房面積（請參照表四，Table-4）：

2、Iksan 加工出口區

Iksan 加工出口區距離南方的漢城約 225 公里而開車需 3
小時即可到達，且它非常靠近 Honam 的高速公路以及鐵路。
Iksan 市的人口數約 330,000 人。Iksan 加工出口區的面積有
292,616 平方公尺，區內有 26 家公司，員工數約有 1,500 人。

導致加工出口區成功或失敗的因素：

● 租金便宜：

● 政府扮演加工出口區發展和管理最主要的角色；

● 提供」全套性」的服務；

● 穩定勞資雙方的關係；

● 吸引外商在國內其他地區投資。

馬山加工出口區及 Iksan 加工出口區所面臨的下列問
題：

　　馬山加工出口區沒有足夠的空地讓公司擴廠。此外，外國公司的家數在逐漸地減少。Iksan 加工出口區的設置地點不理想，所以大型企業都不願來此設廠。

（四）加工出口區的遠景

　　加工出口區有需要轉變為自由貿易區。對於韓國目前的發展階段來說，加工出口區的角色不再侷限只是簡單的加工區而以。所以有必要轉變為吸引外國投資以及擴張國際貿易。

　　加工出口區將由原來的生產導向轉型為多功能的階段來從事國際貿易包括成為配銷中心，倉庫以及 R&D 機構。

　　此外，土地應該是要購買而不是用租的而且外國投資的角色應該要被加強。這樣這些區才能被稱之為新的自由貿易區。

REPUBLIC OF KOREA

Hyeyoung Cho
Korea Industrial Complex Corporation

GOVERNMENT POLICY FOR THE ESTABLISHMENT OF EPZs AND INCENTIVES FOR INVESTORS

Policy

The establishment of EPZs in Korea can be seen in the context of the national development strategy. Towards the end of 1960s, the Korean government decided to pursue an active policy to attract investments. In 1970, Free Export Zone Establishment Act was enacted.

As per the stated objectives, an EPZ was to facilitate economic development by inducing foreign investment, technology transfer and know-how, promoting export and increasing employment. In addition, the Korean government aimed at regionally balanced industrial development through EPZs. Masan FEZ in Kynongnam Province was notified in 1970 and Iksan FEZ in Chonbuk Province came into being in 1973.

The Ministry of Commerce, Industry and Energy is currently contemplating building a new gateway towards the Asia-Pacific era in the 21 Century. One of the ideas floated for this purpose is to transform the newly constructed port （the Kunsan National Industrial Estate） into a sophisticated FEZ. However, as the location of IFEZ is not suitable, Kunsan port city is being considered as a substitute.

Incentives

Units located in the EPZs are provided 「One-stop」 services. All the administrative jobs relating to foreign investment permissions for entry and factory construction and approvals for export-import are under the direct control of the administration office. Investors can do their business without facing any operational problems. For the convenience of investors, factory construction and construction related works in the zone are taken care of by the FEZ authorities while city or provincial authorities deal with permissions for construction, repairing and extension work.

Built factory space and developed plots are leased to investors at low rentals at one-fifth of the market rents. The leasing period is for ten years which can be extended for another ten years. In the standardized factory building, operations can begin as soon as production facilities are provided after obtaining entry permission.

No additional registration procedures are required. Rent for the privately constructed factory building in MAFEZ is charged at the rate of 124 Korean Won/m^2 （US$10,334/$m^2$） per month. For the standardized factory buildings, rates of rent for different floors are detailed in Table-1.

Table-1 : Rent for the Standardized Factory （MAFEZ）（1,200 Won/US$, a month）

	1st Floor	2ed Floor	3ed Floor	4th Floor
Korean Won	925/m^2	822/m^2	793/m^2	398 m^2/
US$	77.1/m^2	68.5/m^2	66.1 m^2/	33.2/m^2

Foreign investors are entitled to a wide spectrum of tax incentives in the FEZs, depending upon the type of business pursued by them. In other areas, however, tax benefits are given only for hifh-technology businesses. These incentives have been listed in Table-2.

Table-2 : Tax Incentives

Nature of Tax	Period & Extent of Tax Reduction & Exemption
Corporate tax, income tax	■ 100% reduction & exemption for 7 years from the date of starting business ■ For next 3-years 50% reduction & exemption
Property tax, acquisition tax, aggregate land tax, and registration tax	■ 100% reduction & exemption for 5 years ■ For the next 3-year 5% reduction & exemption
Corporate tax, income tax on return from foreign investment	■ 100% reduction & exemption for 7-year from the date of commencement of business ■ For the next 3-year 50% reduction & exemption
Duties, special excise tax, value added tax on induction of capital goods	■ 100% reduction exemption

Customs duties on all the imported raw material and consumable are exempt in the FEZs. Accordingly, zones do not require complicated tariff refund procedures when exporting products manufactured out of imported raw materials. However, at present, duties are imposed on goods for domestic sales, which are manufactured out of imported raw materials. Since January 1999, taxation system of levying duties on imported raw materials has come into force.

Resident companies in the FEZs are granted composite permission for undertaking production, export and import activities in relaxation of various provisions.

BRIEF DESCRIPTION OF MAFEZ AND IFEZ MAFEZ

MAFEZ is a coastal industrial complex located in southeast coast of Korea, 412 km south from the capital city of Seoul and 40 km west the city of Pusan. It has a total area of 793,010 ㎡, which is divided into two sections. It has 31 fully foreign owned companies, 17-joint venture companies and 31 domestically owned companies. Most of these companies export up to 98% of their production. In all there are 79 companies in the zone, which have 12,987 employees.

Among the multinational companies are included, SONY, SANYO, NOKIA, CASIO, and CITIZEN. MAFEZ was set up to attract foreign capital and has been accredited by the WEPZA（World Export Processing Zone Association）.

 加工出口區與經濟發展

Table – 3 : area for the Privately Constructed Factories

(Unit : ㎡)

	Total Area	Factory Land Area	Leased Area
Factory Section 1	535,136	409,483	409,483
Factory Section 2	257,874	192,688	192,688
Total	793,010	602,171	602,171

Details relating to total area in Section 1 and Section 2 of the Zone and the factory land and the leased land are given in Table – 3. Details of standardized factory leased area are in Table – 4.

Table – 4 : Area of Standardized Factories

(Unit : ㎡)

Total Area	Factory area	Leased Area	Vacant Area
89,952	83,043	74,086	8,957

IFEZ

Iksan FEZ is 225 km about 3 hours' driver and south from Seoul. It is very close to the Honam （Taejon-Kwangju） Highway and Railroad. Iksan city has total population of 330,000. IFEZ has an area measuring 292,616 ㎡. Number of operational companies in the zone is 26 which employ about 1,500 persons.

PERFORMANCE OF OCCUPANT FIRMS, IMPACT ON THE LOCAL ECONOMY AND BY THE GLOBAL ECONOMY

Investment in the Zones

Despite decrease in the number of firms in FEZs, especially in MAFEZ since the mid-1970, there has been gradual increase in investment as is evident from Table – 5.

Table – 5 : Investment and the Participating Enterprises in FEZs

Year	Number of Firms			Investment （US$ millions）		
	MAFEZ	IFEZ	Total	MAFEZ	IFEZ	Total
1970	4	0	4	1.4	0	1.4
1975	105	6	111	89.0	3.3	92.3
1980	88	12	100	112.9	7.5	120.4
1985	79	20	98	125.9	14.3	140.2
1990	72	25	97	215.8	44.4	260.2
1995	73	24	97	235.3	51.1	286.4
1999	79	26	105	249.5	40.9	290.4

Export Performance

The rate of export growth of EPZs was highest during 1971 – 1976. During 1977 – 1979 also increase in exports was substantial. However, the share of FEZs in the total exports by

1998 was around 1.9% only.

Table – 6 : Export Performance of FEZs

（Unit：US$ million）

Year	Exports			
	Total	MAFEZ（%）	IFEZ（%）	FEZ Total
1971	1,067	0.9（0.1）	0	0.9（0.1）
1976	7,715	303.0（3.9）	5.3（0.1）	308.3（4.0）
1980	17,504	628.1（3.6）	46.1（0.3）	674.3（3.9）
1985	30,283	809.3（2.7）	80.5（0.3）	889.8（3.0）
1990	64,982	1,405.4（2.2）	127.3（0.2）	1,532.7（2.3）
1995	125,233	2,400.9（1.9）	132.1（0.1）	2,533.0（2.0）
1998	132,313	2,378.1（1.8）	96.2（0.1）	2,474.3（1.9）

Employment

FEZ employment peaked in 1987 at 41,518. Thereafter, it gradually came down owing to worldwide economic stagnation. Employment during 1999 was around 15,000. Zone-wise employment details are in Table – 7.

Table – 7 : Employment in FEZs

（Persons）

Year	MAFEZ	IFEZ	Total
1971	1,248	0	1,248
1975	22,586	333	22,919
1980	28,532	2,700	31,232
1985	28,983	3,801	32,784
1987	36,411	5,107	41,518

1990	19,616	3,608	23,224
1995	14,736	2,005	16,741
1999	12,987	1,546	14,533

Foreign Investment

MAFEZ has 79 resident companies of which 48 are foreign companies. But of 48 foreign enterprises, 40 are Japanese, which have invested US$169 million. Besides 2 companies are from USA, 2 from Germany, one from Netherlands, one from Finland, one from Singapore and one from Taiwan respectively.

Table – 8 : Resident Companies and Investment by Country

（Unit：Company, US$ Thousand, %）

Country	Investment		Joint Ventures	Total	
	Domestic Companies	Fully Foreign Owned Companies		Number of Companies	Investment
South Korea	31			31	57,981（23.2）
Japan		27	13	40	169,168（67.6）
EU		3	1	4	22,771（9.1）
USA		2	1	2	187（0.1）
Others			2	2	303（0.1）
Total	31	32	17	79	250,410（100.0）

Impact on the Local Economy

During the formative years, EPZs had substantial impact on regional development as a result of expanded employment opportunities, increase in wages and social overhead

263

expenditures. But recently the importance of EPZs in the development of Masan and Iksan area has relatively declined due to new and substantially large adjacent industrial areas, which are under development.

●Major contribution of MAFEZ to the regional economy was by way of US$80 million in wages and US$183 million in supply purchases every month during 1995. In addition, many participating enterprises source parts and components from outside subcontractors, though it is difficult to assess the impact on this account on regional economic development.

●In 1995, about 45% of inputs used in MAFEZ were supplied by the local firms in the Koreasn customs territory. As many as 40 MAFEZ firms obtained production materials, such as parts, components and other materials from 363 locally sub-contracted firms.

Factors leading to success or failure of EPZs

Following factors account for successful functioning of an EPZ：

●Leasing of land at confessional rates;

●Leading role played by government for the development and management of EPZs;

●Provision of one-stop services;

●Stable labor-employer relations; and

●Attracting inward investment to other areas in Korea.

MAFEZ and IFEZ are faced with following problems：

MAFEZ has insufficient space, especially for the firms,

which plan to expand. Besides, these have been decrease in number of foreign companies. IFEZ has unfavorable location. As a result there is absence of well-performing large enterprises.

ORGANIZATION, MANAGEMENT, AND PERFORMANCE OF EPZs

EPZs are managed by the administrative offices, which are sub-offices of the Ministry of Commerce, Industry and Energy. Zones provide following services：

- Custody of goods and state-owned property;
- Receipt of revenues and lease of land and standard factory contracts;
- Licensing and supervision of supporting firms;
- Management of utilities and welfare facilities;
- Industrial accident insurance service;
- Labor-employer cooperation service;
- Safety management;
- Receipt and processing of foreign investment application authorization;
- Export and import licensing inspection and export promotion matters; and
- Approval for temporary removal of goods from the zone.

FUTURE PROSPECTS OF EPZs

There is need for change of the concept from EPZs to FTZ（Free Trade Zone）.There are limits to the role of simple processing zones in the present development stage of Korea. There is need to shift the focus to induce foreign investment and extend international trade. It is desirable to move the concept from export base to acquiring strategic position for international trade both export and import.

EPZs will have to change from production-oriented to multi-functional estates for international trade including distribution center, warehouse and R&D facilities.

Besides, there should be segmentation in the FTZs and differentiation in allotment of sites. Land purchase rather than leasing alone should be introduced and the role of foreign investment should be reinforced. These zones should be designated as new FTZs.

四、馬來西亞加工出口區（Malaysia EPZS）

（一）政府政策對於興建自由工業區

馬來西亞在 1957 年 8 月完成獨立後即於 1962 年開始實行工業化政策，其第一步為完成進口替代政策。在 1960 年代工業的快速成長起因於進口替代和出口擴張以及國內市場的需求。進口替代的過程在 1968 年完成的情況還算不錯，木製品，煙草，化學製品以及橡膠製品工廠等均被認為有高度可能性足以自給自足的產業。然而，馬來西亞政府也瞭解到進口替代政策的限制已經感到疲乏而且高度工業成長非這項短期性政策能夠滿足。

為了幫助長期工業成長，馬來西亞政府支持採用以出口導向工業化形式的對外政策。在 1970 年到 1990 年間，根據這項新的經濟政策，馬來西亞憑藉著出口導向政策已經成為工業發展的先鋒部隊。

（二）自由工業區的創始

馬來西亞建設自由工業區的兩大主要原因為增加就業機會及達到馬來西亞經濟改善。

失業在低度開發國家是很嚴重的問題，其經濟特性是低資本形成，高自然資源, 缺乏實質的公共建設及出口僅仰賴一，二項農產品。馬來西亞設置自由工業區的三項目的：第

267

一是創造就業機會，第二是吸引外國投資，第三是發展製造工業，這也是馬來西亞經濟最主要的一環，需要指出的即加工出口區或自由貿易區已於 1990 年重新命名為「自由工業區」，其原因是在這個區內並無實質的貿易，故過去應是錯誤的命名。

第二階段的工業發展馬來西亞排定為高科技工業，並列入第二階段工業主計劃之內（1996~2005），焦點轉向高附加價值及資本密集投資；勞動力短缺促使馬來西亞推向長遠工業發展計劃；除設置出口區之外，馬來西亞也提供特別優惠給位在自由工業區之外，具有生產製造倉儲的廠商，（LMWs），LMWs 法優惠規定僅對出口 66% 自製產品的廠商。

馬來西亞自由工業區見表 1：

（三）政府態度以及政策方針對於自由工業區興建和投資者的優惠條件

馬來西亞政府在 1965-1970 年間對於第一階段經濟的政策方針為加強工業的多樣化經營與進口替代政策。其目的為強調以及克服過度依賴在橡膠製品和錫製品以及大量進口的加工物品。在 1968 年馬來西亞政府政策改變於是另外頒布一項投資優惠法案來鼓勵外國投資人將廠房設置在馬來西亞。這代表進入了第二階段。不同的優惠政策包括有免稅，免進口稅和資本津貼補助。而且馬來西亞政府有意重組其經濟結構，將製造加工業加入原有的農業與礦產業。除此

之外，製造加工業特別是指自由工業區，將替年輕族群創造更多的就業機會。第三階段起始於第四個馬來西亞計劃，以經營多樣化方案為目的來發展製造加工業作為馬來西亞經濟的帶頭工業。為期十年的工業總體規劃（1996-2005）已被計劃準備用來實現多樣化經營的目的。而服務產業將被視為第三重要發展重心當製造加工業和農業已被視為重要收入來源。政府在三個經濟階段轉移的政策方針如下：

● 在第一階段為藉由鼓勵進口替代來挽救國際匯兌；

● 在第二階段為在投資優惠政策法案實行期間創造就業機會；

● 在第三階段為改善本身的競爭優勢來爭取更多的國際貿易；

馬來西亞本身的國內消費市場雖然很小，但是確有非常高的購買力。所以馬來西亞政府的優惠政策允許銷售至國內市場的產品有高達60%的產品可以在自由工業區內生產，其目的在於擴大國內消費市場，增加全國稅收而且同時迎合國外市場。加工出口區以及科學園區的相關法令規章已經過特別擬定去除繁文縟節已鼓勵外國投資人。除此之外，特別的優惠條件也提供來鼓勵自由工業區的工業發展，包括進口的機器設備和原物料均不需要繳納關稅。在自由工業區內經營的公司也不需要繳交所得稅。對於要購買或者是建造工廠設施也提供財務援助。

（四）企業促銷和優惠條件的種類提供給投資者以及投資者撤銷投資的原因

下列企業被認可可進駐自由工業區：

● 電器與電子產業；

● 機器製造；

● 金屬裝配產業；

● 化學產業；

● 不含金屬的礦物質產業；

● 塑膠製品產業；

然而，某些產業已確實進駐自由工業區但最後卻失敗的產業有：

● 電器與電子產業；

● 化學產業；

● 金屬裝配產業；

● 紡織產業；

下列優惠條件由馬來西亞提供以吸引外國投資人進駐自由工業區：

● 由自由工業區當局提供簡單的程序以及一元化的服務；

● 免課稅；

● 低廉的設廠費用；

● 提供有技能的勞工；

● 提供當地有強大購買力的市場；

●提供實質上的公共建議例如有電力，水，以及電信設施；

（五）加工出口區與科學工業園區設置與管理的成功或失敗的因素

馬來西亞認為在境內設置自由工業區是成功的案例，因為區內的空間只要有單位空出，馬上就有別的企業進駐。使得自由工業區管理成功的因素有：

●由馬來西亞政府透過 MITI 以及政府經濟發展協會共同合作來制定適當的計劃；

●稅金以及市場的優惠條件；

●提供一元化的服務；

●提供充足有技能的勞工；

MALAYSIA

Jamaluddin Che Sab
MARA Institute of Technology

GOVERNMENT POLICIES FOR ESTABLISHMENT OF FREE INDUSTRIAL ZONES

Malaysia began its industrialization policy in 1962 after achieving independence in August 1957. The first step towards industrialization was the implementation of an import substitution strategy. The rapid industrial growth in the 1960s was due to import substitution and expansion of exports and domestic demand (Hoffman & Tan, 1975). By 1968 the process of import substitution was complete in so far as good, wood products, tobacco, chemicals, and rubber product industries are concerned and the high potential self-sufficiency in these sectors was visible. (Chee, Donald Lee & Foo, 1981). However, the Malaysian government realized that the limits of import substitution had been stretched and high industrial growth could not be further sustained by this short-term gap policy.

Helen Hughes(1971)argued in favor of an outward-looking strategy in the form of export-oriented industrialization for sustaining long term industrial growth. Under its New Economic

Policy （NEP） during 1970 to 1990, Malaysia has implemented the export oriented strategy for spearheading industrial development.

INCEPTION OF FREE INDUSTRIAL ZONES（FIZs）

Free Industrial Zones （FIZs） were set up in Malaysia for two main reasons. These were to generate employment and achieve diversification of Malaysian economy.

Unemployment is a serious socio-economic problem in less developed countries （LDCs）.These economies are characterized by low capital formation, rich natural resources, lack of physical infrastructure and export dependence on one or two agricultural products. There were three major objectives for setting up FIZs in Malaysia. The first was to create job opportunities for the young population in Malaysia. The second was to attract foreign investment into the country and third to develop the manufacturing industry as a major sector of the Malaysian economy. It should be noted that the export processing zones or free trade zones （FTZs） as they were known earlier were rechristened as 「Free Industrial Zones」 （FIZs） in 1990. This was due to the fact that as trading was not carried out in these zones, terming them as Free Trade Zones was a misnomer.

In the second phase of industrial development, Malaysia has accorded priority to hi-tech industries under its Second Industrial Master Plan （1996-2005）. The focus has shifted towards high value-added and capital-intensive investment. The shortage of labor has prompted Malaysia to embark on this strategic move in its long-term industrial planning. Besides setting up specialized export zones, Malaysia has also provided special incentives for firms to be located outside the FIZs in the form of licensed manufacturing warehouses（LMWs）. LMWs status will only be given to firms, which export 60% of their production.

Malaysia has also extablished a special economic zone for Information Technology which in known as the Multi Media Super Corridor （MSC）. This 15x50 km multimedia economic zone provides for future business locations utilizing e-commerce in their business operations.

Table – 1 : Free Industrial Zones in Malaysia

Name of FIZ	Date of Inauguration
1. Bayan Leaps FIZ	27 August 1971
2. Sungei Way FIZ	11 February 1972
3. Batu Berendam FIZ	29 November 1973
4. Seberang Prai FIZ	10 October 1974
5. Pasir Gudang FIZ	3 August 1974
6. Jelapang FIZ	20 October 1989

Source：Royal Customs and Excise Department Report, 1977

ROLE AND FUNCTIONS OF FREE INDUSTRIAL ZONES IN THE PREVAILING ECONOMIC RECESSION IN ASEAN

Malaysia and the other ASEAN nations have gone through a period of economic turmoil during 1997 and 1998. All the ASEAN nations, with exception of Malaysia have sought

International Monetary Fund's （IMF） assistance to rescue their badly affected economies. The economic recession faced by the ASEAN countries, though had profound effect on the ASEAN stock markets, its impact on investments in manufacturing activities in the FIZs has been minimal. Withdrawals of investment from FIZs in Malaysia has also been negligible. FIZs would continue to provide employment opportunities and facilitate technology transfer to the small and medium industry. Malaysia would have to generate home-grown technologies in order to meet the needs of the foreign companies in the FIZs.

GENERAL CONDITIONS OF NATIONAL ECONOMY AND LIVING CONDITIONS OF THE PEOPLE BEFORE THE ESTABLISHMENT OF FIZs

Malaysia is basically a newly industrialized economy. Prior to 1968 it was an agricultural economy with total dependence on exports of its natural resources for export earnings. Rubber and tin industry from the backbone of its economy. Malaysia's economic diversification strategy (First Malaysia Plan 1971-1975) saw the introduction of palm oil and petroleum into its economy.

Malaysia has a total area of 329,733km2 and the population in 1998 was 21.7 million. The most pcpulated city is Kuala Lumpur which has an area of 243km2 and total population of 1,145,342. The second most populated city is Johor Bahru with an area of 1,181km2 and a population of 705,432. The third largest city is Georgetown with an area of 119km2 and its population is 395,714.

The value of Malaysia's gross national product (GNP) in 1970 was RM11.1 billion (at 1965 prices) with a per capita income of RM980. The rate of unemployment was 8% in 1970 as compared to 6% in 1960 and 1965.

Communication Facilities in Malaysia

Malaysia has telecommunication links with other parts of the world via satellite communications. The rate of occupancy of domestic lines is also very high for long distance as well as local calls. Fax and telex facilities are also being used extensively. Internet facilities are available and their usage is widespread both for commercial and official purposes. The Multimedia Super Corridor （MSC） would further promote use of these facilities and business transactions through e-commerce.

GOVERNMENT ATTITUDE AND POLICY GUIDELINES TOWARDS THE ESTABLISHMENT OF FIZs AND INCENTIVES FOR INVESTORS

As mentioned earlier, Malaysian government policy guidelines for economic development in the first phase had laid emphasis on industrial diversification and import substitution during 1965-1970. The objective of this policy was to address and overcome the over-dependence on rubber and tin and high imports of manufactured goods. In 1968 the policy was changed by enacting the Investment Incentives Act to encourage foreign investors to set-up their manufacturing plants in Malaysia. This marked the second phase of the policy. Various incentives in the form of tax holidays, import duty waiver and capital allowances were given. In 1970 the Pioneer Industries Act waved the way to the Free Industrial Zones Act. The Malaysian government is in favor of restructuring the economy in such a way, that the manufacturing sector would supplement the agriculture and mining sectors. Besides, manufacturing sector, especially the FIZs, would generate employment opportunities for the young population. In the third phase beginning with Fourth Malaysia Plan （1986-1990）, the economic diversification program was continued with a view to developing manufacturing as the lead sector in the Malaysian economy. A 10-year Industrial Master Plan （1996-2005） was prepared for realizing this strategy of diversification. The services sector has been earmarked to be the third sector after manufacturing and agriculture as the major source income. The main factors responsible for the shift in policy guidelines for the three phases were to：

- Save foreign exchange by encouraging import substitution in the first phase;
- Create job opportunities in the second phase during the Investment Incentives Act period; and
- Improve the competitive advantage of the country in international trade in the third phase during the IMP I （1986-1995） and IMP 2 （1996-2005） periods.

　　General manpower light industry, general precision light industry, zone-based precision industry and heavy industries in steel-making and automotive industry are given priority. The first priority is for zone-based precision industry, especially in electronics and electrical industries. The second priority is for heavy in steel and automotive industries and the third is for general precision light industry.

In developing export-processing zones, Malaysia has the advantage of abundant supply of semi-skilled and skilled manpower. However, there is a shortage of general or unskilled labor due to its small population of 21.7 million （1998）. Therefore, it is planned to attract high value-added manufacturing industries by upgrading the skills of workers. With this end in view, greater emphasis has been given to technical and vocational training in the educational system in Malaysia. Malaysia has abundant supply of natural resources for the development of resource-based industries in rubber, tin, palm oil, wood and petroleum. Raw materials for electronic industries are mainly imported. An important objective of industrialization policy is to use and enhance the local raw material content in the manufacturing sector.

As regards, capital supply, Malaysia is unable to fully meet the requirement of manufacturing sector. Foreign investment is therefore needed for financing industrial development in Malaysia. The objective is to improve the capital formation of the country and develop local financial market.

Malaysia has reached the threshold of high-tech industrial technology and advanced management technology. The objective is to increase the competitive strength of the country and to achieve the status of an industrialized nation.

Malaysia has a small domestic market, but with a high purchasing power. The Malaysian government has by way of incentive allowed the domestic sale of the product manufactured in FIZs up to 60%. The objective is to expand the domestic market, increase national revenues and also to cater to foreign markets. The laws and regulations for the export processing zones and science parks have specially been formulated to encourage foreign investments with minimum government red tape. Besides, special incentives are given for encouraging industrial development in FIZs. There is no tax or customs duty for machinery, equipment and raw materials, which are imported for own use. No income tax is levied on the companies operating in FIZs. Financing facilities are available for buying or constructing factory buildings.

NECESSARY LOCAL CONDITIONS FOR SITE SELECTION

Extent of Local Industry Support

Malaysia has a strong small and medium enterprise （SME） network of basic industries such as mechanical, electrical, electronics and chemical industries. These SMEs have the capacity and technical expertise to provide small components and engineering services for the foreign companies in the FIZs. Even though SMEs have capabilities to act as vendors and suppliers to foreign manufacturing concerns, the general practice is to outsource major components from the host country. Cost considerations and established business relations with the SME component suppliers are important factors for outsourcing rather than procuring them locally.

Accommodation and Entertainment

Most of the FIZ locations have within 15km radius five-star hotels. Georgetown, Batu Berendam, Pasir Gudang, Sungei Way and Sama Jaya （Kuching, Sarawak） all have five-star hotels.

Malaysia has five TV stations, two of which offer cable TV facilities. High-class cinemas are available in the cities of West Malaysia. There are numerous golf courses, parks, museums and picnic grounds.

Foreign Language Schools （International Schools）

Malaysia has international schools strictly for children of foreign expatriates. Facilities for Chinese education are available in the Malaysian education system. Besides, there is a Japanese International School in Subang. English is widely taught together with the Malay language from primary to tertiary schooling. The University of Malaya has a Japanese Learning Centre while the MARA Institute of Technology has a Korean Language Centre.

Commuting Facilities

Malaysia has an extensive network of highways throughout the country. The road conditions are good and well maintained. Highway users have to pay toll when using these facilities.

Employee Welfare

Foreign companies operating in the FIZs either provide accommodation allowance or dormitories for their employees. In addition, the enterprises provide transportation to and from the factory sites. Employees in FIZs are required to pay for their food in the cafeteria run by the enterprises. The companies, however, arrange health care benefits and recreation facilities for their employees.

Klang Valley provides commuter services. The capital city of Kuala Lumpur has light rail transport system which crisscrosses the city of Kuala Lumpur and its suburbs.

CATEGORIES OF INDUSTRIES PROMOTED, INCENTIVES FOR INVESTMENT AND REASONS FOR WITHDRAWAL OF INVESTMENT

Following industries have been identified for location in the FIZs：
- Electrical and electronic product;
- Machinery manufacturing;
- Fabricated metal products;
- Chemical and chemical products;
- Non-metallic mineral products; and
- Plastic products.

However, industrial units actually set up in the FIZs fall in the following categories：

- Electrical and electronic products;
- Chemical and chemical products;
- Fabricated metal products; and
- Textiles.

Three categories of industries which virtually account for total investment are electronics and electrical industry （80%）, chemical and chemical products （15%） and machinery manufacturing （5%）.

Investment into FIZs has come from eight countries, of which USA, Japan and Singapore are the most prominent.

Following incentives have attracted foreign investors to FIZs in Malaysia：

- Simplified procedures and one-stop services by FIZs authorities;
- Tax exemptions;
- Low set-up costs;
- Availability of skilled labor;
- Strong local market in terms of purchasing power; and
- Excellent physical infrastructure such as power supply, water and telecommunication facilities.

Four cases of withdrawal of foreign investment from FIZs have been reported. Three of these were from the Bayan Leaps FIZ and one from Prai FIZ. In all the withdrawal cases of Bayan Leaps FIZ enterprises were engaged in labor intensive manufacturing operations. They had exhausted their tax holiday incentive period and were looking for cheaper alternative locations in the ASEAN region and China. The Prai FIZ withdrawal case involved investment in the electronics component industry. There was no withdrawal in the Sungei Way FIZ area. The government has taken remedial measures by arranging regular investment promotion campaigns overseas. In line with the Second Industrial Master Plan （1996-2005） the focus is on high capital-intensive industry. The Malaysian Industrial Development Authority （MIDA） has, therefore, reviewed the criteria for selecting foreign investors. The strategic move was made to overcome the shortage of general unskilled labor in Malaysia.

ZONE PERFORMANCE： IMPACT ON THE LOCAL ECONOMY AND BY THE WORLD ECONOMY

Free Industrial Zones contribute 50% to the total exports from Malaysia. The value-added content which averaged 7.4% during 1986-1990 came down to an average of 1.1% during 1991-1995 period. This is attributable to the nature of electronics and electrical industry, which is dominated by multinational corporations. These units are involved mainly in the assembly and packaging of imported electronic parts and components for re-export and have low value addition.

During 1991-1995, labor productivity for the FIZs was estimated at 12.3% compared to 1.6% during 1986-1990. Process efficiency also increased by 1.9% during 1991-1995, compared to 1.8% during 1986-1990.

Table – 2 : Imports and Exports for Malaysia

Year	Exports （RM Million）	Imports （RM Million）
1994	153,921	155,921
1995	184,986	194,344
1996	196,687	197,306
1997	80,258	81,630
1998	81,480	81,791

Source： Malaysia Monthly Production Statistics, Statistics Department Malaysia （1998）

Effect of Technology Transfer

There is very limited or negligible effect of transfer of technology between the foreign firms in the FIZs and local companies. The categories of industries which have some impact, are general mechanical processing and dies fixtures, jigs and repair work. However, there is indirect impact of technology transfer through personnel training either by way of attachment to parent companies overseas of local in-house training. This indirect technology transfer impact is mainly at the technical and vocational levels and not at the managerial lever. Indirect technology proliferation of this type has led to the setting up of enterprises outside the FIZ area. The industries which have benefited the most from indirect technology proliferation are metal working, repair and maintenance services and general electrical components such as capacitors and switches.

Research and Development

Research and development （R&D） activities are not carried out in the FIZs. Most of these activities are undertaken in the parent company overseas. Local research institutions and universities have very little linkage with FIZ manufacturing companies, other than for providing skilled personnel such as qualified engineers and technicians.

Impact on Local Enterprises

Manufacturing companies have been allowed to market up to 60% of their products domestically. This has, however, little impact on the local manufacturing concerns. However, if more than 60% productions is allowed to be sold in the domestic market, there would be some impact on local imports. There is little impact of zones on the local raw material market, as most of the war materials used by FIZs are outsourced for assembly in Malaysia.

Effects on Local Labor Market

The FIZs have provided job opportunities for secondary school leavers, which comprises mainly women. Salary and wage levels in the FIZs are significantly higher than the domestic market including the government sector. Assembly-line workers majority of whom are female workers prefer to work in the FIZs rather than in the service sectors such as retailing and banking.

Impact of Recent Changes in the International Economy （Recession 1996-1997） on the FIZs

The financial thunderstorm that occurred in South Korea, Japan, Thailand, Indonesia and Malaysia and the recent strong appreciation of the Dollar have caused a severe impact on the Malaysian economy. The impact has been severest in the automotive sector of the manufacturing industry. This in turn hit hard the local SMEs which were vendors or suppliers to the automotive and construction industries. The electronic and electrical sector has, however, remained untouched by the recession. Foreign investment withdrawal has been minimal in Malaysia. The high US Dollar exchange rate has no impact on the electronics industry as most of the raw materials are outsourced from overseas and their business transactions are in US dollars.

International Competitiveness among FIZs

On 1979, there were only seven countries in Asia which had FIZs. （Rabbani, F.A., 1980）. These included India, Indonesia, Malaysia, Philippines, Republic of Korea, Sri Lanka and Taiwan. However, lately Thailand has established its own export processing zones. The Chinese Republic has also developed economic zones that encourage foreign investors to operate for export purposes. China, Philippines, Thailand and Indonesia compete with Malaysia as they have much lower labor costs.

The Malaysian government has effected three major policy changes in order to attract foreign investors to invest in Malaysia. The first policy change relates to upgrading the level of vocational education and the enhancement of technical skills among college graduates and school leavers. The second major policy move is to allow manufacturing establishments in the FIZs to sell a major portion of their products in the Malaysian domestic market（currently up to 60%）. The third policy change is to promote partnerships in the form of joint ventures between foreign Multinational Corporations （MNCs） and Malaysian MNCs in high value-added industries such as wafer production.

ORGANIZATION, MANAGEMENT AND PERFORMANCE OF THE ZONE AUTHORITY

In Malaysia, the Ministry of International Trade and Industry（MITI）plans, promotes, and implements policies and guidelines on foreign investment. A corporate entity was specially set up to develop policy guidelines and implementation procedures for encouraging the inflow of foreign investment to Malaysia. The Ministry has also set up one-stop agencies under State Economic Development Corporations（SEDCs）to handle overseas inquiries on investment opportunities in various states in Malaysia. Coordinated efforts by MITI and the SEDCs have reduced the gestation period for foreign companies to commence commercial production. The One-stop agencies under various SEDCs have succeeded in cutting down unnecessary delays caused by bureaucratic red tape and cumbersome procedures. After enterprises are located by foreign investors in the FIZs, the responsibility for the management and administration of the zones devolves upon concerned State Government and municipal authorities. Day-to-Day operations and management are under the various local towns, municipalities and state corporations as in Penang.

Most of the investors build up their own factories on the land allotted to them. These factory lots have requisite infrastructural facilities such as power, water supply and

289

telecommunication cables. As regards environmental protection and waste disposal, companies in the FIZs are required to dispose of the waste material under the supervision of the town councils and municipalities.

Benefits to the General Economy

Immediate benefits of the FIZs to the host country are in terms of employment opportunities, foreign exchange earnings, indirect technology transfer and real estate development around the FIZs. In Malaysia, unemployment was 6.1% in 1965 and 7% in 1970. Penang experienced labor shortage in the manufacturing industry during 1994-1996. As a result, Malaysia had to allow employment of foreign workers by the FIZ manufacturing companies.

As regards foreign exchange earning, the contribution has been in the form of reinvestment by companies whose domestic sales have exceeded 40% of total production. Wages to employees and payment for fees of services also constitute an important component of foreign exchange earnings.

Immediate beneficiaries of indirect technology transfer are the staff at the technical and supervisory levels. Technology transfer at the lowest level is in the form of in-house training provided to line workers for skill up-gradation.

The area surrounding the FIZs is also benefited on account of rise in property values for business premises and domestic dwellings. Rental rates also go up due to the increased demand for accommodation from the factories operating in the FIZs. This represents a direct benefit to property owners and real estate agencies.

FACTORS FOR SUCCESS OR FAILURE IN ESTABLISHING AND MANAGING THE ZONES

The Free Industrial Zones have been reckoned as successful in Malaysia. This is evident from the mortality rate of enterprises in the FIZs and fact that space taken over by other units immediately in vacation. Factors which have led to their successful operations are：

- Proper planning by the Malaysian government through MITI and the State Economic Develop Corporations （SEDCs）；
- Tax and market incentives;
- Provision of one-stop services; and
- Abundance of skilled work force.

SCIENCE PARKS（TECHNOLOGY PARKS）

Malaysia has set up two technology parks for the purpose of providing first-class infrastructure and services for technological innovation and research and development of high-tech industries. The first Park i.e. the Technology Park Malaysia is situated in the Multimedia Super Corridor （MSC） and the second Kulim High-Tech Park is located in the northern region of Malaysia. These parks will focus on three main areas viz. information

technology and multimedia, biotechnology, and manufacturing and industrial engineering.

CONCLUSION – FUTURE PROSPECTS

The establishment of the FIZs in Malaysia has been beneficial as Malaysia lacks research and development in material and process technology. To meet the gap in the availability of domestic capital formation, it is necessary to attract foreign investment. Malaysia is a net investor in terms of foreign investment. Notwithstanding, the recent economic downturn during 1997 and 1998, the Malaysian economy is expected to realize Second Industrial Master Plan （1996-2005） objective of developing high value-added industries. The future for industrial zones is bright especially with the ASEAN Free Trade Area （AFTA） becoming a reality in 2003. During 2000-2003, there will be further reduction in tariff rates in order to harmonize trade between ASEAN nations.

五、菲律賓加工出口區（Philippines EPZS）

（一）政府政策性的建設加工出口區

　　菲律賓國會通過第 5490 號法案後於 1969 年六月即建設了第一個自由貿易區，此反應出為了刺激，鼓勵，及提升國外商務而促使菲律賓為了國際貿易而形成生活中樞，其企圖在強化外幣兌換地位促進工業化減少失業人數，加速國家發展及確保人民經濟安全。

　　此政策目的置自由貿易區在中心的地位在減緩菲律賓當前所面臨的問題，尤其是貧窮及失業。

　　菲律賓設置經濟區管理局的目的：

　　●建立基本的法律架構與管理機制用在對特別經濟區，工業土地／園區，加工出口區以及其他的經濟區的整合，協調，計劃和監督；

　　●將特別挑選的地區轉型成高度發展的農業工業，商業，觀光，銀行，投資以及財務金融中心，並提供給企業公司有受過專業訓練的工作人員及有效的服務；

　　●刺激大量的國內外投資業者來特別經濟區投資，將會創造新的就業機會和建立企業與經濟區的雙向的溝通管道；

　　●藉著提供具吸引力的投資氣候以及優惠條件來激勵菲律賓人的資金回流；

●在現代化科技部份透過技術密集工業促進菲律賓和工業化國家之間的財務金融與產業合作，並藉由新的科技以及管理人的專業來刺激生產力水平；

●在保有菲律賓基本法規架構，主權獨立性以及土地完整性的情況下賦予特別經濟區或某些區域排除關稅障礙條款；

（二）菲律賓加工出口區的優惠條件

●外國人的工作權；

●進口原物料，補給品，設備，機械以及備用零件可免關稅；

●允許第一個五年的營運損失；

●加速折舊；

●免出口稅；

●國際匯兌的援助；

●財政的援助經由貸款，信用，擔保或是政府金融機構其他形式的財務貸款；

●免地方稅以及經營許可證；

（三）對經濟區開發者／經營者的優惠條件

●免所得稅；

●優惠條件根據」建立──經營──移轉法規」執行，包含此政府正式的發展協助及其他財務支援等；

●提供加工區偏遠地帶必要的公共設施；

●可選擇式的繳納 5%的毛利所得稅來替代國家以及地方稅；

●額外地扣除 50%的人事和管理發展訓練的總費用；

●提供永久居留權給外國投資人及其家人；

●外國人的工作權；

●對當地及外國企業題提高在經濟區的協助；

●其餘的優惠條件根據行政命令第 226 條實行，同樣也可由菲律賓加工出口區管理局董事會來裁定；

（四）對經濟區當地投資人的優惠條件

●公司可以有四年的期限免繳納所得稅，最多可延長至 8 年；

●當免繳所得稅的限期已滿，公司可選擇式的繳納 5%的毛利所得稅來替代國家以及地方稅；

●進口的資本設備，備用零件，補給品，原物料，牲畜以及基因的物料或者是可信用的等稅值的項目並源自於當地時，可免關稅；

●國內的銷售津貼相當於 30%總銷售額；

●免碼頭區的進出口稅；

●免檢驗公證費用；

●從 5%毛利所得稅分配中央政府的 3%中扣除勞工和管理發展訓練費用總值的 50%；

●提供永久居留權給外國投資人及其家人；

●外國人的工作權；

●精簡進出口的程序；

●其餘的優惠條件根據行政命令第 226 條實行，同樣也可由菲律賓加工出口區管理局董事會來裁定；

（五）加工出口區內的產業的表現對國內及全球經濟的衝擊

各區在投資，就業及出口等項目的表現分析如下：

在投資方面：

從 1995 年到 1999 年的 9 月為止，經濟區的投資金額達到菲幣 4 千 9 百 43.8 億元。這是五年前即 1990-1994 年投資菲幣 190 億元於舊加工出口區的 25 倍之多。經濟區的投資金額成長了 4.5 倍由 1994 年的菲幣 96 億元上升到 1995 年的菲幣 525 億元。在 1996 年時，投資金額又成長了 25%到菲幣 653 億元。到了 1997 年更暴增了 144% 至 1 千 5 百 97 億元。僅管在 1996 年受到經濟風暴的影響，投資金額還是達到菲幣 969 億元。於 1999 年間，從 1 月至 9 月的總投資額超越去年有 24%之多。

經濟區投資統計（請參照表一，Table-1）：

在就業人數方面：

從 1995 年起，經濟區內的就業人數就快速地攀升，從原來 1994 年 229,650 的就業人數上升到 1999 年 9 月的 635,422 就業人數，結果額外增加了 405,772 個就業機會。

　　經過菲律賓經濟區管理局的統計，替政府每年多製造了13%的就業機會。

　　經濟區就業成長（請參照表二，Table-2）：

　　在出口方面：

　　從 1995 年起，從經濟區的輸出的產品也大量的增加。於 1995 年間，出口值已上升到美金 42 億 8 千 4 百萬元，比1994 年的 27 億 3 千 9 百萬美金出口值高出了 56.4%。到了1996 年出口值成長 51.7%達到美金 65 億元。於 1997 年又上升了 63.5%出口值達 106 億 2 千 6 百萬美元，而在 1998 年增加了 24.9%，出口值達 132 億 7 千萬美元。經濟區宣告在1999 年的前 9 個月間，出口總值達到 115 億 6 千萬美元。

　　此外，菲律賓製造輸出總量中的經濟區的輸出量也呈現穩定的成長。1994 年經濟區的輸出量佔全菲律賓的輸出量的 22%。之後，經濟區的輸出量在 1995 年佔了 27%，在 1996年佔了 35%，在 1997 年佔了 49%，在 1998 年佔了 51%。菲律賓的經濟區對菲律賓的加工製造出口有過極大的貢獻。

（六）加工出口區與科學工業園區設置與經營成功或失敗的原因

　　菲律賓是早期亞洲幾個國家於 1969 年設置第一個加工區的先驅之一。到了 80 年代加工區的出口總值不少於 2 億美元而且雇用了大約 20,000 名員工。

　　菲律賓的經濟區在過去的五年中有了非常大的進步，這個部份已經在先前的章節提過了。這是因為菲律賓經濟區管

理局鼓勵私人企業作先鋒部隊來發展全國的經濟。這項政策
改變了也同時制定新法來管理經濟區而且有吸引人的優惠
條件來推動此計劃，所以為菲律賓的經濟帶來重大的好處。
在行政管理階層面，經濟區的常規有效率地替投資人帶來更
好的服務品質。

除了私人企業在經濟區的發展上居於領先的角色，對有
關法律架構的宣揚，具吸引力的財政優惠條件，有效的作業
程序，有遠見的領導能力以及一群專業的工作人員對於經營
經濟區是同等的重要。

（七）加工出口區與科學工業園區的未來期許

菲律賓的經濟區已經變成投資業，出口業以及就業率的
主要催化劑，尤其是對這過去的五年來說。雖然菲律賓可以
對經濟區的表現感到自豪，但是也不可以就此滿足現狀，因
為菲律賓每年約有 800,000 人進入就業市場。有鑑於此，菲
律賓經濟區管理局必須不停的引進新的事物以便能繼續吸
引外國投資人。這樣菲律賓經濟區管理局和政府就需要定期
去重新探討財政上與非財政上的優惠條件以確定還保有投
資競爭力。目前菲律賓經濟區管理局正審慎評估准予經濟區
當地投資人銷售至國內市場產品的比率由原先的 30%提高
到 50%。因為他們也察覺到本身具有 7 千 4 百 40 萬的菲律
賓人的消費市場對外國投資人而言是有相當大的吸引力。

關於財政上的優惠條件，菲律賓經濟區管理局正在推動
給予新的高科技業投資者只要投資案至少有美金 10 億或以

上的計劃就提供免繳 12 年所得稅。但是這還是需要經過立法機構的同意。

　　經濟區偏遠地帶的公共建設發展是另外一個課題，同樣也需要改進。菲律賓保證基本的公共建設會設在有需求的地方，讓菲律賓鄰近鄉村都同時享有鐵路系統，運輸網，通訊設施，電力以及電信設施。

PHILIPPINES

Lilia B. De Lima
Philippine Economic Zone Authority

GOVERNMENT POLICIES FOR THE ESTABLISHMENT OF EXPORT PROCESSING ZONES （EPZs）

The Philippine Congress passed the Republic Act No. 5490 creating the first free trade zone in the country in June. 1969. This was in response to the need for stimulating, encouraging and promoting foreign commerce to make the Philippines a vital center for international trade. Besides, it was intended to strengthen foreign exchange position hasten industrialization, reduce unemployment accelerate the development of the country and ensure economic security for its people.

There policy objectives have put the free trade zone at the center stage in alleviating the problems confronting the Philippines, especially those of poverty and unemployment.

Three years after the establishment of free trade zone in Mariveles, Bataan, former President Marcos, exercising legislative powers under an authoritarian regime, issued a Presidential Decree No. 66 （PD66） on 20 November 1972 to set up the Export Processing Zone Authority. The decree also authorized establishment of additional export processing zones at strategic locations in the country to hasten the realization of the objective of the government 「to create a new social and economic order for the national benefit.」

Six policy objectives for the Bataan Zone cited above were included in the said decree also as the objectives for other zones. Recognition of the benefits derived by the country from the establishment of the first free zone in Bataan, the government decided to set up additional zones barely two months after the declaration of material law on 21 September 1972.

During the period from 1972 to 1994, PD 66 underwent a series of amendments which strengthened the capability of government to respond to various zone-related concerns. These amendments empowered the Authority to designate certain specific private industrial estates as special export processing zones and review incentive schemes to make them more competitive and attractive to investors in the zone.

In 1995, pursuant to policies mandated in the 1987 Constitution that recognize the indispensable role of the private sector and encourage private enterprise, Republic Act No. 7916 （RA7916） or the Special Economic Zone Act of 1995 was passed by the Congress. This was intended to provide incentives for attracting much needed investment, promoting preferential employment of Filipino labor and use of domestic materials and locally produced goods, besides adopting various measures to help zones become competitive. The Philippine Economic Zone Authority （PEZA） was set up under the Act to accomplish the following objectives：

● To establish the legal framework and mechanisms for the integration, coordination, planning and monitoring of special economic zones, industrial estates/parks, export processing zones, and other economic zones;

- To transform selected areas in the country into highly developed agro-industrial, commercial, tourist, banking, investment, and financial centers, where highly trained workers and efficient services will be available to commercial enterprises;

- To promote the flow of investors, both foreign and local, into special economic zones which would generate employment opportunities and establish backward and forward linkages among industries in and around the economic zones;

- To stimulate the repatriation of Filipino capital by providing attractive climate and incentives for business activity;

- To promote financial and industrial cooperation between the Philippines and industrialized countries through technology-intensive industries for modernizing industrial sector and improving productivity levels by utilizing new technological and managerial know-how; and

- To vest the special economic zones or certain areas thereof with the status of a separate customs territory within the framework of constitution, national sovereignty and territorial integrity of the Philippines.

RA 7916 also stipulated that in pursuance of these policies, the government would actively encourage, promote, induce and accelerate a sound and balanced industrial, economic and social development of the country in order to provide jobs to people especially those in rural areas, increase their productivity and individual and family income and thereby improve the level and quality of their living through the establishment, among others, of special economic zones in suitable and strategic locations in the country and through measures that shall effectively attract legitimate and productive foreign investment.

INCENTIVES

Under the Republic Act 5490, the only incentive granted by law to companies inside the export processing zone was to allow merchandise to be brought in and out of the zone for export without being subjected to customs and internal revenue regulations of the Philippines. In fact, the law merely amended the Traiff and Customs Code of the Philippines to enable the zone to offer this singular incentive.

PD 66 improved the package of incentives granted earlier to companies inside the zone by including the following：

- Employment of foreign nationals;
- Duty and tax free import of raw materials, supplies, equipment, machinery and spare parts;
- Carry over of net operating loss for first five years of operations;
- Accelerated depreciation;
- Exemption from export tax;
- Foreign exchanged assistance;
- Financial assistance by way of loans, credit, guarantees or other forms of financial accommodation by government financial institutions; and

- Exemption from local taxes and licenses.

Under the present law RA 7916 or the PEZA Law, following incentives have been granted to Economic Zone (Eco-zone) Developers/Operators and Locators.

Incentives for Eco-zone Developers / Operators

- Income tax holiday;
- Incentives under the Build-Operate-Transfer Law which includes government support for accessing official development assistance and other sources of financing;
- Provision of vital off-site infrastructure facilities;
- Option to pay a special 5% gross income tax in lieu of all national and local taxes;
- Additional deduction of 50% of the total cost of development training for labor and management (to be applied against the National Government's share of 5% gross income tax);
- Permanent resident status for foreign investors and their immediate family members;
- Employment of foreign nationals;
- Assistance in the promotion of eco-zones to local and foreign locator enterprises; and
- Other incentives under Executive Order No. 226 (The Omnibus Investment Code of 1987), as may be determined by the PEZA Board.

Incentives for Eco-zone Locators

- Income tax holiday （ITH） or exemption from corporate income tax for four years, extendable to maximum of eight years.
- After expiry of ITH period, option to pay a special 5% tax on gross income in lieu of all national and local taxes;
- Exemption from duties and taxes on imported capital equipment, spare parts, supplies, raw materials, breeding stocks and/or genetic materials or the equivalent tax credit on there items when sources locally;
- Domestic sales allowance equivalent to 30% of total sales;
- Exemption from wharfage dues and export taxes, imports and fees;
- Exemption from SGS Inspection;
- Additional deduction of 50% of the total cost of development training for labor and management from the 3% national government share of the 5% special gross income tax;
- Permanent resident status for foreign investors and immediate family members;
- Employment of foreign nationals;
- Simplified import and export procedures, and
- Other incentives under Executive Order 226 （omnibus Investment Code of 1987）, as may be determined by the PEZA Board.

ROLES AND FUNCTIONS OF EPZS AND SPS IN THE LIGHT OF PREVAILING ECONOMIC CIRCUMSTANCES

In the Philippines, economic zones have become an important factor in the development of country's economy, particularly in the areas of employment creation, export diversification, and investment generation. Since 1995 onward, there has been continuing growth of investment in eco-zone development and investment by locators which has led to increased export receipts and additional jobs for the Filipinos.

Economic zones have thus helped to alleviate the impact on the Philippines of the financial crisis that hit Asia in mid 1996. While, a number of small medium scale companies had to scale down the size of their work force and some even had to resort to outright closures, employment needs in PEZA eco-zones remained high due to continuing inflow of investments by new locators. The number of additional jobs created in PEZA zones during 1997 and 1998 was 181,460 and 46,959 respectively.

Export performance of locator companies in the eco-zones during the crisis period 1997/98 was simply astonishing. The total manufactured exports from PEZA eco-zones during 1997 grew by 63.5% to US$10.626 billion and during 1998 by 24.9% to US$13.270 billion.

CONTRIBUTION OF SPs IN STRENGTHENING R&D ACTIVITIES AND TECHNOLOGICAL PROMOTION

Most of the special economic zones approved by PEZA are designed to house high-technology based export manufacturing companies. Most of them manufacture electronic parts and products that are meant for export. A number of these companies also undertake research and development activities in the eco-zones, especially those that do car designs. For example a particular company hired 400 Filipino engineers to do car parts designs which are exported to 16 other countries in the US, Europe, Latin America and ASEAN countries including Japan.

PEZA has also approved during the first semester of 1999, the establishment of the country's first two information technology （IT） parks. These IT Parks are envisioned to become prime world-class locations for exporters of information technology and other computer-based services that include software development for business, e-commerce, education, entertainment and multi-media applications, data encoding and conversion centers, call centers, systems integrators, computer system support and consultancy, and other IT-related activities.

The establishment of science parks and the eventual location of high-technology based export manufacturing firms in these science park special economic zones will significantly contribute to the strengthening of research and development activities and technology transfer to the Philippines.

FUNCTIONAL LINKAGES BETWEEN EPZs AND SPs

In the Philippines, EPZs and SPs are functionally combined with one another. Most special economic zones host high-technology-based locators together with other export manufacturing firms. This particular set-up is normally left to the sole discretion of the private sector developer of the special economic zone. PEZA policy intervention may however be invoked should there be a compelling need to alter the current set-up.

PERFORMANCE OF OCCUPANT-FIRM, IMPACT ON THE LOCAL AND GLOBAL ECONOMY

Performance of zones has been analyzed in terms of investment, employment and exports.

Investment

From 1995 to September 1999 investment in economic zone reached PHP494.38 billion. This is twenty five times more than the investment of PHP19 billion during preceding five year period from 1990-1994 under the old EPZA. Eco-zone investment grew 4.5 times from PHP9.6 billion in 1994 to PHP52.5 billion in 1995. In 1996, investment further grew by

25% to PHP65.3 billion. It further soared by 144% during 1997 to PHP159.7 billion. In 1998, despite economic crisis, investment reached PHP96.9 billion. During 1999, a total of PHP119.9 billion had been invested from January to September, which is 24% higher than last year's full investment of PHP96.9 billion.

Table – 1 : Accumulated Investment in Eco-Zones

Year	Amount （PHP billion）
1994	9.6
1995	52.5
1996	65.3
1997	159.7
1998	96.9
1999	119.9

Employment

Since 1995, employment in eco-zones has been increasing rapidly. It has gone up from 229,650 in 1994 to 635,422 by September 1999, resulting in creation of 405,772 additional jobs （Table – 2）

Since eco-zones are located outside the metropolitan Manila area and other urban centers, creation of jobs has provided much needed additional income to families in outlying areas of the country. With the establishment of economic zones in different parts of the country, other economic activities like those in the services sector, retail, food business, and transportation have also flourished, adding to the local income.

It has been estimated that PEZA have been contributing 13% to the annual employment needs of the country since 1995.

Table – 2 : Employment Growth in Eco-Zones

Year	Persons Employed
1994	229,650
1995	304,557
1996	380,625
1997	562,085
1998	609,044
1999 （up to September 1999）	635,422

Exports

Manufactured exports from eco-zones have also registered rapid growth since 1995. During 1995, exports had risen to US$4.284 billion, which were 56.4% higher compared to 1994 exports of US$2.739 billion. Export growth during 1996 was 51.7% when these touched US$6.5 billion. Export further increased in 1997 by 63.5% to a total of US$10.626 billion and in 1998 by 24.9% to US$13.27 billion. For the first nine months of the 1999, eco-zone manufactured exports had posted a total of US$11.56 billion.

The share of PEZA eco-zones exports in the total manufactured exports of the Philippines has also shown steady growth. In 1994, manufactured exports from eco-zones represented 22% of the total Philippine manufactured exports. Their share increased to 27% in 1995, 35% in 1996, 49% in 1997, and 51% in 1998. PEZA eco-zones have emerged as major contributors to Philippine exports of manufactured goods for the past five years.

FACTORS OF SUCCESS OR FAILURE IN ESTABLISHING AND RUNNING EPZs AND SPs

The Philippines was one of the pioneers in Asia in establishing the first zone in 1969. Until eighties, zones generated less than US$200 million exports and employed about 20,000 workers.

The performance of Philippine eco-zones has tremendously improved in the past five year as has been discussed in the preceding sections of this paper. This is mainly due to the fact that PEZA encourages private sector to spearhead the development of economic zones all over the country. This policy shift together with a new set of laws governing eco-zones and attractive incentive scheme provided the impetus for the eco-zone program to take off and bring about significant benefits to the Philippine economy. At the administrative level, eco-zone procedures were streamlined for better service to investors.

Aside from the lead role of the private sector in eco-zone development, sound legal framework, attractive fiscal incentives, streamlined procedures, visionary leadership and a corps of professional staff have been equally important in making the eco-zone program work.

ORGANIZATION, MANAGEMENT, AND PERFORMANCE OF EPZ AND SP AUTHORITIES

RA7916 as amended by RA8748 bestows upon PEZA all the necessary organizational and administrative powers to successfully fulfill its mission. PEZA has a compliment of professional staff at its Central and Zonal offices to render services to investors, developers and locators, as and when required.

It may also be mentioned that PEZA effected restructuring of its offices that resulted in reduction of officers and other personnel by 41.2%. Whereas its predecessor office EPZA had a total of 1,006 officers and other personnel in December 1994, PEZA had by December 1998 trimmed down the staff complement to only 591 officers and personnel.

PEZA is continuing its efforts to streamline operations so that bureaucratic fat will be eliminated and the clients are assured of the best possible service from a highly motivated corps of staff.

FUTURE PROSPECTS OF EPZs AND SPs

The Philippine eco-zones have become a major catalyst to investment, exports, and employment, especially over the past five years. Although the performance of PEZA is something to be proud of, it cannot however, rest on its laurels because of the pressure on the Philippine economy to provide jobs to about

800,000 new Filipino entrants to the labor force annually. In view of rapid increase in labor force, PEZA has to be on its toes to introduce creative innovations so as to continue to attract foreign investors in the country.

This may require regular review of fiscal and non-fiscal incentives to ensure that PEZA and the Philippines remain competitive as an investment destination. One area, which is currently under review relates to increasing the proportion of domestic sale entitlement for export manufacturing locators. PEZA is very seriously considering allowing locators companies to sell up to 50% of their production in the domestic market instead of the current 30%, provided all the corresponding taxes are paid. PEZA is well aware that a large market of 74.4 million Filipinos（Philippine market）is in itself a great attraction for foreign investors.

With regard to fiscal incentives, PEZA is pushing to increase the income tax holiday period to 12 years for new investments in high-technology based projects involving an investment of US$1 billion or above. This will however, require legislative action.

Off-site infrastructure development is another area, which needs improvement. The Philippines has to ensure that basic infrastructure needs are in place to put the Philippines at par with neighboring countries in terms of road network, transportation, communications, power and telecommunications.

All of these thrust areas are key to sustaining the country's viability in a highly competitive world of investment promotion.

六、越南加工出口區（Vietnam EPZS）

（一）介紹

　　越南於 1991 年在 Tan Thuan 建立了第一個加工出口區以鼓勵外銷出口生產以及吸引外國投資人。隨後又另外建立五個加工出口區，其地點分別在 Linh Trung，Hai Phong 1996，Da Nang，Noi Bai 和 Can Tho。本報告是經亞洲生產力中心對越南加工出口區評鑑的結果。本評鑑的目的在了解加工出口區對國家經濟發展的目標執行績效，本報告企圖測驗出設置加工區的目的，政府的政策及法規，設區位置選定條件，加工出口區內產業特性及投資，以及撤資原因，各產業經營績效，區內管理及加工出口區經營成功與失敗的原因等。

（二）加工出口區的創立及目的

　　1976 年國家再統一之後，越南初期發展根據中央五年計劃目標執行，以發展重工業為優先，而因採中央集權，官僚體制及封閉式管理系統，其結果是農，工生產均無績效。到 1990 年，越南已列為全世界倒數十名貧窮的國家，農業佔了國民生產毛額（GDP）的 45%，失業率高達 10.2%。

　　為了克服低成長，食物嚴重短缺，預算赤字，通貨膨脹，長期貿易赤字等問題，越南第六屆國民大會在 1986 年 12 月

推動一項：全面經濟改革政策，其兩項基本政策為達到食物自給自足改善人民生活標準。至 1991 年第 17 屆國會再確認為多方位及以社會導向的政策；市場經濟仍根據中央政府決定，進行深架構的改革。越南政府了解到一貫作業經濟區可能是走向經濟工業化及現代化過程中最主要的一項工具。

再進行一貫作業經濟區發展時，政府參考了台灣，新加坡，中國等設置越南自己的經濟區；1991 年政府決定設置加工出口區鼓勵來區投資。從 1993 年起又設置了多個工業區，並克服了公共設施及設備提供給外來投資，尤其是對中小企業。這些工業區的管理是在 1993 年新頒布的工業區增設條款。政府對一貫作業經濟區的管理建立在一致的基本標準上，1994 年 4 月 24 日頒布的法規 NO. 36/CP 實用於工業區，加工出口區及高科技園區，以代替早期對加工出口區及工業區的政策。

興建加工出口區與工業園區的目的：

●促成國內生產毛額（GDP）的成長，促進投資和工業生產外銷以及其他經濟面的發展與促進國內消費市場；

●創造一個對環境保護有利的條件，增加土地的長期使用率；

●創造勞工就業機會以及提升勞工的技能；

●引進現代技術轉移；

●設立城市衛星區域以縮短地區與地區間的生活水平差距；

（三）政府建設加工出口區的政策

　　政府的政策經濟方面著重在工業生產及對外貿易，加上服務業。農業及工業同時並重，對外貿易在提高國家年度收入，增加更多的就業機會。有以下幾個主要因素，影響到政策的形成，包括增加就業機會，提高收入及生活標準，環境保護，增加政府年度收入，及提升國家競爭力。無論為何，增加政府年度收入及提升國家競爭力是考慮政策形成最重要的因素，另外次要的因素包括進口工業替代品，貧窮鄉村都市化，提高教育水平，增加土地有效使用及投資。

　　過去農業是越南主要的經濟活動，1990 年佔 GDP 的 41.5%，所用勞動力達 80%，政府企圖改善經濟結構增加農業生產及建設勞力密集工業以增加就業機會。這些可用的廉價勞力，1990 年前越南曾接受前蘇聯提共過時技術的勞力技術密集工業以增家加工作機會。

　　增加工業生產及提高對外貿易是政府政策最重要的構想。如是，一般性勞力輕工業及各區基本上界定為勞力密集的輕工業也該被推廣；一般性勞力輕工業是列為第一優先，其次才是各區基本上界定的勞力密集輕工業。

　　為加工出口區設置人力，原料，資本，技術及市場是有必要的，農業是主要的經濟活動，80%的勞動力來自鄉村。這些人力的供應是充裕的，唯缺少技術，故目標訂在達成全面就業，提升基本技術及人民的生活水準，因為越南缺少技術人力，致有大量畢業於大學，學院，職業學校的學生，1999/2000 年的需求，工業區及加工出口區在胡志明市登記

勞工需求達 26,000 人而合格者為 20%即 5,200 人，職業學校每年訓練 14,000 人，但年度需求則達到此數的兩倍，在新順加工出口區每年就需要 3,000 至 4,000 訓練完成者，而當地可能提供數量僅達 40%。原料在當地只能提供一部份的需求，無論如何本地原料儘可能大量供應而後才向國外買，以降低生產成本及增加市場競爭力。越南本身的企業也不能完全配合資金需求，特別是私人企業。他們需要國外融資或是外國投資參與合資，越南政府也提供少量的貸款，其目的在增進資本供應以增加附加價值，進而達到提升國家資本財的形成；另一目的是確立由生產工業資本的有效應用而增加國家個方面的收入並改善生活水準。

誠如以上所述，越南在建設各區之前只有成舊的技術，越南過去已有的為一般性技術，但缺乏管理及品質控制；從建設了各區之後，有了高科技的設備，品質提升達到國際貿易水準，並賺取了外匯，因此 GNP 也增加，及國家級競爭力也提升。

在工業區內不同的企業，各為專業出口產品生產及提供出口服務與出口相關的行為，他們的產品首先要符合進口國的要求。對外國企業有一些在財務相關的問題上有些限制。1996 年 10 月 12 日政府公佈了有關本地企業與加工出口區的企業間商品交換的辦法。這些交換處理與進出口做法雷同，交換辦法同越南的進出口法律相同，規定各區的產品必須通過海關的檢查如同進口產品一樣，其目的在允許區內產品銷往本地市場而後發展到國外市場。

目前對加工出口區及科學園區並未公佈特別法，越南工業區管理局將「工業區法」延用到加工出口區。目前加工出口區及高科技園區是在政府的法令，規定及部長的指揮下運作，1997 年 4 月 24 日政府發布的 No. 36/CP-1997 公報，工業區為一般級，而加工出口區為特別級，此涵蓋了對工業區，加工出口區及高科技園區的規定，督導及海關負責單位自由的檢查等內容，有關詳細的優惠條件按以下規定給予：

越南加工出口區與工業園區所提供的優惠條件：

● 進口至區內的機器設備，原物料，和商品給予免繳關稅的優惠；

● 從區內運送出口的完成品提供免繳出口稅的優惠；

● 對製造業，營業稅減免稅率 10%，及 4 年免稅，（營利所得稅）此外在接下來的 4 年可繼續享有 50%的免稅；

● 對服務業，營業稅減免 15%的稅率，2 年免稅，此外在接下來的 2 年可享有 50%的免稅；

● 盈利部份的退稅可用於再投資期限為 3 年；

● 外國投資者要將利潤匯款至國外需按總匯款額繳納5%的匯稅即可，而非加工出口區的投資人得繳交的總匯款稅率為 5%，7%，或 10%，依照投資額的等級來界定；

越南對設置加工出口區提供多項優越條件如下：

● 擁有充足的勞動力；

● 有足夠的公共設施；

● 良好的通訊系統；

● 距離海港或是機場皆不遠；

● 當地的企業可提供適時的援助；

- 擁有住宿以及休閒設施給外國投資人；
- 設置外國語言學校提供給外國投資人的子女就讀；
- 有足夠的通勤設施提供給員工使用；

除此之外，加工出口區其他的優惠條件也吸引投資人來投資，包括有：

- 低廉的土地租金；
- 擁有廉價的勞工；
- 提供大量低價的原物料以減少生產成本；
- 對於要出口至先進國家的企業給予優惠；
- 於某特定時期提供免繳稅金／或稅金減輕優惠；
- 提供簡化的手續及一元化服務；

（四）加工出口區設置與經營成功或失敗的因素

成功的因素有：

- 低生產成本及產品在市場上的競爭力；
- 擁有充足的勞動力，原物料及半成品和材料以降低生產成本；
- 高品質與先進的科技加強了加工出口區產品的市場競爭力；
- 擁有良好工作態度的大量勞工；
- 在設置園區前有適當的規劃並提供完善的優惠條件；
- 低廉的土地租金以及低價的廠房建築成本；
- 加工出口區當局提供高效能以及高品質的服務水準；

失敗的因素有：

● 不完善的律法與規範嚴重影響到園區運作；

● 無法打進國際市場是導致園區內的電器與電子產業，紡織與成衣業，和精密工具產業失敗的因素；

● 不適當用途的設備和有缺陷的公共設施或是加工出口區的地點設置不當；

● 由於科技的不更新以及公共設施發展計劃的不完全，造成外國投資人對於投資越南的興趣缺乏；

（五）未來展望

越南政府仍致力於發展其現代化及工業化。加工出口區與高科技園區在改變越南的經濟結構中仍然扮演重要的角色。越南政府計劃要興建更多的加工出口區，工業園區，和高科技園區。到了 2003 年，30 座額外的工業園區，加工出口區，以及高科技園區將計劃設立。

VIETNAM

Dr. Phan Van Hoa
Dr. Duong Dinh Tung
Vietnam Industrial Zone Authority

Mr. NguyenXuan Hong
Ms. Tran Thi Thu Ha
Vietnam Productivity Cebter

INTRODUCTION

The First Export Processing Zone （EPZ） was established in Vietnam in 1991 at Tan Thuan to encourage production for exports and attract foreign investment. Five more EPZs were licensed to be established later at Linh Trung, Hai Phong 1996, Da Nang, Noi Bai and Can Tho. This paper presents the results of survey on Export Processing Zones in Vietnam sponsored by the Asian Productivity Organization （APO）. The objective of the survey is to undertake a fact-finding study on the performance of EPZs with reference to national objectives of economic development. This paper attempts to examine the objectives of setting up of EPZs, government policies and regulations, local conditions for site selection, nature of industries set up and investment in the EPZs and the reasons of withdrawal of investment, performance of enterprises and zone management and factors which contribute to the success or failure of EPZs.

INCEPTION AND OBJECTIVES FOR ESTABLISHING EXPORT PROCESSING ZONES（EPZs）

After the reunification of the country in 1976, Vietnam initiated the development process on the basis of centrally planned mechanism for achieving five-year plan objectives. Development of heavy industry was given priority in comparison with other industries. Centralized, bureaucratic and closed management systems resulted in inefficient industrial and agricultural production. Until 1990, Vietnam was ranked amongst the last ten poorest countries of the world. Agriculture accounted for 45% of GDP and it had high unemployment rate of 10.2%.

To overcome the problems of slow growth, serious food shortages, budget deficits, soaring inflation and chronic trade deficit, the Sixth National Congress of the Vietnamese Communist Party embarked upon the policy of overall economic renovation in December 1986. Two basic objectives of the policy were to achieve food self-sufficiency and improve living standards of people. The Seventh Congress in 1991 reaffirmed the policy of a multi-sector, socialist-oriented; market economy based on state management, and introduced deeper structural reforms. Vietnamese government recognized that integrated economic zones could be one of the most important tools for putting the economy on the path of industrialization and modernization.

While evolving the policy for development of integrated economic zones, government was guided by the experience of similar zones in Taiwan, Singapore, and China and used these models for setting up zones in Vietnam. In 1991, the Government decided to establish EPZs to encourage investment in export production. From 1993, onward a number of Industrial Parks have been set up to overcome critical deficiencies in infrastructure and facilitate foreign investment, especially by small and medium enterprises. These IPs are regulated under the additional Government status on Industrial Parks issued in 1993. To streamline the management of all the integrated economic zones in the country on a uniform basis, the government issued Decree No. 36/CP dated 24/4/1994 stipulating the status on Industrial parks, Exports Processing Zones and High-Tech Parks （known under the common name as Industrial Zone - IZs） which replaced the earlier policy framework for EPZs and IPs.

The objectives for establishing EPZs and IZs are：

• To contribute to GDP growth, promote investment and industrial production for exports and other economic sectors and for domestic consumption;

• To create favorable conditions for environment protection, increase effectiveness of land use on long-term basis;

• To create job opportunities and improve skills of workers;

• To import and transfer modern technology; and

- To establish satellite urban areas and to reduce the gap in living standards between regions.

So far, 60 IPs, 6 EPZs and 1 HTP have been established in the country which operate under the Industrial Zones Regulations No. 36/CP. EPZs have been defined in these regulations as bonded industrial zones that produce export goods and provide supportive services for the production of export goods and other export activities. Within an EPZ, investors may engage in manufacturing, sub-contracting and assembling export products. However, out of six zones, three at Da Nang （1994）, Noi Bai （1994） and Can Tho （1994） have been converted into Industrial Parks （IPs） to widen the scope of their activities for domestic consumption. Thus, Vietnam has now only three EPZs and the number of IPs has risen to 63.

The aim of establishing IZs in general and EPZs in particular is to change the economic structure, attract foreign investment, promote foreign trade, create jobs and to enhance the Gross National Product （GDP） by attracting local and foreign enterprises to invest in these zones.

It is expected that with the establishment of IPs and EPZs, the economic structure of Vietnam would gradually shift in favor of industry. Though the Vietnamese economy has dominance of agriculture, the long-term strategy of the government is to industrialize and modernize the country. As a result, the share of industry in GDP would increase and industry would become relatively more important sector, while the share of agriculture would gradually come down. In other words, after the establishment of EPZs and IPs, industrial growth is expected to be faster than that of agriculture, leading to increase in GNP in a few years time.

The Government also hopes that with the establishment of EPZs, the inflow of foreign investment will increase. This would sequentially crease job opportunities for the Vietnamese and help reduce unemployment, especially amongst the people from the rural areas. EPZs and IPs can also stimulate the country's 「internal forces」 to mobilize potential resources such as labor, land, money and the skills to enhance productivity and competitiveness of 「Made in Vietnam」 products. This would help expand the regional and global market.

GENERAL CONDITIONS OF NATIONAL ECONOMY BEFORE THE ESTABLISHMENT OF ZONES

In 1990, a year before the establishment of the zones, the share of agriculture in GDP was 41.4% while industry accounted for 35.1%（Figure - 1）. In the national economic structure, there was a mix of agriculture and labor intensive industry. The agricultural activities mainly consisted of cultivation of rice, corns, and other vegetables. For processing of agri products out-dated technology was in use.

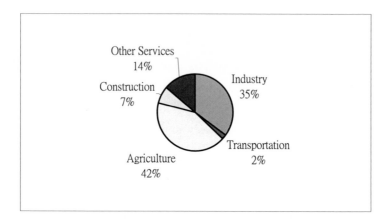

Figure - 1：Economic Structure of Vietnam in 1990
Source：Statistical Yearbook 1992

GNP and annual revenue for the years 1985 and 1990, a few years before the establishment of the zones are depicted in Figures – 2 and – 3 respectively. Values are in VND, since the exchange rates of VND to US$ were not recorded for these years. The growth rate of GNP ranges from 102% to 108% （over the previous year's base）. In 1990, the growth rate of GNP was 26.4% compared to 1985. The index of growth of annual revenues of Vietnam ranges between 102.3% to 106.5% （over the previous year's base）. The growth rate of annual revenues in 1990 was 20.9% compared to 1985.

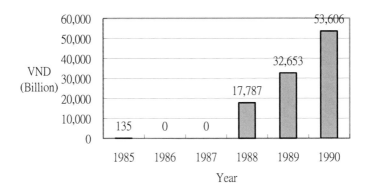

Figure－2：GNP of Vietnam from 1985 to 1990
Source：Statistical Yearbook 1992

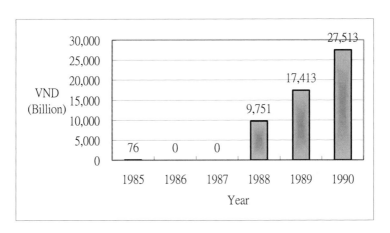

Figure－3：Annual Revenue of Vietnam from 1985 to 1990
Source：Statistical Yearbook 1992

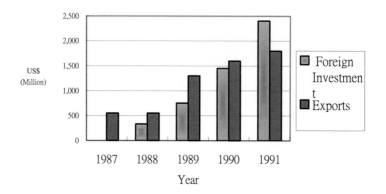

Figure – 4：Foreign Investment and Exports （1987 - 1991）

Source：Vietnam – A Guide for the Foreign Investors

Prior to 1987, there was no foreign investment in the country. After the Communist Party's Sixth Congress launched economic reforms （renovation）, the foreign investment law was passed in December 1987. in 1988, foreign investment projects for US$360 million were approved. Since then, the inflow of foreign investment has increased dramatically. Foreign investment and exports during 1987 to 1991 has been highlighted in Figure – 4.

Before 1990, infrastructure in Vietnam was weak, especially infrastructure for communication and transportation system including airlines, shipping, railways and roads. The Communication Corporation, which was in public sector, controlled all communication facilities. Until 1991, both domestic and international teledensity was very low. Telegraph was used in large parts of the country until 1990. Vietnam has launched Internet and fax services only a few years ago. Before the establishment of the zones, these facilities were not in use.

However, in the field of education, Vietnam is ranked amongst high literacy countries of the world, though the economy is not developed. The rates of enrolment in senior high schools, junior high schools and the primary schools are very high ranging from 89 to 93%. This is due to the fact that government subsidizes tuition fees and enrolment to the primary schools is compulsory for the Vietnamese.

GOVERNMENT POLICIES FOR THE ESTABLISHMENT OF EPZs

Government policy highlighted the lead role of industrial production and foreign trade in the economy, supplemented by the service industry. While agriculture and manufacturing were equally emphasized, foreign trade was intended to raise revenue for the country and create additional jobs opportunities. There were several key factors, which influenced the formulation of policy guidelines. These included increasing job opportunities, raising income and enhancing the living standards, protecting environment, increasing government revenues and improving competitiveness of the country. Increasing government revenues and improving competitiveness were, however, the most important factors taken into consideration while formulating policy guidelines. Other less significant factors which also weighed were the need for providing import substitute for industrial goods, urbanizing poor rural areas, improving education standards and increasing effectiveness of land use and investment.

Realizing that agriculture was the main economic activity in Vietnam which accounted for a share of 41.5% share in GDP in 1990 and employed 80% of labor force, the government attempted to improve the economic structure by increasing agricultural production and setting up labor intensive industries to create job opportunities. In view of availability of cheap labor, some labor-intensive industries for job creation deploying outdated technology were set up, even though prior to 1990 Vietnam had the support of former Soviet Union.

Increasing industrial production and promoting foreign trade were important features of government policy. Therefore, general manpower light industry and zone based labor-intensive light industry were sought to be promoted. The general manpower light industry was the first priority, followed by zone based labor-intensive light industry.

For establishing EPZs manpower, raw material, capital, technology and market are required. With agriculture as the main economic activity and 80% of labor employed in the rural, manpower supply was considered to be abundant, though it lacked technical skills. The objective was to achieve full employment and upgrade basic skills and living standard of the people. Vietnam has faced shortage of skilled manpower, though the number of graduates from universities, colleges and vocational schools is very high. Recent reports suggest that during 1999/2000, Ips and EPZs in Ho Chi Minh City need to enroll 26,000 workers of which 20% or 5,200 should be qualified. Vocational schools have the capacity to train 14,000 workers every year, but the annual requirement is twice as much. A concrete example is that of Tan Thuan EPZ, which alone requires 3,000 to 4,000 trained workers per annum, but the local availability is to the extent of only 40% of the requirement.

Raw material requirement can be met locally only partly. The objective, however, is use local raw material to the maximum possible extent so as to broaden the market and reduce production costs and thereby increase market competitiveness. Vietnamese enterprises are also not in a position to meet capital requirements fully, especially in the private sector. They need either fusion of foreign capital or foreign investment in the from of joint ventures. Government also provides small amounts as loans. The objective of improving capital supply is to increase the value added, and step up capital formation of the country. Another objective is to ensure optimal utilization of capital by productive industries to increase national income in all sectors and improve living standards.

As has been mentioned above, before the establishment of zones production technology in Vietnam was outmoded. Vietnam possessed general industrial technology, but lacked in production management and quality control. By establishing integrated zones, which facilitate use of higher technology, the productivity and quality will be upgraded for promoting international trade and earning foreign exchange. Thus the GNP will increase and the competitiveness of the country will also improve.

Unlike manufacturing enterprises in the Ips, enterprises specialize in the production of export goods and provide support services for the production of export goods and other export related activities. Their products are primarily meant for export to other countries. However, this restriction has caused several problems in terms of financial relationship with outside enterprises. On 12 October 1996, government introduced a new decree on exchange of goods between domestic enterprises and EPZ enterprises. These exchanges are treated as import-export activity and, therefore, must observe Vietnam laws and regulations on import and export. The zone products have to pass the custom check as imported products. The objective of the new decree is to permit zone products access in the domestic market, besides development foreign markets.

Presently, there is no specially promulgated law for the export-processing zone or science parks. The Vietnam Industrial Zone authority is drafting the Law on industrial zones, which will also cover EPZs. The EPZs and Hi-Tech parks presently operate under Government's Decrees, Statutes and the ministerial and inter-ministerial circulars. Industrial zones in general and EPZs in particular are governed by the Government Degree No. 36/CP-1997 dated 24 April 1997 that contains regulations on Industrial Parks, EPZs and Hi-Tech Parks. Under these regulations, supervision and inspection by customs authorities is hassle free. Details of other incentives under these regulations are given below :

Incentives

- Exemption from customs duties on equipment, raw materials and commodities imported into the zone;
- Exemption from export tax on finished products exported from the zone;
- Concessional tax rate of 10% and tax holiday for 4 years, besides tax reduction of 50% for next four years commencing from the year of generating profit for the manufacturing units;
- Tax rate of 15% and tax holiday for 2 years and tax reduction of 50% for next two years commencing from the year of generating profit for service sector enterprises;
- Refund of tax on profits reinvested for three years; and
- Profits transferred abroad by foreign investors are subject only to remittance tax of 5% of the amount remitted as against 5%, 7% or 10% for non EPZ enterprises, depending upon the level of investment and the proportion of equity investment.

LOCAL CONDITIONS FOR SITE SELECTION

Industrial zones（IPs, EPZs, HTPs）are planned in regions, which have favorable conditions for industrial development, such as proximity to large cities, availability of natural resources, convenience in transportation and relatively developed infrastructure. Six export processing zones established in Ho Chi Minh City, Ha Noi, Da Nang, Hai Phong and Can Tho, are in the biggest cities of Vetnam. Following considerations are also reverent for site selection for the zones：

- Manpower supply;
- Adequate public facilities;
- Good communication system;
- Distance from seaport or airport;
- Extent of local industry support;
- Accommodation and entertainment facilities for foreign investors;
- Foreign language schools for children of foreign investors; and
- Adequate commuting facilities for employees and workers.

Vietnam offers many favorable conditions for setting up export processing zones
as discussed below.

Manpower Supply

Vietnam has a high percentage of young population. Besides, literacy rate is over 80%. Vocational training schools, colleges and universities can train work force at all levels including engineers, technicians and workers （Table - 1）. But still there is acute shortage of skilled workers in Vietnam. New enterprises require assistants, supervisors, chief engineers and personnel and marketing executives who need to be professionally skilled and also have experience in the respective positions for at least three to five years. Some companies also require technical workers in skill specific trades such as steamer operator, electricity generator, lifting machines, and operators for electrical and electronic appliances, which are not easily available.

Table – 1 : School and Colleges in Ho Chi Minh City, Danang, and Hai Phong

Cities	Technical Secondary School		Vocational Training School		College and University	
	Number of Schools	Number of Students	Number of Schools	Number of Schools	Number of Schools	Number of Schools
Ho Chi Minh City	18	12,760	5	10,234	13	80,180
Da Nang	11	8,101	2	3,134	4	14,311
Hai Phong	6	4,373	2	4,212	1	5,690

Local Industry Support

Before the Second World War, Vietnamese economy was primarily agrarian in nature. However, since 1975 and especially after 「Doi Moi」 in 1986, the economic system has been restructured and Vietnam has experienced significant economic growth. It is expected that GDP will grow between 8.55 to 9.5% over the next few years. Many investment projects in light and heavy industry sectors have been implemented. The structure of the economy is gradually shifting from agriculture to industry and services.

Vietnam is rich in natural resources including oil, gas, coal, phosphate, iron, bauxite, gold, tin, lead, manganese, granite, marble and gemstone, which can help in developing basic mechanical and chemical industries. Beside these industries, there is potential for developing electrical, electronics, plastics and textile industry. Ho Chi Minh City, Da Nang and Hai Phong cities have these basic industries, which can support the EPZs. However, factories are operating with old and obsolete equipment. Larger investment is required for suppoeting EPZs more effectively.

Accommodation and Entertainment

Hotels of international standards are available in Ho ChiMinh City but their availability is limited in Hai Phong and Da Nang. Budget hotels and guesthouses are, however, available in these locations. Table – 2 gives details about hotel accommodation in the cities where the zones are located.

For entertainment, each city has one TV station with 4 channels in Vietnamese, including 1 domestic and 3 international channels. Besides, channels in Vietnamese also have short news in English and French. All cities have high-class cinemas and many dancing halls, which attract lot of people over the weekends. There are museums, zoos and parks in these cities. Facilities for soccer, golf, tennis, table tennis and badminton are also available. In Ho Chi Minh City, there are several picnic grounds and amusement parks of national standard. Investors have also shown some interest in providing amusement parks and entertainment resorts because of high profitability.

Table –2 : International standard Hotels in Ho Chi Minh City, Da Nang, and hai Phong

City	Four-Start (and above) Hotels		Three-Star Hotels		Under Three-Star Hotels	
	Number of Hotels	Total Number of Rooms	Number of Hotels	Total Number of Rooms	Number of Hotels	Total Number of Rooms

Ho Chi Minh City	6	1,100	21	1,800	43	2,100
Da Nang	2	350	3	320	8	230
Hai Phong	-	-	1	120	4	210

Foreign language Schools for Children of Foreign Investors

Hai Phong and Da Nang do not have foreign language schools because the number of foreign investors is not significant. Ho Chi Minh City has some foreign language schools, specially set up for children of foreign investors （Table – 3）.

Table – 3：Foreign Language Schools in Ho Chi Minh City

Serial Number	Type of Institute	Language	Garde
1	International Schools 1	English	From 6 to 9
2	International Schools 2	English	From 1 to 5
3	Sai Gon People-founded School	English	From 1 to 5
4	College	English	From 6 to 9
5	Japanese School	Japanese	From 1 to 9
6	French School	French	From 1 to 9
7	Fuldino Kindergarten	Japanese	
8	Kindergarten ABC	English	
9	Kindergarten HB	Korean	
10	Tinitots Kindergarten	English	
11	Playmate International Kindergarten	English	

Commuting Facilities for Employees and Workers

All EPZs are located in areas tat have convenient highways. Ho Chi Minh, Hai Phong and Da Nang cities have relatively developed transportation system and employees can commute to workplace by their own motorbikes, bicycles or company buses.

INDUSTRIAL AND INVESTMENT PROFILE OF EPZs

Almost all categories of industries, except the following are projected to be admitted into the EPZs :

- Projects which are prejudicial to the national security, defense and public interest;
- Projects which are detrimental to the historical and cultural relics, customs and traditions of Vietnam;
- Projects which are prejudicial to the ecological environment; projects for treatment of toxic water •imported from foreign countries to Vietnam;Projects for production of toxic chemicals or utilization of toxic agents, which are prohibited under an international treaty; and
- Projects relating to nuclear power, radioactive material, industrial explosives, leather and dyeing.

During 1997 and 1998, some manufacturing enterprises had withdrawn Investment in the wake of economic crisis in the region. But as many as 51 investors have also expanded during this period their operations in the EPZs. During 1998, 20 companies have invested US$25.1 millions to expand manufacturing facilities and improve production lines in Tan Thuan and Linh Trung EPZs.

By 1998, 138 investors had been admitted into the zones with projected investment of US$638 millions. Sectoral break up of these units is given in Table – 4. It is evident that highest investment is in electrical and electronics sectors which account for 25% total investment, followed by textile and garments, and mechanical units with 21% and 14% of total incestment respectively. Investment in these three sectors amounts to US$386 million, which is 60% of the total investment.

Table – 4 : Categories of Industries Admitted into the Zones up to 1998

Category	Number of Investment Projects Approved	Investment Capital (US$ Million)	Ration （%）
Electrical and Electronics	14	158.5	26
Textile and Garment	44	135.3	21
Mechanical	19	92.3	14
Plastics	5	54.6	9
Furniture and Package	4	52.5	8
Foodstuff	9	27.7	4
Sport Equipment	4	13.2	2
Shoes	9	21.3	3
Other	30	82	13
Total	138	637.4	100

EPZ in Vietnam have attracted investors primarily from Asia countries （Table - 5）. Japan ranks first in term of total investment. Japanese investors have set up 48 enterprises and invested US$298.2 million, which accounts for 47% of total investment. Taiwan ranks second with 52 enterprises and investment of US$185 millions. Hong Kong ranks third with 10 enterprises and an investment of US$64 millions. Investment from these three countries accounts for 87% of investment in the zones.

Table – 5 : Country – Wise Break up of Investment

Country	Number of Investors Approved	Investment Capital (US$ Million)	Ration （%）
Japan	48	298.2	46
Taiwan	52	185.3	29
Hong Kong	10	64.2	10
Korea	12	35.2	6
USA	4	13.4	2
Singapore	2	10.5	2
China	2	8.1	1
England	2	9.3	1
Vietnam	2	3.4	1
France	2	5.2	1
Philippines	2	4.0	1
Total	138	636.8	100

During first six months of 1999, the number of investors was higher compared to corresponding period for 1998. This is due to improvement in the economic situation in Asia countries. Besides, liberal incentives have also attracted investors to the zones.

These include：

- Low rentals for land;
- Availability of low cost labor force;
- Abundant supply of low cost raw materials which reduce production costs;
- Favorable treatment for export to advanced countries;
- Tax exemption/reduction for specified period; and
- Simplified procedures and one-stop service.

Since the setting up of zones, only five enterprises have withdrawn investment amounting to US$48 million（Annex - 3）. This was mainly due to the economic crisis in the region.

PERFORMANCE OF OCCUPANTS FIRMS

Analysis of the Trade Performance of EPZs

Trade status of the zones from 1994 to 1998 is detailed in Annex – 4. By 1998, 138 firms had been granted permission for investment in various zones. Of these, 110 were approved for Tan Thuan EPZ, 24 for Linh Trung EPZ, 2 for Da Nang and 2 for Hai Phong 96 EPZ. The operation of these companies in EPZs has had positive impact on the economy in term of trade, transfer of technology and job creation.

So far trade is concerned, the quantum of imported materials by firms in the surveyed EPZs is on the increase since the inception of zones. Annexure – 4 may be perused for year –wise details. This is also reflected in Figure – 5.

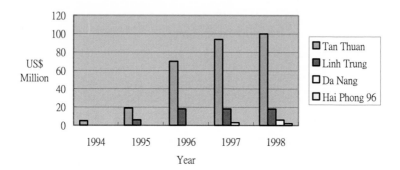

Figure – 5：Import of Raw Material by EPZs

in Tan Thuan EPZ which is the most successful of the zones and has the largest number of enterprises, imports are 8 to 9 times higher than total imports by other zones. Besides imported materials, EPZs also use only small quantities of local materials, as these do not meet their production requirements. Besides, many of the required materials are not available.

Value of local materials used by EPZs in recent years is depicted in Figure – 6.

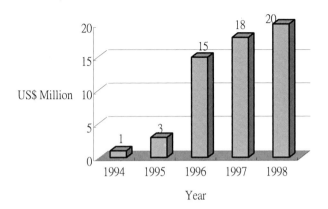

Figure – 6：Value of Local Materials Used by EPZs

It is noteworthy that in value terms there has been increase in the use of domestic raw materials, but it is still relatively small as it accounted for only 15% of raw materials used in 1998. Local raw material suppliers and investors are, however, making efforts to enhance the use of domestic raw material.

EPZs enterprises have effected exported to 44 countries. Since 1994, when the first company in Tan Thuan started operating and exporting, exports have increased rapidly. Exports went up from US$5 millions in 1994 to US$286 millions in 1997. However, during 1998, export turnover slightly came down to US$281 million due to economic crisis. But it picked up again in 1999. The Vietnam Industrial Zone Authority（VIZA）reported that exports of EPZs during the first quarter of 1999 were up by 210% as compared to the first quarter of 1998 and it was expected that the trend would continue as more and more investors have evinced interest in EPZs.

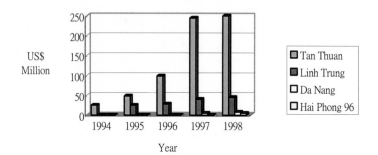

Figure – 7：EPZ Exports

Rising exports have resulted in favorable balance of payments and improvement in value-added. The favorable balance of payments is depicted in Figure – 8.

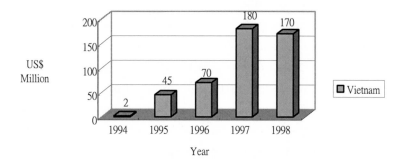

Figure – 8：　Favorable Balance of EPZs

With a view to promoting their mutual business, EPZ enterprises and local industry usually seek cooperation from each other. As mentioned earlier, local materials used by EPZ units constitute 15% of total raw materials. During 1999, EPZs were expected to buy US$ 25 millions worth of raw materials from the local market. Zone enterprises also sell to the local enterprises semi-finished goods such as cotton yarn, electric parts, plastic materials and so on. Details of goods supplied by EPZs to the local market during 1995 to 1998 are given in Table – 6.

Table – 6 : Products Supplied by EPZs to local Enterprises

(Unit : US$ Million)

Product	1995	1996	1997	1998
Synthesized Threads	2.567	5.645	4.936	4.354
Plastic Pipes	0.342	0.646	0.411	0.824
Electronic Parts	0.032	0.130	0.315	1.567
Paper Containers	0.121	0.311	0.484	1.982
Others	0.212	0.412	0.432	0.476
Total	3.274	7.144	6.578	9.203

Bilateral relation between EPZs and local enterprise, however, continue to be impeded by bureaucratic red tape, though there has been considerable improvement recently. Small and medium sized enterprises are not yet permitted to trade directly with companies in the EPZs because the sale of commodities such as food, stationary and materials is restricted. Both foreign companies and local enterprises have a feeling that government regulations and endless red inhibit trade relationship between EPZs and local industries, which can improve substantially with simplification of regulations and removal of irritants.

Effect of Technology Transfer

EPZs have attracted some high tech enterprises, which have made modest contribution in terms of technology transfer. These include units for the manufacture of semiconductor products, computer disks, electronic lighting and computers and these units account for 17% of the total production in the EPZs. Following categories of industry have been instrumental in technology transfer：

- Precision mechanical processing;
- Electronics products of higher technology such as computers and communication equipment;
- Food processing.

The satellite units in the zones have the benefit of technology transfer from the

Parent companies which enhances their productivity and quality and also of the material suppliers. A large number of employees have also been trained which include 110 engineers, 5,000 technicians, 210 line operators, 50 section leaders and 10 manager level executives.

After the establishment of EPZs, some new factories have come up to meet the requirement of raw material in the EPZs. Most of these factories provide packaging materials and material for cotton-stuffed toys pets and light jackets and furniture. Cotton material accounts for 50% while furniture's share is 30%. These new factories have created 12,000 additional jobs in the region.

Research and development is usually carried out by enterprises in order to improve product quality. According to

VIZA, about 50 enterprises are engaged in research and development activities and they spend between 0.5 to 3% of business turnover on R&D activities. Garment and textile units' account for 40% of units engaged in R&D. mechanical industry units rank second with 20% followed by foodstuff units with 15% of units undertaking R&D work.

Effect of EPZs on Enterprises on the Domestic Customs Territory

As mentioned earlier, two-way trade between EPZs and local enterprises is still limited due to government regulations, besides other limitations of low quality of local raw materials and high cost of end products. At present, enterprises in EPZs sell to local companies only products, which have to be imported and cannot be supplied by other domestic companies and buy from them local materials for production. As the volume of local sale is relatively low, it does not affect domestic market for similar products. Annual supply of local raw material to zone enterprises is, however, valued at US$18 millions, which is a reasonably good contribution to the local raw material market.

Impact of EPZs on local labor market is quite strong, as they require highly skilled employees. The educational level of zone employees in 1998 is depicted in Figure-9. The educational level varies between the staff and workers. While those in staff are mostly college or university graduates, most of workers have undergone courses in vocational and junior high schools（Annex - 5）.

347

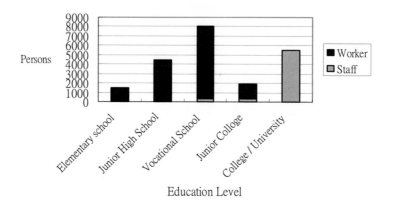

Figure – 9： Education Level of EPZ Employees in 1998

As regards sex ratio of employees, male employees account for about 65% of total work force in the Industrial Zones. By 1998, there were 14,200 male and 7,700 female employees with an average age of 29 and 27 respectively.

At present, wage in Izs are higher than the domestic labor market. Technical workers, on an average are paid US$ 100 to 120 per month, which is higher by 20% compared to domestic market wage rates. The production line workers are usually paid US$50 to 70 per month, which is 30% higher than the domestic market wage rates. Salaries of managerial personnel in the high salary brackets vary between US$ 700 to 1,200 per month, which is 100% to 150% higher than the domestic market rates.

It is obvious that wage rates and working environment in the zones are better than those in the domestic market. As a result, there has been an inflow of technical work force from domestic territory to the zones and workers prefer to work in EPZ enterprises, especially in Da Nang and Hai Phong cities.

Impact of Financial Thunderstorm in East Asia

Recent changes in the international economy have not had much impact on the EPZ enterprises. The financial thunderstorm that engulfed South Korea, Japan and Thailand two years ago and the recent strong appreciation of the dollar and the deep plunge of the Yuan and the New Taiwan Dollar have, however, affected the zones. The financial thunderstorm, and the strong appreciation of the US dollar, caused devaluation of the local currency as a result of which cost of imported raw materials increased up to 20%. Due to difference in exchange rate, the local raw material supply increased by 5%. Besides three as reduction in processing cost by 5%.

However, its impact on international market was adverse which affected the zone-based industries as well. The impact was wide spread in the Asian countries as their markets shrank, and exports of EPZ industries came down by 45% and the two-way trade also slid by 35%.

ORGANIZATION, MANAGEMENT, AND PERFORMANCE OF EPZs AUTHORITY

The management set up and organization structure of Izs in general and EPZs in particular in Vietnam is shown is flow charts in Figures-10 and –11.

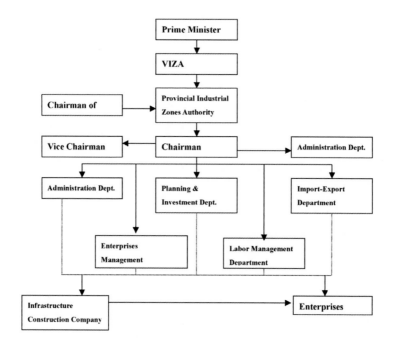

Note：*PPC stands for Provincial People Committee

Figure – 10：Organization set up for EPZs

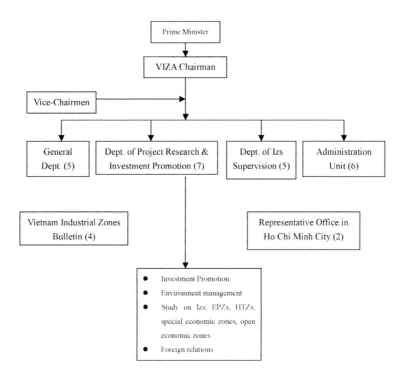

Figure – 11：Organization Structure of VIZA

The zone authority has responsibility and authority to fix targets for the zones in terms of investment, export turn over and employment. Figure – 12 shows the rate of attainment of planned targets of zones since their establishment.

The important services that the zone authority renders include attraction of investment, promotion of foreign trade, provision of industrial and commercial management and services and labor administration. Number of enterprises set up and amount of investment made in the zones from 1994 to 1998 have been depicted in Figures – 13 and – 14 respectively.

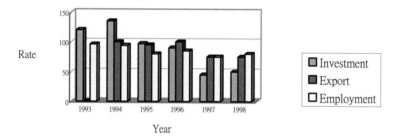

Figure – 12：Targets/achievements for Investment, Export and Employment

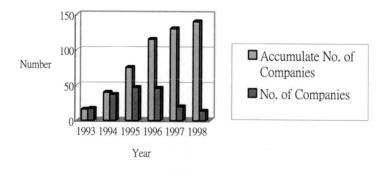

Figure – 13：Number of Enterprises in EPZs

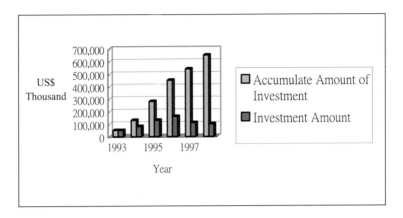

Figure – 14：Amount of Capital Invested in Surveyed EPZs

There was some decline in investment and the number of enterprises during 1997 and 1998 due to regional economic crisis. In the first six months of 1999, however, indicators have shown improvement.

Land in Vietnam can only be leased and not sold. Details of land leased during 1993 to 1998 are given in Table – 7. There are no standard factory buildings or private factory building in the surveyed EPZs in Vietnam. Infrastructure companies provide requisite infrastructure and enterprises themselves construct buildings.

Table – 7 : land leased in EPZs

Name	1998	1997	1996	1995	1994	1993	Leas able Area
Tan Thuan	126	112	93	69	30	7	210
Linh Trung	20	17	11	9	6	2	42

Da Nang	10	10	7	0	0	0	54
Haiphong 96	9	4	0	0	0	0	120
Tota Area	165	143	111	78	36	9	426

Zone enterprise does not control air pollution. However, they control water pollution. Each enterprise conducts on average three inspections on wastewater annually and the persons in charge of environment management of Zone authority carry out six inspections a year to monitor general flux channels.

The survey revealed that the technical training programs are sponsored by the enterprises as per training plan and training needs. The zone authority and enterprise have no responsibility in providing accommodation to the employees, who are supposed to take care of it by themselves. Enterprises as well as zone authority provide buses for commuting. Each zone has public cafeteria run by the zone authority, which provides low cost lunch. About 75% enterprises have their own cafeteria and provide low cost/free lunch to the employees. Zones have health centers （clinic） for providing health service at low cost. Enterprises also pay a certain amount of annual fee to the zone authority to run these Centers. Government hospitals outside the zone help in handling emergency cases since all employees have insurance cards, which entitle them to treatment in these hospitals. About 60% of enterprises organize summer holidays for 3 to 5 days for the employees. Other than this, the zone authority and enterprises do not sponsor any recreational activity.

EFFECTS AND BENEFITS TO THE GENERAL ECONOMY OF THE COUNTRY

With the establishment of the zones, additional job opportunities have been created （Table - 8） and the development of satellite factories has further brought down unemployment rate. The number of unemployed and rate of unemployment during 1988 – 1990, i.e., three years before setting up the zones and the position as in 1997 is given in Table – 8. The average rate of unemployment which was 10% three years before the setting up the zones, had come down to 6.9% in 1997.

Table – 8 : Number of Unemployed and the Rate of Unemployment

1988 ~ 1990 Average		1997
Number of Unemployed （million persons）	2.92	2.74
Rate of Unemployment	10%	6.9%

Source：General statistical Office

GNP has improved rapidly since the establishment of EPZs （Table – 9）. The rate of GNP growth was 327% in 1995 and 481% during 1997. in addition, the successful operation of the zones has created a favorable environment for rapid development of medium and small businesses in the domestic customs territory. This has resulted in increase in income levels and improvement in living standards. The per capita income has

reached VND 655,200 per month （equivalent to US$45）．

Table － 9：Improvement in GNP after Establishing of the Zones

	1990	1995	1997
GNP	53,606	228,892	311,623
Increase over 1990	0	175,286	258,017
Rate of Improvement （%）	0	327%	481%

Foreign investors also bring foreign markets into the host country. Presently, Vietnam exports goods to 42 countries and its trade volume is US$9,185 million, while in 1990, the year before the establishment of the zones, trade was confined to 23 countries only and the trade volume was US$1,700 million.

Industrial technology brought into the zones by foreign investors also enhances industrial development in the rest of the country. To sum up, the zones have contributed immensely by raising GDP and improving the standard of living of people.

FACTORS OF SUCCESS/FAILURE IN ESTABLISHNG AND MANAGING EPZs

Of the six EPZs establishment in Vietnam, one has been highly successful （Tan Thuan）and another one is in process of construction and development. Remaining four zones are not suitable to operate as EPZs. Therefore, three of these have been converted into Industrial Parks （Can Tho, Da Nang and Noi

Bai）. Can Tho zone is in the mixed form of IP and EPZ and now is named as Tra Noc Industrial and Export Processing Zone（I & EPZ）. 60% of production of this zone is also exported.

Factors contributing to Success

The main factors which contribute to the success of EPZs are low production costs and high market competitiveness of products. Abundant supply of labor force, raw material, semi-finished products and parts cut down the production costs. High quality and advanced technology helps to enhance the market competitiveness of EPZ goods. Mr. Yoshitaro Kido of Nidec Tosok, one of the entrepreneurs observed, 「Over the past two years, customers have highly valued the company's products and orders have increased much more than expected.」 He also said that in the year 2000, the company's output would increase by 20% and the 「Made in Vietnam」 goods produced at Tan Thuan and Linh Trung EPZs were competing in the world market.

Availability of labor force with goods working attitude is another important factor. Japanese investors at Tan Thuan EPZ have been surprised at the quick grasp of advanced technology by Vietnamese engineers and workers. Mr. Kazuhiro Kumagai, a Japanese entrepreneur said that the fact that the Vietnamese workers could absorb the technology as well as their Japanese colleagues has encouraged them to invest in Vietnam.

Proper planning before the establishment of the zones （parks） and the package of incentives are also critical to the success of EPZs and Hi-tech Parks. Location of the zones and infrastructural facilities within the zones should be very attractive, particularly for Japanese and Korean investors. Tan Thuan EPZ is a success story in Vietnam. The zone is located 4 km from downtown Ho Chi Ming City, next to Saigon port, the largest seaport in Vietnam and 12 km from Tan Son Nhat international airport. Corporate Location Magazine of United Kingdom had ranked this zone as the third best IP/EPZ or Science Park of the Asia-Pacific Region in July 1998.

Low rental for land and construction costs of factory building are other factors for the success of a zone. Before the regional economic crisis, many foreign investors preferred to invest in Vietnam due to low rentals and construction costs.

Sound and unambiguous policies regarding land rentals, investment incentives and finance and banking services are also important for the success of EPZs. Investors should feel secure in terms of planning, environmental protection and services.

The last but not the least, success of an EPZs also depends on the quality of service. The zone authorities have to ensure efficient and high quality services for the enterprises. Simple investment procedures and one-door policy are the two crucial tools to ensure good quality of service.

Factors OF Failure

Deficient laws and regulations are an important cause of failure of a zone and they tend to hamper its smooth functioning. There have been too many administrative controls on various aspects of operations of zone units. Sometimes the procedures are highly complicated. Even for minor modification such as changing the representative office or size of investment or expanding capacity, etc. permissions are needed to be obtained from the concerned authorities.

Inability to access international market is another factor which causes failure Electrical and electronic parks, textiles and garment, and precision tools are the major industries in the zones, which need to be exported in large volumes. Virtnam has, however, not been able to fully tap international market for these products. It is estimated that the volume of goods exported by EPZ esterprises in Vietnam is half of the volume of similar enterprises in other countries in the region （equal in capital investment）.

Inadequate facilities and utilities and deficient infrastructure or inappropriate location of EPZs are other reasons resulting in failure. To attract foreign investors, the zone authority should provide sufficient facilities and utilities like water supply, electricity power, waste treatment plants, and banking offices. Other support services, especially roads, transportation and communication facilities are equally important.

According to World Bank, foreign investors have lost interest in investing in Vietnam （investment has been declining dramatically since 1998）. This is due to out-dated technology and poor planning for infrastructure development.

Need for Improvements

At present, there is no law to regulate the setting up of IP, EPZs and Hi-tech Parks. All activities including establishment, operation and management of these zones are governed by the government Decree No. 36/CP which stipulates regulations on IPs, EPZs and HTPs and prescribes other legal documents such as the law on foreign investment, the Law on domestic investment, etc. It is proposed to amend the Decree 36/CP.

Other aspects like environmental protection and waste treatment should be adequately addressed in the laws or regulations for establishing the zones. 「One door」 policy should be effectively implemented to simplify the procedures for grant of license. This would attract foreign investors.

Facilities for education and training of workers need to be enhanced. A vocational school near tan Thuan and Linh Trung EPZs, provides 5,000 trained employees to these two EPZs. Government should focus on how workers in sufficient number can be trained for EPZs and HTPs. Government should also improve work attitude among the workers through training courses and mass promotion. Vietnam and Singapore have joined hands to open a technological training center to meet the demands of trained workers. This model could be replicated in the rest of the country.

Local conditions of the area where zones are located also need improvement to suit the requirement of foreign investors. These include improvement in transportation services, medical facilities, banking system, electricity power, water supply, schools, waste treatment plant and telecommunication services. Infrastructure is an important factor, which determines the success or failure of the zones.

The efficiency of the zone management should be improved to make foreign investors feel secure in the zones. The paper-work and procedures for granting license or various permissions by the zone authority need to be simplified and made explicit and transparent.

FUTURE PROSPECTS

Vietnam government will continue to maintain and develop the integrated economic zones including Ips, EPZs and HTPs. Vietnam will intensify effort to attract foreign investors. Proper laws and regulations for the zones and parks will soon be enacted for streamlining their operations. Any unsuccessful EPZ could be converted into an IP and enterprises located therein will then be subject to terms and conditions for IP enterprises. Even in the IPs, existing enterprises can enjoy the status of EPZ enterprise, if they so desire. Vietnam Industrial Zone Authority and other agencies and institutions are carrying out studies to evolve new incentive strategy to encourage the development of science and technology in the IPs, EPZs and Hi-tech Parks.

The government is seized of the problem of shortage of trained labor. To resolve this, a Vietnam Singapore Technological Training Centre, a joint venture has been set up. This would provide 5,000 trained workers per annum for the EPZs and IPs.

In the near future, Vietnam and Japan are also likely to set up technological training center in Ho Chi Ming City.

The 「One door」 policy will soon be given legal backing to simplify the procedures for granting license and reducing paperwork. It is also proposed to delegate powers to the zone authority and provincial councils to enable them to work more effectively. The government will train senior executives in the zones and develop human resources in order to meet the requirements of investors.

Besides, opening domestic market, government will also help the zone enterprises to promote export market in conformity with the general economic plans of the government.

In conclusion, the Vietnam government will continue its endeavor for modernization and industrialization of the country. EPZs and Hi-tech Park are still playing an important role in changing the economic structure of the country. The government has planned to establish more IP, EPZs and Hi-tech Parks. By the year 2003, 30 additional IPs and EPZs and one Hi-tech Park are planned to be set up.

REFFERENCE

1.Circular providing guidelines for financial regime applicable for industrial zones. Export processing zones and hi-tech zones, Vietnam Economic News, No. 28, 1998, pp.38-41

2.Statistical Yearbook – 1992, General Statistical Office, Hanoi.

3.Statistical Yearbook – 1998, General Statistical Office, Hanoi.

4.Annual Report of Vietnam Industrial Zones Authority（VIZA） on IP and EPZs in 1998, VIZA, Hanoi.

5.Export Processing Zones and Science Parks in Asia-Symposium report on export processing zones, Asian Productivity Organization, 1987.

6.Law on industrial zones and export processing zones, the 3rd draft 1998.

7.Ngo Xuam Loc,（1999）, Remark speech of Mr. Ngo Xuan Loc-Vice Prime Minister of Vietnam.

8.Vietnam : a guide for the foreign investor, Price Waterhouse, forth edition, January 1996.

Annex – 1 : Some Key Indicators （Per Capita）

Serial No.	Indicator	1980	1985	1989	1990
1	Food （rice basic）, kg	268	304	332	324
2	Meat （pork basic）, kg	8.3	12.5	14.8	15.2
3	Export, US$	6.3	11.7	30	36.3
4	Import US$	21.5	31	39.6	41.5
5	Number of People to School per 10,000	2,371	2,160	1,877	*
6	Number of Doctors and Nurses per 10,000	8.3	10.4	10,8	10.7

*Data was not collected

Annex – 2 : Education Status before the Establishment of Zones

		1987/88	1988/89	1989/90	190/91
University	No. of schools	100	103	103	106
	No. of Graduates Each Year	19,200	19,600	20,700	21,900

	Rate of Enrolment, %	9.29	11.75	14.27	18.55
Junior College, Vocational school	No. of schools	293	267	270	268
	No. of Graduates Each Year	47,100	46,700	47,200	39,900
	Rate of Enrolment	24.20	25.45	31.38	38.76
Senior High School	No. of schools	1,025	1,047	1,078	1,113
	No. of Graduates Each Year	303,000	272,000	220,000	174,000
	Rate of Enrolment	89.2	90.3	90.1	90.6
Junior High School & Primary School	No. of schools	12,994	13,377	14,308	15,403
	Rate of Enrolment	90.5	91.3	93.2	93.8
	No. of schools	8,423	8,426	8,420	8,412
Kindergarten	Rate of Enrolment	80.5	80.1	82.4	82.1

Annex – 3 : Enterprise Approved, Withdrawn and Currently in operation

Year	Enterprises Approved				Withdrawal of Enterprises				Enterprises in Operation in Current Year	
	No. of Enterprises	Amount (US$1,000)	Cumulative		No. of Enterprises	Amount (US$1,000)	Cumulative		No.	Amount
			Enterprise	Amount (US$1,000)			Enterprise	Amount (US$1,000)		
1991	NA	NA	NA	NA	NA	NA	NA	NA	NA	NA
1992	NA	NA	NA	NA	NA	NA	NA	NA	NA	NA
1993	8	28,410.00	6	26,110	NA	NA	NA	NA	NA	NA
1994	26	94,467.00	34	122,877	NA	NA	NA	NA	2	7,345
1995	39	158,988.00	73	281,865	NA	NA	NA	NA	14	60,620
1996	41	167,024.00	114	448,889	1	5,000	1	5,000	29	148,525
1997	17	116,292.00	131	565,181	1	4,000	2	9,000	57	303,631
1998	7	71,913.75	138	637,095	4	22,560	6	31,560	95	451,170

Annex – 4 : Imports and Exports

Year	Imports				Exports			
	Local Material	Imports	Total	Cumulative	Local sales	Exports	Total	Cumulative
1993	NA	NA	NA	NA	NA	NA	NA	NA

1994	703,200	3,984,800	4,688,000	4,688,000	NA	8,736,000	8,736,000	8,736,000
1995	4,082,400	23,133,600	27,216,000	31,904,000	3,274,000	63,952,000	67,226,000	75,962,000
1996	4,598,750	87,376,250	91,975,000	123,879,000	7,144,000	170,456,000	177,600,000	253,562,000
1997	19,131,920	107,995,413	127,127,333	251,006,333	6,578,000	286,134,000	292,712,000	546,274,000
1998	20,018,040	112,859,960	132,878,000	383,884,333	9,203,000	281,414,000	290,617,000	836,891,000

Annex – 5 : Education Level of Employees

Year		1996	1997	1998
Total Employees		11,498	16,689	22,790
Staff	Vocational school	584	335	658
	Junior College	584	335	658
	College University	4,612	3,002	6,123
	Master	6	3	7
	Sub-Total	5,786	3,676	7,445
	Rate （%）	35	32	33
Workers	Elementary School	1,363	782	1,535
	Vocational school	4,088	2,347	4,604
	Junior College	4,088	3,911	7,673
	College University	1,363	782	1,535
	Sub-Total	10,903	7,822	15,345
	Rate （%）	65	68	67

365

七、美國外國貿易區
（United States Foreign Trade Zones）
John DaPonte

　　美國外國貿易區是因應廣大的國內需求而設立，聯邦法授權每個港口的貨物均可進入此外國貿易區。總數 300 個的港口中有 1/3 是位於海岸線上，1/3 位於與墨西哥及加拿大的邊境，1/3 散佈在美國境內。

　　直到 1970 年止，美國的主要海港港口都有外國貿易區的計劃，這些區的計劃均結合港口的設備使能提供額外的服務給與進口商。至今有相當大的改變，法律並無改變，但是整體經濟環境的改變使我們現在有了 115 個外國貿易區。

　　為了要讓更多想擁有這類型服務的社區能夠接受加工區的觀念，很顯然的我們必須有彈性的配合他們的需求。舉例來說，我昨天剛從一場在內華達州雷諾市舉行的聽證會回來，他們想要設置一個外國貿易區。但是在雷諾市已經有一個貿易分區由一家公司所經營，這家地區性配銷中心已負責了美國境內的西部市場。這家擁有大量進口商品庫存的公司其關稅問題變得更為重要。為了減少費用他們在內華達州拉斯維加斯成立外國貿易區的分區。現在雷諾市有鑑於貿易分區的成功所以想設置自己的外國貿易區。

　　為了要讓外國貿易區的概念能與每個美國社區的利益相結合，我們必須對貿易區略作修改，採取務實原則使之具有可行性。而且我們能夠比照執行而不改變基本型態。

　　但是現在我們正改善我們的規則，因為美國的行銷條例與外國貿易區條例並不一致。我們已經在這些條例下加了許多解釋，即使我們已經讓條例與他們的一致，但是在讀完這些條例並不會讓你對外國貿易區有更深的概念。事實我們一直在修改我們的條例，這修改條例的過程牽涉到兩個部門，一是外國貿易區的董事會，由商業部長擔任主席，另一個部門是美國的海關由財政秘書擔任主席。

　　我所領導的外國貿易區管理處直屬於商業部。我們辦理的對貿易區及分區的申請案，監督和為美國外國貿易區制定章程。我們要求這些貿易區要公佈他們的收費標準而且我們認為收費標準是合理的。我們不直接介入他們如何訂定收費標準，但是我們會針對使用者的抱怨來重新檢視他們的收費標準。而美國的海關部是主管機關每天都參與作業，督導外國貿易區使用邊境的審查標準。他們要求外國貿易區的使用者要有某種形態的加強系統作業而且他們還作抽樣檢查及設立人身安全檢標準。

　　這說明了我們的計劃必須是機動性的──它必須不停的修改。我們發現很多社區，一旦他們有了執照去經營一個貿易區，他們必須照著他們所申請的計劃去經營。我們作了很多的努力很頻繁的修改我們的規則儘可能達成當地居民的需求。因為不是那些居民也不是我們一開始就知道需要那些協助一直到當貿易區經營一段時間後才清楚了解。

　　另產生一種新的觀念稱之為「一貫作業區」，為一種大型操作區，對能力不足的一些小社區如果他們無法証明他們擁有大型的公共建設來經營一個貿易區可能就無法設立外

國貿易區。舉例來說，在工業區裡可能有 10%的使用者可以享受到園區帶來的利益而不是來自海關。假如有可能讓非園區使用者及園區使用者混合在一個工業區內。如果這種模式阻礙了美國海關的監督，美國的海關有權利禁止這樣的經營模式。大多數的情況下，如果持續使用邊境的審查標準，很有可能會造成非園區使用者及園區使用者混合在一個工業區內一起經營下去。

在美國，貿易區變成了州與地方經濟發展的方案。不要認為這個決定的決策權在聯邦政府；我們的態度是儘可能不去控制和不去妨礙。我們要城市去計劃他們所需求的貿易區，讓我們知道什麼樣的改變是必須的，而我們會配合給予必要的協助。另外，當我們要設立及修改貿易區時我們會有一個公開的記錄作業。

在我們 115 個貿易區裡有許多小型私人設備。我們目前大約有 60 億美元的商品在園區內流動。附帶地，這些小型貿易區還需要 2~3 年時間才學會經營。大約有 70 家的小型貿易區已開始生產。其中有大約 80 家的貿易分區已得到營業許可，有 45 家已開始生產了。大部份的貿易分區是從事汽車及其他運輸設備組裝。原因是我們對於汽車工業在關稅法中制定了一項反傾銷稅。美國對於完成品的汽車課稅2.5%. 但對於從國外進口的部份零件卻要課 5%，8 %，或是 10%的稅。所以我很確定你們都知道以及鼓勵這類型的生產來刺激我們國內的經濟。

我們有一個貿易區在亞歷桑那州的鳳凰城，靠近 Flagstaff 的地方，我將引用它作為例子。這個貿易區的贊助

者是鳳凰城本身。它是一個進口港而且得到州政府全力支
持。這個外國貿易區是要來幫助這個社區達成其長遠經濟發
展的目標，其中最重要的是發展其國際貿易經濟。他們的計
劃是請一家私人機構來經營貿易區而他們提供場所。這是一
個很普通的常識，在我們的貿易區方案中是被允許的。我們
發現結合公營企業與私營企業對於貿易區經營成功是很重
要的一環。在合約的規範下這些私人公司可使用 60%的貿易
區場所。這是在鳳凰城的例子。讓一家私人公司來經營一個
工業區然後有許多公有的倉庫位於工業區內。在任何時間，
都大約有 10~15 家公司在使用工業區。還有許多的公司開始
跟他們接觸詢問一些關於在工業區內設廠的手續及費用。
讓他們知道一個重點即區內的設施為吸引他們來區是隨時
都能供應給他們使用的。鳳凰城在未來的 5 年還是前途看
好的。

　　我們其中一項規定是你不可以在沒得到董事會的許可
下在美國的貿易區經營任何一項製造業。大約有 70%商品會
從貿易區直接銷售至美國市場。

UNITED STATES FOREIGN TRADE ZONES

John DaPonte, Executive secretary

U.S. Foreign Trade Zones Board

U.S. Dept. of Commerce

Washington, DC

I appreciate the opportunity to be here at this very important WEPZA session. As director of the U.S. Foreign Trade Zones program, and on behalf of the Secretary of Commerce, I welcome you to the land of the U.S. Foreign Trade Zones.

I associate very much with the WEPZA organization and appreciate the fact that I have associated with it since its beginning. Ted Pena to me, is one of the top examples of an international civil servant. Ted, it is so good to see you again, your presence here has made this of much more importance.

I also want to acknowledge Peter Ryan of UNIDO whose involvement during the setting up of WEPZA is well known. Peter Ryan has played a very important role as champion of information and official involvement in the foreign trade/free zone concept. Nice to see you, Peter.

The U.S. Foreign Trade Zone program is a peculiar one designed to serve the needs of the public at large under this concept in the United States. The fact is that our federal legislation entitles every port of entry to a zone. We have over 300 ports of entry about 1/3 of which are coastal, another 1/3 are on the borders with Mexico and Canada and the other 1/3 are scattered throughout the U.S. interior.

Until about 1970 it was mainly our U.S. seaports that had zone programs. The zone programs were part of their port facilities to provide additional services to the importers who were bringing goods into the United States. Since that time our program has changed drastically. The law has not change but the economic environment has changed so that we now have 115 communities with foreign trade zones.

In order to adapt a concept like zones to the multitude of communities that want to have this type of service, it is obvious that we have to be flexible to match their special needs. As an example, yesterday I came from a public hearing in Reno, Nevada, for a foreign trade zone that they want to establish. Already in Reno there is a foreign trade subzone operating for a company, which has a regional distribution center for its western market in the U.S. For this company with its heavy inventory of imported goods the customs duties become very important. The company was able to reduce its costs by becoming a subzone to a foreign trade zone project already in that states at Las Vegas, Nevada. The city of Reno now wants to have its own full foreign trade zone project because it has seen the success of this subzone.

In order to accommodate the interests of the communities of the U.S. to use this concept, we have had to modify trade zone a little and adopt some practices and principles so that it is workable. And we have been able to cope without changing the basic form.

But now we are changing our regulations. U.S. marketing regulations are really not in tune with the zone that we have today. We have made so many interpretations under these regulations, even though we have always been consistent with them that reading the regulations today do not give you a very good picture. The fact is that we are in the middle of changing our regulations now, a process that involves the Foreign Trade Zone Board, which is chaired by the secretary of Commerce, and the U.S. Customs Service chaired by the Secretary of the Treasury.

The Foreign Trade Zone Office that I direct is part of the Commerce dept. We process the applications for new zone and subzones, monitor zone and do the regulating that is involved in the U.S. Foreign Trade Zone Program. Our zones are required to publish their rates and charges and we see that they are reasonable. We don't get involved in rate making but we do review complaints from users about rates. The U.S Customs Service, on the other hand, is the agency that is involved on a day-to-day basis. It supervises zones using border inspection principles. It requires that Zone users have a certain type of enforceable system and it makes spot checks and sets physical security standards.

Many of our system follow the same principles that you will find in your EPZs, but with differences peculiar to our needs. For example, even a small community that may not have a large amount of international trade at present may be trying to provide the services that an individual importing company needs. In our case the Nissan Plant, a major international investment, was the first automobile assembly factory in the U.S. to operate on a subzone basis. Now all automotive assembly companies in the U.S. have, at least in some of their plants, subzone status to operate as part of a U.S. Foreign Trade Zone. This allows them to maintain inventory of imported parts and pay duty only when they actually used them.

This illustrates that our program must be dynamic – it is always changing. We have found that many communities, once they have their license to operate a zone on the basis of a plan that they have presented to us, believe that have to stick with that plan. But this is not necessary. We make major efforts to change our procedures to make it possible to meet the local needs of that community. Frequently neither they nor we know what those specific needs will be until a few years of operation under the license.

One of the results has been a new concept that you might call a 「piggy back」 or integrated zone, which is part of a larger operation. Many of our smaller communities would not have been able to have zones if it weren't for the fact that they could operate a zone as part of a large facility, which has the same physical infrastructure they need for the zone. For example, in the industrial park environment maybe 10% of the users at any time could benefit from using zone procedures rather than the customs procedures we have today. It is possible to have a mix of non-zone and zone users in the same industrial park. The United States Customs Service has the authority to prohibit operations that interfere with their supervision. But for the most part, using border inspection methods, it is possible to have zone and non-zone operations going on side by side.

Another general policy is to minimize the federal role and emphasize that it is a state and local program. Zones in the U.S. become part of the state and local economic development programs. Don't think of decisions as being made at the federal level; our attitude is to be as non regulatory as possible and non-interfering. We want cities to plan their zone to meet their needs, and to let us know what changes must be made. We will cooperate with them in required procedures, which involve giving public notice of any comments. We have an open record procedure when we are acting on requests to establish and modify zones.

Many of our 115 zone are very small private facilities. We deal in about 6 billion dollars of goods that are moving through our zones today. Incidentally, it takes about 2 to 3 years for zones to get into operation. About 70 of these are in operation. Of the 80 subzone licensed, there are 45 now operational. Most of our subzone are used for auto assembly operations and other transportation equipment. The reason is that we have an inverted tariff on automobiles under the U.S. Tariff Schedule. The duty rate on finished automobiles in the U.S. is 2 1/2 %. The duty rates on some of the parts and components imported from abroad is some cases is 5, 8, or 10%. And I'm sure all of you know what that means in terms of encouraging production in our national economy.

We have a zone in Phoenix, Arizona, which is typical, and, since it is the closest to Flagstaff, I will use it as an example. The sponsor of the zone, the licensee, is the City of Phoenix. It is a port of entry, with the full support of state agencies. The FTZ is a service to the community meeting its long-term economic development objectives, which include international trade as an important part of the economy. Their plan also called for a private operator to run the zone and provide the facilities. This is a common practice, which has always been allowed under our zone program. We find that the mix of the public and private entrepreneur is very important for the success of the zone. Probably private companies under contract operate 60% of our zones with the licensee. This is the case with Phoenix. It is a company that operates an industrial park and public warehousing within the industrial park. Between 10 and 15 companies are using the zone at any time. There are a number of companies contacting them about the procedures and rates they are thinking of setting up. It is important to let them know the zone facilities are available in order to attract them. Phoenix has god prospects for the next 5 years.

One of our rules is that you cannot conduct any manufacturing in a U.S. Zone without board approval. About 70% of the goods leaving zones are destined for the U.S. market. Occasionally a domestic industry, which is getting protection under a higher tariff and would lose it under zone procedures objects to allowing others to manufacture that in a zone.

We have a procedure for them to object and, following public hearings on the issue, can prohibit and restrict some operations in the zones – all under the general authority of public interest.

I hope that from this observation you have learned about the similarities and differences between U.S. Foreign Trade Zone and your own EPZs. My own view has been that any improvements we can make in facilitating customs procedures and eliminating export taxes in EPZs all over the world will help us all with international development. It has been a pleasure to be with you. Good luck with your conference.

八、牙買加加工出口區（Jamaica's EPZS）

　　牙買加的加工出口區發展開始於牙買加的港務局，因為他們對於將貨物分途裝運然後再銷售至許多位於加勒比海的島嶼的生意感到極大的興趣。牙買加的加工出口區的發展過程包括一般的港口發展，例如開發新的港口設施，以及引進自由貿易的觀念。工會的阻力在為工業發展引用了自由區觀念所產生的法律功效而予以克服。

　　在牙買加港務局的計劃下，於 1977 年成立了金司敦工業區並開始運作。在 1977 年運作初期，牙買加港務局投入了美金 1 億 5 千萬在碼頭區興建倉庫及包裝工廠。到了 1979 年，大約有 700 名工人在面積約 15 萬平方英尺大的包裝工廠工作。

　　1982 年，自由貿易區開發者與牙買加港務局達成協商，同意使用免稅優惠政策來發展工業區。自從 1983 年起，金司敦工業區大約增加了 10 萬平方英尺的面積，到目前為止，這個工業區至少有超過 4000 名工人在這個面積有 30 萬平方英尺的包裝及裝配廠工作。

　　我們的計劃是在未來的 18 個月裡在金司敦自由區擴區 40 萬平方英尺的面積，將可增加一倍的勞動力。

　　我們的業務單位已注意到近年來一些廠商不僅對金司敦有興趣，同時也對盟帝歌灣有興趣。這個城市位於牙買加北部海岸，而且早已是具有旅遊中心，國際空運及完善的公

共設施而聞名。於是我們在盟帝歌灣另建設一個加工出口區，如今工廠使用面積已達到一萬兩千平方英尺。我們將於 1986 年另增建擴大一萬五千平方英尺，以及希望到 1986 年底再另增加四萬平方英尺。

金司敦工業區有九十家廠商於其營運，對於盟帝歌灣，雖然是新區，仍已有三家廠商進駐。

我們自由區一直受到各方面的協助，USAID 曾給予過最大的協助。另外，德國及愛爾蘭也曾給予大力的支援。

相較於別的加工出口區。由於我們提供更優惠的待遇，如 100%的區內固定資產免稅，進口的原材料，零配件，甚至廠房所用的藝術品或裝飾品，或只要與生產有關的東西，全部免稅。

加工區的管理及區內的廠商有其一定的架構存在，不管如何，我們覺得一定要讓我們的廠商在完全的自由狀況下運作，不用擔心煩瑣的法令規章，這是我們大部份的廠商營業額為何可以大幅成長的原因之一，兩年內，我們預計出口值將會自 1800 萬美金成長至近 3000 萬美金，同時區內廠商的營利也將大幅成長。

JAMAICA'S EXPORT PROCESSING ZONES

Charles A. Pennycooke
General Manager
Kingston Free Zone Company, Ltd.
Kingston Jamaica

Jamaica's EPZs began with Jamaica's Port Authority and its interest to enter the break-bulk business for distribution of goods to the many Caribbean Islands. It evolved from the general process of port development, including developing new port facilities, and from the free zone concept. Resistance from unions was overcome under the law implementing a strategy for industrial development using the free zone concept.

The Kingston industrial zone became a reality in 1977 out of the plans of the Port Authority. In its early years the Port Authority had invested $150 million in piers with warehouses and packaging facilities. By 1979 there were 150,000 square feet of packing facilities employing about 700 people.

With the new law negotiated by the Port Authority in 1982 the free zone developers used tax exemption to provide an incentive for industrial development. Since 1983 there have been approximately 100,000 square feet added, and to date there are 300,000 square feet of packing and assembly facilities employing just over 4,000 people.

Our plan for the next 18 months is to build another 400,000 square feet to double the work force in the Kingston Free Zone.

Our marketing people noticed in recent years that clients were attracted not only to Kingston but also to Montego Bay. This city, located on the North Coast of Jamaica, has built an outstanding reputation as a tourism center and possesses an international airport and many infrastructure elements. Acting on the requests we decided to do another free zone in Montego Bay and are now operating 12,000 square feet of factory space. We will be building and developing another 15,000 square feet in January of 1986 and hope to add another 40,000 square feet by the end of 1986.

In Kingston there are 90 companies operating within our export processing zone facilities, and in Montego Bay, although it is a new zone, we have 3 companies operating.

Our free zone would not have been a reality without assistance, and the assistance has been very great from USAID. We have also received help from the German colony and the Irish colony.

The higher incentives that we offer than other free zones give us certain advantages. We have a 100% tax freeze on corporate tax profits in perpetuity, there's the duty free import of capital goods, raw materials, consumables, components, articles used for construction or part of the construction of the facilities, and any items that are needed for production.

Relationships between the companies and free zone management require a frame work of bureaucracy. However, we feel that the client company should be able to operate freely, without having worries about meeting endless detailed requirements of bureaucratic regulations within our free zone facilities. That's one reason why sales of these companies have increased tremendously. In a two years we expect exports from here will have grown from US$18 million to close to $30 million. Our projections are the profits of our client companies will also grow.

九、斯里蘭卡加工出口區（The Greater Colombo Economic Commission of Sri Lanka）

斯里蘭卡的加工出口區成立於 1978 年正代表著斯里蘭卡經濟的轉變由控制轉變為自由發展企業經營，而接下來政府也在隨之改變。轉變的目的在利用外國私人投資對本國失業人口增加就業機會，由我們政府提供所需之公共建設，只保留少數的資本投資事業，另一個目的是從事多樣化的出口經營而不專注於農業出口，以能增加我們的外匯收入。

於 1978 年，我們在機場設立了第一個加工出口區。管理委員會的成立具有事權統一功能，對外國投資案逕行核准。委員會對具有潛力的投資人有權與之協商。關於這點，這和其他的加工出口區並沒有多大的不同。

10 年免稅優惠，適用於投資成功，勞工水平及外匯交易所得等。接下來，我們還提供額外的 15 年只收取 2% - 5% 的營業稅來取代公司所得稅。這與別的公司稅法比起來確實是優惠許多。

目前約有 36,000 員工在所有加工出口區內工作。我們的第一個加工出口區尚未完成。在 1983 年，我們在靠近可倫波附近開始興建了另一個加工出口區。

我們目前正朝著高科技產業邁進，但是我們卻選擇了高，中，低水平的產業來發展以解決我們最基本的問題。

　　當我回想起我們第一家工廠在 1979 年開始營運以來，從歷史記錄上看我們沒有損失任何一個人一日的工作時間在罷工上，這是令人喜悅的。之所以沒有發生是代表我們很幸運。委員會投入了非常多的時間與努力來留心觀察勞工與管理階層之間所發生的不愉快。如果發現有衝突發生的可能，委員會的人員會介入試著排解雙方的衝突並且順利的化解歧見。

　　此刻工會還沒成立，但是委員會堅持參與工會管理的協調會。除此之外，委員會利用本身的力量去幫勞工與管理雙方謀取更多的福利。我們曾經有過問題，但是對於整個勞工與管理階層而言，他們曾因藉由我們的協助來幫忙解決了問題。

　　發表演說並不是我的目的——但只希望能提供一些重點告訴您我們委員會是如何的在運作。謝謝各位的關心。

THE GREATER COLOMBO ECONOMIC COMMISSION OF SRI LANKA

Tilak Samarasekara, Chairman
Greater Colombo Economic Commission
Colombo, Sri Lanka

The Sri Lanka EPZ was set up in 1978 as part of our changes from an economy of controls to an economy of free enterprise following a change in government. The major objective was to create jobs for the unemployed in our country using foreign private investment. We provided the infrastructure, retaining a very minor capital investment in the operation. Our other objectives were to diversify our export base which had been primarily agricultural and to increase our foreign exchange earnings.

In 1978 we set up our first Export Processing Zone which is at the airport. The Commission was set up as a single authority which, when it deals with foreign investment, is the approving authority. It has the powers within itself to negotiate with the potential investor. In this it is not very different from many other zones.

The incentive is a tax holiday on profits of ten years maximum depending, of course, on the investment made, employment level, foreign exchange earned, etc. We then follow that with up to 15 additional years of substituting a turnover tax of 2% - 5% for corporate income tax. This compares very well with the corporate tax level on profits.

Current employment totals about 36,000 in our EPZs. Our first zone is not finished yet. In 1983 we began building another zone closer to the city of Colombo.

There is the road to high technology which we are going on, but we still take the high, the low or the middle just so long as it will solve our basic problems.

When I think back to our first factory which we opened in 1979 and recall that we have never lost a man-day to strikes in our history, it is gratifying. This didn't happen just because of good fortune, although we've been fortunate enough. The Commission invests much time and effort in watching for labor and management clashes. If there is a potential for a problem, we go in and act as a buffer between the two sides and smooth it out.

There is no unionization of labor at the moment, but the Commission insists on joint worker management councils. In addition the Commission uses its own powers to work for the benefit of both. We have had problems, but on the whole workers and managers have had a valuable means to work out their problems, but on the whole workers and managers have had a valuable means to work out their problems because of us.

It has not been my purpose to make a speech – but rather to fill you in on some of the highlight of the way we operate. Thank you for your attention.

十、墨西哥邊界工業化計劃（Mexico's Border Industrialization Program）

　　墨西哥的邊界工業化方案已推動 20 餘年企圖要解決邊界的失業問題，因為這個區域遠離墨西哥人口聚集及工業中心。

　　經過幾年的推動，這個方案的觸角已遍及墨西哥各地，但是，至目前為止這個方案在邊界推行的很成功。

　　墨西哥最大的優勢在於其地理位置毗鄰美國──全世界最大的市場。位於邊境的工廠僅需花不到 6 小時時間產品就能送抵美國各主要城市。另一個優勢是墨西哥擁有廉價且可訓練的勞工，目前工資為每小時一美元並包括額外福利。

　　邊界工業化方案非常簡單。墨西哥同意加工生產及裝配完成的產品 100%出口給予優惠進口設備及原物料暫時性的免稅。

　　進口原物料免稅期限達六個月之久。

　　墨西哥並不介意產品將輸出到那一國去。他們並不需要再輸回原產國。有些公司，特別是電視組裝工廠，直接從遠東地區將零件進口至墨西哥將產品加工成成品或半成品然後將產品出口到美國。

　　這些公司允許擁有 100%的外國資本，因為墨西哥不提供任何的優惠方案。

　　所有的公司都必須繳納營業稅，而且要遵守工會及其它法律的規範。墨西哥政府及一些私人公司非常有興建將墨西哥生產零件裝配在這些出口貨品上，雖然目前墨西哥零件的出口值只有 2%。其原因是這類工業將有很大的出口遠景，這也就是我們被人賦予「MAQUILA」—外來零元件加工再出口業，這個西班牙名字。

　　在 1969 年，當這個方案已在墨西哥實行時約有 5000 個輸出品生產的工作機會，有一半的工作機會在華來市（Juarez）這個城市。今天在華來市約有 75,000 個工作機會，而且在全墨西哥有超過 725 個工廠將近有 225,000 個直接生產的工作機會。預測每一個直接生產的工作機會可以產生約兩個間接生產的工作機會，將為這個 maquila 工業帶來超過 600,000 的工作機會。

　　在 1984 年，墨西哥估計 maquila 工業為墨西哥帶來了約美金 11 億 6 千萬的附加價值的收入。其中約美金 6 億元屬於薪資部分的收入，另外約美金 900 萬為墨西哥生產的零件，原物料及包裝材料部分的收入。

　　透過美國海關，我們知道墨西哥出口值將近 48 億 1 千 7 百萬美元，其中包含 25 億 5 千 2 百萬美元是根據海關關稅條款 806 及 807，美國零元件所繳的關稅。這代表著其餘的外國零元件，大部分來自亞洲，由於透過 maquila 方案再將這些產品出口至美國已為我們賺進美金約 11 億零 5 百萬元。

　　我們被這價值 36 億 5 千 7 百萬美元的零件及原材料收益所吸引。我們認為墨西哥的製造業者有相當大的機會借著

maquila 方案實行能夠生產及提供可符合品質，交期及價格要求的產品給國際市場。我們可以生產許多不同類別的產品從最尖端的高科技產品到最普通的金屬衝壓，我們皆可生產。我們目前致力於將 maquila 工業引進給華來市和墨西哥市。

對於墨西哥市來說，maquila 工業愈發的重要因為它是僅次於石油出口第二大的外匯收入，而且更重要的是，它提供寶貴的工作去訓練我們的工人在國際市場上競爭，一個月前，墨西哥總統宣佈要將 maquila 工業列為全國首要發展工業。

將公共設施設置在適當的地區將會促進該地區的成長繁榮。著名的管理學作者 Peter F. Drucker 在 Flagstaff 研究中心的研討會中只出，墨西哥期望在預估增加生產量方面與美國分享。

Drucker 建議美國借著高水準技能及教育的優勢重整他們的勞動力後在未來的幾年在開發中國家將導致約 7-9 百萬的新製造業工作機會產生。根據關稅 806/807 條款，為了維持我們目前在 maquila 工業貿易方面 1/3 的市場佔有率，我們必須設下目標要贏得至少 1-3 百萬這項工作機會。

到目前為止，我們成功的原因在於我們可將自己定位為私人的工業園區從事出口事業並得到墨西哥政府的全力支援。我們的資金來自于民營企業，這些企業大部分在美國。目前只有少數幾家政府資助的工業園區從事 maquila 工業發展。在墨西哥的法律保護下工廠出租及銷售是被允許的。

　　目前我所代表的公司計有 63 家工廠設在區內大約雇用超過 50,000 名員工。我們希望將延伸至墨西哥境內和 Yucatan 半島，刺激新的風險投資設置四個以上的工業區。我們相信借著 maquila 工業方案達到技術轉移和增加出口就業人數以及使用私人工業區管理制度來吸引 maquila 的公司是我們最主要的目的。

　　就這種意義來說，我們支援世界加工出口區會設於 Flagstaff 研究中心的一些改變給予像我們這種的私人出口工業區享有和其他國家由政府所成立的加工出口區同等的地位。我們許諾支援世界加工出口區會為主要的資訊中心與我們便能在國際製造業網路中獲得利益。

MEXICO'S BORDER INDUSTRIALIZATION PROGRAM

Guillermo Ochoa, President
Grupo Bermudez
Cd. Juarez, Chihuahua
Mexico

The Border Industrialization Program of Mexico started 20 years ago in an attempt to solve an unemployment problem in the region which was particularly difficult, in part because the area is so far from the center of population and industry in Mexico.

After a few years of operation the program was extended throughout Mexico, but, so far, most of its success has come in the border region.

The major advantage of Mexico is its location adjacent to the United States, the largest market in the world. Industry along the border is within 6 hours of any major city airport of the United States. Of equal importance is the availability of low-cost trainable labor in Mexico, both along the border and in the interior, at current wage rates of about $1 per hour actually worked including fringe benefits.

The border industrialization program is very simple. Mexico allows the temporary duty-free import of equipment and raw materials for processing and assembly provided 100% of the products are exported.

The duty free import of the raw materials has a grace period of six months.

Mexico does not really care about where the products are exported. They do not necessarily have to go back to the country of origin. Some companies, particularly television assembly plant, now import components directly from the Far East and process them into either finished or semi finished products and then export them to the United States.

Companies are allowed to have 100% of foreign capital. There are no other important incentives offered. All must pay normal corporate taxes in Mexico and comply with all labor and other laws and regulations of Mexico. There is a strong interest by the Mexican government and the Mexican private sector to incorporate Mexican components in these exports, although only about 2% of component value exported is Mexican at present. The reason is the very large future we foresee for growing exports of this industry, to which we have given the Spanish name 「MAQUILA」.

In 1969 when the program really got underway Mexico had about 5000 export manufacturing jobs in this industry, half of them in Juarez. Today in Juarez we have over 75,000 jobs, and in all of Mexico there are over 725 plants with a total of 225,000 direct factory jobs. It is estimated that each direct job generates about two indirect jobs which would bring the total impact of the maquila industry to over 600,000 jobs.

For the year 1984 the Banco de Mexico estimates the total value added by the maquila industry was $1,160 million dollars. Of this about $600 million was in wages and salaries and $9 million was in Mexican components, raw materials and packaging materials.

Through the U.S. Customs we learn that Mexico exported a total value of about $4817 million, including $2552 million of U.S. components under Tariff Articles 806 and 807. This means that other foreign components, mostly from Asia, which we re-exported to the U.S. under the maquila program totaled $1105 million.

It is this flow of $3657 of components and raw materials which interests us. We see considerable opportunity for Mexican manufacturers to link to the manquila program by supplying those components where we can meet quality, schedule, and price requirements of the international market. There are many products ranging from very sophisticated high-tech products to very common small metal stampings which we believe can be made in Mexico. We are marking great efforts in Juarez and Mexico City to stimulate interest in linkages to the maquila industry.

For Mexico today, the maquila industry has become extremely important because it generates foreign exchange second only to petroleum exports and, more important, it provides precious jobs to train our workers to compete in international markets. A month ago the President of Mexico declared that the maquila industry deserved national priority.

Great efforts will be made to put infrastructure in place to promote its growth. Mexico is counting on the growth forecasts for production sharing with the United States such as those made by Peter F. Drucker, noted author on management subjects, at a seminar of the Flagstaff Institute.

Drucker suggests that the restructuring of the American labor force to take advantage of its higher skills and education in future years will result in some 7-9 million new manufacturing jobs being created in the developing world. To maintain our current 1/3 share of 806/807 trade in this industry, we must set as our objective the winning of 1-3 million of these jobs.

Our success so far has been due to the freedom with which we have been able to operate as private industrial parks for export with the full support of the Mexican Government. All of our financing is done through the private sector, must of it in the United States. There are very few public sector industrial parks that deal with this industry. Under Mexican trust law both leasing and selling plants is possible.

At present the company I represent has 63 plants in its industrial parks which provide direct employment to over 50,000 people. We are expanding to the interior of Mexico and to the Yucatan Peninsula to stimulate new ventures through establishing 4 more industrial parks. We believe that transfer of technology and creating export employment go hand-in-hand under the maquila program and that the management concept of using private industrial parks to attract maquila firms is our major asset.

In this sense, we support the changes WEPZA has instituted at Flagstaff to give our private export industrial parks equal status with the government operated EPZs that other countries prefer. We pledge our support to WEPZA as a key information center from which all of us in this fascinating international manufacturing network can benefit.

十一、賴比瑞亞工業自由區

（Update on the Liberia Industrial Free Zone）

賴比瑞亞工業自由區持續運作，不管嘗過多少失敗經驗仍努力以赴以達成目標及任務。

由於世界經濟的衰退導致我們主要出口產品如鐵礦及橡膠產品的需求減少。賴比瑞亞的經濟成長被嚴重的阻礙而且相對影響到賴比瑞亞工業自由區順利的運作。

升級的做法及策略，在世界很多經營成功的自由區都曾經用過，我們的自由區也曾經採用過，但因賴比瑞亞缺乏資金而延緩。

儘管如此，我們還是持續不斷努力以書信與有實力的投資人保持連繫，特別是那些已在本區完成初步設廠準備工作的投資人。

自從於 1975 年依法成立賴比瑞亞工業自由區以來，致力於發揚傳統精神和珍惜自由事業體系使得自由區成為一個具有完善設施及可信賴的投資環境。

設立此區有三個目的：（1）激勵工業發展以達到對賴比瑞亞技術移轉（2）激勵勞力密集工業使用當地原料以降低失業人口比率（3）發展我們的出口貿易。

首先，區內所有基本的公共設施已能充分供應區內既有需求。這些設施包含標準廠房供生產與製造之用，一個大型的倉庫作為原物料及成品的儲存，道路，下水道和停車場，

休閒中心和區內的原工餐廳，健康中心以及水電供應設施，等。此區佔地面積 113 英畝，其中 75 英畝已完成開發。

第二點，對區內投資人已計劃完成一整套的優惠方法。其優惠方法包括：（1）進口機器，設備原物料及其他非關緊要的供應物資等均可免關稅；（2）區內製品或成品免出口稅；（3）製成品可課稅內銷國內市場，其稅率為 5~10%；4）提供最少 5 年所得稅 100%全免，依法視投資規模類別及金額大小得申請延長期限；（5）土地與廠房的租金可延後一年繳交。

除此之外，區內持續不斷收到投資人針對「自由區法規」所制定的嚴利出口條件提出抱怨。因此自由區管理局同意將出口條件放寬 3 年以利企業個體推展自己的出口市場。

我很榮幸向各位報告截至目前維止我們的審核委員會已經核准至少 15 件投資案而初期投資金額預估為 6 千萬美金。

然而，目前只有 3 項投資案完全開工營運，所雇用的總員工人數在 1,000 人以內；由於最近同意將出口條件放寬 3 年，預計其餘的投資案很快會起死回生。

最後，我謹代表賴比瑞亞政府及工業自由區管理局（LIFZA）及其董事會的各位董事表達對世界加工出口區（WEPZA）協會給予我們如此寶貴的機會致上最高的謝意。同時也要感謝 Flagstaff 研究中心的參與。

身為 WEPZA 的創始會員之一，LIFZA 隨時準備與WEPZA 的成員一起合作來完成所付予的任務。

UPDATE ON THE LIBERIA INDUSTRIAL FREE ZONE

Paul H. Perry, Managing Director
Liberia Industrial Free Zone Authority
Monrovia, Liberia

The Liberia Industrial Free Zone （LIFZA） continues to function within the scope of its mandate irrespective of some setbacks experienced in the achievement of its goals and objectives.

Due to the global economic recession which has resulted in a low demand for our iron ore and rubber products which constitute our major exports, Liberia's economic growth has been seriously hampered and this has adversely affected the smooth operation of the Liberia Industrial Free Zone.

The promotional activities and strategies which have been instrumental in the success of other booming Free Zones in the world, most of which were to be adopted by our Free Zone, had to be deferred because of stringent liquidity problems which Liberia now faces.

Notwithstanding, relentless efforts continue to be made through the mail in furthering contacts with potential investors, particularly those with whom some preliminary arrangements for location in the Zone had been concluded.

Since the establishment of the Liberia Industrial Free Zone in 1975 by an Act of Legislature in the true spirit of the country's traditional and cherished free enterprise system efforts have continued to be made to make the Free Zone a fully equipped and reliable investment environment within the Liberian economy.

The zone was established primarily to meet three objectives：1）to ignite industrialization thereby imparting the transfer of technology to Liberians. 2）to stimulate labor-intensive type industries utilizing local raw materials, hence reducing the unemployment rate. and 3）to develop our export trade.

First of all, the basic infrastructure required to support an industrial operation have been made available in the Zone. These include standard factory buildings for production and manufacturing operations, a very large warehouse for storage of raw materials and finished products, roads, drainage and parking, recreation and dining hall to cater to the needs of employees of Zone enterprises, a health center, adequate electrical power and water supply facility, etc. The zone occupies 113 acres of land, 75 acres of which is developed.

Secondly, a package of tax incentives has been formulated to be offered to investors operating in the Zone. The package includes：1）complete exemption from customs duties on imports of machinery, equipment, raw materials and other supplies indefinitely; 2）complete exemption from export tax on exports of manufactured or finished products from the Zone; 3）payment of only excise tax on manufactured or finished products destined for the domestic market. The excise tax rates in most cases are between 5 and 10 percent; 4) 100% corporate income tax exemption for a minimum period of 5 years with provision for extension depending on the type/kind and size of investment; 5) one-year grace period on payment of land and factory rental fees.

In addition, as a consequence of numerous complaints from potential investors regarding the stiff export requirement as stipulated by the 「Free Zone Rules and Regulations」. The Free Zone Authority now grants a 3-year export relaxation period to enable enterprises to develop export markets for their products.

I am pleased to report that so far our Screening Committee has approved about (15) fifteen project proposals with a planned initial investment estimate of US $60 million.

However, only three of these projects are now fully operating within the Zone with a total employment of less that 1,000; but with the recent opportunity granted to investors to enjoy a 3-year export relaxation period, indications are that most of these projects are soon to get off the ground.

In conclusion, I wish to extend my sincere appreciation on behalf of the Liberian Government and in particular the Board of Directors of the Liberia Industrial Free Zone Authority (LIFZA) for the opportunity offered us by WEPZA and The Flagstaff Institute to participate on this unique occasion.

As a founding member of WEPZA, LIFZA is always ready and prepared to work cooperatively with all WEPZA members to ensure that the goals and aspirations of this body are effectively achieved.

十二、哥倫比亞加工出口區

（The Colombian Industrial Free Zones）

Fernando Llinas Toledo

　　哥倫比亞加工出口區被利用作為一政治手段工具發展成為出口業中心來刺激經濟，社會，地區性以及全國的發展。目前哥倫比亞有 6 個加工出口區正在營運中。這 6 個加工出口區被視為擁有治外法權的地區並無海關的控制，著重於出口貨物。基於這個原因哥倫比亞政府賦予他們特別的條件。

（一）免稅區的建立與發展

　　在 1958 年 12 月 31 日哥倫比亞立法開發免稅區，根據第 105 條法規設置了巴蘭給拉（Barranquilla）加工出口區，巴蘭給拉加工出口區於 1964 年開始營運。隨即又在布維那文士（Buenaventura），卡利（Cali），喀他基那（Cartagena），Cucuta 以及聖瑪塔（Santa Marta）設立新的加工出口區。

　　1981 年免稅區的法規經歷了一次改革，伴隨著普通法第 47 條引進為已建立的免稅區制定共通的法律。在 1982 年將兩條修正法案第 1753 條及第 1754 條加入，以替免稅區補充制定組織，行政以及功能上的法規。

　　在 1983 年政府又制定外國貿易法，為免稅區樹立基本原則來遵守。

（二）目的

　　自由區的經濟政策在引進進出口貨物及服務，刺激工業公司，邀請外國投資，創造就業機會，引進新技術，總括而言在促進已建設地區的經濟發展。

（三）優惠

　　目前所有的哥倫比亞加工出口區有幾項優惠條件是對使用者有益處的。

　　1、所有免稅區的大樓都附帶基本設施，而且租金相對比其他國家還要低廉，一個月的租金大約是每平方公尺 0.84 美元。

　　2、外國進口的原物料及商品免關稅。

　　3、免稅區可在政府有關規定限制下以外國貨幣來經營。

（四）經濟的成果

　　在免稅區的工業生產成衣，皮製品，金屬產品，國內電子設備，玻璃器皿，化學產品，食物以及飲料。在 1984 年成衣及化學產品的生產量為最大宗。

　　免稅區的商品大部份主要銷售至美國，委內瑞拉，大小安第列斯群島，巴拿馬，巴西，秘魯以及西德。

（五）出口額約佔全國的 50.8%。

1980 年生產量加速成長（從 2 千 6 百 50 萬美金上升至 5 千 2 百 10 萬美金）。免稅區的產量高於全國的生產量，使得全國的生產量由原先的 0.19% 上升至 0.32%。在 1981~1984 年間，產量以美元估計仍然不景氣。1984 年的產量約在 5 千零 80 萬美原元少於 1980 年的產量約 2.5%。

雖然哥倫比亞的出口工業面臨小部份的衰退（從 1980 年的 12 億美元跌至 1983 年的 11 億 8 千 5 百萬美元），免稅區的的跌幅最大。原因是製衣類及金屬產品類多集中於免稅區所受到的不景氣衝擊更甚於其他產業。

因為有如此的不順遂發展，免稅區對於總工業出口的產值從原先的 1.5% 下降至後來的 0.7%。

（六）巴蘭給拉（Barranquilla）加工出口區

巴蘭給拉（Barranquilla）加工出口區在所有的哥倫比亞加工出口區中面積是最大的，它在 1980 年時生產量達到 78%，其出口量有 70.6%。

巴蘭給拉（Barranquilla）加工出口區就其本身而言，為其他的工業區提供良好的示範。在 1980 年時巴蘭給拉加工出口區的生產量就有 4 千 5 百 20 萬美金，在 1983 年時減少 20%，在 1983 年又掉了 20%

目前巴蘭給拉加工出口區有 52 家企業，分別有製衣類，金屬產品類，機械裝配業，皮革製造業，玻璃，聚乙烯，

木材類，鞋類，掃帚及刷子類，國內電器，玩具，香水，食品飲料的罐頭加工業，化學製品等等總共創造出 2,500 個工作機會。在 1984 年這些產業替國內增加了約 1 千 100 萬美金的附加價值或換算為每一個工人可帶來約 4,400 美金的附加價值。

巴蘭給拉加工出口區的公共建設涵蓋了 14 萬 2000 平方公尺面積大的大樓以及約 13 萬平方公尺面積大的道路，另外這裡也設有電話，電傳機，電器設備以及天然氣服務。

THE COLOMBIAN INDUSTRIAL FREE ZONES

Fernando Llinas Toledo

Zona Franca Industrial y Comerical de Barranquilla

Barranquilla, Colombia

The Colombian Industrial Free Zones were created to serve as a political instrument to develop centers of production in exportable goods that would foment economic, social, regional and national development. At present tere are 6 functioning free zones in the country.

These are considered as extraterritorial areas free of customs controls, primarily dedicated to exporting goods. For that reason the national government has allotted them special conditions.

Constitution and Evolution of the Free Zones

The legislation of the free zones in Columbia was started on December 31, 1958, with Law # 105 which created the Industrial Free Zone of Barranquilla. This zone started operation in 1964, the development spread to new zones in Buenaventura, Cali, Cartagena, Cucuta, and Santa Marta.

In 1981 the regulation of the Free Zones underwent a change with the introduction of common law #47, which established a common statute bringing together all zone legislation. In 1982 amendments # 1753 and #1754, were added to this law, to complement the statute in regulating the organization, administration and functions of the free zones.

In 1983, the government issued the Foreign Trade Law, which established the general principles that the Free Zones should follow.

In October 1984, the government introduced a new customs law that stipulates customs rules in one special chapter. Finally, in the past special session of Congress, a law was in debate to convert the free zones into export poles of the country.

Objectives

The Free Zone are instruments of economic policy to induce the importing and exporting of goods and services, to stimulate industrial enterprise, to invite foreign investment, to create employment, to introduce new technology, and in general to promote the economic development of the regions where they are established.

Incentives

Currently in all the Colombian Free Zones there are certain incentives that are advantageous to the users.

1.The Free Zones have buildings with basic services, where rents are low compared to other countries. A monthly rate of US$0.84 per square meter applies.

2.The importing of raw materials and goods from abroad is exempt from paying customs duties.

3.The Free Zone can operate with foreign currencies under limited government regulation.

Economic Results

Industry in the free zones produces garments, leather goods, metal mechanical products, domestic electrical appliances, glassware, chemical products, food and beverages. In 1984, the largest volume of production was in garments and chemical products.

The free zones export a major part of their products to the United States, Venezuela, the Antilles, Panama, Brazil, Peru and West Germany.

The value of the national component of such exports was 50.8%.

There was an enormous accelerated growth in production in 1980 （from US$26.5 million to 52.1 million）. The output of the zones grew faster than national production. The Free Zones contribution to national production increased from 0.19% to 0.32%. Between 1981 and 1984, the value of production, measured in current U.S. Dollars, remained stagnant. The last year, 1984, was $50.8 million, 2.5% less that in 1980.

There was a dramatic decrease in the exports beginning in 1981. By 1984 the zones exported only $10.5 million.

Even though there was a minor reduction in total Colombian exports of industrial products （from US$1,200 million in 1980 to US$1,185 million in 1983）, Free Zone production decreased at a much faster pace. The reason for this was that garment and metal-mechanical production, which is concentrated in the Free Zones, experienced a faster reduction in exports than the rest of industry （from $107 million to $59 million in the first, and from $43 million to $19 million in the second）.

Because of this unfavorable evolution, the Free Zones contribution to total industrial exports decreased from 1.5% to 0.7%.

FREE ZONE EXPORTS
Millions of Dollars

1979 26.5
1980 52.1
1981 53.2
1982 45.2
1983 50.5
1984 50.8

The Free Zone of Barranquilla

Of the Colombian Free Zones, Barranquilla is the largest, contributing in 1980 78% of production and 70.6% of exports.

As such, Barranquilla provides a good measure of the behavior and tendencies of the industrial activities of all the Free Zones. In 1980 production of the Barranquilla Free Zone was US$45.2 million. After staying relatively stable in 1981 the production reduced 20% in 1983, and then fell again in 1984. The level reached in this past year was 13.2% less than in 1980.

FREE ZONE OF BARRANQUILLA INDUSTRIAL PRODUCTION AND EXPORTS
(1979 – 1984)
(MILLION US DOLLARS)

YEAR	GROSS PRODUCTION	GROSS EXPORTS
1979	22.326	14.786
1980	45.237	26.265
1981	46.984	22.008
1982	37.517	14.936
1983	43.967	12.194
1984	39.254	7.396

At present The Barranquilla Free Zone have 52 industries dedicated to textile garments, metal-mechanical production, assembly of machinery, leather manufacturing, glass, polyethylene, wood, shoes, brooms and brushes, domestic electronics, toys, perfumes, heliographic paper, processing and canning of food and beverages, and chemical products that generate 2,500 direct jobs in a land area of 1 million square meters. The national value added in 1984 of these industries was US$11 million, or about $4,400 per worker.

Infrastructure consists of a constructed area of 142 thousand square meters of industrial buildings and 130 thousand square meters of roads. Also there are telephone, telex, electricity and natural gas services available.

十三、歐洲加工出口區（European EPZS）

　　五年前有一位比利時的商人問我要怎麼做才能吸引更多的生意至安特衛普港。我回答說：設立一個免稅區。建立一個免稅區就像設立自由航空站在愛爾蘭的香農河，在那裡有 100 多家的公司行號極力想減低財政及管理的負擔。

　　在 1981 年，免稅區被視為一種吸引外國投資人到一個落後國家或地區投資的手段。最典型的例子為在愛爾蘭香農河的免稅區或在台灣高雄的免稅區。他們被稱作為加工出口區是因為在區內所大量生產的產品可以出口到其他地區。

　　我的構想是在比利時的工業心臟——安特衛普港將免稅區的概念注入該地，雖然當地的景氣還不夠蓬勃發展。這個城市有大約 30,000 個的失業人口，我計劃要減少財政及管理的負擔不僅是在出口上而且要顧及到免稅區內的任何的生意 1.5 個月過後——在 1982 年的 12 月——比利時人採用了所謂的勞工雇用區法令，規定將在一個大約 300 公頃的土地旁設立高科技產業。在這區內公司既不用付營業所得稅也不用繳交公司稅。另一個讓人感興趣的是對於那些在比利時免稅區投資的外國人也可隨心所欲的決定採用政府所提供的社會福利方案。

　　可是比利時的免稅區實行起來卻是失敗的。這裡有兩種原因：第一種是區內的財政免稅政策是有時間限制的，時間太短了。免稅措施無法持續超過 10 年，比利時政府本身的

免稅政策可長達 18 年但是歐洲經濟共同體委員會建議 10 年就已足夠了，事實上是不正確的。第二個原因是區內無提供任何的公共建設，整個免稅區只是個有著免費的土地但卻沒有任何設備的工業區。

英國政府在同一時間也頒布一項名為自由企業區法案，顯然比比利時政府要聰明的多了。這個法案為英國的 24 個企業區提供多項的服務。可是這個法案既沒有減少區內財政及管理的負擔且提供給區內的服務也不是很完善。在這 24 個英國自由區及 6 個英國自由港中只有三個區是成功的。其中一個自由企業區位在 Corby 市──大約有 300 家公司聚集，共創造約 5,000 個工作機會。

三個月之前，法國政府，比利時政府及盧森堡政府提議在位於三國邊界連接處距離盧森堡不很遠的地方設立一個自由區。在準備有關法律的法規上給了我們一個很好的範例就是不要任意的起草有關政府的規章。這三個政府的部長迫不及待的想建立第一個跨國的自由區，而它他們只對一件事取得共識那就是創立一個跨國區管理法並設有公職人員並制定跨國區計劃來爭取補助款。有 2 個很重要的元素是促成自由區成功的原因在這裡卻失去了：第一點是這個區的管理最好是讓私人企業來執行比較好。第二點是區內的財政及管理的負擔必須有實質上的降低。

造成比利時，英國及法國的自由區失敗的一個原因為他們的提倡者不瞭解立法程序。在一個民主制度下，立法程序是要與增加政府財政及管理上的負擔相適應的。民主政治的權力總是握在那群遊說議案通過的人手中──短期內──

將從政府增加的規章下得到利益。事實上，針對任一個政府條款都有它的守衛者。通常對於某些條例都會由一些政府人員構成一個壓力團體來作其第一條防守線。他們很容易接近新聞界而且不擇手段地利用它。對於廢除某一特定法律的擁護者正相反，是會被驅散而且不容易組織。法律的廢除不會攸關他們的生或死，他們不會為了這個去反抗的。

　　基於這樣的原因為一位立法委員來起擬自由區法規是相當愚蠢的。自由區法規最好不要在特定的政府條例中被提起不然會被廢除的。

　　關於我用特別的方法寫一個自由區法案就與傳統的方法有相當大的不同。這不是說說而以，那一個政府條例並不適用，則自由區法案就應該詳加說明於那一個條例適用。我最喜愛的自由區法案會簡易的說明在特定的區內那些私人的權利將被尊重而那些權利將會被政府強力執行。自由區法案應該規定：區內使用者有權利做他們想做的事以及生產或取得商品只要他們同樣地尊重其他不管是在區內或區外的使用者也有同樣的權利。

　　某些個國家的立法委員或許不是那麼理智或優秀的接受我提出的建議。既然這樣我有 3 種設立自由區的法規草稿：

　　1、立法委員只說明設置自由區的目的，例如這樣做會創造出 10,000 多個工作機會。

　　2、立法委員陳述這樣做會讓外國投資人有選擇法規的機會。他們可以選擇自己國家的法規也可選擇地主國家的法規，如此那個對他們而言是最少的負擔呢？一個特別的法庭應當有解決這樣國際間衝突律法的能力。

3、立法委員陳述某些法律及經濟學說將成就留給自由區的董事或是給特別法庭。這些學說包括：

(a)不應該對公司徵收稅款，應當對個人課稅。(b)不應該對生產徵收稅款，應當對消費課稅。(c)政府不應該對產品及服務的價錢或品質制定規章。(d)政府不應該對自由區行使任何壟斷權益。(e)政府不應該在自由區內從事任何的經濟活動。(f)政府不應該對自由區內的任何經濟或政治活動給予資助。

這三種不同的立法技巧與我喜好的立法技巧分享一個好處就是——這樣他們就不會在某一政府法規上詳加說明它將被廢止。法令的廢除不是經過政治官員之手就是經過法官或者是內閣之手。我的偏好是一項法律的廢除應該由法院來完成的。

每當自由區的使用者發現某一政府法規正好侵犯到他的權利時，他也許會試著不去理會。政府接著會試著去執行這項法令。接著法官可能會裁決這項法規與一些基本人權或憲法相抵觸。只要有上述的有關法律的覆審不被接受時，才會由內閣或被政務協調會委派的人員來審理廢除法令的判定。

接著我想要把土耳其共和國也納入我的簡報，即使土耳其共和國大部份的領土位在小亞細亞只有少部份的土地在歐洲。土耳其目前有四個自由區正在興建中。

其中位於安塔利亞市及梅爾辛市的自由區已差不多建造完成即將可以使用，而另一個自由區位於土耳其南部的亞德那市。第四個也是最大的一個自由區將設置在位於 Nemrut

灣距伊士麥北方 50 公里之處。Nemrut 自由區的面積非常大約莫 10 平方公里。這個自由區將專門為外國企業家提供服務，並把注意力放在輸出品的生產上，預計在 1987 年開始經營。

土耳其的國會於 1985 年的 6 月 6 日採用了土耳其的自由區法規。其中有三項最種重要的主張為：

（1）將不會課稅

（2）將不會對外幣交易流通予以管制。

（3）將不會對價格，品質，以及標準立法限制。

我的報告即將到了尾聲，為了達成我的報告的完整性我還是必須要提到在西班牙，希臘以及安道爾共和國也設有自由區。在德國的漢堡市有設立一處重要的關稅自由區，在那個地方一些工業擁有完整的製造權利而不用考慮到任何的關稅條例。同時我應當提到在盧森堡以及倫敦也設置有所謂的離岸的自由銀行區，在這兩個城市的自由銀行區內，銀行業的財政及管理的負擔已經大幅度的被降低了。

現在我要針對在歐洲的自由區下個結論，我的結論是歐洲的自由區在 1959 年當愛爾蘭在香農河建立自由區有了一個美好的開始。另外也是個值得注意的進步就是 1915 年在德國的漢堡市設立一處關稅工業自由區。但是模仿愛爾蘭自由區所建立的自由區就不是那麼令人滿意的，尤其是設在比利時，法國以及英國的自由區。原因是在這幾個地方被大量的發現缺少立法技能儘管在歐洲有許多的立法委員。期盼土耳其的自由區能為歐洲的自由區人民帶來良好的示範。我知道義大利及挪威也有計劃要興建自由區。歐洲不久將遭逢經

濟的衰退以及改變。在歐盟的 12 個會員國，大約有 1 千 4
百萬人處於失業狀態。唯一辦法來改善這個問題是撤銷管
制規定。而最快的辦法來進行撤銷管制規定是採用自由區
的概念。因此我想我們將會看到有越來越多的自由區在歐
洲設立。

EUROPEAN EXPORT PROCESSING ZONE

Michael van Notten, Director

Institutum Europaeum

Brussels, Beginum

Legend has it that the search for the Holy Grail is a difficult and life-long pursuit. It seems to be no different with Export Processing Zone. I started my first efforts to establish an industrial free zone （IFZ） some five years ago. As a result, seven zones were erected. But, it will take much more time than 5 years to establish the first real free zone, as I will call this interesting political device to promote production.

It was 5 years ago that a Belgian businessman asked me what could be done to attract more business to the port of Antwerp. I answered： make a free zone. Make a free zone just like the Free Airport Zone in Shannon, Ireland, where, as you know, for some one hundred companies government has considerably reduced the fiscal and regulatory burden.

In 1981 Free Zones were thought of only as devices to attract foreign investors to an underdeveloped country or to an underdeveloped region of a given country. The Free Zones in Shannon, Ireland, or Kaohsiung in Taiwan, were typical example of this economic philosophy. They were given the name Export

Processing Zones because the idea was that the bulk of the goods produced in those zones could be exported.

My idea was to use the free zone concept in the industrial heart of Belgium – in the port of Antwerp – where biz was booming, yet not booming enough. The city had 30,000 unemployed, and something had to be done. My idea was to reduce the fiscal and regulatory burden not only on exports but also on any business that was being conducted within the free zone. 1.5 years later – in Dec. 1982 – the Belgians adopted the so-called Employment Zone Act, which stipulated that an area of 300 hectares of land would be set aside for high-technology industry. Within that zone corporations would neither pay the corporate income tax nor any of the other half dozen so-called corporate taxes. Another interesting aspect of the Belgian Free Zones is that foreign businessmen are free to decide which government social security scheme they will follow – that of Belgium or that of their home country.

Interesting as all this may sound in theory, the Belgian Free Zones don't work at all in practice. Biz shows little interest. There are 2 main reasons. One is that there is a time limit on the fiscal exemption in the zone, which is far too short. The tax freedom will not last longer then 10 years. The Belgian government itself had opted for 18 years but the EEC-Commission advised that 10 years would be enough, which simply isn't true. The second main reason for the failure of the Belgian Zone is, that no infrastructure has been provided to bring the Free Zone to life. The Belgian zone is an empty price of land and not a full-service industrial park.

The British government, which enacted its Free Enterprise Zone Act at about the same time as the Belgian government, was much smarter. It arranged for each of its 24 Enterprise Zones to supply a number of services to the zone occupants. Yet neither the fiscal and regulatory relief in these zones, nor the service to the zone occupants proved to be sufficient. Out of these 24 British Free Zone and 6 British Free Ports only 3 succeeded. One of these free enterprise zones is located in Corby where – in 5 years time – about 300 companies started up. They created some 5,000 new jobs.

For some of you it may be of interest to know that the Employment Zones in Belgium and the Free Enterprise Zones in England do not grant special exemptions from customs duties. The companies in these zones do not particularly cater to import or export biz. Therefore no particular measures have been taken to relieve the zone occupants from customs regulations. Neither can it be said that these zones cater in particular to foreign investors. In actual fact foreign industrialists constitute only a small percentage of the zone occupants.

3 months ago, the French, Belgian and Luxembourg governments solemnly proposed to create a free zone on the junction of their borders, not far from the city of Luxembourg. The preparations for the legal statute are a good example of how not to draft government regulations. The ministers of these 3 governments were so eager to establish the first multinational free zone in Europe that they shied away from anything controversial. Practically the only things they agreed upon were the creation of a multinational zone management full of national

civil servants and a multinational scheme for granting subsidies. 2 important elements for the success of a free zone were missing. One is that the management of the zone should be done by private enterprise. Another is that within the free zone the fiscal and regulatory burden on biz must be substantially reduced. In the French-Belgian-Luxembourg zone of Longwy/Athus/Petange, nothing like that will occur in the foreseeable future.

One reason for the relative failure of the Belgian, English, and French free zones is that their promoters do not understand the legislative process. In a democracy, the legislative process is almost exclusively geared to increasing the fiscal and regulatory burden of government on biz. The democratic power are invariably in the hands of those lobbyists who – in the short run – will benefit from the increase in government regulation. They will almost always resist any reduction in the amount of government regulation. In fact, for each government regulation there is a separate little group of defenders. The first line of defense of such pressure groups usually consists of the civil servants who make a living out of the particular regulation. They are a well-organized lot of people when it comes to defending their cozy corner. They have easy access to the press and unscrupulously take advantage of it. The proponents of the abolition of a particular law on the contrary, are dispersed and difficult to organize. Abolition rarely is a matter of life or death for them. They will not fight for it.

For this reason alone it would be quite stupid for a legislator to draft a free zone law, which is too explicit. A free zone law should preferably not mention at all which specific government

regulations will be abolished. If a legislator says for example :
the following 15 government regulations will not apply in the
free zone, exactly 15 protests will be heard, one from each
particular pressure group. The more freedom you ask in this way,
the more lobbyists the legislators will have to appease. Only in
very unusual circumstances can a legislator overcome the fiercest
resistance against the abolition of any particular law.

One such an exception can be found in Ciskei – one of the
former South African homelands, which is fast becoming one of
the world's largest free zones. Last year, the Ciskei parliament
abolished – with one single stroke of the pen – some 80 different
legal statutes, which were burdening the biz community. That
was done through the Small Biz Deregulation Act of June 1984.
Two dozen similar Acts of Parliament are in the process of being
adopted in Ciskei. They deal with the following subjects : tribal
land, deeds registration, land survey, local authorities/zoning, law
courts, liquor, labor relations, company registration and auditing,
banking, education, land transfer tax, environmental protection,
sale of farm produce, medical aid, income and corporate tax,
export processing/customs duties, gambling, apartheid, donations
and inheritance tax, immigration, nationalization, housing,
government-owned biz, constitutional control of legislation and
the government budget. But again Ciskei forms an exception to
the general rule, which says : it is hundred times more difficult
to abolish a particular law, than to adopt one.

My favorite recipe for writing a free zone Act is quite
different from the traditional technique. Rather than saying,
which government regulations do not apply, the free zone statute

should spell out which regulations do apply. My favorite free zone law would simply state that within the confines of the zone the rights to private property will have to be respected and will be enforced by government. Stated differently, the Free Zone Act should stipulate： The zone occupants have the right to do what they like with their own body and with the goods which they produce or acquire with it as long as they respect the same right of all other citizens, be they inside or outside the zone.

Some people will ask whether this is enough. The answer is YES. The general laws on private property and the general principle of freedom of contract are good enough to settle any conflict that may arise in any society. All efforts of legislators to improve on the law of property usually ends with infringing upon it. My sown favorite free zone statute is only one page long. It states only the basic principle of private property. It further applies it to various problems and conflicts, which may arise within the zone or the area around it.

The legislator of a particular country may not be intelligent enough or sufficiently strong to adopt my legislative proposal. In that case I have 3 types of draft statutes for the establishment of a free zone：

1.The legislator states only the purpose of zone, for instance that it must create 10,000 additional jobs. Such a zone statute leaves the task of temporarily reducing the fiscal and or regulatory burden of government regulation to a special government commissar.

2.The legislator states that foreign businessmen will have a choice of law. They may choose between the laws of their own country or that of the host country, whichever is the least burdensome to them？ A special court of justice should solve any conflict of law that might arise in such an international setting.

3.The legislator states certain principles of law and economics, and leaves their implementation to the zone directorate or to a special court of justice. These principles could include the following：

    a.No taxation shall be levied on corporate entities, only on individuals.

    b.No taxation shall be levied on production, only on consumption.

    c.Government shall not regulate the price or quality of goods and services.

    d.Government shall not exercise any monopoly powers in the zone.

    e.Government shall not engage in any economic activity in the zone.

    f.Government shall not subsidize any economic or political activity in the zone.

In Ciskei this letter legislative technique has been adopted in the Small Business Deregulation Act of 1984. Thee, the following principles were enacted：

    a.No person should violate the common law rights of another and no person should initiate coercion against another, except by way of lawful self-defense or retaliation in protection of personal or property rights by reasonably necessary means.

b.All persons should be free to engage in mutually volitional transactions upon mutually and volitionally agreed terms.

c.There should be freedom of contract, exchange, association and disassociation.

d.The law should respect personal and property rights.

e.The principles of liberty, the rule of law and natural rights should be upheld.

f.No persons should use fraudulent or dishonest means of trade.

These three different legislative techniques share one advantage with my preferred type of statute – they do not spell out which particular government regulation is going to be abolished. The abolition is either to a government official, or to a judge or to the Council of Ministers. My preference is that the abolition is done by a court of justice.

Whenever a zone occupant finds a government regulation infringing his rights, he may ignore it. The government will then try to enforce the regulation. The judge may then rule that a particular government regulation contradicts some fundamental human right or constitutional principle. Only if such a legal review is not acceptable, should the particular abolition be done by the council of ministers or someone appointed by this council.

We have seen that under normal circumstances it is not possible to abolish a particular government regulation. The reason is that the abolitionists are dispersed and not very motivated whereas the defenders are a close-knit group, which is, highly motivated.

With a good zone status the abolitionists can turn the odds in their favor. If the proponents do not spell out in detail which regulations they wish to abolish and if they abolish regulations only for a particular town or a particular industrial park, they can win. Then the proponents will be all the politicians of that particular town of whatever political party. It will be a concentrated close-knit group of people. The defenders on the contrary will not be able to organize themselves. First they do not know whether their particular government regulation will be under attack or not. Second, they will only loose one tiny geographical part of their vast empire. They therefore may not be able to call up their usual troops.

I would like to include Turkey in my brief, even if only a small part of Turkey lies in Europe and a very large part in Asia Minor. Turkey has at present four free zones under construction. Those in Antalya and Mersin are almost ready and soon operational. Another zone will be in Adana/Yamutalec. A fourth and a very large zone will be established 50 Km north of Izmir, at the bay of Nemrut. The Nemrut zone will be a big zone, some 10 kilometers square. It will particularly cater to foreign industrialists and it will concentrate on production for export purposes. It should be operational in the year 1987.

The Turkish free zone law was adopted by the Turkish parliament on June 6. 1985. The three most important sentences in the Turkish free zone law are the following :

(1) There shall be no taxation.

(2)There shall be no foreign currency exchange controls.

(3)There shall be no government regulation of prices, qualities and standards.

Basically this is all one needs in order to assure a complete freedom for the occupants of the zone. If the council of ministers, whose task it will be to issue the implementing regulations, will be generous, the burden of government regulation on the employers and employees in the zone will indeed be nil.

I have nearly come to the end of my brief survey of free zones in Europe. For completeness sake I must still mention that Spain, Greece and Andorra have free zones. In Hamburg there is an important customs free zone where a number of industries have received the right to manufacture completely without regard to custom duty regulation. Also I should mention that in Luxembourg and London there are so-called offshore free banking zones. The fiscal and regulatory burden on banking has been sharply reduced in these cities.

I have some to the end of my survey of free zones in Europe. My conclusion is that Europe made a good start in 1959 when the Irish government established a Free Zone in Shannon. That was a remarkable improvement over the customs industrial free zone of Hamburg, which was established in 1915. But the imitations of Irish free zone have been less that satisfactory, especially in Belgium, France and England. The reason for this is largely to be found in the lack of legislative skills with the various legislators in Europe. There is some hope however that the new Turkish free zones will improve upon the Irish concept and that the Turkey will become the new model for European Free Zone nations. I know that in Italy and Norway there are plans for the creation of one or more free zones. Europe is presently going through a period of economic decline and change. In the 12 member states of the European Community alone, there are some 14 million unemployed. The only way in which Europe can change this terrible situation is by deregulation. The quickest way to get the deregulation process going is by adopting the free zone concept. I therefore think that we will see more free zones being established in Europe pretty soon. Let's hope that at the next WEPZA conference I can report on some spectacular successes in this field. Thank you.

十四、波多黎各工業發展公司及波多黎各區
（Pridco and the Puerto Rico Zones）

波多黎各工業發展公司（PRIDCO）的成立，正代表著波多黎各的經濟在自力更生，和平改革逐漸由農業社會轉變為工業社會。

波多黎各工業發展公司於 1942 年 10 月開始營運初期投資金額約為美金 50 萬元。

剛開始，公司投入許多工業開發計劃（後來轉賣給私人企業）及觀光設施，例如 Caribe 希爾頓飯店。之後，公司轉為走向直接促銷島上興建的私人工業廠房。

由於經濟發展局（FOMENTO）的成立，波多黎各政府轉變為財務支援負責興建工業廠房建築及開發工業園區，提供財務優惠措施給投資人，興建和出租觀光旅館及設施並提供其他與經濟發展有關的功能。

旅館出租業，公司公開募股，廠房租售及由政府立法機關編列預算用作表揚多年來表現良好的公司。

到目前為止，我們擁有 2,071 家製造工廠開工，雇用了 152,614 名員工。大多數的員工受到美國聯邦政府的保障享有最低工資福利。根據州勞動力及人力資源局的報告，經濟發展局（FOMENTO）促成 1,578 家工廠業績成長及 137,168 個工作機會。

為了吸引美國資本來波多黎各投資，我們提供了特別的優惠。只要是美國公民，波多黎各人及他國居民經過國會和波多黎各政府同意就可享有會計年度自治權及聯邦政府的免稅措施。

目前，波多黎各工業發展公司總資產超過 5 億 1 千萬元比前幾年多增加了 2 千 6 百萬元。在 1984 年新的土地投資，包括營建及設備便超過了 2,600 萬美元。1985~86 年度中，我們正在研擬以及幾年獲得土地的新計劃方案，尤其在自治區內有比較少可用的場所，同時在 1985~86 年間，公司最新的投資計劃為 3,790 萬美元，到今年底，我們收到聯邦政府允諾的 430 萬美元，另 1,180 萬美元由政府立法撥款及 2,180 萬美元由政府銀行及私人銀行提供。公司近來也希望透過基金收入刺激某些項目的工業發展，可能會促進波多黎各經濟發展，此構想包括特別優惠條件以加速新廠的成長。

（一）波多黎各的外國貿易區

在 1961 年於 Mayaguez 市建立了第 7 號外國貿易區，Mayaguez 市位於波多黎各島的西南方是一個參議院的行政區及深海港的重鎮。

這個貿易區屬於波多黎各工業發展公司的一部份，土地面積約有 42 英畝靠近港口。這個計劃起源於聯邦當局審慎的考量下，因為經營這個貿易區不需要波多黎各工業發展公司的太多經濟支援，而且工廠設備是現成的。再者，此區已

圍起來並設有必要的安全設施，目前區內只要求少許的投資來保養維護及支付連帶的花費。

這種類型的貿易區建立在以進出口業為中心並享有免關稅及貨物稅的優惠。貨物可允許運入區內，再加工，最後運出也不必付稅。

不像其他位於美國境內的區，我們的第 7 號外國貿易區強調產品的製造過程。原物料及零件運送至區內，完成品再運送出區都不需要付稅。現在，在新法律之下，任何完成品從區內要運送至美國境內不徵稅卻要有附加價值的要求。

預期未來的承租人也許會承租土地然後蓋自己的廠房，或者與波多黎各工業發展公司簽訂合約由波多黎各工業發展公司蓋廠房然後再出租給他們。

Mayaguez 市成功的設立第 7 號外國貿易區鼓舞了島上的投資人在波多黎各的首都聖胡安市的主要海港旁建立另一個新的外國貿易區。

第 61 號外國貿易區土地面積約 60 英畝，其中的 42 英畝將最先被開發。目前這個區已被貿易發展公司及政府的代辦機構列為優先發展階段。這個區將會是聖胡安市作為經營大型國際貿易中心的主要部份，而且它將使得波多黎各成為加勒比海及西半球的主要貿易據點。

Mayaguez 市的外國貿易區有 8 家工廠在運作大約雇用了 869 名員工及每星期支付 19 萬元的員工薪水或每年支付員工薪水大約 1 千萬元。與之前的 12 個月比較起來，在 1984 年這個區的活動力顯示了重大的改善。在 1984 年這個區的商品進口和出口總價值約在 5 千 5 百 80 萬元。這包含了商

品的進口總額在 2 千 5 百萬元及商品輸出總額在 2 千 8 百
80 萬元。

在 1984 年間總計有 14,442 短噸的貨物進口及輸出從
Mayaguez 市的外國貿易區內，這其中包括有 8,061 短噸的貨
物進口，經過加工後再出口的貨物有 6,381 短噸。

（二）Penuelas 的石油化學製品分區

煉油及石油化學聯合企業設立在 Penuelas，位於
Guayanilla 的南部海港，是美國的商業部在 1982 年 8 月特別
選定作為 Mayaguez 市第 7 號外國貿易區的分區，代號為 7-B.
本規劃將加強此煉油廠的重要性以達成原油加工區免稅，再
轉載至加勒比海區其餘較小的煉油廠。

（三）加勒比海盆地的倡議

波多黎各，透過加勒比海盆地的倡議美國雷根總統的支
持下，可專注於改善及增強其鄰近區域的經濟。

我們目前正參與雙子星工廠的開發計劃，其中一個位於
加勒比海盆地的工廠將著重於勞力密集工業，而另一個姐妹
廠將設於波多黎各完成其最終製造業然後將產品運送至美
國及其他市場。位於波多黎各的外國貿易區對於雙子星工廠
的發展期望將扮演一個舉足輕重的角色。

（四）結論

　　波多黎各曾致力於發展我們的經濟和提高我們的生活水準。目前我們的國民所得為 4,294 元，是美國範圍以外其中幾個高收入所得的國家之一。波多黎各的政府及人民仍然堅守其私人企業體系及持續的發展其社會，經濟和工業成長。我們目前也幫助鄰近的國家一起提高生活水平，同時，也幫助他們穩定其政治及經濟就像我們現在所享有的。

PRIDCO AND THE PUERTO RICO ZONES

Mario Martinez-Camacho

The Puerto Rico Industrial Development Company （PRIDCO） was established as a part of the social and economic peaceful revolution which marked the beginning of 「Operation Bootstrap」 – the transformation of the Puerto Rican economy from an agricultural to an industrial society.

The company started operations with an initial appropriation of $500,000 dollars in October of 1942. Initially, it involved itself in several industrial projects （later sold to the private sector） and tourism facilities, such as the Caribe Hilton Hotel. It then moved into direct promotion of the initial private industrial plants established on the island.

With the establishment of the Economic Development Administration （FOMENTO）, PRIDCO came to be the financial arm of the Administration with the responsibility for constructing industrial buildings and developing industrial parks, financing the incentives offered to prospective investors, construction and leasing of tourism hotels and facilities and other functions related to economic development.

The hotel-leasing operation, the sale of bonds as a public corporation, the sale and leasing of industrial buildings and appropriation of funds by the state legislature provided the necessary funds for the successful performance of the company throughout the years.

So far, we have 2,071 manufacturing operations with a total of 152,614 workers. A great percentage of them are covered by U.S. Federal minimum wage legislation provided for the various categories in interstate commerce. FOMENTO promotion accounted for 1,578 of those plants and 137,168 jobs of the total, according to the State Department of Labor and Human Resources Reports.

To attract American capital to the Puerto Rican industrial community we provide unique benefits. As American citizens, Puerto Ricans and other residents enjoy benefits provided by our close political ties to the United States by virtue of such citizenship as well we the unique Commonwealth status established in 1952 by a compact ratified by Congress and the people of Puerto Rico. Those benefits include fiscal autonomy and the exemption from Federal taxes of profits resulting from island manufacturing operations.

At present, PRIDCO has total assets of over $510 million which represents an increase of $26 million over the previous year. New investments in land, buildings and equipment amounted to over $26 million in 1984. During fiscal 1985-86 we are initiating a vigorous program for the acquisition of land during the next few years, particularly in those municipalities with fewer available sites. Also, during 1985-86 the company proposes to initiate a program of capital investments in the amount of $37.9 million. To this end we accept income of $4.3

million from Federal grants：$11.8 million from Legislative appropriations and $21.8 million from financing to be provided by our Government Development Bank and private financing institutions. The Company also expects income from a fund recently created to stimulate the development of certain types of industries that might contribute to the Puerto Rican economy. This includes the granting of special incentives to accelerate the promotion of new plants.

Foreign Trade Zones in Puerto Rico

Included in the overall performance of PRIDCO is the creation, administration and preservation of the island's U.S. Foreign Trade Zone Number 7, established since 1961 in the city of Mayaguez, head of a senatorial district and site of a deep-water port in the southwest part of the island.

This zone was part of the general structure of the Company which separated 42 acres of its land close to the port. The project was started after due consideration with federal authorities. Since it started operations the zone has required very little financing from PRIDCO, in the sense that the facilities existed in the beginning. The zone area was duly marked and fenced and the necessary security system was established. A minimum investment has been required for maintenance and other incidental expenses.

This type of trade zone, as you all know, is established primarily as an import-export center exempt from custom duties and excise taxes. Goods may be brought into the zone, altered in some way, and then shipped out without paying any duties.

Unlike many other such zones in the United States, our Foreign Trade Zone Number 7 has emphasized manufacturing processes. Raw materials and components are shipped in, and finished products shipped out without incurring duties. Now, under a new law, no duties will be exacted on the value added to these finished products sent from the zone to the United States mainland.

Prospective tenants may either lease land and construct their own facilities, or enter into a construction-lease agreement to have facilities built to their own specifications by the Puerto Rico Industrial Development Company.

The success of the zone in Mayaguez has motivated planners on the island to establish a new foreign-trade zone in the main seaport area of San Juan, the capital in the north.

Foreign Trade Zone Number 61 will contain 60 acres, 42 of which will be initially developed. It is currently in the advanced planning stages by the Trade Development Company, a government agency. The zone is to be a major part of a large international trade center to operate in San Juan. The whole complex will give a strong thrust to Puerto Rico's growing role as a major Caribbean and Western Hemisphere trading hub.

The Mayaguez Foreign Trade Zone is the site of eight （8） industrial operations which employ a total of 869 people with a weekly payroll of $199,000, or approximately $10 million a year. Activities in the zone showed significant improvement during fiscal 1984 when compared with the preceding 12-month period. The value of merchandise received at and shipped from the zone during fiscal 1984 totalled $55.8 million. This included

433

merchandise received amounting to $25 million and merchandise shipped out amounting to $28.8 million.

A total of 14,442 short tons of merchandise moved into and out of the zone during the period, including merchandise received, 8,061 short tons, and processed merchandise shipped out 6,381 tons.

Penuelas Petrochemical Subzone

The oil refinery and petrochemical complex in Penuelas, in the south coast port of Guayanilla, was designated by the United States Department of Commerce as special purpose subzone 7-B of the Mayaguez Foreign-Trade Zone in August 1982. This designation enhances the refinery's appeal as a potential tariff-free regional processing center of crude oil for reshipment to smaller foreign refineries in other Caribbean locations.

The Caribbean Basin Initiative

Puerto Rico, through the Caribbean Basin Initiative sponsored by President Reagan, is involved in the process of renovating and strengthening the economies of neighboring countries in the area.

We are participating in the development of twin-plant manufacturing projects in which one plant emphasizing labor-intensive operations is located in a CBI beneficiary nation and its twin plant located in Puerto Rico carries out final manufacturing for shipment to the United States and other markets. The Foreign Trade Zones in Puerto Rico are expected to play a key role in the development of twin-plants under the CBI.

Our recently elected Governor Rafael Hernandez Colon's proposal to the United States Government, that Puerto Rico support the implementation of the Caribbean Basin Initiative on the condition that Section 936 of the U.S. Internal Revenue Code remain unchanged, gained new impetus on August 29 when the Governor outlined specifics on how the commitment is to be fulfilled.

In announcing the details of his five-stage industrial development plan, the Governor revealed that he has pledges from 21 companies now operating in Puerto Rico as Section 936 corporations to invest $65 million in complementary plant projects in CBI countries which will create 5,500 direct jobs.

Conclusion

We in Puerto Rico have gone very far in the development of our economy and in raising our standard of living. Presently, our per capita income is $4,294, one of the highest in the hemisphere outside the United States. The government and the people of Puerto Rico remain firmly committed to the private enterprise system and the continuing social, economic and industrial growth of the island. Also, we are now in the process of helping others around us to progress and to attain a better standard of living as well as the political and economic stability that we already enjoy.

十五、中華民國加工出口區

洪瑞國副處長　孔長江博士著
經濟部加工出口區管理處

（一）加工出口區，政府的政策及優惠條件

1、政府政策

台灣於 1960 年代致力於發展基本民生工業。為了加速經濟發展，中華民國政府在高雄建立了第一個加工出口區，就是現今大家所熟悉地高雄加工出口區（KEPZ）。在短短的三年間，高雄加工出口區的使用空間就額滿了，因此決定再興建另外兩個加工出口區。

在過去的 30 年間，加工出口區對於我們致力於發展出口工業扮演一個相當重要的角色。它的目的有：吸引工業投資，擴充對外貿易，引進現代工業以及創造就業機會。到目前為止，當初興建加工出口區所設立的四個目標已圓滿達成。

在 1995 年加工出口區管理處（EPZA）以配合成為亞太平洋地區營運中心的計劃為目的，針對原有的目標再重新給予定義。這些目標為：加強工業競爭的優勢條件，結合世界市場需求，提昇國內科技水平以及引進跨國企業投資。

2、優惠條件

●投資人可依照提昇產業條例有權享有 5 年（或 4 年）的所得稅減免優惠條件。此外，股東享有延期繳交所得稅的優惠措施。

●轉運業的營業所得稅按轉運收入 10%的比率課稅。

●進口稅　日用品稅，營業稅以及契約稅均免課稅。

（二）科學園區，政府的政策及優惠條件

1、政府政策

經過 60 年代以及 70 年代的持續擴充對外貿易和增加就業機會，台灣於 80 年代將焦點轉移至發展高科技產業。考量到工商製造業的快速轉變，使得引進高科技產業以及募集人力來從事工業技術的研究與創新變成政府一項非常緊急的任務。於是在 1980 年，第一座以科學為基礎的工業園區在新竹成立。在 1995 年，政府又在台南增設另一座科學工業園區來加強高科技產業的發展與加速經濟發展的腳步。台灣科學工業園區的興建確立了三個目的：

■引進技術產業以及人力；

■鼓勵工業研究以及創新；

■促進高科技產業的發展；

2、優惠條件

■投資優惠條件給予合於產業升級條例的公司。新設立的公司可享有選擇性 5 年期（4 年期對於額外投資）免徵商

業所得稅或是可減免的投資。超過 5 年的免稅期，可享有課營利所得稅不超過 20%.

■進出口稅　日用品稅，營業稅以及契約稅均免課稅。

（三）加工出口區與科學工業園區在機能上的結合

加工出口區與科學工業園區均屬於高科技以及高附加價值的特別區，而且均以高科技電子業作為其主流產業。但是他們分屬於不同時期產業發展階段。以積體電路（IC）產業以及液晶顯示（LCD）產業為例，加工出口區專注於中，下游製造業例如積體電路，包裝和液晶顯示。而科學工業園區則著重於上游之晶片製造業，光罩業，IC 設計以及液晶顯示。所以加工出口區與科學工業園區形成勞力垂直整合不同區域的產業。事實上，有些企業例如南茂科技公司和飛利浦台灣公司，均在兩個特別區分別投資。因此，加工出口區與科學工業園區在機能上巧妙的相結合在一起而且成為密不可分的合作夥伴。

（四）加工出口區內與科學工業園區內的產業對於國內經濟以及全球經濟的影響和貢獻

加工出口區對於國內經濟以及全球經濟的影響和貢獻：

●投資金額方面：在 1966-1995 年間，累積總投資金額達到美金 36 億元。在 1996/97 年間，又投資了美金約 21 億

元。總計投資金額至 1998 年高達新台幣 130 億元。

　　●就業人數方面：在過去的十年間，加工出口區的就業人數平均在 59,000 人。然而在 1987 年時，加工出口區的就業人數以超過 90,000 人。在 1976–1998 年間，加工出口區內工作的就業人數佔全部就業人數的 0.78% 至 1.27%，而加工出口區內製造業的就業人數就佔 2.13% 至 4.42%。

　　●引進現代化技術：現代化技術是由日本以及美國介紹引進的，而荷蘭更是幫助我們將當地產業提昇至更高階層的貢獻者。

　　●政府的歲收：可替政府每年收到將近 4 億美元的收入。

　　●外匯存底：總計貿易盈餘可達到美金 346 億元。

　　●對於國內生產總值的貢獻：僅就 1987 一年而言，加工出口區的國內生產總值佔全國內生產總值的 1.6%，而僅就製造業部份，佔國內製造業生產總值的 5.81%。

　　●促進國際間的合作：由於加工出口區成功的經營與管理使得加工出口區成為國內企業的投資天堂，同時也成為各國的領導者與經濟學者作為學習以及複製的對象。已經有超過 600,000 人次的政府官員首長，學者專家。訪問者從世界各國來參觀加工出口區，其中包含有國家元首，經濟學專家以及企業管理專家。這樣的交流為我們促進了國際間的合作和友誼。不僅如此，我們舉辦了加工出口區營運與管理研討會並邀請發展中國家派代表參加，這項研討會的最大貢獻在重整這些國家的經濟結構及提升全球性的貿易。在 1989年，加工出口區成功地贊助在高雄舉辦世界加工出口區國際

會議。於 2000 年 10 月，很榮幸地高雄又成為世界加工出口區國際會議的主辦城市，期望這將促進全球經濟的合作以及經驗的交換。

　　科學工業園區對於國內經濟以及全球經濟的影響和貢獻：

- 吸引投資；
- 創造就業機會以及帶來當地繁榮；
- 促進工業的發展；
- 增加財政稅收以及外匯存底；
- 引進現代化技術；
- 增加國際間的聲望以及間接的對全球經濟有所貢獻；

　　促成加工出口區與科學工業園區成功的因素：

- 藉由法律以及地方法則來管理這兩個特別區和合理的徵稅措施以及優惠政策；
- 完備的公共建設，高品質的勞動力以及熱忱的工會和管理關係；
- 提供一元化的服務和有效率的管理；
- 出租土地並收取低廉租金可減少投資者過大的投資金額以及增加土地使用率（每年每平方米 NT400.）；
- 便捷的地理位置和有彈性的營業策略；
- 透過代工生產（OEM）形成衛星工業體系

（五）加工出口區與科學工業園區的未來期許

1、對於加工出口區的未來期許

（1）成為高科技電子產業的運作中心

（2）成為高科技產業研發，市場行銷，品質保證以及
配銷中心

（3）成為全球高科技電子產業的後勤中心

2、對於科學工業園區的未來期許

期望科學工業園區的發展能將經濟發展與社區文化相
結合，促進台灣的科技發展，使得台灣島能成為名副其實的
科技島。

（六）加工出口區將成為中華民國倉儲轉運專區

1、專區的目的

其目的在繼續發展以生產製造及倉儲轉運為基礎的工
業，促進台灣向科技島發展，多國企業將擔任起本國企業與
數以千計的亞太生產線之間的橋樑，專區將協助本國企業與
外國企業緊密合作，如此台灣將成為本國與外國企業在亞太
地區的生產總部，而至再造台灣經濟榮景。

2、專區的位置及面積，見表一（Table - 1）

　　優惠條件及設施（概括要點）：

　●特別稅的優惠條件

　●一元化及高行政效率的服務

　●低土地租金

　●提供最適宜的投資環境

REPUBLIC OF CHINA

Juay-Kuo Hong
Chang-Chiang Kung
Export Processing Zone Administration
Ministry of Economic Affairs

Shiann-Far Kung
National Chen Kung University

GOVERNMENT POLICIES FOR ESTABLISHMENT OF EPZs AND SPs AND INCENTIVES OFFERED

Policy and Incentives for EPZs

Policy : Taiwan laid the foundation for basic livelihood industry during 1960s. With a view to accelerate the pace of economic development, the government of the Republic of China established the first EPZ which is known as Kaohsiung Export Processing Zone （KEPZ）. Barely within three years, the zone was fully occupied. It was, therefore, decided to establish two more zones.

During the past thirty years, the export processing zones have played an important role in developing export-oriented industries in the country. They were set up to attract industrial investment, expand foreign trade, introduce modern technology and create job opportunities with a view to upgrade the national economy. By now, these four original goals for setting up EPZs have been fully achieved.

With a view to coordinate with the plan for Asia Pacific Operation Center, the Export Processing Zone Authority （EPZA） redefined the original goals in 1995. The rested goals for the zones are to strengthen industrial competitive edge, combine global market demand, upgrade domestic technology and introduce multinational business investment. EPZA is determined to pursue these new goals vigorously. In addition, the EPZA has recently established warehousing transshipment special zones to engage in product R&D. parts composing, certification, and distribution with a view to making EPZ the distribution and global logistics center. However, hi-tech and high value-added manufacturing industry would still be welcome in the zone. For purposes of ease of comparison, original and transformed goals for EPZ are given below： --

Original EPZ Goals：

2.Attract industrial investment

3.Expand foreign trade

4.Introduce modern technology

5.Create job opportunities

Transformed EPZ Goals：

2.Strengthen industrial competitive edge

3.Combine global market demand

4.Upgrade domestic technology level

5.Introduce multinational business investment

Incentives：Following incentives are admissible in EPZs：

- Investment made in accordance with the Statute for Upgrading Industries is entitled to relevant incentive measures such as five （or four） years exemption on profit-seeking enterprise income tax for investment （increased investment） or deductible investment. Besides, shareholders may have the benefit of deferred payment of consolidated income tax;
- The business income tax for transshipment is leviable at the rate of 10% of the transshipment revenue; and
- Import tax, commodity tax, business tax and deed tax are exempt.

To facilitate investor's business promotion, all matters concerning investment, screening, industry/commerce registration, building permit, import and export endorsements are handled efficiently by the EPZA.

Policy and incentives for Science Parks

Policy： Having expanded foreign trade and created job opportunities during sixties and seventies, Taiwan shifted focus on developing high technology during eighties. In view of rapid changes in industrial manufacturing, introduction of hi-tech industry and recruitment of technical manpower to undertake research and innovation of industrial technology became an emergent task for the government. In 1980, the first Science-based Industrial Park was established at Hsinchu. In 1995 the government started work for establishing the Tainan Science-based Industrial Park to further strengthen the development of hi-tech industries and accelerate the pace of economic development. The Science Parks of Taiwan have been established with three goals in view, viz :

- To introduce technology industry and manpower;
- To encourage industrial research and innovation; and
- To promote the development of hi-tech industry.

Incentives :

- Investments made in compliance with the Statute for Upgrading Industries are eligible for relevant incentive measures. Newly established firms can enjoy selective five-year （four year on additional investment） tax holiday of business income tax or deductible investment. After the expiration of five-year tax holiday period, business income tax rate will not exceed 20% ; and
- Import and export duties, commodity tax, business tax and deed tax are exempt.

All matters concerning investment application, screening, industry/commerce registration, building permit, import and export endorsement are handled efficiently by the Science Park authority.

ROLES AND FUNCTIONS OF EPZs AND SPs IN THE PREVALING ECONOMIC ENVIRONMENT

In Taiwan, the export processing zones and science parks are the two important citadels for hi-tech manufacturing industry. Furthermore, the booming industry of IC and LCD specifically converges in the EPZs and SPs. Now that the EPZA is also promoting a warehousing transshipment special zone, which if it succeeds, would become the hi-tech operation and logistics center for the Asia Pacific region. Science Park Authority is now actively engaged in the establishment of Tainan science park and expansion of Hsinchu science park. As a result of these developments, EPZs and SPs will instrumental in expanding Taiwan's new hi-tech industry and enhancing its competitive edge, thus laying solid foundation for developing it into a hi-tech manufacturing center in the Asia Pacific region. Currently, EPZs and SPs are playing a pivotal role in upgrading Taiwan's industry and sustaining its economic development.

CONTRIBUTION OF SPs TOWARDS R&D AND TECHNOLOGICAL PROMOTION

The National Science Council under the Executive Yuan has been promoting for many years supportive R&D programs on products keeping in view the industrial characteristics of the Science Park. It has made significant contribution to R&D and up gradation of technical levels. The science parks have played a pivotal role in making Taiwan the third largest country in information industry and the first largest country in mass production technology in semi-conductor such as chip OEM and packing. In this context, following facts are quite revealing. For example, during 1997 : -

- Expenditure on R&D was NT$24.5 billion which accounted for 6.2% of the total turnover;
- The number of applications for patents was as high as 1,583 of which 1021 were domestic cases and 561 foreign; and
- There were 54 proposals of subsidy for R&D involving an amount of NT$400 million.

The National Science Council has established an academic and industrial R&D enter and a hands-on design center in the science park. This has encouraged collaboration amongst academicians and industrialists, which has good potential for encouraging R7D and enhancing technical skills.

FUNCTIONAL LINKAGES BEWTEEN EPZs AND SPs

EPZs and SPs are hi-tech and high value-added special zones which have hi-tech electronic industry as their mainstream industry. But they represent different stages in industrial development. While in the case of IC and LCD, the focus of EPZs is on mid-and down-stream manufacturing such as IC, packaging, and LCD, SPs are characterized by up-stream chip manufacturing, mask, IC design, and LCD. Thus EPZs and SPs form vertial industrial division of labor. In fact, some firm such as Nan-Mao Technology Company and Philips Taiwan Company have investment in the zone and also in the Science Park. EPZs and SPs have thus been functionally combined into one zone and have very close cooperation.

By appropriate planning of vertical industrial division of labor, the EPZs and SPs can in future be developed into high-tech inlands of Taiwan. Besides, proper integration of EPZs & SPs with the Asia Pacific Operation Center plan can push Taiwan's industry into higher levels.

PERFORMANCE OF OCCUPIED FIRMS, IMPACT ON THE LOCAL ECONOMY AND BY THE GLOBAL ECONOMY

EPZs

During 1960s, EPZs become a household name for Taiwan's booming industry and their contribution to its economy is well known. Due to their successful operation in Taiwan, EPZs become a model for replication by other developing countries. Their major contribution to the local and global economy is detailed below：

- Investment ： During 1966-1995, accumulated capital investment reached US$3.6 billion. During 1996/97, further investment of US$2.1 billion was made while the amount of investment for 1998 was as high as NT$1.3 billion.

- Employment：During the past decade, the number of workers in EPZs on average was around 59,000 persons. However, in 1987 EPZs employed over 90,000 persons. During 1976 – 1998, workers employed in EPZs accounted for 0.78% to 1.27% of total employment and 2.13% to 4.42% of total employment in manufacturing sector.

- Introduction of modern technology：Modern technologies introduced through Japan, the United States, and Holland have made great contribution to the advancement of local industry.

- Government revenues：Around US$400 million are collected per annum towards government revenues.

- Foreign exchange reserves：Accumulated trade surplus reached US$34.6 billion.

- Contribution to GDP：For 1987 alone, EPZs accounted for 1.6% of the nation's GDP and 5.81% of GDP from manufacturing sector.

- Promotion of international cooperation： Successful operation and management of the EPZs has made them investment paradise for the local entrepreneurs. They have also become an object for study and replication by foreign policy leaders and economists. Since their inception, over 600,000 government officials, scholars, and visitors from all over the world have visited EPZs, of which many were presidents, economists and experts on business management. This has made significant contribution towards promotion of global cooperation and friendship. In addition, over the years EPZA organized seminars on EPZ operations and management in which representatives from developing countries were invited. These seminars have made notable contributions to the program of economic reconstruction of their economies and promotion of global trade. In 1989, EPZA successfully sponsored WEPZA International Conference in Kaohsiung. In October 2000, EPZ will again host WEPZA Conference in Kaohsiung which, we hope, will be conducive to global economic cooperation and exchange of experience.

SCIENCE PARKs

Since inception in 1980, due to favorable government policy and active involvement of the enterprise in R&D, science parks have made significant contribution to industrial advancement, which is well known in Taiwan's technology. Science Park have successfully：-

• Attracted investment;
• Created job opportunities and brought about local prosperity;
• Promoted industrial advancement;
• Increased tax revenues and foreign exchange reserves;
• Introduced modern technology; and
• Increased international fame and indirectly contributed to the global economy.

Due to rapid industrial growth, by 1998 over 200 firms were in operation in the Science Park employing more than 70,000 workers. The science park has become a new show window for decentralizing Taiwan's industrial development and economic miracle.

FACTORS CONTRIBUTING TO THE SUCCESS OF EPZs AND SPs

Following factors have contributed to the success of EPZs & SPs in Taiwan : -

- Unambiguous laws and bylaws governing these enclaves and sound taxation and incentive policies;
- Developed infrastructure, high quality work force and cordial labor and management relations;
- One-stop service with efficient administration;
- Lease only policy for land and low rentals （per square meter costing only NT$400 per annum） which reduces investment substantially and optimizes land use;
- Accessible geographic locations and flexible business strategy; and
- Establishment of industrial satellite through OEM.

For the science park, a team of experts was loaned by EPZA to park authorities during 1979-81 to help in formulating statutory systems and plan development of infrastructure. Factors contributing to the success of SP are similar to those for EPZ. Further more, the Hsinchu area where the Science Park is located has excellent technical manpower and professional academic and research institutions and universities such as Technology Institute, National Chinghua University. Introduction of 「Innovation Technology Research and Development Project Subsidy」 system has been another key factor for the success of Science Park.

ORGANIZATION, MANAGEMENT, AND PERFORMANCE OF EPZ AND SP AUTHORITIES

Both EPZs and SPs have comprehensive organizational set up. All functions in relation to the enterprise are relegated to relevant departments and each department adopts the policy of one-stop service. All procedures, starting from investment application, screening, and company registration to issue of building permit are administered by the EPZA and SPA with such speed and efficiency that it has won widespread acclaim from the enterprises.

FUTURE PROSPECTS OF EPZs AND SPs

EPZs

EPZs are being given new development orientation through the establishment of warehouse transshipment special zone and developing them into hi-tech operation center and hi-tech R&D, marking, certification and distribution center as well as a global logistics center.

Hi-tech Operation Center： Taiwan is the third largest country in information industry, next only to the United States and Japan, whereas in the case of mass production technology for semi-conductor it tops the world. During 1998, the turnover of IC and LCD enterprises accounted for 60.68% of the EPZ's total turnover. These enterprises have as high as 78% share in the total investment. EPZs have become the main citadel of Taiwan for manufacturing IC packaging, testing, and LCD. By making IC and LCD as the core industry and developing related industries such as composing, testing, certification, and distribution, the EPZ can be developed into one of the best electronic manufacturing and R&D centers in Asia.

Hi-tech R&D, Marketing, Certification and Distribution Center︰ For the development of hi-tech industry, Taiwan can utilize existing technology manpower to keep on strengthening its R&D capabilities. By way of compound transport model of land, sea and air, enterprises at home and abroad can be attracted to send to the EPZ key components and semi-finished products for R&D, testing, certification and distribution and sales all over the world. This will provide impetus to the development of relevant industries and make Taiwan the headquarter of global multinational enterprises in the Asia markets.

Global logistics center︰With the rapid development of hi-tech industry, especially hi-tech electronic industry, a key problem that cannot be ignored is how to deliver the product to the consumer （raw material → production → sale → consumer →） within the shortest time. Therefore, development of rapid and effective logistics system will be the direction for future. Thus, the development of a set of logistics model which can combine the six Asia Pacific Operation Centers and closely cooperate with global logistics center is currently one of the main tasks for the EPZA.

SP

The aim is to develop Science Park into a technology cultural city and realize the goal of making it Technology Island of Taiwan. With a view to promote industrial growth and balanced area development and to coordinate with the Asia Pacific Operation center, Hsincha Science Park established Taiwan Science Park in 1995. The new science Park by creating linkages of city with countryside in terms of economic development and community culture, will develop Taiwan into a technology island not only in name but in reality.

EXPORT PROCESSING ZONES WAREHOUSING AND TRANSSHIPMENT SPECIAL ZONES REPUBLIC OF CHINA

Objectives of Special Zones

Over the past 30 years, the export processing zones, which have helped in accelerating the pace of economic development of Taiwan, are now being transformed into warehousing transshipment special zones. These second generation zones will upgrade their level, enrich their functions, and develop pre and post stage of manufacturing industries and warehousing-transshipment based industries. They will be instrumental in transforming Taiwan into a technology island. Multinational enterprises located in these zones will act as bridges between the domestic industries and thousands of the Asia Pacific production lines. The special zones will thus help domestic and foreign enterprises bind together closer. Taiwan will become the base for the Asia pacific multinational operational headquarter for local and foreign enterprises. They will offer another opportunity for economic boom in the country.

Location and Area of the Special Zones

All the kaohsing warehousing transshipment special zones are located near the airport and port. Three special zones will be located as under :

- Chungtao special zone is being set up by enlarging the area of the existing Kaohsing export processing zone from 68 hectares to 72.3 hectares;
- Cheng-kung special zone including 81 hectares of land for state-run enterprises is being set up along the Cheng-kung road; and
- Hsiaokang airport warehousing transshipment special zone has an area of 32 hectares and is located north of Kaohsuing international airport.

Besides, Taichung harbor warehousing transshipment special zone will have an area of 182 hectares. Establishment of special economic zones at Chiang Kai-shek International airport and Keelung airport is also under consideration.

Table – 1 : Planned scope and Target for the Warehousing Transshipment Special Zones of Kaohsiung Area

Zone	Area (ha)	Land Use	Current Status	Planned Target
Chungtao	72.3	EPZ Port area	Kaohsiung EPZ	Mainly manufacturing

			37-2-38-2 wharves warehouses of Kaohsiung Harbour Bureau	industry assisted with warehouse transshipment and related industry
ChengKung	80	Class AIZ	CPC：Kaohsiung District Office Tang Eng：Steel Plant （will be transformed into Hsin-Tang District Park） Taipower：power Station Taifertilizer：Kaohsiung Plant Taisuger：Warehouse and truck transfer center Cargill Taiwan Corp：Feed plant	Warehouse Multinational regional operation center and related services
Hsiaokang	32.0	Airport facility – use land and farm land	Sugarcane field	Air warehouse transshipment, general and air-related services
Total Land Area：184.3 ha			Total Production Value by 2006：US$50 billion/year	

Remaeks：

CPC：Chinese Petroleum Corporation

Tan Eng：Tang Eng Iron Works Company

Taifertilizer：Taiwan Fertilizer Corporation

Taipower：Raiwan Power Company

Taisugar：Taiwan Sugar Corporation

Salient features of the special Zones

• Warehousing transsshipment special zones are being established under the current policy for export processing zones policy in conformity with the Asia Pacific Operation Center Plan;

- These zones will become a base for composing, inspection, and distribution by the manufacturers of Asia region, thereby promoting international division of labor;
- They offer enterprises opportunities for setting up global operation headquarters and regional operation centers;
- These zones combine characteristic of Singaporean distribution park, multinational enterprise operation headquarters and harbor warehousing; and
- These are essentially second generation export processing zones which, besides being manufacturing centers of first generation, include （a）R&D designing as well as composing and distribution activities, （b）warehousing and transshipment operations （international logistic industries）, and （c）related service industries.

Operational Model of the Special Zone

- The warehousing transshipment special zones provide a platform for division of labor in terms of composing, inspecting and distribution by the three global economic systems viz： American, European, and the Asian Pacific system. Let us take the example of an electronic company, which is engaged in the manufacture of high quality TY and has two production lines in Taiwan and one line each in the USA, Japan and Malaysia. The finished components and parts fro each regional production line can be transported to the special zone for processing, composing, packaging and distribution. With the establishment of the special zone, the enterprise can set up a distribution plant and run business in the special zone. Otherwise, it may have to move to other location for understanding these activities;

- These zones will emerge as the inspection and distribution centers for the Southeast Asia. For example, a company manufacturing card machine in the mainland China may send its product to other countries for inspection and distribution. In the special zone, all the functions of inspection, distribution, and delivery can be undertaken to save shipping costs and exports can be effected to all parts of the world, which enhances the competitiveness of the product;

- For the Taiwanese businessmen, the zones will be a center for the purchasing, inspecting and delivery. For example, a textile company which has 12 plants in Taiwan and 27 plants in mainland China, can in future engage in purchase, inspection, packing delivery and transshipment in the special zone;

- These zones are also international marketing and inspecting centers. For example, a foreign aeronautics company manufacturing high level technology parts can, if matched with domestic aeronautics manufacturing industry, export complete components and parts to the southeast Asia region after going through inspection process in the special zone;

- These zones will also become the warehousing transshipment operation center for eastern Asia. Products can be transferred to the zone enterprise from foreign countries for inspection, simple processing, packing warehousing transshipment and distribution; and

- Special zones are also the joint domestic warehousing operation

centers. The domestic （or foreign） industries can utilize the joint warehousing operation center for communication, warehousing, delivery and distribution operations.

Incentives and facilities

Special Tax Incentives：
- Profit seeking income earned from the transshipment business will be taxed in accordance with 10% of business revenue;
- The most advantageous law, viz. statute for Upgrading Industries is applicable to zone enterprises;
- Customs duty on local sales will be levied after deducting added value （bonded factory will be levied at 70%）; and
- There will be no customs duty on sale of five-year-old machinery.

「One-Stop」 Shop and Higher Administrative Efficiency：
- All matters from the stage of issue of certificates concerning investment application, screening, company registration, profit-seeking enterprise registration and factory building permit etc. are handled by the export processing zone administration;
- Customs services and banking facilities have been provided in the zone. Exports, domestic market sales, labor services and environment protection measures can all be completed within the zone; and
- Efficient warehousing and transportation services have also been provided.

Land Rentals are Low：
The Zone Have Proximity to the Port and Airport：

Medical, Catering and Cleaning services and Related Infrastructure are Available
Which Reduces Operational Costs：

The Zone Offers a Secure Environment：
Investment Opportunities in the Special Zones

The zones offer good investment opportunities for the following reasons：

- Salary of the local managerial and technical employees is lower than in Singapore and Hong Kong;
- The zones are located in the very center of the Asia Pacific region. The shortest distance between the six main ports of the Asia pacific and Taiwan is 53 hours only by sea, which substantially reduces shipping cost;
- The zones have solid foundation of advanced technology for manufacturing industry;
- The manufacturing industry in the zones has multinational investment for exports, besides numerous production lines in foreign countries and adequate business information;
- Direct transportation and transshipment costs are 40% lower than Hong Kong;
- With the unified use of land, sea and air services in conjunction with internet, commodity flow is improved and operation costs are reduced; and

- The Offshore Shipping Centre is presently in the first stage of implementation. In the second stage later, commodities imported directly from mainland China will move into the export processing zone and re-exported. This would substantially reduce freight costs. The warehousing-transshipment center can be the base for multination operation center for the Taiwanese investors in the mainland China.

Annex-1：

Export Processing Zone Administration Announcement

SUBJECT : ANNOUNCEMENT OF INVESTMENT REQUIREMENTS AND SCREENING PRINCIPLES

Statutory basis

- Statute for establishment and management of export processing zones and measures government screening of application for establishment of enterprise in the export processing zone.
- Outlines of establishment of Taichung Harbor Transshipment Special Zone and Kaohsiung Warehousing Transshipment Special Zones（including Chungtao,Chengkung and Hsiaokang special zones） as approved by the Executive Yuan letter Tai （86）Chin 18448, 8 May 1997.

ANNOUNCEMENT DETAILS

Investment Requirements

Investor should meet the following requirements;

The Minimum capital （NT Dollar）Requirements：（1）Manufacturing industry：40 million;（2）warehousing industry：80 million;（3）transportation industry：50 million;（4）trading industry：5 million; and （5）transportation service and others; 1 million. However, if other laws have regulations on the minimum capitals regarding the above-mentioned industries, which are higher than the said standard, latter would be applicable.

The Minimum Leasing Land Area for Constructing a Self-Designed Factory Building：

（1）Manufacturing industry： 2,000 ㎡;（2）warehousing and transportation sector： 3,000 ㎡; and （3）there is no limit for other industries.

Table - 2：Building and Coverage Rate for Self-Designed Factory Building

Zone \ Item		Building Rate （%）	Coverage Rate （%）	Remarks
Chungtao Special Zone	Factory Area	60	500	
	Industrial/Commerical service Area	70	1000	
	Warehousing/Transportation Service Area	60	300	
Chengkung special Zone （CSZ）		60	600	
Tangjung special Zone		In line with CSZ	In line with CSZ	
Hsiaokang special Zone		60	No Limit	
Taichung Harbor Special Zone		80	600	

Note：For Hsiaokang special zone there is no limit on coverage rate, but the high-rise building should comply with the regulation regarding airport limitation on building.

Annual Production Value Per Hectare： After operating for 10 years the enterprise should achieve the following standards.
- Warehousing Industry： US$100 million; and
- Manufacturing and other Industries： US$200 million.

Industries permissible in the zone： （Annex – 2 ）
Industries that can economically use land, water and electricity：
and Industries that will not pose danger to public safety, environment and sanitation.
Screening Standards

Priority for screening and land allotment will be on the following criteria：
- Capital investment;
- Business revenue;
- Annual production value per hectare;
- Profit making percentage and outlook including market competitiveness, marketing strategy and so on;
- Pollution possibility and preventive measures;
- Investors credit and business performance;
- Industry category （multi-national operation center, the first 1,000 national large enterprises, large hi-tech enterprises, warehousing distribution center and so on will be given priority）; and
- Advantage for the export processing zone and national development in the zone.

Matters not mentioned in this announcement shall be decided as per relevant law and regulation of the export-processing zone.

Annex – 2

Industries Permissible in the Special Zones

- Precision Machinery Manufacturing;
- Electricity and Electronics Manufacturing
- Metal products Manufacturing;
- Machinery Equipment Manufacturing;
- Chemical Products Manufacturing;
- Food Manufacturing;
- Transportation Tools Manufacturing;
- Apparel & Accessories Manufacturing;
- Miscellaneous products Manufacturing;
- International Trading;
- Consulting Service;
- Information service;
- Warehousing, Transshipment and Assembling, Reassembling, Examining, Repairing and Realigning, categorizing, Cutting, Inspecting and Distributing;
- Machinery Appliances Repairing;
- Transportation Tools Repairing;
- Electricity and Electronics Repairing;
- Industry-related Services; and one of Other Hi-tech, capital-intensive, High Quality and High Value Added Industries Approved for Establishment.

參、世界加工口區協會收集有關加工出口區專題報導

一、加工出口區最佳財務規劃
John E. Jent Vice President

美國曾有工業開發園區因發展過大，造成投資過多的公共建設及甚多閒置的廠房而至破產；另外在政府方面也有投資在不同的工業區，加工出口區，其投資十分完善，耗用龐大資金在公共建設，廠房及行政辦公樓等方面，其資金的來源多從政府，世界銀行，國內美國開發銀行等單位，數十億的資金最後是花費而無結果；這兩種情況的產生在於投資在公共建設費用上的金額太大，而到開始運作時反而沒有錢可運用，這種現象維持達數年之久，導至工業區，加工出口區空無所有。

這是由兩點錯誤造成，第一，應該先將道路建好，水電供應完成及海關人員配合，如此便可吸引到如 G.M，飛利浦或三菱之類公司駐進，然而他們並沒有這麼做，第二點是貸款公司作業問題，規定」所貸金額限用於公共建設，而且限 20 個月內使用，否則失效」，因此而造成計劃者，建築師，工程師，營建公司等都倉促趕工。

為了謹慎及成本效益考量，在投資公司來區之前先建好一棟廠房備便，而並不須建六棟或一打的廠房閒置空等待，

公共設施中的用水，污水管線，雨水排放，電及其他項目，雖設計齊備，但不必馬上建設安裝，等到廠房確實有使用者，而且也付了費才做，因為公共建設費用是非常貴的開支，每人都知道好的加工出口區必須有完備的硬體設施，但不宜過分。

有兩個字要記住即「階段及彈性」。

階段是將進度分成多個階段進行，第一階段性工作完成且已使用，再進行第二階段工作，如此類推；彈性是階段性工作有必要調整時可以改變，完全根據實際需要而定。

世界銀行，或聯合國工業發展組織，或是美國國際發展局等可能給我們一筆龐大的金額達一千萬之數，用於公共建設，建廠房，行政大樓等，但卻不給一分錢用於園區成長或市場行銷上；何不將一千萬改成五百萬元，其中兩百五十萬元用作硬體建設，另兩百五十萬元用作園區升級或成長用呢？如此可使園區變為具有吸引力及維持營運的工業區。

DESGINING AN EPZ FOR OPTIMUM FINANCING John E. Jent Vice President International Parks, Inc. Winchester, Massachusetts USA

Eight years ago the most successful and best-managed industrial park developer in the U.S. went into bankruptcy. Cabot, Cabot & Forbes （CC&F） had begun developing industrial parks in 1952 and the result – due in large part to its efforts – was Route 128, Boston's Technology Highway. The company, a recession year in the U.S., CC&F had simply built too much infrastructure and had too many empty buildings.

In another scenario, we have a different kind of industrial park： an export processing zone in an underdeveloped country. We see wide paved roads, electric power lines, water and sewer facilities, a dozen or twenty beautiful factory buildings and an impressive zone administration building. It is a picture post card of what an EPZ should look like. The trouble is that there are no trucks, no machinery, no customs activity and NO people. A government, the World Bank, the Inter-American Development Bank or some other agency has spent millions of dollars, pesos or rials and nothing is happening.

The problem in both cases – the private industrial park and the publicly-financed export processing zone – is that it is very expensive to develop the facilities. Millions must be spent before the first semiconductor is bonded or the first blue jeans are sewn.

And, until those activities start, there is no money coming in to start paying for all that pretty construction. Worst of all, that situation can go on for years. We have all seen those empty industrial parks, industrial estates and export processing zones.

The fault, as I see it, lies in two places. First, each of us thinks that the world is going to beat-a-path to his doorway. All we have to do is put up a sign, pave the streets, supply electricity and water, and get the customs people to cooperate. Then, General Motors or Phillips or Mitsubishi will come. We cannot understand why they don't.

The second fault lies in the way the lending agencies operate. The say（after years of negotiating and waiting）,「Here's the money for the infrastructure. You have 20 months to spend it or you lose it.」 It's no wonder that the planners, architects, engineers and construction companies have a field day.

The prudent and cost-effective way to design and build an export processing zone is to stay one building ahead of the customer or tenant.

That means that you always have a building ready for a prospective company to occupy within a reasonable time. But, you don't have six or a dozen idle and empty buildings on your hands waiting for users.

The same principle applies to streets and sidewalks, water and sewer lines, storm drains, electricity and the rest of the infrastructure. You design it on paper of course, but you don't build and install it until you absolutely have to – that is, when the prospective user is ready to occupy the building and the money is about to flow in.

Infrastructure is terrible expensive and the idea of not spending money to provide it before it's needed sounds naive and unrealistic. Everyone knows that you can't attract an industrial company unless you have the physical facilities to prove you have a bona-fide export processing zone. Furthermore, it takes a long time to build an EPZ. True, but you don't have to overdo it!

There are two key words to remember : PHASING and FLEXIBILITY.

PHASING means that you design and construct your industrial park or export processing zone in a series of steps or phase : Phase 1, Phase 2, Phase 3, etc. You take one step at a time, and you don't begin Phase 2 until Phase 1 is completed and occupied or nearly so.

FLEXIBILITY is part of the phasing process in that you build into your planning the ability to change things as the part or zone develops. Once a 30 foot-wide road is built or an eight inch water main is installed, it is awfully hard to move them. However, if the roads and water mains are still only designs on paper, they can be changed easily.

Let's take a concrete example. We have the land for an export processing zone of 100 acres or about 40 hectares. That's big enough for about 10,000 workers or about 30 manufacturing plants. The typical way that such an EPZ has been developed in the past is to build the roads, install the electricity and the water and sewer systems, and construct maybe 10 factory buildings. At a cost of $8million!

Now we wait for the customers – U.S., Japanese or European companies – to move in and manufacture TV sets or automobile engines. The trouble is that they don't and we wait, and wait.

We have a beautiful industrial park or zone with good roads, excellent utilities and nice factory buildings （and, of course, an office building for the management）. By now, we have spent $10 million, including salaries and other administration expenses and we are still waiting for the first industrial job to show for it.

Naturally, the World Bank or UNIDO or USAID could give us a grant or a loan for $10 million for infrastructure, buildings and administration. But, they could not give us one dime for promotion or marketing.

Wouldn't it be better to have $5 million instead of $10 million, and to spend $2.5 million of it on physical things and $2.5 million on promoting the zone？ For $2.5 million, we can install about 25% of the ultimate road and other infrastructure systems and construct two buildings, one of 10,000 square feet and another of 30,000 square feet. We then have concrete evidence that we have an attractive and a viable industrial park and, most important, we can accommodate a tenant-company in a matter of months.

On our engineering and architectural drawings we show the plants for Phase 1, which is already constructed, and for Phase 2 and 3, the ultimate development of the zone. When we have our first tenant occupying the first building, we proceed to build the next building. We are always one building ahead of the demand; when we fill one building, or are about to, we build the next one. When promotion slows down due to a recession, we stop. When we are close to filling the Phase 1 area of the zone we begin to build the roads and infrastructure for Phase 2.

The flexibility part of the process comes from our ability to adjust the plans and designs. We can adapt them to the market demand. For example, we can lay out the road pattern around lots of, say, four acres. If our experience shows that most companies want 20,000 square-foot buildings on only one-acre lots, we can subdivide the bigger lots into smaller ones and add new streets. Similarly, we can subdivide a 40,000 square-foot building into 20,000 square feet for each of two companies, or even 10,000 each for four tenants.

The foregoing is a commonsense approach based on good physical planning and prudent economic development. Phasing and Flexibility are the keynotes. However, it is also based on the premise that the funding or investment money will be available on that basis, and that is the difficulty.

To the members of the financing agencies among you, I say that you must find ways to be more prudent, realistic and flexible in your allocating funds. You must be able to say to developers of industrial parks and export processing zones, 「Here are the funds for Phase 1, and we give you a 100% guarantee for the funds for Phase 2 and later phases when you show us that you are ready for them. 」

You must also begin to finance the EPZ 「business」 by including administration and promotion costs in your lending packages. These represent very significant changes in the way development funds are currently approved and made available.

Let us hope that the World Bank, the Asian Development Bank, the Inter-American Development Bank, and all the regional and national development banks are listening!

二、投資成長——優惠條件的影響（Investment Promotion–The Effect of Incentives）

從經驗總括的來看投資優惠條件，最好的優惠條件是政局穩定及有好的環境，而一些開發中國家慷慨所給的優惠條件如免各種稅，免進口關稅之類的用以滿足吸引新的投資者，而時間證明是不正確的。

事實上要非常小心的作長期打算，因為自由區的投資成本回收很慢，很多地主國借了大筆資金投資工業區，而僅能從來區投資者方面收到租金至無法支付借貸，而行政管理及海外招商變成政府的一項經常性負擔。

一些成功的地主國家，如印度，菲律賓，他們不將免稅包括在優惠條件之內，而他們利用了得力的會計作業使應繳的稅延後數年繳交，也有用加速折舊的辦法一樣可以達到免稅的效果。

站在地主國的立場要察查之處在於公平原則，任何地方都要付稅，很多投資者比起地主國的資源多得多，也有能力合理付稅，給予免稅作為最大優惠條件即是否認了地主國稅賦的功效。而這些稅是為這些國家的基本收入，當然公司採用了海外控股公司複雜網路作業，海外操作利潤分配，利用這樣的基金在避免或僅付給最少的稅。

如是，對優惠必須小心架構平衡，工業自由區對長期還本應認真的計算，很不幸的，並未如此的做，而今世界加工

出口區協會可以從這個領域中已有經驗的發展中國家將其經驗提供給正在發展中的國家參考。

還有不幸的是，有些顧問公司根據純理論提供參考而誤導開發中國家，有些國家當他們已設定好他們的優惠條件後，來到聯合國工業發展組織希望得到往後的建議，但是為時已晚。

我們都了解優惠條件，而新投資人會問優惠條件在實務上要如何運作；採用優惠條件的要點是要有適當的行政運作及中央政府不要強加壓力予以限制或以不明確的法規考慮貨幣兌換或利潤攜回。在加工區管理處的任何延遲或困惑，包括承辦職員頻繁的更換都將損及到優惠的目的。

加勒比海共同市場為免稅區有助於優惠行政作業，15個會員國同意給予三大國家即牙買加，古雅納及 Trinidad 在某種條件下 10 年免所得稅，另一方面對低開發國家就應該給予 15 年免所得稅，巴布杜已有大量的開發但國家小，是另一例外不同結構的國家。

區域協定可能用在其他地區，區與區之間因競爭而提供長期的免所得稅是沒有幫助的；值得一提的是地主國政府可以善用稅收付清貸款；總括的講，我們要了解免所得稅不是優惠辦法最重要的因素，而最為重要的因素是：

i 政局穩定

ii 明確的投資法規

iii 有效的區內行政管理

還有一些次要的因素如實際的勞動成本對生產的關係，但很多投資者誤估了這項頗為重要的因素。另關於每小

時工資方面，亞洲國家是 30 美分，而加勒比海國家是 75 美分至 1.07 美元。如果沒有穩定的政局，或不明確的投資法規就不會有投資人來過問，當然，建設已久的區各有不同的優惠條件，因為他們有能力吸引他們所喜歡類型的投資人並與之直接連繫，並可能徵對不同程度的投資人給予適當的優惠條件。

有些新區對某些事不能完全了解，有那些重要議題會形成非優惠條件。我們都知道的有準備不恰當的說明資料，對拜訪者的接待不週，或問題答覆得太慢等都將成為非優惠條件。

特別一提的是財務制度強調對償還貸款索取租金價碼的管理，誠如所知，廠房租金標準的多少要為國際間所接受，如果租金要求太高就造成非優惠條件；廠房租金的了解是世界性的，也是一種服務，此項服務世界加工出口區協會可以提供。

對世界加工出口區協會的建議：

我想對世界加工出口區協會成就的檢討將會有益，而未來的成就又將如何？特別是未來將要比上一個世紀困難得多了；

自 1974 年開始，勞動力的需求跟不上工業的成長，一部份原因是自動化減少勞動力的需求，還有機器人的替代，以及電子設備微小控制系統的高速度及高精密度的工作等，從這種傾向來看，對任何案件來規範勞動力就變成非常敏感，因為這些案件可能會減少勞動力的需求，或者是「工

作輸出」而導致聯合國很多的懷疑，聯合國曾責備自由區的很多工業問題並不真正的歸咎在自由區本身。

還有的問題就是「區」對地主國的價值，公共設施成本高達兩千萬美元之普的爭議，而來區的投資者不付稅金僅付廠房租金，工資相較偏低，附加價值的爭議，以及對投資還本的不關心等，此形成外國大的投資人在繳稅支出方面要求金額補助。

還有就是相同的裝配工作不斷地重覆，不努力就得換工作，一些可預見的操作危險及工作負責人堅持要求超時工作或延長工作時間。

我在意這些責備是因為我認為世界加工出口區協會能夠有效的改進與勞工組織的對話，協會最初的意願是要做這件事，你們大部份的人都會記得 1974 年由 Niall O'Bren 先生所簽的文件，協會會員可能為自己的理由加強自己與投資人之間的談判實力，如果「訴訟法」簽成，則建築工程師協會也會知道。

加勒比海共同市場曾對優惠條件予以限制；例如為了工資調升 5 到 10 分而致使製造廠商離開，這對紡織業是否會很遺憾呢？1984 年曾發生一些公司在處理成衣問題而由墨西哥搬遷到海地。這樣非常自由的改變可能對生意很好，但對地主國卻無任何的承諾；很多國家很感激一些投資人因短時間搬遷重建困難而留下來維持生產，免稅進口設備限制等等；我不認為輕微的限制會對投資人是嚴重的障礙，這要問對如此自由改變的公司應該要完全給他們優惠條件嗎？有些投資人失敗而非他們本身的錯而是肇因於參謀作業時間

疏失，及區作業管理漫無目標；實在的，應對投資人要限制不允許在兩年內搬進又搬出。

世界加工出口區協會可能放掉督導任務，然而這將變成國際間標準規範的認知，如果世界加工出口區協會在這方面不行動，嚴重的要問協會真心要服務的目的是什麼？何以會員要付會費呢？我希望這些話不會造成某些人的不悅。我深深感覺有些人應該要有行動就像是撒旦的提倡者一樣，假如我能確認世界加工出口區協會是完全有效率的話，則前面所講的都不會是事實。

就以上總結，協會會員應該認同類似的制度「訴訟法」，它包括了最低額度投資的優惠限制，最大時限免稅規定及優惠條件選用管制，例如加速折舊還有最低工資的同意及工資談判組織。同時還要管制的是避免投資人將生產機器等轉移用以避免支付最低工資的調整，對這種投資人我們都應該將之列為問題人物。

聯合國工業發展組織的角色：

我未曾考慮聯合國工業發展組織服務於這個領域，其原因你們都很了解。我們在實行有需要的可行性研究。參與投資成長會議，市場評鑑及提供有經驗的專家到主辦國解決問題，這類服務的需求也不多，但經常的，年年都有，聯合國工業發展組織在這方面很有經驗，而且對地主國及投資人都一樣有效（對顧問公司卻無效，因為他們已接受自由區提供服務的合約）。

聯合國工業發展組織依然如故，特別是它本身擔任一項新角色好比是專業代理公司準備好服務這個領域，例如工業

投資計劃，加工出口區，各種投資區或對相關領域的可行性研究，小型工業之類的服務。

　　本書作者註：彼德‧瑞先生是聯合國工業發展組織加勒比海高級工業發展顧問，同時也是派任世界加工出口區協會的指導委員，對世界加工出口區協會的支持很具影響力，本篇文章很有價值，值得參考。

INVESTMENT PROMOTION – THE EFFECT OF INCENTIVES
Peter F. Ryan
Senior Industrial Development Field Advisor （Caribbean）
United Nations Industrial Development Organization
Bridgetown, Barbados

I am very glad to be able to attend this meeting at Flagstaff since I was also present seven years ago in Manila when WEPZA was established. It is good also to see familiar faces.

To sum up my experience with investment incentives, the best incentives of all are political stability and an atmosphere of friendliness towards new industrial investments. However, some developing countries assume that generous incentives in the area of tax exemptions, duty free import and the like, are sufficient to attract new investors. Time has proved this to be incorrect.

In fact, the long term calculation has to be very carefully done, because the return on capital invested in a Free Zone is very low. Some host countries have borrowed large capital sums to construct industrial estates, only to find that the rentals paid by investors do not cover repayments, and that the cost of administration and overseas promotion cause a constant drain on government resources.

The is probably why some successful host countries, such as India and the Philippines do not include in their incentive package any tax exemption. In part, this is because in reality an investor with competent accountants can postpone its tax liability for several years. Also, other provisions, such as accelerated depreciation, can have the same effect as tax exemption.

The position of the host country has to be examined here. It is a main principle of equity that tax must be paid somewhere. Many investors have very great resources as compared to developing countries, and can well afford to pay reasonable taxes on corporate profits. Giving tax exemption as a main incentive can in fact have the effect of denying the host country taxes which are eventually paid in the country of origin. Of course, some companies operate complex offshore holding company networks into which they pay the profits of offshore operation, using these funds in such a way as to avoid or minimize taxation.

Incentives therefore, have to be very carefully constructed as a balanced package. The long term returns on an industrial Free Zone should be realistically calculated. Unfortunately this has not been done, and it could be a very useful function of WEPZA to make available to developing countries the experience in this field of more experienced developing countries.

Again unfortunately, there are consultant companies who offer advice in this area based on pure theory, and this can be quite misleading for developing countries. Some countries subsequently come to UNIDO for further advice after having set up their incentives, but it can be and frequently is, too late.

We here all know that whatever the incentive package is, the new investor will ask how the package is administered in practice. This is the vital part of the incentives, that they are properly administered and that Central Government does not vitiate them by imposing restrictions or having unclear regulations concerning currency exchange or repatriation of profits. Any delay or confusion in Zone Authority administration, including frequent staff changes, can also defeat the purpose of incentives.

The Caribbean Common Market is an interesting example of what can be done to assist in effective incentive administration. The fifteen member countries agreed that the three largest countries. Jamaica, Guyana, and Trinidad, should be entitled to five tax holidays on certain conditions for only 10 years, whereas the lesser developed countries should be allowed to give tax holidays for up to 15 years. Barbados, being more developed but very small is an exception with a different structure.

This sort of regional agreement could well be applied elsewhere, since competition between zones to offer longer periods of tax holiday is not helpful. For one thing, all host governments can well use the tax income to help in paying off the loans taken to finance construction. On the whole, we should all realize that tax holidays are not the really critical factor in incentive package. The critical factors are：-

　i. Political Stability.

　ii. Clear Investment Laws.

　iii. Efficient Zone Administration.

There are also lesser factors such as the actual cost of labor related to productivity, but some investors wrongly count this factor as the most important. In this regard, consider that hourly wages in some Asian countries are 30 US Cents, but in the Caribbean they are 75 cents to $1.07 in US Dollars.

Needless to say, if there is no political stability, or the investment laws are not clear, few investors will be attracted. Also investors who find themselves talking to different staff on every visit, are put off.

Of course, long established Zones have different incentives because they are able to target what type of investor they prefer and then make direct approaches to them, possibly tailoring incentives to each different potential investor.

This is something which newcomers find very difficult to comprehend, as well the the subject of disincentives. We all know how badly prepared literature, poor visitor reception, or slow correspondence are disincentives. We need not dwell on them here.

Specifically, the financial institutions have lately insisted on some managements charging rent commensurate with loan repayments. As we know, there is a norm for rentals of factory space, more or less internationally accepted. If higher rents are demanded, a disincentive is created. Knowledge of factory rents worldwide would be useful and is the sort of service which the WEPZA Secretariat could provide.

Suggestions for WEPZA

I think is would be useful to review what WEPZA has achieved. And what is could in future achieve, especially as the future is likely to be more difficult then the last decade.

Since 1974, the demand for labor has not kept pace with industrial growth, partly because automation has reduced the need for human guidance, replacing it with robots, with electronic devices and with miniaturized control systems working at high speeds with great accuracy. In view of this trend, it is natural that organized labor has become very sensitive to anything which may be seen to reduce the demand for labor, or to quote, 「export jobs」, unquote. Any kind of industrial estate which uses the phrase 'Free Zone', attracts the suspicions of the Unions, who have blamed on 'Free Zones' many industrial problems not really attributable to the Zones themselves.

Called into question also, is the value of such zones to the host economy. The argument is that the infrastructure costs upwards of US $20 million, and the investors do not pay taxes but only rent space. As wages are comparatively low, the added value, it is argued, regardless of the volume of turnover, must also be low, This, it is claimed, subsidizes large foreign investors at the expense of the taxpayer.

It is also alleged that the type of assembly work done is repetitive, and that no effort is made to vary the work, that some operations damage eyesight; that supervisors insist on over-time and longer hours that agreed.

I mention these accusations here because I think that WEPZA could be effective in improving the dialogue with organized labor. WEPZA was originally intended to do this, as many of you will remember from the paper written in 1974, by Mr. Niall O'Brien. WEPZA members could further their own cause, and strengthen their own bargaining power vis-à-vis new investors, if a Cold of Practice was drawn up, similar to that which associations of architects and engineers have.

In this way, incentives could be limited, as was done by CARICOM. Also, is it not regrettable that in the textile industry, a rise of 5 to 10 cents in wages is enough to cause manufacturers to leave, and to move to countries with lower wages. This happened in 1984 when companies making disposable garments moved from Mexico to Haiti. This sort of footloose changed may be good business but, it certainly does not show any basic commitment to the host country. Most countries also owe it to themselves to make this kind of move more difficulty by establishing a minimum time which investors must remain in production, to qualify for duty free import of equipment, etc. I do not consider that such a minor restriction would deter serious investors. Rather the question should be asked, should incentives be given to footloose companies at all？ Some investors will fail through no fault of their own, causing a loss staff time, and involving Zone management in expenses to no purpose. It is surely sensible to insure against investors who move in and out within two years.

WEPZA could lay down guidelines on this and similar matters to become internationally recognized standard norms. If WEPZA does not act in this way, the question has to be asked seriously as to what real purpose does it serve？ For what do members pay their fees？

I hope that these few words will not cause offense to anyone. I do feel that someone has to act here as the Devil's Advocate, and it would not be true if I assured you all that I though that WEPZA was fully effective.

To sum up, WEPZA members should agree, as similar institutions do, on a Code of Practice. This should cover minimum investment periods to qualify for incentives; maximum time limits for tax relief and guidelines on alternative incentives, such as accelerated depreciation. If should lower minimum wage agreements and wage negotiating machinery.

There should also be guidelines to avoid situations where investors transfer production machinery merely to avoid paying a minimum wage increase. The value of hosting this type of investor must surely be questioned by all of us.

UNIDO's Role

I have not gone into UNIDO's services in this field, partly because most of you know them. We carry out on demand full feasibility studies, investment promotion meetings, market surveys, and we also provide expertise to host countries in trouble-shooting in cases where an objective view is needed.

The demand for such services is not very great, but it is regular, year by year. UNIDO has a great deal of experience in this field, and it is a available to host countries and investors alike. （It is not available to consultant companies, who, having accepted a contract to offer services in the Free Zone field, turn to UNIDO for advice）.

UNIDO remains, especially in its new role as a Specialized Agency ready to offer its services in the field of planning of industrial estates, export processing Zones, investment Zones or in the related fields of feasibility studies, small scale industry and the like.

三、The Nogales 市風雨棚計劃——管理工具

（ The Nogales Shelter Plan, A Management Tool. ）

查理 卡碑爾

墨西哥 蘇羅拉省 Nogales　Nogales 工業區局長

　　要想將出口工業區填滿投資客並不容易，我們曾找了三佰家有實力的投資客，結果只有一家成功，所以我耗用了我半生的時間在芝加哥、波士頓、費城以及遍及美國其他地方，只是為了找到投資客，我們採用研討會的方式進行，但都浪費了，而每次研討會都要花一萬五仟元至三萬元，有時無一家參加，有時又來了二佰家工作非常困難，你可能會問在過去的日子到底有多困難，其實現在也不容易。

　　關於我們計劃的一些明確的資訊，我帶來了一些我們客戶所製造的樣品，及告訴你如何吸引到這些成功的製造業者，那就是 Nogales『風雨棚計劃』。

　　這裡有一件 Samsonite luggage 的樣品，Samsonit 是美國最大行李車的製造商，也可能是世界經營最成功的一家，Samsonite 在 1970 年是 Nagale 市的第一個投資客，條件之一是 Samsonite 在我們工業區期間我們不會對任何人公開 Samsonite 市 Nogales 的事實，他們曾在墨西哥生產遭遇很大的困難，但四、五年後他們成功了，而且在紐約週刊及時代

雜誌上有他們全版的廣告並披露了他們的大名，Sonara 廠的行李車 Sonora 廠是在我們墨西哥 Sonora 省，今天你可能買到由 Sonora 廠生產，那麼昂貴的行李車，但是之前要說服他們在墨西哥生產如此好品質的產品是非常困難的。

這塊線絡板是聯合科技公司的產品，這家公司在 1971 年剛開始到我們這裡用了四千平方英尺的廠房面積，他們給我們的只是一位生產工程師及用手工具生產，他們沒有自動設備，這家工廠的特性是在長條桌上由人工用手工具像鉗子之類的加工，幾年後，他們進步到生產非常府複雜的線絡板，用自動化設備生產及儀器做測試，同時也生產世界最進步的電話，品牌 Lexar，它會告訴你氣溫、時間、股市、叫你起床，非常貴也非常先進，是由墨西哥的工程師製造出來的，這家公司目前已使用了十萬平方英尺的面積，而將會繼續的擴充。

另外一個很嚴重的問題是，在開發中國家設有工廠的投資人的市場，會衝擊到那些國家本身市場，美國一家水錶公司，將近 95% 的產品都是賣給市政府，當市政府一旦發覺這些水錶都是由墨西哥製造，他們就不願意再買了，原因是認為品質太差，這家公司問是否可能在風雨棚計劃下九年的時間租我們的工廠及勞動力，使用五至廿五位工作人員，而不登記他們的名字，這在那段時間對我們是無利可言，而現在他們 Nogales 市向我們租了四萬平方英尺的面積，用了 200 位工人，二班工作，他們已不再夢想搬到別的地方去，事實上 Nogales 生產的產品已 100% 的賣給了市政府及墨西哥，產品已廣為聞名。

你會看到沿著邊界有很多捆好的馬具產品，這些都是要進到 Lowiy Organ 去的，都是名牌，製造十分困難，但因延著邊界有很多我們好品質的勞工在服務我們的客戶，我們在台灣、東京都沒有辦公室，同時我們也從我們的客戶方面進口一些有競爭單價的零件——這在先進國家是不會了解一般工業區的生產力的；我們提供熟練的製造服務給客戶，其服務成本是在他們可能得到的成本之下。

生產分享——一個很好的實例，汽車房門開關器，當我們的客戶在芝加哥開始生產，而後賣給 Sears 銷售，得到美國 20% 的市場，他們根據這個經驗，開始向海外採購零件而在 Nogales 生產製造，12 年後，牠們有了美國全部市場的 65% ，同時這買到日本、西班牙、德國、法國，他們從台灣、日本買零件，自己做塑膠件、金屬成型及在 Nogales 裝配，而後賣到全世界，他們保持成本不變，僅有一次乃是過去 10 年工程進步的原因，這就是生產分享。

GE 公司是我們主要的客戶，他們在 Nogales 生產金屬延長線，是屬非常勞力密集的製造作業，當我們在 Nogales 提升海外生產製造時，在 1960 年代後期或 1970 年代先期銷售的觀念是不太容易理解的，而 10 或 12 年後的今天這已不是十分嚴重的問題，我的意見是墨西哥的成功是因為日後建立了一些簡單的法規，墨西哥政府讓私人公司在墨西哥私人工業區內配合做到生產分享。

風雨棚計畫

1968 年開始，我們立即從經驗中了解到一些有實力的投資人，因我們工業區的問題而嚇得遠走海外到別的地方，甚至有在墨西哥鄰近的地方，我們所聽到的原因有客戶、勞工、曠職者、生產容量、工作品質、員工態度、語言障礙、水電及服務、稅、交通運輸、缺乏工業公共設施、美墨兩方官僚延誤及文化背景的差異等問題，這些問題自然對生產製造者是無法克服的。

1969~70 年 Nogecles 風雨棚計畫為了增加我們的銷售發展，在風雨棚計畫下，我們（工業區發展負責人）採取了一項危險的做法，即供給我們的客戶低成本現代化，最好設備的廚房、水電、警衛安全服務，以保持廠房的清潔，廠房保養；全部直接勞工及人事行政管理等全由工廠自理。

我們作了一些很重要的事情，例如員工考試、雇用及解雇，同時還提供會計作業、薪水帳冊，還提供處理美國人在墨西哥的工作許可，我們允許有海關經紀人的服務，我們也做美墨海關的界面服務，做從建廠開始至生產中間的顧問，我們也有堆置場所供給美國方面的原料、機器及成品轉運之用，在風雨棚計畫下，客戶會提供原料、機器及負責生產的經理人員。

一開始進度很快，因為客戶過來組成他們在墨西哥自己的公司，僅只與我們在亞歷桑納州的附屬公司簽約，付給使用我們工廠的費用及墨西哥依小時計的勞工工資，很多大型公司包括 GE、Samsonite、洛克威爾國際公司等，發現風雨

棚計畫，一開始便能很快生產，比之要等六月建造他們自己規格的廠房要方便的多。在時間方面，廠房已備妥，他們也訓練好一半的工人，同時在產品方面也開始賺錢；一個典型的風雨棚計畫客戶先簽六個月至二年的合約，而後視需要再延長。

客戶也知道利害關係，如果他一旦決定終止合約，馬上便會有成本發生，所以他會在開始時就了解即可能接受的最低風險。我們深信所發展的風雨棚計畫是非常重要的單一銷售工具。

此有注於填滿工業區，而當今的作為是培育新的企業有利於墨西哥的競爭性，並能保持工業區內隨時備便有空間給新的有潛能，競爭力的客戶進駐。

THE NOGALES SHELTER PLAN, A MANAGEMENT TOOL
Richard P. Campbell, President
Nogales Industrial Park
Nogales, Sonora, Mesico

It is not easy to fill an export industrial park with customers – and keep it full. We have to see 300 potential customers to get just one. So I spend about half of my life in places like Chicago, Boston, Philadelphia and elsewhere across the U.S. just to get customers. We do it by holding seminars similar to this one, but it's expensive; it costs between US$ 15-30,000 for each seminar. Sometimes no one comes, sometimes 200 comes. It's a very difficult process. You may talk about how difficult it was in the old days—it's no easier now.

To give you explicit information about our program I have brought a few samples of what our clients are manufacturing and will tell you about a method of attracting manufacturers that has been very successful – the Nogales Shelter Plan.

Here is a sample of Samsoniteluggage. Samsonite is one of the biggest luggage manufacturers in the U.S., and probably one of the most successful in the world. Samsonite was one of our first customers in Nogales in 1970. One of the conditions that Samsonite made at the time they came to our industrial park was that we would not disclose to anybody the fact that Samsonite was in Nogales. They were almost embarrassed about manufacturing in Mexico. After about 4 or 5 years they were so successful that they took out a full page advertisement in Newsweek and Time magazines and renamed their luggage the Sonora Line; that's our State...Sonora, Mexico. And to this day the most expensive Samsonite luggage you can buy is the Sonora line. But, in the early days to convince them that we could produce such quality in Mexico was very difficult.

The printed circuit board is a product from United Technologies. When this company started with us in 1971 they used only about 4000 square feet of factory space. They sent us only one production engineer and were making things with hand tools. They had no automatic equipment whatsoever. The factory was characterized by long tables with people with hand tools like pliers. Over the years they have evolved into producing very complex circuit boards with automatic production and testing equipment, such as this one which goes into the most advanced telephone system in the world, the Lexar. It will tell you the temperature, the time, the stock market, it wakes you up; it does everything. The company was kind enough to lend me the board for the seminar. It's quite expensive, very advanced, and is manufactured by Mexican engineers. The company is now utilizing 100,000 square feet and is looking to expand.

Another problem in marketing for clients with factories in a developing country, a serious one, is the impact of the perception of that country in its home market. Here is one of the best water meters in the United States. Nearly 95% of these are sold to city governments. When the cities found out the meters were manufactured in Mexico they didn't want to buy them because they thought the quality would be bad. The company asked if it could rent its factory and labor force from us under our Shelter Plan for 9 years, using 5 to 25 people but without identifying its name. It was not profitable for us at the time, but now they rent about 40,000 square feet from us, they have 200 workers in Nogales on both shifts. They wouldn't dream of moving anywhere else. In fact, almost 100% of their production for cities is now made in Nogales and the fact that they produce in Mexico is widely known.

One of the things that you see along to border is a lot of wiring harness production. This one goes into a Lowry Organ, a well known brand. It is quite difficult to manufacture, but because of the quality of out labor you see a lot of this along the border. To service our customers we have opened an office in Taiwan and another in Tokyo, and we import components at competitive prices for our customers –- an activity unknown to ordinary industrial parks in advanced nations. We provide sophisticated manufacturing services to our customers at costs below those they could obtain themselves.

Production sharing … a good example of this is this garage door opener.

When our client began producing this in Chicago, they sold their output to Sears and obtained 20% of the U.S. market. They undertook an experiment, and started buying their components offshore and manufacturing in Nogales. Today, in 12 years later, they have 65% of the total U.S. market, and they sell to Japan, Spain, Germany and France. They buy components from Taiwan and Japan, and they mold the plastic, bend the metal, and assemble in Nogales, and sell the product all over the world. They have kept their costs in line, raising the price only once due to an engineering improvement in the past 10 years. That's production sharing.

General Electric Company is a major customer of ours; they mold these extension cords in Nogales – quite a labor intensive manufacturing process. When we began promoting offshore manufacturing at Nogales, selling the concept in the late 1960's or early 70's was not easy. It's not quite the ordeal today that it was 10 or 12 years ago. In my opinion, Mexico is successful because, after establishing a few simple rules, The Mexican government lets the private sector set the tone and pace for production sharing the Mexico through private industrial parks.

The Shelter Plan

When we began in 1968, we soon learned from experience that many potential tenants for our industrial park were being frightened away with the thought of going offshore to a distant land, even one as close as Mexico. The problems that we would hear about were customs, labor, absenteeism. Production volume, quality of work, employee attitudes, language barriers, utilities and services, taxes, transportation, lack of industrial infrastructure, bureaucratic delays in both the U.S. and the Mexico, and culture differences. And of course these all seemed insurmountable to the manufacturer.

In 1969-70 through the necessity to increase our sales we developed the Nogales Shelter Plan. Under the Shelter Plan we, the developer of the industrial park, took the risk of providing to our clients at low cost a modern well-equipped building, utilities, the janitorial services to keep the building clean, the maintenance to keep the building going; all the direct labor, and the personnel administration to operate the factory.

We do the important things like employee testing, hiring and firing, as well as provide accounting and payroll. We provide arrangements for work permits for the United States personnel to work in Mexico. We have a licensed customs broker on staff, we interface with Mexican customs and U.S. customs. We consult during startup and ongoing operations. And we also have a staging area on the United States side where raw materials, machinery, and finished products are transferred. Under the Shelter Plan the client provides materials, equipment, and a manager who knows how to make the product.

Startup is rapid because the client does not have to form his own Mexican company – he merely signs a contract with our Arizona subsidiary under which he is charged for the use of our factory and labor in Mexico at an agreed hourly rate. Many of the largest companies including General Electric, Samsonite, and Rockwell International have found the Shelter Plan a convenient way to begin operations quickly rather than waiting six months while we construct their building to their specifications.

By the time the building is ready they have already trained up to half their work force and have been making a profit on their production in the meantime. A typical Shelter Plan customer signs up for an initial 6-months to 2 years trial, then extends for additional time as needed.

The client knows in advance what it will cost if he decides to terminate during the contract term, so his downside risk is knows and acceptable to him before he starts.

We believe the Shelter Plan is the most important single sales tool we have developed.

It helped fill out industrial park originally and now acts as an incubator for new firms to try out Mexico for themselves and to keep a steady stream of new potential customers to compete for space in our industrial park as it becomes available.

四、聯合國工業發展組織投資成長計劃
（Unido，s Investment Promotion Program）
William R. Millager

聯合國工業發展組織了解專業發展計劃乃全球投資成長計劃的一部份，當我們談到關於投資時會參照各種工業公司的型態，包括了合資，授權許可，或者生產分享等。

我們的計劃是由四種主要因素組合而成的一項完整計劃：

（1）投資成長會議在世界各地召開，對有意的伙伴或投資人提供詳細工業投資案機會的簡介資料，這類會議每年舉辦六或八次。

（2）在巴黎，東京都設有投資成長服務的辦公室，目前共有八處辦公室，其用意在促進贊助國的投資及技術流向世界各發展中的國家。

（3）投資資訊系統提供了在開發中國家有關工業投資案的訊息。最重要的訊息是由幾頁簡介資料提供了一些整合的資訊，約有 5 億及 10 億的金額是由 1500 至 2000 個當前這類訊息所促成的。

（4）投資成長專業發展——我將專注在本案的發展。

專業發展在投資市場國家裡，我們都設有投資服務辦公室；此乃基於唯一的信念即邊作邊學。訓練人員對投資成長的最佳途徑是給他們開始的機會並由他們負責執行，如此他們會直接的學到經驗。他們必須自己努力的打電話，或與人

497

開會，比之只看到別人如何的做要好。在紐約，自 1978 年
開始如此進行，其有絕對需要的理由是我們用了很低的成本
達到幫助了一些國家進入到投資成長的事業裡。在這一段時
間有 40 個國家已執行了這項計劃。我們已有了來自全世界
的訓練學員，雖然我們確認了加勒比海的分支機構，同時也
有了非洲投資中心。

　　每個參與國家均從事這樣的工作，目前有 6~9 個國家
設有辦公室，設備支援，工作人員及實驗設備，所必需要的
裝備包括了電腦等，還有研究助理，教練及多項服務。你可
能說這是相反於 Nagales 的 Shelter 計劃，那要有一種適當
的解釋，除非我們在將來有一小步的進展。生產設備由我們
提供，而你所要做的是提供主管人員或是投資成長負責官
員。這位負責主管需要某種程序的合格條件以便能動態的擔
任操作員的工作，較之於北美的投資環境他必須安於現況，
也就是具有某種程度的堅韌個性的人。

　　在這幾年裡，這些國家在會同紐約聯合國工業發展組織
中心的運作已建設了多座工廠，總金額約在 1.5 億到 2 億美
元。那並不是一筆龐大的金額，但我想，我們需要考慮的一
項事實即在這條發展的路上這些國家已起步在做。由他們的
人民吸取了技術同時也做出了他們的信心，更進一步約超過
100 人不但已經學習到他們的工作經驗，同時也促成個人與
網路接觸，這是超過了任何有形資產的價值，因為如果你為
他們這般安排，他們將會持續終生。這些國家在本計劃之下
停留 1 至 3 年，這些國家中的某些國家曾一次或多次的提出
參與本計劃，例如 Cartagena 自由區參與我們的計劃達三年

之久，Dakaar 自由區過去也在這裡。還有，Greater Colombo Economic Commission 也是。很多國家如印尼，菲律賓從這裡離開而後接著利用了他們曾建立起的背景而設置了自己的辦公室。

本計劃一開始在紐約及華盛頓有一個月的密集訓練，受訓者有機會面對銀行負責人，政府官員及公司經理人等有利於相互的認識。最後幾天專注於模擬談判練習，我們有一位先生來自 Princeton 隨身帶來了他的影像裝備及一些衣袖裡的魔術表演，他將這一群人分成幾個小組，進行一些競賽並穿插一些恐怖的魔術助興。

第二個月，我們工作在學員方面，協助個別國家的代表利用目標技術規劃其北美成長會議等，試圖達成他自己國家，或者是自己家鄉的研究單位所設定的目標。他們代表了開發公司，加工出口區, 財務部等等。

第三，全力的支援。誠如我曾提過的成長所需的設備，訓練以及研究助理等等。

第四，我們教導適應，工具使用及技術，以促進生產力增加。為了達到某一水平的生產力不致使同樣水平在這個世界停留 20 分鐘，我們如是使用了電腦，Dun 及 Bradstreet 基本資料檔，我們也與石油輸出國組織及美國商務部連線，我們非常專注找低成本或無成本的達成目標，所以我們只有不到 100 種刊物，州發展代理，小型商務服務處，北美當地或區域商務會所，以及中間繁衍點的組織。我們利用電腦推動工作，選取公司，個人網路似乎是促進成功的根本。最後的成效驗收及回饋對本案是非常重要使得受訓學員知道他們

將如何的做，當然也使得對本案的贊助人知道他們將如何做，而找出成長之路。

　　基金的來源有聯合國發展計劃局（UNDP），世界銀行，其他發展基金機構，聯合國工業發展組織本身，美國國際發展局（USAID）或發展國家本身。從長遠看，根據我們的經驗，技術及方法的成長要繼續不斷的推展。我想，世界加工出口區協會是很好的媒介，使它本身的會員間各別的接觸，交互了解彼此的作為。投資成長是一項無限量的工作，它必須是在國際競爭條件下不斷的進步及改進。

UNIDO' S INVESTMENT PROMOTION PROGRAM William R. Millager Head Investment Promotion Service – North America United Nations Industrial Development Organization New York USA

UNIDO has a rather comprehensive professional development program which is part of a global investment promotion program. When we talk about investment we refer to all type of industrial cooperation, whether it be joint ventures, licensing, or production sharing.

Our program is an integral one with four major components：

(1)Investment promotion forums are held around the world to present specific industrial project opportunities in profile form to prospective partners or investors. These are held on every continent – in all about 6 or 8 each year.

(2)Investment promotion service offices of which mine is one are located in places like Paris and Tokyo, a total of 8 these days, to promote the flow of investment and technology from the host country to the developing countries around the world.

(3)Investment information systems provide information about industrial projects in developing countries. The most important provides a little summary of each one backed up by a several-page profile. There are 1500 to 2000 of these currently active totaling somewhere between 5 and 10 billion dollars in value.

(4)Investment promotion professional development – the program which I will concentrate on.

Professional development in the investment market countries where we have these investment development services offices is based on a unique concept – learn by doing. The best way to train people to do investment promotion is to give them a start and put them in charge of doing it so that they get the direct experience themselves. They must personally experience picking up a sweaty telephone or meeting people in meetings like this rather than observing how other people do it. In New York this has been going on since 1978, and for reasons of absolute necessity we concentrate on the low cost approach to helping countries get into this investment promotion business. Forty countries have gone through the program in this period. We have had trainees from all over the world, although we do identify a Caribean subgroup and also have an African investment center.

The way this works is each of the participating countries, and there are 6-9 at any given time, has an office, a support facility, staff and physical facilities, necessary equipment including computers and so on. It has research assistants, coaching and a variety of services. You could say this is a Nogales 「Shelter Plan」 in reverse. That is an apt description except that we go a few steps further. Production equipment we supply – all you do is supply the director or the investment promotion officer. He needs to have certain qualifications to become a dynamic operator, and he should be comfortable in more than the North American investment environment, which is certainly a tough one.

Over these years a number of plants have been landed by the countries operating from their offices with the UNIDO center in New York. The total value is somewhere between 150 and 200 million dollars. That's not a tremendous value, but I think that we need to take account of the fact that this has been done by countries which have been starting out on this road – by people who have been picking up the skills and confidence while they have been doing it. Furthermore, over 100 people have developed not only operating experience, but also personal contact networks which are beyond any assessment of value because they last a lifetime if you work on them. Countries stay in the program for 1 to 3 years. Several of the countries represented here have participated at one time or another. For example, the Cartagena Free Zone was with us for three years. Dakaar Free Zone was also there, as was the Greater Colombo Economic Commission. Many of the countries such as Indonesia and the Philippines have gone through and have subsequently set up their own offices marking use of the background that they've built up.

The program begins with a one-month intensive orientation which is held in New York and in Washington where people have face to face interaction with a number of leading bankers, government officials, and company managers. This ends with a few days devoted to a simulated negotiation exercise. We have a gentleman who comes from Princeton with his video equipment and a lot of tricks up his sleeve. He breaks the group into a number of teams so there's a lot of competition, and he intervenes with dirty tricks to make it a little more interesting.

The second month we work in a collegial way to help each individual country representative in the design of his North American promotion campaign using techniqu3es of targeting, etc. to try to fulfill objectives that have been established by his own country, perhaps by his home institution. They represent development corporations, EPZs, ministries of finance, and so on.

Third, there's implementation support. As I mentioned the promises in equipment and coaching and research assistants and so forth. That's what this point is about.

Forth, we teach adaptation and use of tools and techniques that make productivity go up. What it takes to achieve some level of productivity doesn't stay the same for more than 20 minutes in this world. So, we are using computers, Dun and Bradstreet databases; we have links to OPEC and the U.S. Commerce Department. We are very much looking for low cost or no cost means of reaching target audiences. So we have a few hundred publications, state development agencies, the small business administration, local and regional Chambers of Commerce in North America, organizations as intermediary multiplier points. And we use our computer equipment to move through them or use them to target selected companies. Personal networking seems to be the most productive root to eventual success. Finally, the monitoring and feedback is the most essential part of this program to let the trainees know how they are doing and, of course, let their sponsors back home know how they are doing, and to seek ways to improve.

As for funding our sources are UNDP, the World Bank, other development financial institutions; UNIDO itself, USAID or the country itself.

Looking at the future, based on our experience, promotion techniques and tools are continuing to evolve. I think that WEPZA is a good vehicle to keep it's members in touch so individuals can crossfertilize what they are doing now. Investment promotion is a frontier activity, and it must rapidly improve and change to keep up with international competition.

附　錄

附件（一）

加工出口區的人肉機器吟悲歌

——中國時報記者　張志清 1994. 元. 4

陳美娟今年四十一歲，在加工出口區工作已經廿一年，
這份工作是她的第一份工作，原本她也希望是最後一份工
作；但是，眼看一家家工廠關門、一批批工人被資遣，自己
公司的業務同樣一天不如一天，她有點宿命、幾分無奈的說
「對退休已經不抱太大希望」，在政府有關單位拿不出實際
因應辦法的情況下「加工出口區還會繼續萎縮下去」。

話雖如此，但是與其他多數加工區的勞工一樣，陳美娟
總還是認為，如果政府有心做，加工區會有轉型成功的一天。
只是，自己的公司能不能撐到那個時候、明天會不會被資遣、
失業之後怎麼辦等，這些問題令他們每天晚上經常失眠。

加工出口區　風光不再有

台灣經濟發展史上，加工出口區在過去廿幾年來一直扮
演著火車頭的角色。當時，美援剛剛停止，紡織、電子、塑
膠加工正待起步，五十五歲的經濟部長李國鼎為刺激經濟發

展，決定在高雄成立「加工出口區」鼓勵工業品出口，吸引外資，以賺取更多的外匯。

陳美娟上班的日商電子公司就是在這樣的獎勵政策下，民國五十六年以三億元的資本額開始設廠，當陳美娟在六十二年到公司時，員工人數已經有三千四百多人，而加工出口區類似規模的公司比比皆是。外商投資設廠製造許多就業機會，吸引大批來自屏東、台南等鄰近外縣市農業人口投入生產線。

投資生產揚聲器的豐達公司董事長陳榮華便有相當的感觸，他回憶指出，當時應徵工作的勞工十分珍惜得來不易的這份工作，應徵三十人往往一口氣來了三百人，勞工的安定性很高，十分聽話，不像現在，要找三十個卻只來了三個，所謂待沒多久就跑了，到附近 KTV、MTV 當公主、小姐去了。這位老闆表示，現在會來這裡找工作的主要還是以結了婚的家庭主婦為主，另外澎湖等離島居民也逐漸成為人力主要來源。

老闆算盤精　藉口遣散人

加工出口區工會聯合會理事長何棲鴻以南部腔調的台語說，「現在比以前稀微多了」，工廠不是外移到大陸就是申請引進外勞，被資遣的勞工平均工作年資在十年以上，男的多半在這裡成家、立業、買房子，女的有許多人也結了婚甚至剛懷孕。辛苦了大半輩子換來的只是認識到社會的現實罷了。

　　因為，有的老闆在投資設廠廿幾年之後算算，如果再不找個理由離開，再幾年就有一大筆的退休金要發放，景氣已經不好了，如果再要給退休金可能要貼上老本才夠。因此，多數公司的作法是先到大陸設廠，將訂單轉往大陸；然後以訂單減少經營困難、台灣勞工工資上漲、人事成本增加等各種理由宣布歇業、關廠，然後資遣員工。

　　有的老闆是將最早設廠的高雄廠收起來，然後希望員工能夠到楠梓加工區，藉此使員工因路途遙遠而自動離職，節省公司支出。

　　鄭英華本身就經歷過一次資遣。她說，當時公司老闆約談每個人，但是時間只有五分鐘，如果沒有特殊理由，就必須領取資遣費走路。由於不知道自己什麼時候會被點名叫到，每個人都提心吊膽，公司那幾天氣氛很差。不過，與其他公司沒有經過個人面談就張貼名單宣布資遣的作法相較，鄭英華認為他們公司已經相當夠意思了。至於給多少資遣費，她也不是十分清楚，只說「都是照規定」。

加班費廿元　食之如雞肋

　　何理事長說，他曾經接獲一個申訴案例，一個年輕人為他的母親向工會申訴，理由是他母親公司給的加班費一個小時只有廿元。這個案子經過工會調查確有其事，但是當事人卻有另一套教人十分感心的想法。這位母親說，「反正現在媳婦也娶了，家裡不再需要我去煩心，早回家晚回家其實都一樣；而且同事可以邊做邊聊，每天加班二小時四十元又剛好可以買一大包「落葉仔」的龍眼（指掉落地面一顆顆不是

整把的龍眼），回去洗好澡之後可以與孫子一邊看電視一邊吃，有什麼不好。」

在記者走訪期間，發現一家可能在明年關廠的製鞋公司。這家設在高雄加工出口區的唯一製鞋公司有一百多名員工，日商在台的廠長山本克己在接受訪問時表示，製鞋業無法在台灣生存是因為鞋品製作無法以機械自動化來取代，必須靠手工；而台灣的加工費用太高，除非生產高單價產品，否則實在不容易在國際競爭中存活下來。不過，該公司員工則認為公司設廠、人才培養訓練不易，在台灣政府有意開放國內市場情況下，日本公司應該可以考慮繼續經營，將高單價產品送到台灣來做，另外，也製造一些產品供應台灣市場。員工積極爭取工作機會的意圖清晰可見。

何棲鴻指出，在台中加工出口區有一家外商公司在關廠時，就做得很有誠意。他說，這家公司在要結束營運前四個月就明白跟員工表明經營不下去，並願意與公司員工面對面解決問題，毫不逃避；是個很好的典範。他指出，高雄有一家公司在二年前資遣員工五百六十人，到大陸投資設廠；結果最近向管理處說想再回來。對於這個個案他認為，當初被這家公司資遣的員工有許多目前仍然在加工區工作，如果讓它再回來以同一家公司名稱繼續經營，勞工心裡怎麼想！

憑勞力賺錢　竟成壞榜樣

過去，加工出口區能夠吸引勞工是因為區外沒有其他工作，如今服務業在國內盛行，加上文憑主義作祟，加工出口

區竟成了附近學校教育學生應認真讀書的反面活教材，國中、國小老師在教堂上教誨學子一定要好好唸書，不然就只有到加工區工作。加工出口區推動台灣經濟多年以後，竟然變成了「壞」榜樣，年輕人不再想到這裡求職，為了國際競爭，加工區的新進人員薪水也一直維持在比基本工資稍高一點的程度，與區外工業區或者民間工廠每月一、二萬元的薪水無法比較，人力的流失是自然的現象。

只是，被資遣之後的勞工哪裡去了？

陳美娟說，他們以前的同事在被資遣之後，大約一半以上是在自己家裡附近隨便找工作做，有的則是改行開計程車或擺地攤。

在高雄鳳山市老爺四街附近自己買機器接單自己做的魏昌五，過去是加工區的勞工，也是公司工會的常務理事。被資遣時已經工作了廿年。

公務員調薪　民間跟不上

外商老闆及部分高級幹部認為，我國政府每年調整公教人員薪水幅度過高，影響民間企業運作。業者表示，韓國政府在不久前宣布該國政府科長級以上官員五年內不得調整薪水，日本在得知之後也隨即宣布三年內調薪幅度不得超過三％，而台灣官員似乎不知民間疾苦，不斷的調高薪水。

但是，對應加工區老闆的言詞，在加工區內、外或大或小的人事廣告卻明白標示新進人員每月薪資為一三五〇〇元，只比勞委會才公布的基本工資每月一三三五〇元多了一百五十元，在領了這些錢後，許多勞工還要寄回家，還要買

衣服、化妝品、租房子、交通費。這些投入加工出口區勤奮
工作的勞工會不會「沒有明天」？這些大問題他們雖然想
過，但是卻始終找不到答案。

附件（二）

加工出口區力圖轉型何來悲歌？

——中國時報　余光亞／高市（加工出口區老兵）1994. 1. 13

　　元月四日見貴報第六版之「加工出口區的人肉機器吟悲歌」宏文報導，閱後令人為之搖頭嘆息，曾身為加工出口區之一員，且曾奮力為該區服務之老兵，對加工出口區之了解，自認較一般人略深一層，因此，有些話想說。加工出口區民國五十五年十二月三日正式在高雄港成立第一個高雄加工出口區後，相繼在楠梓、台中成立楠梓加工出口區及台中加工出口區，其創設加工出口區及因當時我國經濟環境之所需，經政府十年長期之研究而成立。

　　其成就 27 年來，已為各界所公認，蜚聲中外，更於一九八九年十一月六日至九日世界加工出口協會之年會在高雄市由我加工出口區舉辦，使世界參與大會之 27 個國家代表一致認同中華民國加工出口區之成就為世界之最；我加工出口區在相對利益之理論基礎下，達到三利原則之目的，即「國家的利益，廠商的利益，員工的福利」，因而廿多年來，建立起國家豐富之資本財，由於外商之投資帶入了廣大之國際市場及最新之生產技術及設備，更為我國每年創造平均約七萬人之就業機會及區外數萬人之衛星工廠之工作機會，促成小康社會之基礎而至形成小資產密集到中小企業之發展，激發社會經濟活力及社會安定力，此於世界加工出口區

年會中，美國開發銀行基辛博士所發表之論文中特別對我加
工出口區大加稱讚其對國家之貢獻，甚而強調因我加工出口
區之成功而延伸到中鋼公司及新竹科學園區之建立，及對日
後世界各國相繼成立加工出口區之影響，按目前我國政府尚
在接受中美洲哥斯達尼加之要求協助其成立加工出口區，派
員管理，同時我國有興趣之投資人，前往投資且已實際協助
其外銷美國，逐漸其因我國加工出口區之成功而希望我國協
助者眾。

　　時間之巨輪在不停的旋轉前進，加工出口區之歷史任務
已圓滿達成，但工業不因階段性任務達成而捨棄不要，而且
更要認識「只有夕陽產品，而無夕陽工業」，因而我國經濟
環境之變遷，加工出口區之經營環境亦隨之改變，當初以勞
力密集之加工、裝配工業已為高科技、自動化生產之高附加
價值產品工業所取代，所以區內洋傘、製鞋、假髮、人造
花……等工業已不復存在，成衣、初級電子裝配產品亦逐漸
減少，取而代之者為光學、高科技電子、精密機械……等工
業產品，故而形成公司「新陳代謝」之正常現象發展，否則
加工出口區早已不復存在，區內如此，區外工業亦復如此，
此即表示我國工業升級之良性轉型發展，亦即呈現出我國與
亞洲鄰國有所區別之所在；惟公司「新陳代謝」所影響到者，
即是對辛勤工作多年之勞工朋友生活之保障未盡合理之照
顧，勞基法推出太晚，內涵亦不夠周全，對勞資雙方均不能
得到滿意之保障，是為最大之不幸！

　　筆者於加工出口區任職期間，約三百家廠商，均為誠懇
敬業者，若有故意逃避退休金而關廠者，鮮有耳聞。又部份
公司撤資到他處投資，區外亦有類似之情況，國資亦不例

外，此乃大勢所趨，非加工區僅有；員工對工作之安定性不夠，招考不易亦為當前全國之通病，如此等等非加工出口區之罪，乃大環境使然，雖如此，當前加工出口區每年之業績仍不斷成長，前述之貢獻亦繼續未輟，能不令人感佩及感激加工出口區全體員工之努力麼？何來悲歌之有？

加工出口區在滿足於當前成就之同時，亦應考慮未來之發展，就筆者淺見有以下幾點供政府及讀者大眾參考：

一、勞基法對退休金提撥辦法不夠落實，宜比照新加坡之公積金方式辦理較妥。

二、加工區管理處應速擬轉型方案，以配合國家經濟政策之改變，其中對區內管制項目宜大量放寬。

三、勞動力不足，勞工安定性降低的事實，開放外籍勞工刻不容緩。

四、工業廢棄物政府如不能有效協助業者處理（業者應合理付費）將迫使再投資減少，甚而拆資外移。

五、非經濟因素造成事業投資安全性降低，而致減少就業機會，政府不能坐視。

六、政府應重視非生產性經濟快速成長之嚴重性及對勞工安全性之影響，而致力改進員工工作意願、敬業精神。

七、社會大眾對加工區宜深入了解，鼓勵鞭策及支持，尤其新聞界朋友，如其嚇人聽聞之不實文詞打擊加工出口區七萬員工之士氣情緒，不如以懇切關懷之建言嘉惠於加工區使之改進缺失，創新未來，則加工出口區全體員工將感激不盡，幸甚！

附件（三）

加工出口區 28 年來之貢獻及其轉型

——經濟日報　余光亞 1994.05.20、21

一、我國加工出口區建區之背景及目的：

我國加工出口區於民國 54 年 12 月 3 日成立至今已達 28 年之久，今之社會各界及年輕的一代多只知加工出口區之名，而不知其由來及其對社會國家之貢獻，筆者願以較深入之了解，以其誠懇之心記述加工區發展里程之貢獻及轉型供讀者參考指教。

民國 39 年政府遷台後其時社會處於貧困狀態，經濟結構仍為農業經濟體制，人民亟需就其機會，通貨膨脹影響民生，就以當時環境背景而言，簡述如下：

在台灣三萬平方餘公里之土地上　三分之二為山地，可耕面積約四分之一，天然資源極度貧乏，然而在 40 年代的人口成長率卻高達 3.5%，每年需要增加十萬個就業機會方能滿足社會需要，按 40 年代，農業生產占全國 56%，工業僅占 26%，故 GNP 僅及二百美元，約為美國的十分之一，屬於未開發之貧窮國家，尤其於民 40 年韓戰爆發，美國經援停止，使本已脆弱之經濟體質頓失支持，因此政府決定著手經濟改革，以因應國家需要。

我國經濟改革發展分三個時期推動：

第一時期為進口替代時期（民國 40~50 年）（1951~1961）

第二時期為出口擴展時期（民國 50~60 年）（1961~1971）

第三時期為調整經濟結構，加速經濟發展時期（民國 60~70 年）（1971~1981）

各時期之任務且不予贅述，但第二時期人口成長率增高，失業率相對增加。此時，唯有發展經濟，獎勵工業投資，給予良好之投資環境以吸引外人投資，增加就業機會，乃有「加工出口免稅區」初期意念之產生，按 40（1950 年代）年代香港因大陸遷往之企業家在當地建立了製造業之基礎，同時香港亦為自由貿易港，除極少數商品外，機器原料等均不收關稅，故前往投資之外商甚多，發展快速，1963 年香港出口總值為六億美元，其中 80% 為工業加工品，而台灣僅出口一億美元，幾乎全為農業產品，故以香港為借鏡，促成對成立加工出口區之研討而至建區。政府從民國 42 年至 55 年正式創設加工出口區共經歷 11 寒暑，其中最主要時刻在民國 51 年李國鼎先生隨同財政部長嚴家淦先生赴美歐開會中途赴義大利 Trieste 港參觀自由貿易區作業情形，回國後詳加研討，提案將自由貿易區及工業區合併經營，並擬議為「加工出口區」此乃加工出口區之由來，民國 52 年 9 月由經合會，邀請財政部長嚴家淦先生、經濟部長楊繼曾先生、交通部長沈怡先生、外貿會主任委員徐柏園先生、國防部副部長馬紀壯先生及省政府有關廳處長等十餘政府首長往高雄港內視察由濬港所產生之新生地（即現高雄加工區之所在地）及聆聽簡報初步構想藍圖，各首長均表贊同，而儘

速推動立法，民國 53 年 7 月加工區設置管理條列草案完成
送請立法院審議，審議期間，面臨民國 54 年 6 月美經援即
將停止，政府必須採取多項措施因應，遂於 53 年秋起，分
批安排立法委員視察美援支持之各項計畫，其中亦包括建立
加工出口區計畫，視察期間均由陶聲洋先生、李國鼎先生及
吳梅村先生等陪同，立法委員視察後，深深了解建立加工出
口區計畫之重要性，在立法院院會中均踴躍發言支持，尤其
甚者湖北省籍立委王開化委員大聲疾呼「政府已將在高雄港
中挖出砂土變成黃金，我們如不支持加工出口區設置條例，
實在沒有理由。」因而於民國 54 年 1 月 31 日經協調會議後，
立法院審議通過，完成立法手續，並呈　總統公布實施，此
刻甫接任經濟部長之李國鼎先生幾經考慮決定邀請曾任基
隆市長，其時正擔任經合會參事之謝貫一先生擔任加工出口
區籌備處處長，謝先生即為加工出口區之第一任處長，籌備
期間便有數家外資廠商來區設廠，至民國 55 年 12 月 3 日籌
備工作完成舉行建成典禮，由嚴副總統兼行政院長主持揭
幕，加工出口區如是正式成立。

　　加工出口區於民國 55 年 12 月 3 日正式成立，其建區之
目的有四：

　　1、吸引工業投資。

　　2、拓展對外貿易。

　　3、創造就業機會。

　　4、引進最新技術。

　　其中按當時實情，創業就業機會為首要任務，當務之
急，其他三點則為創造就業機會之共生目的。

二、20 餘年加工出口區之貢獻及轉型：

　　民國 55 年 12 月 3 日加工出口區成立，以其特有之設置管理條例及授予吸引投資最優惠之辦法，便有一百多家廠商申請設廠，投資金額達 2.5 億美元，因而政府即時規劃增設楠梓加工出口區及台中加工出口區，並分別於民國 60（1971）年建立開始營運，此其時，我國勞動力非常充沛，民國 59（1970）年僅一個高雄加工出口區便有 3.5 萬多人就業，62（1973）年三個加工出口區同時營運達 7 萬人，以後每年約維持在 7.5 萬人，76（1987）年高達 9 萬多人，加工區外之衛星工廠亦有數萬人之就業，人人工作勤奮及政府對國民教育的重視，勞工知識水準提高，至生產之產品品質優良，為我國產品在國際市場踏出有利之第一步，又勞動中有極大比率為女性員工，家庭婦女（按加工區員工中女性約占 70%）彼等較安於工作，收入相對得到保障，對改善家庭生活助益頗大，因而促進了社會之祥和安寧，如此連鎖反應，使國家經濟日益繁榮，乃有目共睹之事實。

　　加工出口區之繼續不斷成長茁壯，數以萬計之勞工朋友在加工區辛勤工作，也不斷的學習上進，一方面外來投資還繼續大量湧進，另一方面，人們生存權及上進心之驅使，國人以其勤儉美德，由小企業開始萌芽發展到中企業之擴展。使國家經濟有了較為明顯之轉變，民國 60（1971）年以後，由南部到北部幾乎每一城市都有加工區個人出來投資開業者，如服務業、製鞋業，甚至以後之高科技產品亦不乏自立門戶，此對勞動生產力及產品附加價值亦相對提高，勞工收入增加，形成社會良性循環反應，至為可喜。

　　民國 70（1981）年以後，我國經濟結構屬於第三個經
濟發展時期，亦即經濟發展升級期，加工出口區踏著與政府
政策齊一步伐，推動自動化發展，同時也鼓勵研發新產品，
提高附加價值及國際市場競爭力，例如民國 72（1983）年
台中佳能公司配合以上政策，申請海外技術研發訓練有成，
至該公司每年均有自行研發之新的照相機問世，使之得以永
續經營，又如民國 75（1986）年台灣飛利浦建元電子公司
在加工出口區內成立研究中心，推動了我國 VLSI 之發展，
及民國 76（1987）年台中加工出口區亞洲光學公司在國科
會之協助下，研發產製高倍數醫學用顯微鏡成功，民國 80
（1991）年楠梓日月光半導體電子公司之關係企業，日月冠
子公司自行研發個人電腦，成功打開美國及歐洲市場，成為
國內一枝獨秀之電子企業，尚有不勝枚舉之案例，在在說明
加工出口區在進步，轉型，與其同時社會大眾心態亦在改
變，此刻之勞工朋友，對加工區較固定方式之工作意願漸感
不適，加之服務業之蓬勃發展，部分勞工朋友對固定八小時
辛勤之工作亦乏興趣，因而全國各生產事業漸感勞動力不
足，甚而有更嚴重者，加工出口區亦不例外，如此變更時期
之來臨，激發了投資人必須朝向高科技產品及自動化生產發
展，否則生存困難，促使加工出口區產業與區外企業一樣，
加快了腳步積極轉型，其成效至為彰顯。
　　由於加工出口區之轉型，使建區初期之加工生產功能，
產生極大之變化，除產品加工生產外，研發也為主要之工作
項目，如前述所舉實例，其經營程序為先生產而後研發新產
品成功，再對新產品生產，如此良性循環，與科學園區之先

研發再生產而後繼續研發新產品，此兩兄弟區對國家之貢獻
實殊途同歸無分軒輊，但國家對加工出口區之投資遠不及科
學園區之豐厚，加工出口區人當不致氣餒，而仍會繼續努
力，更求精進！倘若加工出口區再接再厲與南部各大學繼續
加強合作、推動研發工作及改善工作環境，則加工出口區將
具有科學園區之實質功能，政府是否有必要再作大金額之投
資於第二科學園區，甚值得商榷深思。

三、加工出口區有傲視全球之生產力及貿易實績：

　　加工出口區自民國 56（1967）年開始經營以來，各項
成就均為國內外所肯定，尤其在三區僅有之 192 公頃土地面
積上，創造了傲視全球之高生產力及貿易實績，茲分別簡述
如下：

　　就生產力（產值）而言，值得一提者如勞動生產力及土
地生產力，按民國 56（1967）年勞動生產力為 1,800 美元／
人，77（1988）年增為 45,000 美元／人，十年增加了 25 倍，
至 82（1993）年再增加為 82,000 美元／人，達 45 倍之多，
然而勞工人數卻逐年減少，民國 77（1988）年勞工人數達
86,863 人，而 82（1993）年底僅有 53,189 人，又在土地生
產力方面，民國 56（1967）年為 11 萬美元／公頃，77（1988）
年為 1,960 萬美元／公頃，增加 178 倍，82（1993）年增加
到 2,298 萬美元／公頃，增加了 209 倍，以上數據顯示在有
限之土地上，勞工數逐年減少，而生產力卻不斷以高倍數成
長，此在說明加工出口區產品之附加價值在不斷提高，乃因

加工出口區之產品品別，品級均在日新又新的改變、提升，即表示加工出口區產業轉型成功之事實證明；又加工出口區每年貿易實績亦不斷成長，至民國 68（1979）年其出口金額超過 12.4 億美元，進口總額達 6.8 億美元，順差 5.6 億餘美元，占當年全國順差之 42.46%，以後每年進出口貿易均持續成長，及至民國 78（1989）年出口金額更超過 39 餘億美元，民國 82（1993）年出口金額達 43.2 億餘美元，至民國 82（1993）年止，累計出口總金額達 451 億餘美元，進口 230 億餘美元，進出口合計高達 681 億餘美元，其總順差高達 221 餘億美元，按我國目前外匯存底約以 830 億美元計，加工出口區之貢獻約占 26％強，此 28 年來之成效貢獻，確實嘆為觀止，非同小可，如此傲視全球之生產力及貿易實績，當可告慰國人及在加工區不斷繼續努力經營之全體員工及各事業之投資人。

四、加工出口區對國家經濟效益之貢獻：

其最顯著之效益有以下五點：

1、對國家初期資本財之形成，有利於政府外匯之運用。

2、就業機會之增加，促成小康社會之基礎，而至形成小資本密集到中小企業之發展，更而促進社會經濟活力及社會安定。

3、因加工出口區之成功，促成新竹科學園區之成立，帶動國家高科技工業之發展。

4、加工出口區外商帶進國際市場及國際貿易，有利於國產品之連帶輸出，形成政府外匯存底增加，累積了國家整體財富。

5、加工出口區現已成為我國在世界之櫥窗功能，仍繼續配合政府需要協助開發中國家建設加工出口區，以發展經濟。甚而於目前對欲了解我加工出口區之友邦人員開班訓練，以廣被其影響、受益。

五、加工出口區成功之要因：

加工出口區成功之因素甚多，諸如正確之設區觀念，給予投資人最大之優惠條件，一元化之整體服務，高品質低成本之勞動力，區內良好之基本設施等，但最為重要者乃在先有一部完善之法律──設置管理條例，是為世界各國加工區所不及者。也因此，政府原為增加就業機會，增加外銷而設計之加工出口區，其壽命預定不過十餘年，而今卻已達 28 年之久，再就了解世界其他各國加工出口區雖有充沛低工資之勞動力，卻因法之不夠週全而窒礙難行者眾，此乃我加工出口區之幸也。

六、國人對加工出口區應有之正確認識：

我國加工出口區從初創到茁壯，乃至轉型發展，我們對它亦應隨時序之推進而有更深一層之認識，謹列舉以下四點供參考：

1、創造高附加價值之就業機會：

由前段勞動力之貢獻及轉型，已說明勞工朋友心態，隨社會經濟結構之改變而轉換，如今已不再是低勞動成本及勞動力充沛之時刻，由於加工出口區因應得宜轉型有成，故而已轉變為創造高附加價值之就業機會所在。此實有別於建區伊始時之勞力密集之加工出口區。

2、淘汰了夕陽產品，便無夕陽工業：

加工出口區之轉型在使產品國際化，初期之裝配產品已不復存在，而今均邁向高附加價值及高科技產品工業發展，故在加工出口區內無夕陽工業之存在。

3、加工出口區為我國經濟發展中之一環，不可或缺：

我國 40 多年來之經濟發展，重點在發展工業，加工出口區亦為工業中之一環，自有其存在之道理，事實證明加工出口區之經營不輟，及為現有勞資雙方所共同賴以為生存發展之所在。

4、具有舉世最好之管理制度：

前已說明國加工出口區具有一部最為完善之法律——設置管理條例為基礎，只要加工出口區能繼續有效的據以運用執行，則加工出口區將有無限之前程遠景，當然適時修法，以應當前環境需要，是為應繼續努力之要項。

根據以上成效說明及正確理念之認識，吾人應了解到加工出口區之前進不應因歷史成因而否決當前存在之必要性，而應視實質發展成就之連續性，即加工出口區不但適應勞力密集之生產事業同時亦適應於高科技資本密集之工業，如此適應兩個層面（Two Phases）之加工出口區，得以

證實並肯定其繼續經營之意義及必要性，切盼社會各界深入
理解，給予鼓勵支持，乃加工區之幸也！

附件（四）

大陸經濟區　三部可能變八區

——中國時報 2004 年 6 月 5 日

學者建議未來五年發展走向　更符合實際需求

據香港《文匯報》報導，中共國務院發展研究中心發展戰略和區域經濟研究部部長李善同表示，中國未來五年區域發展的思路脈絡可能改變以往太粗的東部、中部、西部的劃分方法，而以八大經濟區來取代，令政策制定更符合當今經濟發展的實際和要求，更加科學、可行。

報導指出，中國八大經濟區的基本區域情況如下：

東北地區：包括遼寧、吉林、黑龍江三省。面積七十九萬平方公里，二○○一年總人口一億○六九六萬。這一地區自然條件和資源稟賦結構相近，歷史上相互聯繫比較緊密，目前，面臨的共同問題多，如資源枯竭問題、產業結構升級換代問題等。

北部沿海地區：包括北京、天津、河北、山東二市兩省。面積三十七萬平方公里，二○○一年總人口一億八一二七萬。這一地區地理位置優越，交通便捷，科技教育文化事業發達，在對外開放中成績顯著。

　　東部沿海地區：包括上海、江蘇、浙江一市兩省。面積廿一萬平方公里，二○○一年總人口一億三五八二萬。這一地區現代化起步早，歷史上對外經濟聯繫密切，在改革開放的許多領域先行一步，人力資本豐富，發展優勢明顯。

　　南部沿海地區：包括福建、廣東、海南三省。面積卅三萬平方公里，二○○一年總人口一億二○一九萬。這一地區面臨港、澳、台，海外社會資源豐富，對外開放程度高。

　　黃河中游地區：包括陝西、山西、河南、內蒙三省一區。面積一百六十萬平方公里，二○○一年總人口一億八八六三萬。這一地區自然資源尤其是煤炭和天然氣資源豐富，地處內陸，戰略地位重要，對外開放不足，結構調整任務艱巨。

　　長江中游地區：包括湖北、湖南、江西、安徽四省。面積六十八萬平方公里，二○○一年總人口二億三○八五萬。這一地區農業生產條件優良，人口稠密，對開放程度低，產業轉型壓力大。

　　西南地區：包括雲南、貴州、四川、重慶、廣西三省一市一區。面積一百三十四萬平方公里，二○○一年總人口二億四六一一萬。這一地區地處偏遠，土地貧瘠，貧困人口多，對南亞開放有著較好的條件。

　　大西北地區：包括甘肅、青海、寧夏、西藏、新疆兩省三區。面積三百九十八萬平方公里，二○○一年總人口五八○○萬。這一地區自然條件惡劣，地廣人稀，市場狹小，向西開放有著一定的條件。

附件（五）

上海「全球扶貧大會」

——2004 年 5 月 28 日（星期五）香港大公報 A6 版

中國政府發表《政策聲明》「五統籌」消除貧困

中國政府今天在上海發布的《中國政府緩解和消除貧困的政策聲明》中明確提出，緩解和消除貧困，實現全體人民的共同富裕，是中國政府始終不渝的宗旨。中國政府致力於本世紀前二十年建設惠及十幾億人口的更高水平的小康社會。

這份在此間舉行的全球扶貧大會上發布的聲明說，截止去年底，中國農村仍有近三千萬人沒有解決溫飽，收入水平處於最低生活保障線的城市居民有二千多萬人。由於歷史、自然、經濟等諸多因素的影響，城鄉之間、地區之間、社會成員之間的差距還在持續擴大。這是中國在全面建設小康社會進程中必須解決好的重大問題。

聲明稱，中國通過實施以農村貧困人口為重點的扶貧開發，走出了一條符合中國國情的「政府主導、社會參與、自力更生、開發扶貧」的扶貧道路，大規模減少了農村貧困人口數量，基本解決了農村貧困人口的溫飽問題。這在中國的發展史上具有標誌性的深刻意義。

　　聲明同時指出，雖然中國扶貧開發的歷史性成就得到了國內各界和國際社會的高度評價，但中國是一個人口眾多、資源不足、發展不平衡的發展中國家。特別是在廣大內陸的深山區、荒漠地區、邊疆地區以及一部農村和城鎮，貧困現象仍然比較突出。

　　聲明說，中國政府將統籌城鄉發展、統籌區域發展、統籌經濟社會發展、統籌人與自然和諧發展、統籌國內發展和對外開放，以更堅決的態度、更有力的措施，全面推進緩解和消除貧困的進程。

附件（六）

悼念世界加工出口區之父的殞落──李資政國鼎先生

　　1949 年中華民國政府在台灣，開始從事經濟發展以解決民生之所需，工業發展則視為最佳途逕，在推動發展過程中，首先著重在民生必需品進口替代工業之發展，但卻在短時間內遭遇到國內市場有限舜即達到飽和現象，因而必須拓展外銷，但即面臨必須進軍國際市場，舉步為艱可想而知，復而於 1965 年 6 月面臨美國經援停止，國內資金短缺，加之人口快速成長，農村勞動力過剩，嚴重缺乏就業機會，至需有效大力之改善投資環境，以便吸引僑外投資，拓展對外輸出，增加外匯收入及創造就業機會，但以當時國內環境法規之複雜，限制之嚴格，需要改進改善之處可謂千頭萬緒，諸如外匯匯率之多元制，關稅管制之多所不便及關稅過重等；而香港當時為自由港，機器及原料除極少數商品項目外，皆不收關稅，鑑於上情，政府為求便利吸引投資，促進工業進一步之發展，至對投資環境必須作實質之改善，乃有加工出口免稅區初期意念之產生。

　　1953 至 1958 年間，資政時任職於工業委員會，與海關總稅務司張申福先生會同研究劃出特定區域設立加工廠之可行性，1959 年底，資政兼任美援會工業發展投資研究小組招集人，推動財經措施，草擬獎勵投資條例，因而促成

加工出口區設立可行性之大環境。1962 年，資政隨嚴前總統（時任財政部長）赴美開會，自歐返國途中，前往意大利 Trieste 港參觀其自由貿易區作業情形，回國後即與嚴部長詳加研討後決定設置符合我所需之加工出口區，此區兼具有自由貿易區與工業區功能之綜合體。其設置之架構原則為：

1、在人的方面，投資人出入境仍維持原有手續。

2、在錢的方面，外匯管制仍屬必要，仍維持原有手續，但在區內辦理。

3、在物的方面，因加工出口區產品全部限外銷，其製造所需機器及零件，與原料零組件一概免關稅及貨物稅。

設區架構原則決定後即著手草擬立法，1963 年 9 月，資政服務經合會，邀請經濟、財政、交通、國防、外貿會及台灣省政府等單位首長同赴高雄港視察濬港新生地及聆聽簡報有關建區構想藍圖，並決定儘速推動立法，由是 1964 年 7 月加工出口區設置管理條例草案送請立法院審議，而於 1966 年 12 月 3 日創設建成高雄加工出口區，為我國第一個加工出口區，同時也是全世界加工出口區之首創。由於加工出口區集自由貿易區及工業區功能之長，又不同於該兩區之特性運作，而其功能績效立即顯著呈現，一時為世界各國所讚譽並爭相仿效，更而受到聯合國工業發展組織（UNIDO）、世界銀行（IBRD）、亞洲生產力組織（APO）等國際組織之重視，以至有世界加工出口區聯合會（WEPZA）之成立。

加工出口區之創建里程，由於資政在各個不同職務上不斷持續推動及政府各首長、民意代表等大力支持，歷經 10

年之研究而終於達到設區之目的，使得我國經濟發展加快了
成功的腳步，績效彰顯，由外資投入增加就業機會，促成小
資本之形成而拓展到本土中小企業之形成，乃至大企業之成
長，外匯累集曾達千億美元以上，位居世界前三名，人民由
赤貧到富有之社會轉型，皆因加工出口區確曾提供了相當大
比例之貢獻，乃至今之世界各未開發國家及開發中國家多有
學習我國比照設置加工出口區作為促進該等國家經濟發展
之最佳途徑。1987 年 9 月 11 日應世界加工出口區聯合會
（WEPZA）之邀請，恢復我加工出口區會藉，成為該會正
式會員，並任理事會員國，尤其難能可貴者，與會各會員理
事一致同意，1989 年世界加工出口區年會在我國高雄市召
開，由我加工出口區管理處主辦，參加開會者共 27 國 121
人代表，另國內貴賓近 200 人，盛況空前；資政應邀為大會
主講人，其講題為「加工出口區制度的建立及其功能」，內
容精粹，震驚全會場，入會者共同讚頌不愧為世界加工出口
區之先導，並於大會理事會中一致通過頒贈資政為「世界加
工出口區之父」褒獎獎牌一面及書面頌揚賀詞一份，由是觀
之，資政不僅為我國數十年來之經濟、科技發展貢獻至鉅，
對世界各未開發國家、開發中國家亦貢獻出頗大之助益，即
使美國也為了增進就業而設置類似加工出口區之「外國貿易
區（Foreign Trade Zone）」及「外國貿易區分區（Sub-Foreign
Trade Zone）」，由是可見加工出口區之成功及貢獻之宏偉。
從我加工出口區建成 35 年餘至今，最令世人尊敬讚譽之一
代偉人，世界加工出口區之父　李資政國鼎先生已然仙逝，
魂歸天國，留下世人無限的深思，感嘆哲人其萎，誰能任後

世之師？！耑撰本文　追思悼念一代偉人世界加工出口區之父　李資政國鼎先生在天國之靈！

作者：余光亞

中華民國經濟部加工出口區前任處長

2001.08.10

附　　圖

1963 年月財經首長視察高雄港港區預留加工出口區建區用地

加工出口區位置圖

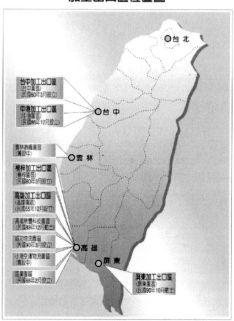

加工出口區各區名稱一覽表

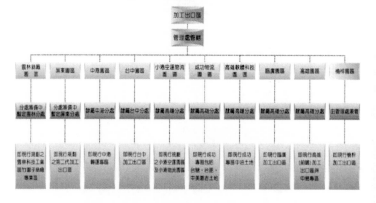

台灣高雄加工出口區

台灣楠梓加工出口區

台灣台中加工出口區

中國昆山出口加工區（之一）

中國昆山出口加工區（之二）

越南新順出口加工出口區

中國 2004 年上海全球扶貧大會

1984 年 5 月 14 日經濟部吳梅邦次長偕余光亞處長等赴日促進投資說明會

1989 年 11 月 6 日至 9 日世界加工出口區協會 1989 年年會在高雄市舉行

K. T. Li – The father of Taiwan's industrial development, Dr. Li helped create the EPZ at Kaohsiung while chairing the Industrial Development Investment Center.

L.A. Chen – Minister of Economic Affairs, Republic of China. A noted engineer and mathematician, Dr. Chen was chairman of the National Science Council 1984-88.

Donald B. Keesing – Dr. Keesing is Principal Economist, Trade Policy Division, The World Bank, Washington D.C. His paper will suggest "Which EPZs Make Most Sense in the Light of Spillover Benefits and Practical Needs of Manufactured Exports."

Derek T. Healey – Professor, Department of Economics, University of Adelaide, Australia. His study with United Nations Industrial Development Organization (UNIDO) of Korea's EPZ linkages to the local economy will serve as a focal point for discussion.

INTERNATIONAL
Conference:

How to Profit from Linking the Export Processing Zone to Local Industry

"A meeting designed for managers of Export Processing Zones to exchange views with managers of global enterprises using or considering EPZs"

The Ambassador Hotel
Kaohsiung, Taiwan, R.O.C.
November 6 – 9, 1989

1989 年世界加工出口區協會年會大會主講貴賓李資政國鼎先生

the WEPZA newsletter

WORLD EXPORT PROCESSING ZONES ASSOCIATION   NUMBER 1989 - 4

FIRST WEPZA AWARD OF MERIT TO K.T. LI

The Honorable K.T. Li addresses WEPZA

Resolution of the WEPZA Council:

WHEREAS, Mr. K. T. Li was the Guest of Honor at the Opening Ceremony of the WEPZA 1989 Conference and General Assembly at Kaohsiung, Taiwan, Republic of China on November 6, 1989;

WHEREAS, Mr. K. T. Li is recognized as the father of the Export Processing concept and the architect of Taiwan's industrial and economic miracle;

WHEREAS, the creation of WEPZA is the logical consequence of the success of the EPZ concept;

NOW THEREFORE, BE IT RESOLVED by the WEPZA Council in meeting assembled to extend due recognition to Mr. K. T. Li by honoring him with an Award of Merit for his creativity and achievement;

BE IT FURTHER RESOLVED that an appropriate plaque be designed which, together with a copy of this Resolution shall be presented to Mr. K. T. Li at appropriate ceremonies.

DONE at the City of Kaohsiung, Taiwan, Republic of China on the 8th day of November 1989.

TEODORO Q. PEÑA   CARLOS J. T. RÖMER
PRESIDENT   SECRETARY GENERAL

HIGHLIGHTS OF THE FIFTH GENERAL ASSEMBLY

WEPZA's Fifth General Assembly at Kaohsiung, Taiwan, Republic of China, November 6-9 attracted 70 EPZ participants from 25 countries and 55 manufacturing companies from Taiwan.

The Export Processing Zone Administration of Taiwan, R.O.C. received the plaudits of all attending for its amiable hosting and excellent management of a smoothly-flowing intense program. The facilities at The Ambassador Hotel were outstanding — and the friendly young people of EPZA mingled with guests to see that their welcome was sustained throughout the conference.

1. ELECTIONS

The General Assembly with 13 Member EPZs participating re-elected Teodoro Peña, President, and Carlos Römer, Secretary General, and kept the WEPZA Council which has served so well during the past two years in place for the next two.

2. AWARD OF MERIT

The Honorable K. T. Li, architect of Taiwan's economic miracle, addressed the conference on the first day and received the first WEPZA Award of Merit as the father of the Export Processing concept which, through the success of EPZs around the world, ultimately resulted in the creation of WEPZA.

THE WEPZA NEWSLETTER is published quarterly at 3421 South Moore Circle, Flagstaff, Arizona 86001, USA (Mail address is P.O. Box 588, Flagstaff, Arizona 86002, USA) by The Flagstaff Institute, a non-profit corporation under the laws of the United States of America and the State of Arizona, by agreement between The Institute and the World Export Processing Zones Association (WEPZA).

Telephone: (602) 779-0052 FAX: (602) 774-8589 Telex: 910361 2568 (INTL PARKES) · Editor: Richard L. Bolin
© The Flagstaff Institute, 1989, all rights reserved · ISSN 0887-9990

1989 年世界加工出口區協會年會新聞報導

2000 年世界經濟加值區（原加工出口區）協會第 20 屆年會在高雄市舉行

參考資料

1、「加工出口區制度之創立」——李國鼎著
（傳記文學民國 76 年 9 月（1987.9）號第 51 卷第 3 期）

2、管理實務——案例——余光亞著

3、台灣加工出口區統計月報

4、Philippine Economic Zone Authority , Special Economic Zones Matrix June, 30,1999

5、ASIA'S Export Processing Zones and Science Parks in Global Markets – Asia Productivity Organization , APO.

6、台灣的對外經濟合作與加工出口區——李國鼎著

7、APO Study Meeting on Science Parts and Export Processing Zones – APO Korea Productivity Center 23~26 November, 1999

8、二次大戰後歐美亞與台海兩岸政治經濟重大變革對照表

9、兩岸工業園區若干問題之探討——東南大學李永泰教授，鄭斯彥先生著（海峽兩岸經濟貿易與信息傳播學術研討會論文1997 南京）

10、中國加工出口區——中國海關學會主辦 2002.9

11、中國加工出口區招商、運作累計情況表 2002.9.30 （昆山出口加工區十週年慶提供）

12、APO Survey on Export Processing Zones and Science Parks, 1999.11

13、印度、大陸經濟有如龜兔賽跑——2004.2.9 經濟日報

14、越南新順加工出口區統計資料

15、李國鼎與台灣財經——茅家琦著 1998.9

16、中華民國，台灣地區經濟現代化的歷程——行政院經濟建設委員會 1991.2

17、使台灣變成一個加工出口區——1988,2.1 天下雜誌 81 期，李國鼎著

18、台灣經濟發展背後政策演變——李國鼎著

19、台灣經濟轉捩時刻——尹啟銘著

20、我國產業發展的重要夥伴——工業技術研究院 1988.6.2 工程特刊

21、我國光電產業回顧與展望——工業技術研究院 1988.6.2 工業特刊　楊玟萍文

22、中國統計年鑑 2001——中國統計出版社

23、中國統計摘要 2001——中國統計出版社

24、中國經濟熱點透視——企業管理出版社 王曉鳴主編

25、台灣經濟快速成長的經驗——李國鼎著

26、台灣經貿發展祕錄——武冠雄，中外雜誌 2003 年 2 月號第七十三卷第二期

27、蓽路藍縷共建園區——何宜慈遺稿，中外雜誌 2003 年 8 月號第七十四卷第二期

國家圖書館出版品預行編目

加工出口區與經濟發展 / 余光亞著. -- 一版. --
臺北市：秀威資訊科技, 2006 [民 95]
　　面；　公分. -- （社會科學類；PF0022）

ISBN 978-986-6909-21-4(平裝)

1. 工業區 – 臺灣 2.經濟發展 – 臺灣

555.9232　　　　　　　　　　　95023323

社會科學類　PF0022

加工出口區與經濟發展

作　　者 / 余光亞
發 行 人 / 宋政坤
執行編輯 / 周沛妤
圖文排版 / 郭雅雯
封面設計 / 林世峰
數位轉譯 / 徐真玉　沈裕閔
銷售發行 / 林怡君
網路服務 / 徐國晉
出版印製 / 秀威資訊科技股份有限公司
　　　　　台北市內湖區瑞光路 583 巷 25 號 1 樓
　　　　　電話：02-2657-9211　　　傳真：02-2657-9106
　　　　　E-mail：service@showwe.com.tw
經 銷 商 / 紅螞蟻圖書有限公司
　　　　　台北市內湖區舊宗路二段 121 巷 28、32 號 4 樓
　　　　　電話：02-2795-3656　　　傳真：02-2795-4100
　　　　　http：//www.e-redant.com

2006 年 12 月 BOD 一版
定價：650 元

讀 者 回 函 卡

感謝您購買本書，為提升服務品質，煩請填寫以下問卷，收到您的寶貴意見後，我們會仔細收藏記錄並回贈紀念品，謝謝！

1.您購買的書名：_____

2.您從何得知本書的消息？

　　□網路書店　　□部落格　　□資料庫搜尋　　□書訊　　□電子報　　□書店

　　□平面媒體　　□ 朋友推薦　　□網站推薦　　□其他_____

3.您對本書的評價：(請填代號　1.非常滿意 2.滿意 3.尚可 4.再改進)

　　封面設計____　版面編排____　內容____　文/譯筆____　價格____

4.讀完書後您覺得：

　　□很有收獲　　□有收獲　　□收獲不多　　□沒收獲

5.您會推薦本書給朋友嗎？

　　□會　□不會，為什麼？_____

6.其他寶貴的意見：_____

_____

_____

_____

讀者基本資料

姓名：_____　年齡：_____　性別：□女 □男

聯絡電話：_____　E-mail：_____

地址：_____

學歷：□高中(含)以下　　□高中　　□專科學校　　□大學

　　　□研究所(含)以上 □其他_____

職業：□製造業 □金融業 □資訊業 □軍警 □傳播業 □自由業

　　　□服務業 □公務員 □教職　□學生 □其他_____

To：114

台北市內湖區瑞光路 583 巷 25 號 1 樓

秀威資訊科技股份有限公司　　　收

寄件人姓名：

寄件人地址：□□□

- -

(請沿線對摺寄回,謝謝!)

秀威與 BOD

BOD（Books On Demand）是數位出版的大趨勢，秀威資訊率先運用 POD 數位印刷設備來生產書籍，並提供作者全程數位出版服務，致使書籍產銷零庫存，知識傳承不絕版，目前已開闢以下書系：

一、BOD 學術著作—專業論述的閱讀延伸
二、BOD 個人著作—分享生命的心路歷程
三、BOD 旅遊著作—個人深度旅遊文學創作
四、BOD 大陸學者—大陸專業學者學術出版
五、POD 獨家經銷—數位產製的代發行書籍

BOD 秀威網路書店：www.showwe.com.tw
政府出版品網路書店：www.govbooks.com.tw

永不絕版的故事·自己寫·永不休止的音符·自己唱